# RESEARCH METHODS IN PSYCHOLOGY

## Third Edition

# RESEARCH METHODS IN PSYCHOLOGY

## Third Edition

**DAVID G. ELMES**
Washington and Lee University

**BARRY H. KANTOWITZ**
Battelle Memorial Institute

**HENRY L. ROEDIGER, III**
Rice University

**WEST PUBLISHING COMPANY**
St. Paul/New York/Los Angeles/San Francisco

*Copyeditor:* Carol C. Danielson
*Cover photograph:* Copyright © Rob Atkins and The Image Bank®
*Interior Design:* Lois Stanfield

**Library of Congress Cataloging-in-Publication Data**

Elmes, David G.
    Research methods in psychology / David G. Elmes, Barry H.
Kantowitz, Henry L. Roediger, III.
        p.    cm.
    Bibliography: p.
    Includes index.
    ISBN 0-314-46962-1
    1. Psychology—Research—Methodology.    2. Psychology,
Experimental.    I. Kantowitz, Barry H.    II. Roediger, Henry L.
III. Title.
BF76.5.E44 1989                                        88-28266
150'.724—dc19                                          CIP

# |||| Contents

# |||| **Preface**

The textbook you are reading is the third edition of a book first published in 1981. Presenting you with this revision gives us great pleasure. Our earlier efforts were rewarded by your acceptance, and we hope that you, in turn, are rewarded by the new version. As with the first two editions the purpose of this book is to present the methods of psychological research so that you can understand the nature of valid and reliable research. Whether you become a producer or a consumer of research, it is vital that you be able to evaluate and appraise psychological research.

## |||| **TEXT ORGANIZATION**

The text is divided into four parts or sections. The first part includes an introductory chapter in which you are invited to try an experiment; four other chapters focus on the bases of science and of scientific psychology. The second part, which is composed of four chapters, emphasizes experimentation and how to do experiments. The next portion consists of two chapters devoted to non-experimental research methods. The final section and appendices A and B treat the pragmatic aspects of conducting and analyzing research.

  We recommend that the first part be read first, but the other parts may be read in any order. The chapters within a section are best read in the order given, except for those in the fourth and final section, which are self-contained and thus may be assigned at any time.

### Pedagogical Features

Each chapter contains several features designed to improve comprehension and enhance interest. The **Facing Page** provides a summary of the upcoming chapter. The facing page will alert you to important concepts and will provide a convenient aid for review. The **Overview** introduces the substance of each chapter. Within the chapter there are frequent **Concept Summaries,** which are designed to drive home important concepts and to assist in study and review. At the end of each chapter are several features: a point-by-point **Summary;** a list of **Key Concepts;** thought-provoking **Exercises;** and **Suggested Readings.** These features will help you derive maximum benefit from the contents of the chapter—they will reinforce and extend your understanding. Most of the chapters are followed by an **Application** section, which describes how the concepts discussed in that chapter can be applied outside of the laboratory, and a **Psychology in Action** section, which presents a project for you to undertake. These applications and projects are intended to further your interest in scientific psychology and to encourage you to undertake scientific projects.

## |||| CHANGES FROM THE SECOND EDITION

Users of the previous edition will notice several changes in this edition. Our own experience, the suggestions of readers, and the advice of our capable reviewers have resulted in changes to the content and organization of certain chapters. As we enter the final decade of the twentieth century, improvements in the technological and scientific sophistication of society seem essential for our survival. The knowledge explosion in science demands that practitioners and consumers of science be equipped to conduct reliable and valid scientific research and to understand theory. Thus, the first two chapters emphasize current philosophy of science more strongly now than in the earlier editions. Chapter 1 has been thoroughly revised. In it we examine the nature of theory construction and of scientific reality from the viewpoint that science is an ever-evolving, self-correcting process for solving problems—or for approaching the solutions to problems. The development of scientific knowledge is examined under the unifying theme of a research area that has both immediate practical interest as well as theoretical interest—the problem of social loafing. The second chapter is a new one. We and many of our reviewers believe that the importance of reliability and validity should be considered before these qualities are examined in detail. Although aspects of reliability and validity comprise the core of the book and are discussed throughout, a unified exposition (and a little distributed practice) should result in better comprehension and awareness of the issues that are involved. Our intent in the first two chapters is to make sure that the student is cognizant of the underlying rationale of psychological science and will, therefore, be challenged to master the nuts and bolts of scientific research.

The major organizational change is that the chapter on ethics appears earlier in the book than it did before—it is now chapter 4. The reason for this change is that we believe, and many of our readers concur, that neophyte scientists have an obligation to confront ethical issues and dilemmas prior to undertaking research. Moving the chapter on ethics forward is more than a mere symbol of this concern. Advances in scientific knowledge will lead us in ways that are now unknown. Thus for science to serve society in the most beneficial ways, responsible scientists and consumers of science must be in a position to make informed judgments about the ethics of research procedures just as they must be able to evaluate the scientific merit of these procedures.

In several places we have chosen new examples to illustrate the concepts and principles that are discussed. As was true with earlier editions, students intrigued by nearly any aspect of scientific psychology will find examples to both challenge and interest them. For example, research on the sleeper effect in persuasive communication is used to illustrate the concept of an interaction, and current research on brain injuries that lead to memory disorders is discussed to show the importance of following a research protocol. Elsewhere, the reader will find discussions of a variety of research problems, including the bases of learning, the higher cognitive processes, pain detection following acupuncture, social loafing, compensatory education, the bases of attachment, and individual differences in physical and cognitive development. Our goals in choosing each of the examples were threefold: to illustrate the proper ways of conducting research, to convey the importance and the tremendous scope of psychological science, and to impart a sense of the fun and excitement that can be found in scientific psychology. We hope we can continue to be successful in attaining these goals.

## | | | | ACKNOWLEDGEMENTS

Writing a text involves many people in addition to the authors. Users of the second edition provided many helpful comments. In addition, we benefitted from the sage advice of several able reviewers. We would especially like to thank the following: Charles Brewer, Furman University; David Hogberg, Albion College; John Jahnke, Miami University; Richard Lehman, Franklin and Marshall College; James McCroskery, SUNY at Oswego; Fred Meeker, California State Polytechnic University; Theron Stimmel, Southwest Texas State University; Lori Temple, the University of Nevada at Las Vegas; and Royce White, Marist College. We appreciate the help of the staff at West— a group of competent people who made our job easier and the product better. Mary Schiller, our editor, deserves special recognition for her wit and organizational skill. Others have provided invaluable technical help, and it is a pleasure to recognize the contributions of Julie Cline, and Kyra Draves who labored over many details with such skill that the book would still be in limbo without their fine assistance. The support of the Psychology Department at Washington and Lee, especially that of Len Jarrard and Joe Thompson, is gratefully acknowledged. We would like to acknowledge the help of several authors and publishers. We are grateful to the Literary Executor of the late Sir Ronald A. Fisher, F.R.S. to Dr. Frank Yates, F.R.S., and to Longman Group Ltd. London, for permission to reprint Table C–5 from their book *Statistical Tables for Biological, Agricultural and Medical Research* (6th edition, 1974).

Finally, we owe an incalculable debt to our teachers who encouraged us to pursue scientific psychology. We would like to dedicate this work to the memory of three outstanding individuals who shared the fun and excitement of experimental psychology with us: **David A. Grant, William M.**

**Hinton,** and **L. Starling Reid.** Each of them, in his own way, encouraged students to engage in sound psychological research. Their enthusiasm led us into experimental psychology, and we hope that you find a similar model to lead you in the same direction.

**D. G. E.**
**B. H. K.**
**H. L. R. III**

## | | | | ABOUT THE AUTHORS

**David G. Elmes** has been on the faculty at Washington and Lee University since 1967. After receiving his B.A. with High Honors from the University of Virginia, he completed both the M.A. and Ph.D. degrees in psychology at that same institution. He has spent a year as a research associate in the Human Performance Center of the University of Michigan and was recently a visiting fellow at University College of the University of Oxford, England. He has published numerous articles in the areas of human and animal learning and memory which have appeared in the *Journal of Experimental Psychology, Physiological Psychology, Memory & Cognition,* and the *Journal of Comparative and Physiological Psychology,* among others. He is the editor of *Readings in Experimental Psychology* and is currently a consulting editor for the *Journal of Experimental Psychology: Learning, Memory, and Cognition.* He is coauthor of *Experimental Psychology, Third Edition,* with B. H. Kantowitz and H. L. Roediger.

**Barry H. Kantowitz** is a Senior Research Scientist at Battelle Memorial Institute, Seattle. He received a B.A. and M.A. from Queen's College of the City University of New York and a Ph.D. from the University of Wisconsin in 1969. He has directed the Human Information Processing Laboratory at Purdue, and has spent a year on a National Institutes of Mental Health Post-doctoral Fellowship at the University of Oregon and has also served as a senior Lecturer at the University of Trondheim in Norway. Dr. Kantowitz's research interests are in attention and reaction time, and he has published numerous articles on these topics which have appeared in the *Journal of Experimental Psychology, Memory & Cognition,* and *Acta Psychologica,* among others. He is coauthor of several textbooks, including *Psychology: Understanding Behavior* (with R. A. Baron and D. Byrne), *Human Factors: Understanding People-System Relationships* (with R. D. Sorkin), and *Experimental Psychology, Third Edition* (with H. L. Roediger and D. G. Elmes). In addition, Dr. Kantowitz edited and contributed a chapter to *Human Information Processing: Tutorials in Performance and Cognition.* In 1974 he was elected a Fellow of the American Psychological Association.

**Henry L. Roediger, III** received a B.A. degree in psychology from Washington & Lee University in 1969 and a Ph.D. from Yale University in 1973. He is now Professor of Psychology at Rice University, following a 15-year appointment at Purdue University. His research interests lie within the field of cognitive psychology, particularly human learning and memory. He has published over 40 articles and reviews, most of which have appeared in the *Journal of Experimental Psychology: Learning, Memory, and Cognition,* the *Journal of Verbal Learning and Verbal Behavior,* and *Memory & Cognition.* He has coauthored two other texts, *Psychology* (with J. P. Rushton, E. D. Capaldi, and S. G. Paris) and *Experimental Psychology, Third Edition* (with B. H. Kantowitz and D. G. Elmes). In addition, Dr. Roediger has served as Consulting Editor of *Memory & Cognition* since 1978. He has been Editor of the *Journal of Experimental Psychology: Learning, Memory, and Cognition* since 1985.

# BASES OF PSYCHOLOGICAL RESEARCH

# |||| Introduction

As a beginning to your study of psychological research, we would like you to take part in an experiment. We hope that your participation in this project will bring out the kinds of questions about psychological research that psychology students and experimental subjects often ask. This experiment will also serve as an outline of the problems and questions that confront a researcher in psychology.

The purpose of the experiment is to determine whether aspects of reading and naming occur automatically. Much of your intellectual activity involves reading words and numbers. Much of that activity also concerns naming or enumerating objects that you encounter. You probably believe that reading and naming are rational, deliberate processes. Are they? Do you have to think about reading and naming, or do those processes occur automatically, without conscious effort? To be a subject in this experiment, you will need a clock or a watch with a second hand (a digital watch that records elapsed time in seconds will do), and you will also need a pen or a pencil.

## |||| DIRECTIONS

As a subject in this experiment, you are to read through or name a series of digits or symbols as quickly and as accurately as you can. The digits and symbols are in a single column, and you should start at the top and go to the bottom of the column without skipping any items. You will go through three different columns on three different pages. Be sure to do them in order. At the top of each page are directions—read them carefully because the directions on each page are different. The phrase **Start Time** is also at the top of each page. If you are using a clock or a watch with a second hand, write down the exact time in minutes and seconds, and then begin the task. If you are using a watch that records elapsed time, start the time and then begin the task. When you have finished the task on a particular page, either note your finishing time or stop your watch and write down the elapsed time. To begin the experiment, please turn to page 7. Do not continue reading here until you have participated in the experiment.

## | | | | WHAT WAS IT ALL ABOUT?

Let us consider the results of the experiment. For each column of digits or symbols, figure out how long it took you to read through it. If you recorded elapsed time, this is straightforward. If you wrote down your start and finish times, calculate the total time by subtracting the start time from the finish time. When you compare the results of the three tests, you will probably find that naming the number of numbers (the last task you did) took the longest amount of time, and that reading the digits took the shortest amount of time. Why is it difficult for you to name the number of digits when your answer is not the same as the name of the digit (that is, saying "4" when you see 3 3 3 3)?

To answer this question, we will outline a theory that seems to account for the results. Researchers have found that people usually are slower in naming the quantity of digits when the names of those digits conflict with that quantity. Apparently, we automatically read the name of the digits as we are enumerating the quantity. So when we have to respond "2" when we see 3 3, we simultaneously have the responses "2" and "3" available, and since we cannot say two things at once, there is competition between the available responses.

You can think of this as a mental race between two processes that lead to different responses when you see 3 3. One process is naming the digits ("3"); the other is counting them and saying the number ("2"). Since the naming process is greatly practiced, it wins the race, and the naming response ("3") comes to mind before the correct counting response ("2"). Thus there is response competition, since you must inhibit the faster naming response to permit the slower counting response to be spoken. Even if you try to completely ignore the names of the digits, you will discover that you are slower in counting numbers than you were in counting pluses (check the results of the second test you took). This outcome can be interpreted as showing that reading is an automatic process, because even when you try to avoid reading the numbers 3 3, you cannot completely suppress the response "3."

Several questions about this general finding are reasonable to ask. Is the difference in naming time between symbols and conflicting digits a real one or just a fluke? If you combine your results with those of your classmates, statistical procedures described in appendix B will allow you to determine whether the difference is a reliable one worth considering or whether it is merely the product of chance.

## | | | | WHAT IS EXPERIMENTAL PSYCHOLOGY ALL ABOUT?

The purpose of experimental psychology is to determine why people think and act as they do. As a discipline, experimental psychology relies on scientific procedures. In determining why people think and act as they do, we must deal with four general issues. We will illustrate these in the context of the reading and naming experiment.

## How Do I Study Reading and Naming Scientifically?

The nature of science requires that knowledge be based on observable events. In the experiment in which you just participated, the time taken to go through an entire column of naming or reading was the observable aspect of those tasks. For us to understand how reading and naming occur, we needed to have something tangible to observe. How else could we study the psychology of an event that is going on inside a person and is, therefore, unobservable? How else do we make reading and naming observable so that we can have a scientific analysis of them?

Before you apply the procedures of psychological science, you need to know something about the event you plan to study, which means that there are other issues to be confronted. What is known about reading and naming? Are there theories that refer to the processes presumed to underlie reading and naming? Where and how do you find out about previous research and theory? How do I conduct an ethical research project?

## What Is an Experiment?

A second general research issue has to do with the nature of experimentation. You participated in an experiment concerned with reading and naming. Your time to name the number of pluses was compared with your time to name the number of digits (3 3) when the name of the digit conflicted with the number of digits. What is an experiment, and how does an experiment differ from other modes of scientific investigation? Experimentation is usually considered the most powerful scientific tool, and this is just as true for scientific psychology as it is for biology, chemistry, or any other science. Because experimental science is so valuable and important, it is necessary for you to understand the details of experimentation.

## How Else Can I Study Reading and Naming?

Experimentation is not the only way to gain scientific understanding. You may have considered alternative ways of studying reading and naming. Instead of doing an experiment by having people name different symbols and digits, you could simply go out and observe people as they attempt to read or name real-life objects. Furthermore, you may be interested in the reactions of different types of people to naming conflicting digits. For example, you could attempt to relate people's personal characteristics, such as age or intelligence, to their ability to read and name quickly.

## How Do I Actually Do Research?

You may have asked this question first, or at least one something like it. Conducting a research project entails numerous pragmatic problems. How is a testable hypothesis developed? How do you select participants and treat them appropriately? When you obtain results, what do you do with them?

Other potential problems revolve around you, your participants, and the task. Have you been an objective, unbiased researcher? Do all humans respond to the conflicting digits the same way that college students do? Is this laboratory task similar to what occurs during "real" reading and naming?

|||| **ORGANIZATION OF THIS BOOK**

This textbook is organized around the four general issues we have just outlined. Initially, we examine the general nature of science, including an examination of theories, data, general research methodology, and ethics. The second and major part of the text concerns experimentation. The design and conduct of reliable and valid experiments are stressed. In the third portion of the book, we detail nonexperimental research procedures. These techniques, including observation, correlation, and quasi-experimentation, often involve interesting but less well controlled problems than is the case with true experiments. The final section of the text considers a number of additional pragmatic problems, such as researcher bias and generality of results.

Neither the practice nor the use of science is easy. The benefits that can be derived from scientific knowledge and understanding depend upon critical and well-informed citizens and scientists. Your involvement with a career, a family, and social affairs will be partially determined by scientific findings. You must be in a position to evaluate those findings accurately and accept those which seem most reliable and valid. Unless you plan to hibernate or drop out of society in some other way, you are going to be affected by psychological research. As a citizen you are a consumer of the results of psychological research, and we hope that the material discussed in this book will help to make you a more intelligent consumer.

Some of you, we hope, will become scientists. We also hope that some of you budding scientists will focus on why people and animals think and act as they do. We wish you future scientists good fortune. Your scientific career will be exciting, and we hope that your endeavors will be positively influenced by the principles of psychological research presented herein.

About a hundred years ago, T. H. Huxley, a British scientist, said: "The chessboard is the world, the pieces are the phenomena of the universe, the rules of the game are what we call the laws of Nature. The player on the other side is hidden from us. We know that his play is always fair, just, and patient. But we also know, to our cost, that he never overlooks a mistake, or makes the smallest allowance for ignorance."

**THE EXPERIMENT** DIRECTIONS: Name the numbers below as fast as you can.

START TIME

_____

2
1
4
3
3
2
4
1
4
1
3
2
2
1
3
4
3
1
4
2
4
3
2
1
1
3
2
4
2
3
4
1

FINISH TIME                    To continue the experiment, please go to next page.

_____

ELAPSED TIME

_____

**THE EXPERIMENT**   DIRECTIONS: Name the number of +s in each row as fast as you can.

START TIME

_____

```
                              +
                              +  +  +  +
                              +  +  +
                              +  +
                              +  +  +  +
                              +  +
                              +  +  +
                              +
                              +
                              +  +
                              +  +  +
                              +  +  +  +
                              +  +
                              +  +  +  +
                              +
                              +  +  +
                              +  +  +  +
                              +  +  +
                              +
                              +  +
                              +  +
                              +  +  +
                              +
                              +  +  +  +
                              +
                              +  +  +  +
                              +  +
                              +  +  +
                              +  +  +
                              +  +  +  +
                              +
                              +  +
```

FINISH TIME

_____

To continue the experiment, please go to next page.

ELAPSED TIME

_____

**THE EXPERIMENT** DIRECTIONS: Name the number of digits in each row as fast as you can.

START TIME

_____

```
2
1 1 1 1
4 4 4
3 3
3 3 3 3
2 2 2
4 4
1 1
4
1 1
3 3 3 3
2 2 2
2 2 2 2
1 1
3
4 4 4
3 3 3 3
1 1 1
2
4 4
3 3
4 4 4
2
1 1 1 1
3
1 1 1 1
4 4
2 2 2
4 4 4
3 3 3 3
2
1 1
```

FINISH TIME

You are through participating in the experiment.
Please return to the introduction.

_____

ELAPSED TIME

_____

| | |
|---|---|
| **BASES OF SCIENTIFIC PSYCHOLOGY** Why do people and animals think and act as they do? | **Research** satisfies curiosity solves basic and applied problems **Sources of Belief** authority tenacity a priori assumptions empiricism **Scientific Procedures** observation correlation experimentation induction deduction strong inference **Scientific Theories** organize and predict are parsimonious precise testable **Scientific Data** illustrate psychological processes demonstrate what can happen |

# 1  ||| **Bases of Scientific Psychology**

What is scientific psychology all about? How does science differ from other modes of knowing? What are some of the assumptions underlying the scientific method? What procedures do psychologists use to study behavior? We will pursue these questions in this chapter by examining a social psychological phenomenon called social loafing. Because the answers to the questions we will examine provide a framework for the rest of the text, you need to understand what is meant by science and scientific psychology.

The goal of scientific psychology is to understand why people and animals think and act as they do. In contrast to the informal and secondary sources of knowledge relied on by nonscientists, psychologists use a variety of well-developed techniques to gather information and develop theoretical explanations. As one example of this scientific approach to understanding, consider the following case study of the research process.

## |||| MAKING SENSE OF THE WORLD

### Social Loafing

A common observation—one you probably have made yourself on many occasions—is that people working in a group often seem to "slack off" in their effort. Many people in groups seem willing to let a few do the work. Bibb Latané, a social psychologist, noticed this tendency and decided to study it experimentally. Initially, Latané examined the research literature to see if there were any evidence for this phenomenon of people's working less hard in groups, which he named **social loafing.** One of the earliest studies of social loafing was conducted by a German psychologist named Ringelmann (reported in Moede, 1927), who asked people to pull on a rope as hard as they could. The subjects pulled by themselves or with one, two, or seven others. A sensitive gauge was used to measure how strongly they pulled the rope. If people exert as much effort in groups as when alone, then the group performance should be the sum of the efforts of all individuals. Ringelmann discovered that groups of two pulled at only 95 percent of their capacity, and groups of three and eight sank to 85 percent and 49 percent, respectively. So, it is probably not just our imaginations when we notice others (and ourselves?) seeming to put forth less effort when working in groups: Ringelmann's research provides us with a good example of social loafing.

Latané, and his colleagues went on to perform a systematic series of experiments on the phenomenon of social loafing. (Latané, 1981; Latané, Williams, and Harkins, 1979; Harkins, Latané, and Williams, 1980). They first showed that the phenomenon could be obtained in other experimental situations besides that of rope-pulling. They have also demonstrated that social loafing occurs in several different cultures, including that of the Chinese, who are supposed to be so work-oriented (Gabrenya, Latané, and Wang, 1983), and even holds for young children. Thus social loafing seems to be a pervasive characteristic of working in groups.

Latané has related this work to a more general theory of human social behavior (Latané, 1981). The evidence from the experimental studies points to *diffusion of responsibility* as a possible reason for social loafing. People working by themselves think they are responsible for completing the task; when they work in groups, however, this feeling of responsibility diffuses to others. The same idea accounts for behavior in other group situations: If one of your professors asked a question in a class containing only two other people, you would probably feel responsible for trying to think up an answer. However, if there were two hundred other people in the class, you would likely feel much less responsible for answering. Similarly, people are more likely to help in an emergency when they feel the burden of responsibility than when there are several others about who could help out.

One possible benefit of such basic research into a phenomenon is that the findings may be applied later to solve some practical problem. A great problem in American society is the declining productivity of the work force. Although social loafing is, at best, only one factor involved in this complicated issue, Marriot (1949) showed that factory workers working in large groups produce less per individual than do those working in small groups. Thus, basic research that would show a way to overcome the problem of social loafing may be of great practical import. In fact, Williams, Harkins, and Latané (1981) did find conditions that eliminated the effect of social loafing in their experimental situation. When individual performance (rather than just performance of the entire group) could be monitored within the group situation, the individuals worked just as hard as they did when they worked alone. Certainly more research must be done, but it may be that simply measuring individual performance in group situations could help eliminate social loafing and increase productivity. The proposed solution may seem simple, but in many jobs only group performance is measured: Individual performance is ignored.

We have taken the trouble to discuss Latané's studies of social loafing as an example of psychological research to illustrate how an interesting problem can be brought into a laboratory setting and studied in a controlled manner. When carefully conducted, the experiments performed will promote a better understanding of the phenomenon of interest than will simple observation of events and reflection about them. This book is largely about the proper conduct of such experimental studies—how to develop hypotheses, arrange experimental conditions to test the hypotheses, collect observations (data) within an experiment, and then analyze and interpret the data collected. In short, in this book we try to cover the fundamentals of scientific inquiry as applied to psychology.

Before examining the specifics of research, we will discuss some general issues in the remainder of this chapter. The research on social loafing will be used to illustrate several aspects of psychological science—its purposes, its sources, and its nature.

## |||| PURPOSES OF SCIENTIFIC PSYCHOLOGY

### Curiosity: The Wellspring of Science

A scientist wants to discover how and why things work. In this desire he or she is not different from a child or anyone else who also is curious about the world we inhabit. The casual observer may not feel terribly frustrated if some observation (for example, that water always goes down a sink drain counterclockwise, or that individual effort in a group is low) cannot be explained. However, the professional scientist has a strong desire to pursue an observation until an explanation is at hand or a problem is solved. It is not so much that scientists are more curious than other people as that they are willing to go to much greater lengths to satisfy their curiosity than are nonscientists. This unwillingness to tolerate unanswered questions and unsolved problems has led science to develop several techniques for obtaining relief from curiosity. It is the careful application of these techniques that distinguishes scientific curiosity from everyday curiosity.

Of what use is scientific curiosity? What purpose does it serve? We have stated that psychologists try to determine why people and animals think and act as they do. Let us explore what this means in more detail.

### Knowledge: Basic and Applied

A convenient way to summarize the purposes of the research on social loafing in particular and scientific psychology in general comes from Rom Harré, a philosopher of science at the University of Oxford, who said, "Experiments ... offer glimpses of a mysterious reality ... [and] they are the basis of tightly disciplined means for the acquisition of certified practical knowledge" (1983, pp. 1–2). These two purposes of science, the glimpses of reality and the acquisition of practical knowledge, are usually called *basic research* and *applied research*, respectively. Although the scientific quest for knowledge may be for one purpose only, usually basic and applied interests eventually intermingle in interesting ways, as demonstrated by the various kinds of research done on social loafing. Ringelmann's early observations of social loafing in the laboratory were also documented in the workplace (Marriot, 1949). A potentially useful way to improve group productivity then arose from the laboratory work of Latané and his colleagues, who found that individual performance assessment can reduce social loafing.

The interplay of basic and applied interests in the social loafing example is of interest because scientists have disagreed about the relative merits of basic and applied research. Some, referring to the primacy of practical knowledge, believe that "the proof is in the pudding." On the other hand, some scientists prefer "pure" research, because they believe that mundane interests seem to subvert attempts to understand nature and acquire knowledge for its own sake.

One reason some scientists prefer to focus on applied research is that it often takes quite a while for a concept developed by basic research to find some useful application in society. Adams (1972) discusses a study that traced five socially important products to discover the impact of basic research, if any. Although basic research accounted for 70 percent of the significant events, these events occurred twenty to thirty years before the ultimate use of the product. This long time lag can obscure the crucial role of basic research, so that many people incorrectly believe that basic research is not very useful to society. Frequently, it is difficult to tell which basic research project being done today will have an impact thirty years from now, but this inability to predict hardly means that we should stop doing basic research.

Basic research often precedes applied work, but this is not inevitably the case: Applied problems and research can lead to basic research. For example, a substantial amount of serious work on complex human intelligence was not undertaken until a practical problem spurred the interest of psychologists. Near the beginning of this century, the French psychologists Binet and Simon undertook a career-long examination of intelligence after they had been asked to develop a way of discriminating between mentally retarded and normal schoolchildren (Cairns and Ornstein, 1979).

Often, basic work and applied work are intertwined. Studies of human depression are one example. Examinations in the clinic done to determine the nature of depressive symptoms coincided with research on rats and dogs that attempted to determine some of the causes of depression. As in the case of social loafing, work in each area had implications for the other (Seligman, 1975). The lack of motivation often seen in human depressives was observed in dogs when they were treated in certain ways. Then at least one cause of this decrease in motivation was determined. Finally, for both dogs and humans, a therapy was devised that tended to alleviate the drop in motivation that often accompanies depression.

 By now, we hope you have a good feel for some aspects of the research process: Problems (whether pure or applied) are attacked, and answers are sought. Although the division of research into basic and applied categories is common, a far more important distinction is that between good and bad research. Understanding social loafing, intelligence, or depression requires the appropriate application of good scientific methodology. Determining why people and animals think and act as they do is the goal of a scientific approach to psychology. The primary purpose of a research project may be basic or applied, but understanding is ultimately a two-way street between the two purposes. The principles and practices covered in this text apply with equal force to basic and applied research. You can and should use them to evaluate all the psychological research you encounter, whether as a student, a professional psychologist, or an educated person reading the daily newspaper.

| **CONCEPT SUMMARY** | Research is conducted to<br>**satisfy curiosity**<br>**solve basic and applied problems** |
| --- | --- |

## |||| SOURCES OF KNOWLEDGE   *imp. section*

### Fixation of Belief

Science and scientific psychology in particular are valid ways to acquire knowledge about the world around us. What characteristics of the scientific approach make it a desirable way to learn about and arrive at beliefs about the nature of things? Perhaps the best way to answer this question is to contrast science with other modes of fixing belief, since science is only one way that beliefs are formed.

 More than a hundred years ago, the American philosopher Charles Sanders Peirce (1877) compared the scientific way of knowing with three other methods of developing beliefs. He called these the **authority, tenacity,** and **a priori** methods. According to Peirce, the simplest way of fixing belief is to take someone else's word on faith. A trusted authority tells you what is true and what is false. Young children believe what their parents tell them simply because Mommy and Daddy are always right. As children get older they may discover, unhappily, that Mom and Dad are not always correct when it comes to astrophysics, macroeconomics, computer technology, and other specialized fields of knowledge. Although this may cause children to doubt some of their parents' earlier proclamations, it may not result in utter rejection of this method of fixing belief. Instead, some other authority may be sought. Religious beliefs are formed by the method of authority. Long after children have rejected their parents as the source of all knowledge, they may still believe that the pope is infallible insofar as religious doctrine is concerned. Believing the evening news means that one accepts Dan Rather or some other news commentator as authority. You may believe your professors because they are authorities. Since people lack the resources to investigate everything they learn, much knowledge and many beliefs are fixed by the method of authority. Provided nothing happens to raise doubts about the competence of the authority setting the beliefs, this method offers the great advantages of minimum effort and substantial security. In a troubled world, it is pleasant to have complete faith in beliefs handed down to you.

 Another method of fixing belief is one in which a person steadfastly refuses to alter acquired knowledge, regardless of evidence to the contrary.

*refuses to consider data*

The method of tenacity, as it was termed by Peirce, is commonly seen in racial bigots who rigidly cling to a stereotype even in the presence of a good counterexample. Although this method of maintaining a belief may not be entirely rational, we cannot say that it is completely without value. Bigots are still around and somehow manage to find a few others to share their beliefs. The method of tenacity allows people to maintain a uniform and constant outlook on things, so it may relieve them from a certain amount of stress and psychological discomfort. For people who have difficulty handling stress, the method of tenacity may be a reasonable way to fix belief.

③ The third nonscientific method discussed by Peirce fixes belief a priori. In this context the term *a priori* refers to something that is believed without prior study or examination. Propositions that seem reasonable are believed. This is an extension of the method of authority. However, there is no one particular authority being followed blindly in this method. The general cultural outlook is what seems to fix belief a priori. People once believed that the world was flat, and it did seem reasonable to suppose that the sun revolved around the earth as does the moon. Indeed, the world does look flat if you are not in a spacecraft.

*The scientific method*

The last of Peirce's methods, the *scientific* one, fixes belief on the basis of experience. If we define scientific psychology (as well as science in general) as a repeatable, self-correcting undertaking that seeks to understand phenomena on the basis of empirical observation, then we can see several advantages to science over the methods just outlined. Let us see what we mean by **empirical** and **self-correcting,** and examine the advantages associated with those aspects of science. First, none of those other methods relies on data (observations of the world) obtained by systematic observation. In other words, there is no empirical basis for fixing belief. The word *empirical* is derived from an old Greek word meaning *experience.* Having ① an empirical basis for beliefs means that experience rather than faith is the source of knowledge. Having one's beliefs fixed by authority carries no guarantee that the authority obtained data before forming an opinion. By definition, the method of tenacity refuses to consider data, as does the a priori method. Facts that are considered in these other modes of fixing belief are not ordinarily obtained by systematic procedures. For example, casual observation was the "method" that led to the ideas that the world was flat and that frogs spontaneously generated from the mud each spring, as Aristotle believed.

② The second advantage of science is that it offers procedures for establishing the superiority of one belief over another. Persons holding different beliefs will find it difficult to reconcile their opinions. Science overcomes this problem. In principle, anyone can make an empirical observation, which means that scientific data can be public and can be obtained repeatedly. Through public observations, new beliefs are compared with old beliefs, and old beliefs are discarded if they do not fit the empirical facts. This does not imply that each and every scientist instantaneously drops outmoded beliefs in favor of new opinions. Changing scientific beliefs is usually a slow process, but eventually incorrect ideas are weeded out. Empirical, public observations are the cornerstone of the scientific method, because they make science a self-correcting endeavor.

| CONCEPT SUMMARY | Methods of fixing belief: |
|---|---|
| | **authority** |
| | **tenacity** |
| | **a priori** |
| | **empirical (scientific)** |

## Scientific Procedures

The remainder of this book details appropriate ways to make empirical observations. Here we will outline the nature of the scientific procedures used to gather empirical data.

Science usually begins with analysis: the breaking down of a complex problem into its elements. Psychological analysis of thought and behavior involves **description, prediction,** and **explanation.** With regard to social loafing, description refers to what social loafing entails and when and where it occurs. Prediction in this case specifies relationships, such as the one relating ethnic group and social loafing. How things affect each other allows the psychologist to predict future behaviors. But ultimately psychologists want to be able to explain the behavior. Explanation here means that the psychologist can determine some of the conditions under which social loafing occurs, that is, the causes of social loafing.

The analytic activities of *description, prediction,* and *explanation* correspond to the three major classes of research techniques used in scientific psychology: **observation, correlation,** and **experimentation.** Observation procedures include naturalistic observation. Latané's initial views about social loafing were shaped by his observations in natural settings. Another way of obtaining descriptive data is by means of surveys, in which substantial numbers of people are systematically interviewed about some aspect of behavior. The case study is another observation technique. In a case study, one person (or perhaps a few people) are interrogated in detail to provide a descriptive history of that individual.

Very often the results from these observation procedures allow further research. A correlation technique might be used for the purpose of prediction or selection. Even though you may not have been aware of it, it is likely that you were selected by your college admissions office on the basis of the results of correlation research. College admissions offices correlate such things as high school grades with freshman college grades so that they can predict who will succeed (at least in the freshman year). Thereafter, students with certain high school credentials are selected on the basis of the previous correlation, and the admissions officer can then predict that the selected students have a particular chance of success. You should note that a correlation specifies how variables are related and does not specify that one caused the other (high school grades cannot cause college grades).

If the goal is, for example, to explain or determine the causes of social loafing, then the psychologist will have to engage in experimentation. Experimentation involves manipulating or changing some aspect of the situation and observing the effect this has on some thought or behavior. In a laboratory setting, an experimenter might vary the number of other people in a group (from zero to seven) and note the differences in effort that result from changes in group size. The comparison the experimenter produces (manipulates) is called the **independent variable** (group size in this case). The **dependent variable** is what is observed or measured (some measure of work effort).

A type of research that is not quite an experiment, the **quasi-experiment,** uses natural manipulations that are selected rather than imposed by the researcher. In a quasi-experiment, the "manipulation" could be ethnic group (social loafing in Chinese people contrasted to that in Americans), or it could be any other naturally occurring attribute or event, such as age, intelligence, the occurrence of a strike in industry, and so on. Quasi-experiments do not allow as much control as true experiments do; this means that the conclusions drawn from a quasi-experiment usually cannot be as strong as the explanations derived from a true experiment with a controlled manipulation. However, quasi-experiments have the twin advantages of being concerned with intrinsically interesting variables and being able to study the effects of variables that would be unethical to manipulate directly.

*advantages!*

The appropriate use of these research techniques and an adequate analysis of the data obtained from them provide the backbone of scientific psychology. Before considering the details of these procedures, we will examine the nature of the scientific method.

| **CONCEPT SUMMMARY** | **Data-Collection Procedures** | | |
|---|---|---|---|
| | *Descriptive Data* | *Predictive Data* | *Explanatory Data* |
| | Naturalistic observation | Correlational | Quasi-experiments |
| | Case study | approach | independent variable |
| | Survey research | | is not controlled |
| | | | directly |
| | | | True experiments |
| | | | the independent |
| | | | variable is varied by |
| | | | the experimenter |

## | | | | THE NATURE OF THE SCIENTIFIC METHOD

Empirical observation and self-correction are the hallmarks of the scientific method. In this section we will examine how these work in science and scientific psychology.

Let us first step back and look at the social loafing research in a general way. Casual observation and some applied work suggested the problem area to be investigated. Laboratory experiments indicated some characteristics of social loafing and tested some predictions about its nature. Eventually, the data from the experiments suggested a solution to the practical

*Francis Bacon*

aspects of social loafing, and the same data were related to diffusion of responsibility, a more general theory in social psychology. This summary seems to capture how science typically works: Empirical observations made on the basis of either casual observations or more formal theories reveal something about those theories, which in turn can lead to further empirical work.

According to Harré (1983), this cyclical and self-correcting nature of science was first recognized by Francis Bacon (1561–1626), who has been credited with being the leading force in the scientific revolution that began in the seventeenth century (Jones, 1982). Although his analysis might today be seen as somewhat primitive, Bacon anticipated several important aspects of modern science that we will explore in detail.

## Induction and Deduction

Certain basic elements are shared by all approaches to science. The most important of these are **data** (empirical observations) and **theory** (organization of concepts that permit prediction of data). Science needs and uses both data and theory, and our outline of research on social loafing indicates that they can be interlinked in a complex way. However, in the history of science, individual scientists have differed about which is more important and which comes first. Trying to decide this is a little like trying to decide whether the chicken or the egg comes first. Science attempts to understand why things work the way they do, and, as we will argue, understanding involves both data and theory.

*Bacon*

Although Bacon recognized the importance of both data and theory, he believed in the primacy of empirical observations. Many modern scientists also emphasize data and view progress in science as working from data to theory. Such an approach is an example of **induction,** in which reasoning proceeds from particular data to a general theory. The converse approach, which emphasizes theory predicting data, is called **deduction;** here, reasoning proceeds from a general theory to particular data. Because many scientists and philosophers of science have argued for the primacy of one form of reasoning over the other, we will examine induction and deduction in some detail.

Since empirical observations distinguish science from other modes of fixing belief, many have argued that induction must be the way that science should work. As Harré (1983) states it, "observations and the results of experiments are said to be 'data,' which provide a sound and solid base for the erection of the fragile edifice of scientific thought" (p. 6). In the case of social loafing, the argument would be that the facts of social loafing derived from experimentation produced the theory of diffusion of responsibility.

The inductive approach seems to be a straightforward one. According to this view, general explanations are induced from a set of empirical observations. Once enough information has been collected, an explanation occurs to the researcher that organizes and describes the data. However, if taken literally, the inductive approach by itself cannot provide a satisfactory account of scientific understanding. A purely inductive approach does not

*One problem!*

seem to capture the way in which science corrects itself. In the case of social loafing, casual observations provided an informal theory that provided the impetus for the initial experiments. The results of these experiments then suggested a theory that guided subsequent empirical work. Stated another way, the initial experiments that had to be done were *deduced* from the informal notion of social loafing, and the data then *induced* a more formal theory.

A second problem with a purely inductive approach has to do with the finality of empirical observations. Scientific observations are tied to the circumstances under which they are made, which means that the laws or theories that are induced from them must also be limited in scope. Subsequent experiments in different contexts may suggest another theory or modifications to an existing one, so our theories that are induced on the basis of particular observations can (and usually do) change when other observations are made. This, of course, is a problem only if one takes an authoritarian view of ideas and believes in clinging tenaciously to a particular theory. Thus, theories induced from observations are tentative ideas, not immutable truths, and the theoretical changes that occur as a result of continued empirical work exemplify the self-correcting nature of science.

*deduction*

The deductive approach, which emphasizes the primacy of theory, takes as its point of departure the two problems of induction that we just mentioned: the importance of general ideas determining the kinds of observations that are made, and the temporary nature of induction. According to the deductive view, the important scientific aspect of the social loafing research is the empirical guidance provided by the formal theory of social loafing. Further, the more general theory, diffusion of responsibility, provides understanding of social loafing. The deductive approach holds well-developed theories in high regard. Casual observations, informal theories, and data take second place to broad theories that describe and predict a substantial number of observations.

From the standpoint of the deductive approach, scientific understanding means, in part, that a theory will predict that certain kinds of empirical observations should occur. In the case of social loafing, the theory of diffusion of responsibility suggests that monitoring individual performance in a group should reduce the diffusion of responsibility, which in turn will reduce the amount of social loafing that is observed. This prediction, as we have seen, proves to be correct.

But what do correct predictions reveal? If a theory is verified by the results of experiments, a deductive scientist might have increased confidence in the veracity of the theory. However, since empirical observations are not final and can change, something other than verification may be essential for acceptance or rejection of a theory. Popper (1961), a philosopher of science, has suggested that good theories must be fallible. That is, the empirical predictions must be capable of tests that could show them to be false. This suggestion of Popper's has been called the **falsifiability view.** According to the falsifiability view, the temporary nature of induction makes negative evidence more important than positive support. If a prediction is supported by data, one cannot say that the theory is true. However, if a theory leads to a prediction that is not supported by the data, then Popper

*Popper*

would argue that the theory must be false, and it should be rejected. According to Popper, a theory can never be proved; it can only be disproved.

There are two problems with the deductive view just outlined. One of these problems is similar to the one that plagues the inductive approach; namely, falsifiability depends on empirical observations. As Harré (1983) has put it, "to use the results of experiments positively to prove laws rests on the unprovable assumption that the world will be similar in important ways in the future and at distant places. So too to use the results of experiments negatively to disprove hypotheses rests on the unprovable assumption that the world will *not* become *dissimilar* in important ways in the future and at distant places" (p. 11).

A second problem with the deductive approach has to do with the theories themselves. Most theories include many assumptions about the world that are difficult to test at any one point and may, in fact, be wrong. In  Latané's work, one assumption underlying the general theory is that measuring a person's behavior in an experimental context does not change the behavior in question. Although this often is a reasonable assumption, we will show later that people can react to being observed in unusual ways, which means that this assumption is sometimes wrong. If the untested assumptions are wrong, then a particular experiment that falsifies a theory may have falsified it for the wrong reasons. That is, the test of the theory may not have been fair or appropriate. It can be concluded, therefore, that the deductive approach by itself cannot lead to scientific understanding.

At this point you may be wondering whether scientific understanding is possible if both induction and deduction are not infallible. Do not despair. The fact is that science is self-correcting, and it can provide answers to problems, however temporary those answers may be. What this means in general is that scientific understanding changes as scientists ply their trade. What this means in particular is that we know more about the causes and cures for a disease such as AIDS than we did five years ago, and we have a better understanding of social loafing now than we did before Latané and his co-workers undertook their research. Through a combination of induction and deduction, science progresses toward a more thorough understanding of its problems.

By way of concluding this section, let us reexamine social loafing. Initially, positive experimental results bolstered our confidence in the general notion of social loafing. These results, in turn, suggested hypotheses about the nature of social loafing. Is it a general phenomenon that would influence even a group-oriented individual such as a Chinese person? Does it occur in the workplace as well as the laboratory? Positive answers to these questions are consistent with a diffusion-of-responsibility interpretation of social loafing.

In the next phase of the research, Latané and his colleagues attempted to eliminate other explanations of social loafing by falsifying predictions made by these alternative theories. In their earlier work, Latané and his colleagues tested a particular person's effort both when alone and when in a group. They subsequently reasoned that under these conditions a person might rest during the group test so that greater effort could be allocated to the task when he or she was tested alone. To eliminate the possibility that allocation of effort rather than diffusion of responsibility accounted for social loafing, they conducted additional experiments in which a person was tested either alone or in a group—but not in both situations. In this kind of experiment, a person tested alone cannot allocate resources differentially, because that person is tested only in one condition. Contrary to the allocation-of-effort hypothesis, the results indicated that social loafing occurred when a person was tested in just that one condition of being in a group (Harkins, Latané, and Williams, 1980). Therefore, it was concluded that diffusion of responsibility was a more appropriate account of social loafing than was allocation of effort.

Note the course of events here. Successive experiments pitted two possible outcomes against each other in the hope that one possibility would be eliminated and one supported by the outcome of the research. As Platt (1964) has noted, this eliminative procedure, which he calls **strong inference,** should, ideally, yield one remaining theory (if the procedure of strong inference is used repeatedly). Of course, it is likely that subsequent tests of the diffusion-of-responsibility theory will contradict it or add to it in some way. Thus, the theory might be revised or, with enough contradictions, rejected for an alternative explanation, itself supported by empirical observations. In any event, where we stand now is that we have constructed a reasonable view of what social loafing entails and what seems to cause it. It is the mixture of hypotheses induced from data and experimental tests deduced from theory that results in the theory that diffusion of responsibility leads to social loafing.

---

**CONCEPT SUMMARY**

The scientific method involves

**deduction**—reasoning from general to specific cases
**induction**—reasoning from specific to general cases
**strong inference**—eliminating possible alternative explanations

---

## | | | | THE NATURE OF SCIENTIFIC REALITY

Thus far we have argued that scientific understanding is tentative: Incorrect theories are modified and additional information is gathered through empirical tests about the problem at hand. In this section we will explain what theories are and will focus on what experimental results may mean.

### What Is a Theory?

A theory can be crudely defined as a set of related statements that explain a variety of occurrences. The greater the number of occurrences and the fewer the statements, the better the theory. The law of gravity explains falling apples, the behavior of roller coasters, and the position of bodies within the solar system. With only a small number of statements about the mutual attraction of bodies, it explains a large number of events. It is therefore a powerful theory. (This does not necessarily mean that it is a correct theory, since there are some events it cannot explain.)

Theory in psychology performs two major functions. First, it provides a framework for the systematic and orderly display of data; that is, it serves as a convenient way for the scientist to **organize** data. Even the most dedicated inductive scientist will eventually have difficulty remembering the outcomes of dozens of experiments. Theory can be used as a kind of filing system to help experimenters organize results. Second, it allows the scientist to generate **predictions** for situations in which no data have been obtained. The greater the degree of precision of these predictions, the better the theory. With the best of intentions, scientists who claim to be testing the same theory often derive from the theory different predictions about the same situation. This unfortunate circumstance is relatively more common in psychology, where many theories are stated in a loose verbal fashion, than in physics, where theories are more formal and better quantified through the use of mathematics. Although psychologists are rapidly becoming equipped to state their theories more precisely through formal mechanisms like mathematics and computer simulations, it is still true that the typical psychological theory is not as precise as theories in more established, older sciences.

Let us see how the theory devised by Latané to account for social loafing stacks up with regard to organization and prediction. The theory of diffusion of responsibility organizes a substantial amount of data about social loafing. More importantly, the theory seems to account for a remarkable variety of other observations. For example, Latané (1981) notes that the size of a tip left at a restaurant table is inversely related to the number of people in the dinner party. Likewise, proportionately more people committed themselves to Christ at smaller Billy Graham crusades than at larger ones. Finally, work by Latané and Darley (1970), discussed in detail later in this book, shows that the willingness of people to help in a crisis is inversely related to the number of bystanders present. The entire pattern of results can be subsumed under the notion of diffusion of responsibility, which asserts that people feel less responsibility for their own actions when they are in a group than when they are alone—so, they are less likely to help in an emergency, less likely to leave a large tip, and so on. Latané's theory also makes precise predictions about the impact of the presence of other people on a person's actions. In fact, one version of the theory (Latané, 1981) presents its major assumptions in terms of mathematical equations.

Theories are devised to organize concepts and facts into a coherent pattern and to predict additional observations. Sometimes the two functions of theory—organization and prediction—are called description and explanation, respectively. Unfortunately, formulating the roles of theory in this manner often leads to an argument about the relative superiority of deductive or inductive approaches to science—a discussion we have already dismissed as fruitless. According to the deductive scientist, the inductive scientist is concerned only with description. The inductive scientist defends against this charge by retorting that description is explanation; if a psychologist could correctly predict and control all behavior by referring to properly organized sets of results, then that psychologist would also be explaining behavior. The argument is futile because both views are correct. If all the necessary data were properly organized, predictions could be made without recourse to a formal body of theoretical statements. Since all the data are not properly organized as yet, and perhaps never will be, theories are required to bridge the gap between knowledge and ignorance. Remember, however, that theories will never be complete, because all the data will never be in. So, we have merely recast the argument between inductive and deductive views about which approach more quickly and surely leads to truth. Ultimately, description and explanation may be equivalent. The two terms describe the path taken more than the eventual theoretical outcome. So, to avoid this pitfall, we shall refer to the two major functions of theory as *organization* and *prediction* rather than as description and explanation.

| | |
|---|---|
| **CONCEPT SUMMARY** | A theory |
| | **organizes data** |
| | **predicts new outcomes** |

## Evaluating Theories

The sophisticated scientist does not try to determine whether a particular theory is true or false in an absolute sense. There is no black-and-white approach to theory evaluation. A theory may be known to be incorrect in some portion and yet continue to be used. In modern physics, light is represented, according to the theory chosen, either as discrete particles called quanta, or as continuous waves. Logically, light cannot be both at the same time. Thus, you might think that at least one of these two theoretical views must be false. The physicist tolerates this ambiguity (although perhaps not cheerfully), and uses whichever representation—quantum or wave—is more appropriate. Instead of flatly stating that a theory is true, the scientist is much more likely to state that it is supported substantially by data, thereby leaving open the possibility that new data may not support the theory. Although scientists do not state that a theory is true, they must often decide which of several theories is best. As noted earlier, explanations are tentative; nevertheless, the scientist still needs to decide which theory is best for now. For that to be accomplished, there must be explicit criteria for evaluating a theory. Three such criteria are **parsimony, precision,** and **testability.**

One important criterion was hinted at earlier when it was stated that the fewer the statements in a theory, the better the theory. This criterion is called *parsimony*, or sometimes Occam's razor, after William of Occam. If a theory needs a separate statement for every result it must explain, clearly no economy has been gained by the theory. Theories gain power when they can explain many results with few explanatory concepts. Thus, if two theories have the same number of concepts, the one that can explain more results is a better theory. If two theories can explain the same number of results, the one with fewer explanatory concepts is to be preferred.

*Precision* is another important criterion, especially in psychology (where it is often lacking). Theories that involve mathematical equations or computer programs are generally more precise, and hence better, than those that use loose verbal statements (all other things being equal, of course). Unless a theory is sufficiently precise so that different investigators can agree about its predictions, it is for all intents and purposes useless.

*Testability* goes beyond precision. A theory can be very precise and yet not be able to be tested. For example, when Einstein proposed the equivalence of matter and energy ($E = MC^2$), nuclear technology was not able to test this relationship directly. The scientist places a very high value on the criterion of testability, because a theory that cannot be tested can never be disproved. At first you might think that this would be a good quality, since it would be impossible to demonstrate that such a theory was incorrect. The scientist takes the opposite view. For example, consider ESP (extrasensory perception). Some believers in ESP claim that the presence of a disbeliever is sufficient to prevent a person gifted with ESP from performing, since the disbeliever puts out negative signals that disrupt ESP. This means that ESP cannot be evaluated, because only believers can be present when it is demonstrated. The scientist takes a dim view of this logic, and most scientists, especially psychologists, are skeptical about ESP. Belief in a theory increases as it survives tests that could reject it. Since it is logically possible that some future test may find a flaw, belief in a theory is never absolute. If it is not logically possible to test a theory, it cannot be evaluated; hence, it is useless to the scientist. If it is logically possible but not yet technically feasible, as was once the case with Einstein's theory, then evaluation of a theory is deferred.

| | |
|---|---|
| **CONCEPT SUMMARY** | Good theories are<br>**parsimonious**<br>**precise**<br>**testable** |

## Evaluating Laboratory Research

Basic research is a reasonable and sometimes successful way to discover why things work the way they do. Certainly, laboratory research is not the antithesis of applied research; indeed, as noted earlier, the two can work together cooperatively to produce understanding. Nevertheless, students of psychology typically demand a high level of "relevance" in their psychology courses. This demand for relevance is not as apparent in their expectations of other sciences. Students who are not at all dismayed that their course in introductory physics did not enable them to repair their automobile are often disturbed that their course in introductory psychology did not give them a better insight into their own motivations, did not cure their neuroses, and did not show them how to gain eternal happiness. If you did not find such information in introductory psychology, we doubt that you will find it in this text either. If this seems unfair, read on.

The data that psychologists gather may at first seem unimportant, since it may be difficult to find an immediate relationship between basic psychological research and pressing social or personal problems. It is natural then to doubt the importance of this research and to wonder why the federal government, through various agencies, is funding researchers to watch rats press bars or run through mazes.

The difficulty, however, is not with the research but with the expectations of how "useful" research should be conducted. As noted by Sidman (1960), people expect progress to occur by the establishment of laboratory situations that are analogous to real-life situations: "In order to study psychosis in animals we must learn how to make animals psychotic." This is off the mark. The psychologist tries to understand the underlying *processes* rather than the physical situations that produce these processes. The physical situations in the real world and the laboratory need not be at all similar, provided that the same processes are occurring.

Suppose we would like to know why airplane accidents occur or more specifically, what the relationship is between airplane accidents and failure of attention on the part of the pilot, the air traffic controller, or both. A basic researcher might approach this problem by having college sophomores sit in front of several lights that turn on in rapid succession. The student has to press a key as each light is illuminated. This probably seems somewhat removed from midair collisions of aircraft. Yet, although the physical situations are quite different, the processes are similar. The accuracy and speed of pressing a key are often used as indexes of attention. Psychologists can overload the human operator by presenting lights faster than the operator can respond. This simple physical situation in a laboratory allows the psychologist to study failure of attention in a carefully controlled environment. In addition to the obvious safety benefits of studying attention without having to crash airplanes, there are many scientific advantages to the laboratory environment (see chapter 5). Since failures of attention are responsible for many kinds of industrial accidents (DeGreene, 1970, chapters 7 and 16), studies of attention by use of lights and buttons can lead to improvements outside the laboratory.

By the same token, establishing similar physical situations does not guarantee similarity of processes. One can easily train a rat to pick up coins in its mouth and bury them in its cage. But this does not necessarily mean that the "miserly" rat and the miserly human who keeps coins under his mattress do so because the same psychological processes are controlling their behaviors.

Not only should we be concerned with the psychological processes that may generalize from the laboratory to an application; we should also be aware of two important reasons for doing research, the purpose of which (at least initially) may not be directly related to practical affairs (Mook, 1983). One reason that basic research aids understanding is that it often demonstrates what *can* happen. Thus, under controlled conditions, it can be determined whether social loafing does occur. Furthermore, the laboratory affords an opportunity to determine the characteristics of social loafing more clearly than does the workplace, where a number of uncontrolled factors, such as salary and job security, could mask or alter the effects of social loafing (see chapter 5).

A second reason for the value of basic research, as Mook (1983) has argued, is that the findings from a controlled, laboratory setting may have more force than similar findings obtained in a "real-life" setting. Showing that the human operator can be overloaded in a relatively nonstressful laboratory task suggests that attention factors are crucial for performance; individuals could be even more likely to be overloaded under the stressful conditions of piloting large passenger planes in crowded airspaces.

Of course, if a researcher wants to test a theoretical prediction or apply a laboratory result in an applied setting, then "real-life" tests will be necessary. Installing a way of assessing individual performance to reduce social loafing in a group manufacturing situation without first testing its applicability in that setting would be foolhardy. The moral, then, is that the researcher needs to be concerned with the goal of the experiments. The researcher or the evaluator of a piece of research should consider well that goal.

---

**CONCEPT**          Good laboratory research
**SUMMARY**
                     **mimics psychological processes**
                     **often shows what can happen**
                     **may have more force than "real-life" research**

---

One way to summarize the material presented in this chapter is to say that engaging in experimental psychology can be stimulating and enjoyable. The attempt to understand why people and animals think and act as they do arises out of curiosity and the search for solutions to basic and applied problems. Although empirical procedures that rely on induction and deduction offer advantages over other methods of fixing belief, the advantages come with a cost. The cost is that theoretical understanding is always tentative because alternative theories lead to the search for new data, and new data provide the bases for modifications of existing theories. Paradoxically, the cost provides the scientific psychologist with a payment by helping to satisfy curiosity, at least temporarily, and by stimulating that curiosity into additional research and theory. Trying to answer questions about ourselves and animals is an exciting challenge. We hope that you are spurred by this challenge and are gratified by the application of sound psychological science to the understanding of thought and behavior.

| | | | **SUMMARY**

**1.** Scientific psychology is concerned with the methods and techniques used to understand why people and animals think and act as they do. This curiosity may be satisfied by basic or applied research, which usually go hand in hand to provide understanding.

**2.** Our beliefs are often established by the method of authority, the method of tenacity, or the a priori method. The scientific method offers advantages over these other methods because it relies on systematic observation and is self-correcting.

**3.** Scientific procedures include naturalistic observation, correlation, true experiments, and quasi-experiments.

**4.** Scientists use both inductive and deductive reasoning to arrive at explanations of thought and action.

**5.** A theory organizes sets of data and generates predictions for new situations in which data have not been obtained. A good theory is parsimonious, precise, and testable.

**6.** Laboratory research is concerned with the processes that govern behavior and with showing the conditions under which certain psychological processes can be observed.

## Key Concepts

| | |
|---|---|
| a priori method | independent variable |
| applied research | induction |
| basic research | method of authority |
| correlation | method of tenacity |
| curiosity | observation |
| data | parsimony |
| deduction | precision |
| dependent variable | prediction |
| description | quasi-experiment |
| diffusion of responsibility | scientific method |
| empirical | self-correcting |
| experimentation | social loafing |
| explanation | strong inference |
| falsifiability view | testability |
| functional | theory |

## Exercises

**1.** Make a list of five statements that might be considered true. Include some controversial statements (for example, men have lower IQs than women), as well as some you are sure are correct. Survey some of your friends by asking if they agree with these statements. Then, ask their justifications for their opinions. Classify their justifications into one of the methods of fixing beliefs discussed in this chapter.

**2.** Compare and contrast inductive and deductive approaches to science. Clarify your answers by referring to at least one branch of science outside experimental psychology.

**3.** Discuss social loafing research from the standpoint of strong inference.

**4.** Is it necessary (or even desirable) for experimental psychologists to justify their research in terms of applied benefits to society?

**5.** [*Special Exercise.*] (Some of the exercises listed at the end of the chapters ask that you critique a research project in some way. You are provided with enough information in the question to answer it. If some procedural detail is omitted—for example, the time of day the research was conducted—you may assume that the detail is irrelevant. Base your discussion on the information provided.) In 1983, a researcher studied how three age groups felt about war. One group contained 10-year-olds, a second group consisted of 35-year-olds, and the last group was made up of 60-year-olds. Marked differences in their attitudes about war were observed. There is an important confounding variable in this study. What is it? Speculate on the effects of this confounding with regard to the attitudes of each age group. (Hint: You might think about this question in terms of the generation gap.)

## Suggested Readings

Further information about the nature of science and scientific psychology may be found in: Kantowitz, B. H., and Roediger, H. L., III, and Elmes, D. G. (1988). *Experimental psychology: Understanding psychological research* (3d ed.). St. Paul: West.

Excellent discussions about the nature and importance of scientific psychology appear in these publications: Broadbent, D. E. (1973). *In defence of empirical psychology.* London: Methuen. Hebb, D. O. (1974). What psychology is about. *American Psychologist, 29,* 71–79. Sidman, M. (1960). *Tactics of scientific research.* New York: Basic Books.

For those of you who are particularly interested in the philosophy of science, we recommend these two books: Kendler, H. H. (1981). *Psychology: A science in conflict.* New York: Oxford. Mayr, E. (1982). *The growth of biological thought.* Cambridge, MA: Belknap Press.

---

## APPLICATION
### Research Careers in Psychology

Many of you may view a course about psychological research as a necessary hurdle for a major in psychology, but of little intrinsic interest. We hope that this book will convince you that psychological research is important and exciting. One reason you may not be particularly interested in psychological research is that you are unaware of the variety of fields open to qualified researchers. You do not have to have a Ph.D. to do good psychological research, and good psychological research does not necessarily deal with esoteric theoretical problems. In fact, we believe there are many careers that demand sound psychological research.

The range of opportunities for a person with training in psychological research is surprisingly broad. Most of these areas require an advanced degree in psychology, but that is not always the case. In any event, almost all aspects of our life need and use psychological research. Here is a list of some of the less obvious careers involving psychological research.

1. A police psychologist who serves as an expert witness on a variety of topics. The psychologist may do work on eyewitness testimony, profiles of criminals, and incentive programs for the department members.

2. A psychologist who does library and laboratory research on the causes of traffic accidents, and who evaluates safety programs. Or, a psychologist who does the same kind of work but specializes in industrial or home accidents.

3. A research psychologist who specializes in population trends: migration, fertility, marriage trends, and the effects of population density. Federal, state, and local governments often need qualified psychologists to conduct such research.

4. A research psychologist who designs effective computer displays and "user-friendly" components and software. Such psychologists are in high demand throughout private industry.

5. A research psychologist who determines effective ways of increasing energy conservation. These researchers might study personality dynamics, or they might examine ways to teach people to conserve energy.

6. A research psychologist who tries to determine the brain mechanisms involved in alcoholism and drug addiction. Such a researcher is likely to work in a government hospital or hold an academic position.

7. A research psychologist in human-factors engineering who is interested in one or more of the following: urban transportation, military training, hijacking, equipment design, or the effects of fatigue on performance.

If you are interested in additional descriptions, the following book may be helpful: Woods, P. J. (1976). *Career opportunities for psychologists*. Washington, DC: American Psychological Association.

## PSYCHOLOGY IN ACTION
### An Ethogram

Naturalistic research of interest to psychologists is perhaps most prevalent in the area of **ethology,** the study of behavior in natural settings. A recent example, which has been popularly noted, is Jane van Lawick-Goodall's investigations of wild chimpanzees. Simply observing the behavior of animals or humans allows us to gain a general impression of the characteristics and range of behavior, but we may soon desire more systematic observation. One way ethologists make systematic observations is by listing different categories of experience for the organism under study and then recording the number of times the organism engages in each behavior. For example, suppose it were possible to follow a college professor and unobtrusively record his or her daily behavior. Borrowing the checklist technique and scheme of activities developed by ethologists to study nonhuman behavior, we could record the frequency of his or her typical daily behaviors and their approximate durations, as in table 1–1, which is often called an **ethogram.** Psychology, like any science, begins with observation. The ethogram is a good way to delimit your initial observations. Another good place to begin is with yourself, but you need some additional guidelines. Perhaps a valuable way to start would be to prepare an ethogram of your studying behavior. The "Psychology in Action" section in chapter 8 describes how you might use an ethogram for improving your studying, but for now we will simply gather some data.

The particular format you use for your ethogram is not important, but it should be similar to table 1–1. You will need to indicate time, type of behavior, and place (or

**TABLE 1-1**
An illustration of the ethogram technique developed by ethologists. The typical daily behaviors of a hypothetical college professor are recorded, as well as their approximate duration.

| Activity | | 1–15 min. | 16–30 min. | 31–45 min. | 46–60 min | Over 1 hr. | Total |
|---|---|---|---|---|---|---|---|
| Eating | | | XX | X | | | 3 |
| Sleeping | | | | | | X | 1 |
| Drinking | Alcoholic | | X | | | | 1 |
| | Nonalcoholic | XXX | XX | | | | 5 |
| Eliminating | | XXXXX | | | | | 5 |
| Working | Lecturing | | | | XX | | 2 |
| | Preparing lectures | | | | | X | 1 |
| | Grading Papers | | | | | X | 1 |
| | Talking with students | | | | | X | 1 |
| | Writing research report | | | | | X | 1 |
| Tennis | | | | | | X | 1 |

setting). Also, you will want to put some measure of frequency or duration of particular behaviors in your ethogram.

If you have never systematically observed some aspect of your behavior before, you might be in for some surprises. Some of the things you might want to watch out for are total amount of study time, study time per course, and duration of uninterrupted study time. Most students find that they actually spend less time studying than they had thought. If grades are a problem for you, you might want to read the "Psychology in Action" in chapter 8 now.

It might be worthwhile for you and your classmates to standardize your ethogram format so you can compare results. There could be some revealing individual differences in patterns of study behavior.

**RELIABILITY
AND VALIDITY
IN RESEARCH**
Effective research
is consistent and
answers the
questions it was
designed to solve

**Reliability**

*Consistency can be achieved by*
  using operational definitions
  following a protocol

*Consistency of research results can be assessed by*
  statistical techniques
  replicating the experiment

*Consistency of test results can be assessed by*
  test-retest methods
  parallel forms of the test
  split-half techniques

**Validity**

*Sound measurement takes into account the measurement scale used:*
  ratio scale
  interval scale
  ordinal scale
  nominal scale

*Sound measurement depends on the technique:*
  indirect measurement
  direct measurement
  sampling
  random assignment

Internally valid research permits causal explanation

Externally valid research permits broad generalizations

Construct validity determined by converging operations assures
inferential validity

*Test validity is assessed by*
  convergent procedures
  discriminant procedures
  ability to predict criterion behavior

# 2 |||| Reliability and Validity in Research

Clear answers to research questions require reliable and valid measures and procedures. Reliable research is consistent research, and valid research does what it is intended to do. In this chapter we will focus on the many ways that reliability and validity enter into the research process. Since reliability and validity are cornerstones of the research process, many aspects of reliability and validity will be reconsidered throughout the text.

The outcome of a successful research project should be a clear answer to a question or a clear solution to a problem. In the previous chapter, we indicated that strong inference is a general procedure that can be used to eliminate possible but incorrect answers or solutions. Successful use of strong inference depends on the appropriate application of scientific procedures, and their correct use should leave the researcher with a reasonable idea about why he or she obtained particular results. Just what these appropriate ways are is the focus of this book, but before we examine them in detail, we will present an overview of many aspects of the research process that can lead to unclear answers.

Generally speaking, a researcher seeking a clear answer to a question wants to be as sure as possible that all aspects of the research project are **reliable** and **valid.** Both reliability and validity have multiple applications in research, so defining them by analogy first and then providing the specifics may be helpful. We will use the analogy of what good friends are supposed to be. One characteristic of good friends is that they are consistent. We need to know what to expect from our friends even if their behavior occasionally is erratic. When we say that we "know" someone, part of what we mean is that we have some ability to predict what they will do. If we can predict someone's behavior, then there is some consistency in it, and we say that the person is reliable. Being reliable is not enough for friendship, however, because a person could be reliably nasty or even reliably unreliable. A true or honest friend is one we can count on no matter what the circumstances—one whom we can call a valid friend. Likewise, with regard to science, research that is reliable is consistent, and research that is valid is true or honest in the sense of doing what it is supposed to do.

Reliability and validity are rarely perfect in science, just as perfect friends do not exist except as an ideal. Nevertheless, to obtain clear answers to our questions, we need to make our research as reliable (consistent) and valid (true) as possible. Reconsider the research on social loafing discussed in the previous chapter. Clear answers about the nature of social loafing would be missing if the procedures and results were inconsistent or if they did not eliminate the possibility that something other than loafing produced the results.

In this chapter we will provide an overview of the many ways in which the problems of reliability and validity enter into the conduct of a research project. Because reliability and validity are crucial components of good research, many of the topics discussed in this chapter are examined again later in the book in more detail.

---

| **CONCEPT SUMMARY** | Reliable research is consistent |
|---|---|
| | Valid research does what it is supposed to do |

---

## | | | | RELIABILITY

### Reliability of Research Procedures

In the "Psychology in Action" section of chapter 1, an observational exercise using an ethogram was suggested as a way for you to examine your study behavior. One purpose of an ethogram is to define the classes of behavior that are to be observed. If the ethogram is explicit, then different observers should be able to agree on the behaviors that they are to count or measure, and they should each examine studying in the same way. If you want to observe studying and if you want to obtain reliable results, then the definition of studying must be clear and the procedures for observing must be carefully specified. These two aspects of procedural reliability are *operational definitions* and *following a protocol*, respectively.

**Operational definitions.** Suppose that you read a journal article that reported poorer comprehension of reading material by speed readers than by average readers (Homa, 1983). To understand that article, you need to know precisely what is meant by *speed readers* and *comprehension*. Understanding among scientists is enhanced by the use of operational definitions. Operational definitions specify the conditions that result in the production and measurement of research procedures, manipulations, and concepts (Kerlinger, 1986). A speed reader can be operationally defined by reading rate, such as the number of pages turned per minute. In Homa's research, the two speed readers he studied saw about twenty-five pages per minute. This is substantially faster than the average reading rate, which is less than one page per minute. Homa did find poor comprehension in his two extraordinarily fast readers. He operationally defined comprehension as performance on a multiple-choice test derived from the reading material. Note that this definition of comprehension may not be the best one; nevertheless, it can be a reliable one because the operations used to define comprehension are clearly specified and can be consistently applied by Homa and other researchers.

Operational definitions can be viewed as a set of instructions (or a recipe) that informs others about what to observe in a particular research problem, as well as how to observe the problem. Since science begins with observation and analysis, operational definitions are a crucial component of reliable research and consistent scientific communication.

**Research protocols.**   A protocol, of which an ethogram is a particular kind, can be viewed as a collection of operational definitions. A protocol for a research project contains the rules for observing particular behaviors (as in an ethogram), the procedures for handling or instructing the participants, and the specification of other methodological details.

Let us consider a specific example to illustrate the importance of following a research protocol. A substantial amount of research is being done to determine the brain mechanisms associated with Alzheimer's disease. Alzheimer's disease is a debilitating loss of memory and other cognitive processes sometimes suffered by older people. Much of the brain research examines the spatial memory of animals following surgery on different parts of their brains (e.g., Bouffard & Jarrard, 1988). To make sure that the brain surgery and not some other factor influences memory, it is crucial that the only difference in treatment among the animals be the site of brain surgery. All animals, regardless of their surgery, must be handled, fed, housed, and tested for retention in exactly the same way every time they are tested. Otherwise, the results would probably be unreliable. Momentary changes in behavior could result from mishandling or alterations in the feeding regimen rather than from the brain surgery. Furthermore, consistent treatment of all animals increases the likelihood that animals within a particular condition will perform similarly, which reduces some of the differences that naturally occur within a group even when the participants are treated the same way. Finally, uniform treatment and measurement should make the behavior of any particular subject more consistent across time.

Therefore, because each participant is treated and measured the same way, strict adherence to a protocol enhances the reliability of a research project. In true experiments, such as the one by Bouffard and Jarrard, subjects are treated the same *except for* the variation of the variables of interest (the independent variables). Consistent treatment also helps enhance the validity of the research (see the discussion of internal validity later in this chapter).

| **CONCEPT SUMMARY** | Operational definitions and protocols provide recipes for doing reliable research |
|---|---|

### Reliability of Results

Usually when psychologists speak of reliability, they are referring to the consistency of their measure of some quantity. You might suppose that several attempts to measure the same thing would all yield the same numbers, unless of course someone had made an error. In fact, there is always some variability, or differences among scores, in a group of measures, even of the same thing. The amount of variability determines the reliability of the measuring instrument and procedure. Highly variable measures indicate low reliability, and vice versa. The measurement "error" to which psychologists and statisticians often refer is meant to imply not that someone made a mistake, but merely that certain unavoided factors caused unpredictable variability in the data. As noted above, psychologists try to reduce this variability, hence increasing the reliability of their measures, by taking their measures under the same conditions.

**Statistical reliability.**   Given a set of results, one way to assess the reliability is statistical. The methods of inferential statistics (see appendix B) allow the reliability of data to be assessed by showing how likely it is to obtain those results by chance. In an experiment, for example, inferential statistics are used to determine whether a difference obtained between conditions is due to operation of the independent variable or to chance factors. If the difference between the conditions is great enough so that it would occur by chance in fewer than one case in twenty, then the researcher rejects the possibility that chance factors produced the result and instead accepts the result as evidence for a real effect of the independent variable. In their experiment, Bouffard and Jarrard (1988) performed the appropriate inferential statistics and concluded that the difference in spatial retention among their groups was not caused by chance factors but was a result of the site of brain surgery. Thus, we can conclude on the basis of such tests that the difference is *statistically reliable.*

Another statistical factor influencing the reliability of data is the number of observations. The greater the number of observations, the more confident we can be that our sample statistics approximate the true population parameter values. For example, if a random sample of persons in the United States are asked about their preference in an upcoming presidential election, we can be more confident that the results accurately represent the population if the sample consists of 100,000 people than if it consists of only 100.

The thing to keep in mind, then, is that our confidence in the reliability of a particular result increases with the number of observations on which the result is based. So, in general, we should attempt to maximize the number of observations in the conditions of our experiments. This not only increases our confidence in the reliability of the result, but it also increases the **power** of the statistical tests we employ, or the ability of the tests to allow rejection of the null hypothesis if it is in fact false.

**Experimental reliability.**   Statistical reliability is a necessary condition for taking seriously an experimental result, but many researchers prefer to see an experimenter also establish **experimental reliability.** If the experiment is repeated under essentially the same conditions, a **replication,** will the results be the same as they were before? An adage among researchers is that "one replication is worth a thousand *t*-tests." (The *t*-test is a well-known statistical test used to evaluate the statistical reliability between two conditions.) The gist of the adage is that many researchers are more convinced by replications of the experiment than by inferential statistics applied to the original outcome. Although an outcome may be deemed statistically reliable, the possibility remains that it could have occurred by chance (statistical reliability still allows a 5 percent error rate) or because of some unintentional confounding or error on the part of the experimenter. For example, perhaps smarter subjects happened to be assigned to one condition rather than to another. Although these possibilities might seem unlikely, they do sometimes occur. In some experiments, subjects are randomly assigned to conditions (see below), and then, prior to the main experiment, the various groups are given a pretest to determine whether the groups are actually equivalent (on the average) in ability. Occasionally, pretests of this sort turn up differences, before the independent variable has been introduced (see, for example, Tulving and Pearlstone, 1966). Since such problems can occur even in well-controlled research, researchers encourage replication of experiments, even when inferential statistics indicate that some effect is reliable.

| | |
|---|---|
| **CONCEPT SUMMARY** | The reliability of research can be assessed by<br>**inferential statistics**<br>**replications** |

**Test reliability.**   The reliability of the results of tests and other nonexperimental measures of thought and behavior is often checked by taking measures under the same conditions on successive occasions. If identical conditions could be assured, then variability in measurement would have to be caused by a real change in the measured quantity. If your height is measured on two occasions, with the results 5'8" and 5'10", is this variability owing to error or to a real change in your height? The answer could be either, or both. But the more similar the conditions—shoes worn, posture—the less likely you would be to attribute the difference to error. Also, the closer the two measures were in time, the less likely you would be to attribute the difference to a real change in stature. You have some notion of how quickly stature can change, or of the stability of a person's true stature.

Intelligence and other psychological processes are more difficult to measure than stature, however. It is also more difficult to develop a notion of their stability. Do they vary at all, or do they remain fixed throughout life? If they change markedly, can they do so within a week, a month, a year, or ten years? If something changes, can we determine those factors which produce the change or are the changes the result of unreliable measurement? These are questions that psychologists would like to answer; the answers require measurement. But the alert reader will realize that we have now reasoned ourselves into a logical circle. Let's go around again, and try to get out.

Several measures of the same quantity will not, in general, exactly agree. This variability may be a result either of error or of a real change in the measured quantity. We cannot tell, without some additional assumptions, how much error there is in our measurement. Thus, how can we ask if a psychological process changes? A useful assumption—one that allows the logical circle to be broken—is that the measured quantity is stable over relatively short periods of time. (If a researcher measures your intelligence in the morning and then again in the afternoon under the same conditions, any change can be assumed to be caused by measurement error rather than a real change in intelligence.) With this assumption, a psychologist can estimate measurement error and attempt to improve and specify the reliability of the measuring instrument.

We will examine test reliability in the context of the concept of intelligence, which is not well defined theoretically and is difficult to measure. Some theorists postulate a number of separate mental abilities, perhaps more than a hundred (Guilford, 1967). Others believe that there is one primary mental ability and that although other more specific abilities may be isolated, they are less important. This primary ability has been described as "a capacity for abstract reasoning and problem solving" (Jensen, 1969, p. 19). To test for this ability, collections of problems or tasks are presented to individuals to solve, generally within a specified time period. The score that an individual achieves is then compared with scores obtained by others. Before placing much confidence in an individual's score, however, we need to know how reliable it is. Would the individual achieve about the same score if we were to test him or her again the next day, or a week later? Because we do not believe that the underlying ability changes appreciably over so short a time, we attribute a large change in scores to measurement error, indicating unreliability in our test. This procedure of giving the same test twice in succession over a short time interval is used to determine what is called the **test-retest reliability** of a measure. It is generally expressed as a correlation between first and second scores obtained from a large sample of subjects.

A slightly different procedure can be employed to avoid problems such as specific practice effects. This technique involves giving alternate or **parallel forms** of the test on the two testing occasions. Again, if correlations between first and second scores are high, they indicate reliability of the tests. Also, the equivalence of the two forms of the test can be determined in this way.

A third procedure can be used to evaluate reliability with a single test presentation. This technique provides **split-half reliability;** it involves dividing the test items into two arbitrary groups and correlating the scores obtained in the two halves of the test. If these correlations are high, the test reliability is confirmed. In addition, the equivalence of the test items is established.

| | |
|---|---|
| **CONCEPT SUMMARY** | Test reliability is assessed by<br>**test-retest method**<br>**parallel forms technique**<br>**split-half method** |

|||| **VALIDITY**

Reliability, as we have just seen, refers to consistency. Validity refers to "trueness" or "honesty," and valid measurements and procedures are usually described as being ones that are doing what they are supposed to do. It is important to note that a reliable measure or procedure does not have to be valid; however, to be valid a measure or procedure must also be reliable. Let us consider a specific example. We could easily devise a consistent measure of people that is a product of their SAT (Scholastic Aptitude Test) verbal score and their foot size—that is, the measure equals verbal SAT $\times$ foot size. However, it is not clear what, if anything, this consistent measure represents. To determine what this measure means, and hence its validity, additional information is necessary, as will be described below. Let us turn this example around. Suppose we find that SAT scores are valid predictors of college grades (see the "Application" section at the end of this chapter). In order for the scores to have predicted college grades, the scores must also have been reliable. This is so, because if a person scored markedly differently on two different occasions, it would have been impossible to predict his or her grades on the basis of the inconsistent scores. Thus, an unreliable measure, in this case the SAT score, would also prove to be invalid, because it would not do what it was meant to do—predict academic success.

## Validity of Measurement

When we assign names or numbers to objects or to their attributes, we are measuring those objects or attributes. The way we assign those numbers determines a **measurement scale,** and a measurement scale determines the conclusions we can draw about those attributes as well as the statistical analyses we can perform on them (see appendix B). Thus, the measurement scale used to assign numbers provides information about the quality and validity of the numbers. To see how this is the case, we need to consider the characteristics of several measurement scales.

**Types of measurement scales.**   All measurement scales are not equivalent. Different scales result from different measurement operations. A scale type is mathematically defined (Suppes and Zinnes, 1963) by the kinds of transformations, such as adding a constant or multiplying by a constant and so forth, that can be performed without altering the unique properties of the scale. Psychologists are most concerned with four types of scales—

nominal, ordinal, interval, and ratio—although other types exist. These four scale types are listed here according to increasing power of measurement, with each successive scale type having the properties of preceding types in addition to new properties. One thing this means is that data obtained using a ratio scale could be statistically analyzed by methods appropriate to any of the three lesser scales, but statistics appropriate only for a ratio scale would not fit the other scales (see appendix B).

It is interesting that one of the simplest measurement operations (counting) produces the highest scale type (ratio). A **ratio scale** remains unique if all the scale numbers are multiplied by a constant. Any other arithmetic operation destroys the ratio properties of the scale. The easiest way for you to tell whether a scale has ratio properties is to look for two characteristics. First, the scale has a real zero corresponding to no objects, or none of the scale property. A physical scale that satisfies this condition is weight in grams. Zero grams truly means no weight. The second characteristic of the ratio scale, from which its name derives, is that ratios of scale values make sense. Thus, a 10-gram weight has the same relationship to a 5-gram weight as a 24-gram weight has to a 12-gram weight, since the ratio of the two weights is 2.0 in both cases. A scale that satisfies these conditions for a person, say Barbara, would be study time. Zero study time truly means no time spent in study. Also, three hours of study time has the same relation to one hour as does six hours of study to two hours, since the ratio of the two study periods is 3.0 in both instances.

An **interval scale** is unchanged if a constant is added or if scale values are multiplied by a constant. In an interval scale there is no real zero, and although distances between adjacent scale numbers are equal, the actual size of the intervals is not very important. Ratios of pairs of scale values are not meaningful. Fahrenheit and Centigrade are interval scales. Although the zero value will change depending on whether Fahrenheit or Centigrade scale units are chosen, the distance between adjacent units is equal. A temperature increase from 34° to 35° produces the same change as an increase from 35° to 36°. An interval scale of some attribute of Barbara could be her grade in a particular course. It is usually assumed (that is, the grading scales are so devised) that the intervals between $A$s and $B$s are about the same as the intervals between $B$s and $C$s, and so on. However, on the typical letter-grade scale, there is little reason to assume that a person who received an $A$ did twice as well as someone who did $C$ work, or that the $A$ student is half-again better than the $B$ student.

In fact, most grading schemes and most intelligence tests are best viewed as examples of ordinal scales. An **ordinal scale** is unchanged by any monotonic (steadily increasing or decreasing) operation, such as taking the square root, adding or multiplying by a constant, or taking a logarithm. It lacks an absolute zero, and the distances between adjacent scale values are unequal. This scale type is achieved most often by asking people to rank order a set of objects, for example, to list all their friends of the opposite sex according to attractiveness. If $Person_1$ is the most attractive, $Person_2$ the next most, and so on, the difference in attractiveness between adjacent persons changes as we go down the list. Likewise, in the case of intelligence, without making some questionable assumptions, we might not be able to say that the difference between a hypothetical IQ score of 120 and a score of 110 represents the same difference that exists between scores of 85 and 95. All we can usually say is that 120 represents greater intelligence than does 110, and, in turn, 95 represents more intelligence than does 85.

A **nominal scale** is the weakest type of measurement, since it merely sorts objects into different categories. Just about any arithmetic transformation can be used without changing the scale properties—as long as objects are not pulled out of one bin and pushed into another. Numbers on athletes' jerseys represent nominal measurement since all they do is identify particular individuals without telling us anything about them. (For that we need a scorecard.) It would be silly to add the numbers that two athletes are wearing and expect the result to be meaningful. Sex is also a nominal measurement, since almost all individuals can be classified into one of two categories: male or female. Calling a person by a particular name or label merely categorizes and does not necessarily tell us anything about the person as an individual. Barbara is female and also a college freshman—pieces of information that help us identify her but do not assist us in measuring her attributes with any depth.

**Importance of measurement scales.**   Some of our discussion of scales may have seemed to you too abstract to be pertinent to an understanding of why people or animals think and act as they do. The examples we included about the different measures of Barbara's behavior should have indicated that the different scales provide different kinds of information. Since a ratio scale represents the most powerful form of measurement, psychologists should always strive for ratio measurement of thought and action. Unfortunately, this is easier said than done. It turns out that the majority of psychological measurement is at the ordinal and interval level. What does that mean to you? One thing it means is that when you evaluate the assertions of a researcher, you should be able to identify the measurement scale underlying the assertions. You should recognize that it is invalid to say that "Barbara is twice as lazy as Tom," unless your measure of laziness is at the level of a ratio scale. Scale type will also play an important part in your own research. If you know that Barbara is lazier than Tom but you do not know how much more (an ordinal scale), then you are constrained in what you can say about the differences between Barbara and Tom. You are even further limited if all you know is that Barbara is lazy and Tom is not (a nominal scale). Thus, the validity of our conclusions rests, in part, on the measurement scale. The different measurement scales are indicating different things.

**Developing measurement scales.**   The type of measurement scale on which a psychological attribute is measured plays an important role in determining the kinds of conclusions that can be made. Since we believe it is crucial that you understand the importance of measurement scales, we will examine two different types of scaling procedures (in addition to counting) that might help us understand more about Barbara. If you desire additional information about measurement, we recommend Gescheider (1976) as a more detailed source on measurement.

The **counting** of aspects of thought and behavior is fundamental to scientific psychology. In examining Barbara, we could count the following (among others): the number of friends she has, the number of dates she has, how often and how long she studies, and the frequency with which she misses class. Some of Barbara's attributes cannot be measured so easily, which means that other types of psychological measurement will have to be used.

A common form of psychological measurement is a variant of the **rating technique.** Everything from students' grades to the intensities of lights has been measured by this technique. Generally, what a person does in a rating task is to arrange the attributes in question into groups or categories that lie along some continuum. Thus, an observer might be shown lights of differing intensities and asked to place the dimmest-appearing light in category 1 and the brightest-appearing light in category 7. Lights of intermediate intensities are to be assigned values between 1 and 7, according to their relative perceived brightness. At the very least, therefore, a rating scale should yield an ordinal scale of measurement: Lights rated 5, 6, or 7 appear brighter than those rated 1, 2, 3, or 4. Likewise, 4 appears brighter than 3, and so on. If we have devised a good category scale and if we have some knowledge of the underlying physical scale (for example, some measure of the physical intensity of light), then it may be that our rating procedure has yielded an interval scale.

How might we apply the rating technique to Barbara? Let us suppose that we decide to measure her friendliness as compared to the friendliness of other freshmen in her dormitory. Our procedure will be like this: We will develop a rating scale, then we will have twenty sophomores who know our eleven stimuli (Barbara and ten other freshmen) sort the freshmen into the categories. Finally, we will determine the average rating for each freshman. Let us assume that we have developed the following seven-category rating scale:

**1.** A mean, nasty person who goes out of the way to be unfriendly

**2.** Mean and unfriendly, but not as aggressive about it as a Category 1 person

**3.** Not as friendly as most people; doesn't get along well

**4.** Typical person; neither overly friendly nor unfriendly

**5.** More friendly than average; pleasant to be with

**6.** A very friendly person; enjoyable to be with

**7.** Extremely friendly; goes out of the way to be nice to others

Our observers' task is to sort the eleven people into these categories. Typically there is no restriction on the repeated use of a particular category (some observer might perceive all our stimuli as 4s), or on which categories should be used, except, of course, that the rating follow the observer's perceptions of the stimuli.

The results of our rating procedure might look something like that shown in table 2–1. Here we have the number of times each of the freshmen was

**TABLE 2–1**
Hypothetical Frequency of Friendliness Ratings

| Freshman | 1 | 2 | 3 | 4 | 5 | 6 | 7 | Mean | Median |
|----------|---|---|---|---|---|---|---|------|--------|
| 1 Barbara | 2 | 17 | 0 | 1 | 0 | 0 | 0 | 2.00 | 2.00 |
| 2 | 0 | 0 | 4 | 11 | 5 | 0 | 0 | 4.05 | 4.00 |
| 3 | 1 | 1 | 2 | 15 | 1 | 0 | 0 | 3.70 | 4.00 |
| 4 | 0 | 2 | 1 | 11 | 3 | 2 | 1 | 4.25 | 4.00 |
| 5 | 0 | 0 | 0 | 17 | 3 | 0 | 0 | 4.15 | 4.00 |
| 6 | 0 | 0 | 2 | 15 | 3 | 0 | 0 | 4.05 | 4.00 |
| 7 | 0 | 1 | 5 | 14 | 0 | 0 | 0 | 3.65 | 4.00 |
| 8 | 0 | 0 | 3 | 15 | 1 | 1 | 0 | 4.00 | 4.00 |
| 9 | 0 | 0 | 0 | 0 | 2 | 15 | 3 | 6.05 | 6.00 |
| 10 | 0 | 1 | 1 | 18 | 0 | 0 | 0 | 3.85 | 4.00 |
| 11 | 0 | 0 | 1 | 14 | 4 | 1 | 0 | 4.25 | 4.00 |

Note: This table shows the frequencies with which each freshman was assigned to each friendliness category. For example, seventeen of the observers rated Barbara as a *2* in friendliness, two observers rated her as a *1*, and one observer rated her as a *4*. The mean rating in the right-hand column is derived from dividing the sum of the ratings by the number of observers (there were twenty). To calculate the mean rating for Barbara, we add 2 (2 × 1—two observers gave a *1* rating), 34 (17 × 2—seventeen observers gave a *2* rating), and 4 (1 × 4—one observer gave her a *4* rating). Then we divide this sum (which is 40) by 20, the number of observers. The result is a mean = *2*. Barbara received the lowest mean rating, and Student 9 received the highest mean rating (6.05). Since this is likely to be an ordinal scale, the preferred measure of central tendency is the median (middle score). The median is given in the rightmost column. An interval scale is needed to take the mean.

rated in each of the categories. Also shown are the median and the mean (average) rating for each freshman. The mean (usually abbreviated $M$ or $\overline{X}$) is calculated by dividing the total score by the number of scores that yielded the total (in this case, the total rating was divided by 20, the number of sophomores who made the ratings). Barbara's mean rating ($M = 2.0$) indicates that she is the least friendly, according to the sophomore raters. Freshman 9 is the most friendly, with a mean rating of 6.05. Note that the extreme values of the scale (categories 1 and 7) were not used very often; nevertheless, there was good agreement in assignment to categories—only in one case (freshman 4) was there any obvious disagreement.

There are a couple of things that may have bothered you about our rating procedure. In the first place, the rating task is an **indirect measuring technique.** Indirect measurement scales force the observer to limit judgments to a small set of categories, and from this limited set the observer is supposed to develop a scale appropriate to the attributes in question. A second problem has to do with the metric that is supposed to underlie our scale. Is category 1 as different from category 2 as category 6 is from category 7? To have an interval scale, we would have to answer that question in the affirmative, but in this instance we have no way of doing so. So, if we don't know precisely what the scale is, the validity of our measures is indeterminate. We could say that person 9 is friendlier than Barbara. Is person 9 three times as friendly as Barbara? A third, related problem, has to do with the categories themselves. Suppose you tried rating your friends on this scale. We bet you would find it difficult to classify some of them. You might have two average friends, so you would have to rate them both as 4s on our scale. Suppose, however, that one of the friends is just a little friendlier than the other. How do you rate them? Does one friend receive a 4 and the other a 3? Or do you rate the more friendly one as a 5 and the less friendly one as a 4? You may want to give one friend a 4 and the other a 4.5, but in this rating scheme you cannot. Thus, the categories artificially limit the scale and we have another reason to question the validity of our scale.

What we need is a procedure for **direct measurement** that will give us some flexibility in assigning judgments at the interval or ratio level of measurement. With a direct measurement procedure the attributes are measured directly rather than being assigned to arbitrary categories. Such a scaling procedure exists; it is called the method of **magnitude estimation.** As the term implies, observers assign numbers (magnitudes) to the attributes in question, usually without any particular restriction except that the numbers are assigned proportionately to the judged magnitude of the attributes. This means that if something has a value twice as large as another, then the larger receives a magnitude estimate twice as great as the other. In contrast to the rating procedure, magnitude estimation is more direct because it allows the observer to use his or her own scale and also permits considerable flexibility in the assignment of numbers. Sometimes an anchor point or **modulus** is used in magnitude estimation so that the observers use roughly equivalent numbers. In the case of estimating the magnitude of friendliness, there might be instructions to the effect that 50 (or 100 or 136.2) represents average friendliness and all other estimations are to be based on that modulus. Since we want to provide flexibility and also have observers directly scale attributes, we probably would not want to provide a modulus that might artificially limit the range of estimations.

To generate a friendliness scale by means of magnitude estimation, we could instruct our observers to assign the lowest possible scores to the nastiest, least friendly people and the highest estimates to the nicest, friendliest people. People who fall between the extremes receive proportional estimates such that someone twice as friendly as another would receive twice the magnitude estimate. Usually it is assumed that magnitude estimation yields a ratio scale. Fictitious results of magnitude estimation for our eleven freshmen (including Barbara) are in table 2–2. The results agree with the rating data shown in table 2–1: students high on one scale received high scores on the other and vice versa. Note, however, that there is a much greater range of estimates than possible ratings, which has the effect of spreading out our scale. Therefore we can probably observe finer differences using magnitude estimation than would be the case using a rating procedure. A comparison of the two tables also indicates that there are somewhat greater differences among our average people according to the magnitude estimates than according to the ratings. Again, this result suggests that magnitude estimation is more sensitive than the rating technique and is, therefore, more likely to provide useful information.

If magnitude estimation yields a higher scale than does rating (that is, a ratio scale instead of, at best, an interval scale), and if the technique is more direct and flexible than rating, why is it that the rating (and other less powerful) techniques are used at all? One reason is the controversy over *what* the magnitude-estimation procedure actually measures (Natsoulas, 1967). The relative freedom of this procedure could lead observers astray. The controversy centers on whether observers report the magnitude of their judgments or instead report falsely on the basis of some confounded attribute that is somehow linked to the stimulus. In this context **confounding** refers to something systematically related to the attribute of interest that biases the estimation. For example, judgments of loudness could reflect

**TABLE 2–2**
Hypothetical Magnitude Estimates of Friendliness

| Observer | Barbara | 2 | 3 | 4 | 5 | 6 | 7 | 8 | 9 | 10 | 11 |
|---|---|---|---|---|---|---|---|---|---|---|---|
| 1 | 2 | 265 | 25 | 400 | 270 | 260 | 22 | 255 | 400 | 100 | 375 |
| 2 | 90 | 600 | 270 | 500 | 600 | 500 | 180 | 455 | 900 | 400 | 800 |
| 3 | 3 | 250 | 90 | 320 | 300 | 200 | 60 | 190 | 375 | 160 | 350 |
| 4 | .05 | 50.5 | 25 | 25 | 40.5 | 50 | 5.5 | 50 | 100 | 45 | 90.5 |
| 5 | 1 | 100 | 50 | 175 | 130 | 105 | 20 | 95 | 200 | 90 | 180 |
| 6 | 1 | 530 | 150 | 560 | 550 | 525 | 80 | 500 | 1000 | 350 | 800 |
| 7 | 100 | 5800 | 250 | 6200 | 6000 | 5500 | 200 | 5000 | 10000 | 700 | 7000 |
| 8 | 25 | 175 | 75 | 250 | 175 | 160 | 55 | 150 | 275 | 150 | 250 |
| 9 | 20 | 1200 | 300 | 2000 | 1300 | 1110 | 200 | 100 | 2000 | 900 | 1900 |
| 10 | .1 | 60 | 40 | 25 | 65 | 55 | 2 | 50 | 100 | 45 | 90 |
| Mean | 24.2 | 903.1 | 128.5 | 980.1 | 956.1 | 846.5 | 82.4 | 763.5 | 1535 | 294 | 1183.6 |

Note: In each row are the estimates given by a particular observer to each of the eleven freshmen. For example, observer 1 estimated Barbara's friendliness as a 2, and gave freshman 6 an estimate of 260. The column means are the average magnitude estimates for each freshman. The means are obtained by adding up the estimates for a particular freshman, and dividing the sum by the number of estimates (10; one from each observer). In Barbara's case, we add 2 + 90 + 3 + ... + 20 + .1 and divide that sum by 10 to get a mean estiamte of 24.2. Barbara received the lowest mean estimate, and freshman 9 received the highest mean estimate (1535).

one's experience that softer sounds are farther away than louder ones (Warren, 1963). In a similar way, friendliness estimates concerning Barbara might have been low because she is not a good student or because she reads unscholarly fiction. Thus, we could have an invalid measure of friendliness—it is not assessing what we want. You should note that these are also potential problems for the rating method. In any event, we should not forget that the magnitude-estimation technique allows us to do something very important: We get a good measure of people's opinions.

When we use scaling techniques such as the ones just described, we are doing research in the oldest problem area in psychology; namely, the specification of psychological characteristics. This is usually called **psychometrics,** which simply means that we are trying to obtain a *metric* (a measurement) of *psycho*logical characteristics. If we are measuring the judgment of stimuli along a known physical dimension, for example, how bright lights of different intensities appear, we are engaging in **psychophysics.** Edwin G. Boring (1950), the eminent psychologist and historian of experimental psychology, claimed that the introduction of techniques to measure the relation between internal judgments (the "psycho" of psychophysics) and the external world (the "physics") marked the onset of scientific psychology. Psychophysics began in about 1850 and was then concerned with dimensions less complex than friendliness (such as brightness, heaviness, loudness). However, scaling techniques can be applied to almost any psychophysical or psychometric problem, so they continue to be very important, and additional psychophysical procedures are described in chapter 8. Science begins with analysis and analysis requires measurement. These scaling techniques and other data-collection procedures discussed elsewhere in the text will help you to measure thought and behavior.

**Sampling.**    Earlier we noted that the reliability of your observations increases with increases in sample size, which is the number of observations that are collected. Sample size is often represented as *n;* for example, if twenty people serve as subjects in an experimental condition, then $n = 20$. How sampling is undertaken can determine the validity or representativeness of the sample. Because only a sample of an entire population is usually studied in a research project, you need to try to obtain a sample that accurately represents the characteristics of the population. How can you be sure that sophomores taking introductory psychology at your institution are representative of all sophomores in colleges?

Sampling is discussed further in appendix B, and other aspects of representativeness are considered later. For now, we want to emphasize two important aspects of sampling: random sampling and sample size. **Random sampling** means that each member of a particular population has an equal chance of being selected for the sample. Unbiased random selection guarantees in the long run that the sample represents the population. This does not mean that a particular sample will be perfectly representative of the population, and hence a perfectly valid sample of the population; that cannot be guaranteed. What random selection does mean is that you can make a statistical or probabilistic guess that the sample is representative of the population.

You probably believe, intuitively, that large samples are more representative of the population than are small samples. You might expect, for example, that one unusual member of a small sample will distort your results more than if that deviant member was part of a larger sample. You can test this yourself by tossing coins. The more coins you toss (the larger your sample is of all coin tosses), the closer you get to seeing the ideal of 50 percent heads show up (Thompson and Buchanan, 1979).

The value of random selection is related to sample size in an interesting way. Kerlinger (1986) suggests that large sample sizes allow the effects of random selection to work. Very small samples are less likely to be representative of the population because even random selection can yield a limited or biased sample if the sample size is very small. An unusual member of a small random sample can have unfortunate effects even when that individual was selected at random. Thus, a large random sample is likely to yield a more valid representation of the population than is a small one. The effect of selecting by chance one unusual individual is diluted in large samples.

Random selection is an ideal that is rarely attained in psychology because it is extremely expensive and time consuming to try to sample from an entire population, such as all college sophomores. Since individuals differ in many ways, we can often assume that the population of possible scores in a research project can vary in a random way (Glenberg, 1988). If that is the case, then it is crucial that participants be assigned to experimental conditions on a random basis. In conducting an experiment on the effects of a brain operation on memory, it is necessary that the operation be the only difference between the operated and unoperated animals. Otherwise, random differences among the subjects could be confounded with the independent variable, and a clear answer to the research question might be unlikely. In this context, *confounding* refers to differences between groups that do not result from the independent variable. Differences attributable to the characteristics of the subjects can be minimized by randomly assigning subjects to conditions. **Random assignment** means that any given subject has an unbiased chance of being in any condition of an experiment. When subjects are assigned randomly, the chances of individual differences confounding the outcome are minimized. Random assignment to conditions helps to increase the validity of the research procedure, a topic to which we now turn.

---

| **CONCEPT SUMMARY** | The types of measurement scales are<br><br>**ratio**<br>**interval**<br>**ordinal**<br>**nominal**<br><br>The major measurement techniques are<br><br>**indirect measurement by category ratings**<br>**direct measurement by magnitude estimation**<br><br>Random sampling can assure a representative sample<br>Random assignment minimizes confounding |
|---|---|

---

## Validity of Research Procedures

The issues addressed in this section can be viewed as trying to answer the following question: How does a researcher determine whether the research technique is doing what it is supposed to be doing? Answers to this question are, as you might expect, related both to the particular procedure being used and to the purposes of the research project.

We noted in chapter 1 that the three main classes of research methods—observation, correlation, and experimentation—are related to description, prediction, and explanation, respectively. As was true of measurement scales, the procedure used determines the kinds of conclusions you can draw about your results. Also, as we go from observation to experimentation, each procedure can do what the preceding ones can plus some additional things. So, we can predict and describe with correlational procedures, but we cannot draw causal conclusions by them or by observation; causality is limited to experimentation. To see why this is the case, we need to consider internal validity.

**Internal validity.**    *Internal validity* refers to the validity with which a researcher can make causal or explanatory conclusions on the basis of the results of a research procedure (Cook and Campbell, 1979). The conditions necessary for arriving at causal conclusions were set forth in the nineteenth century by the philosopher John Stuart Mill (1843).

Mill argued that three interrelated factors allow the researcher to determine causality from research results. In the first place, it is necessary to show that a particular result (we will call the result X) occurred after a particular event, which we will call A. The second essential is that A and X vary together, or that X does not occur without A, and vice versa. The third element is to be able to demonstrate that alternative interpretations of the relation between A and X can be ruled out.

To demonstrate causality, Mill argued that three research methods are necessary. The first of these methods is the **method of agreement,** although by itself this method cannot determine causality. The method of agreement asserts that A is followed by X, which means that it is a *possibility* that A causes X. A causal interpretation based on agreement (A and X covary) may not be valid unless the researcher has direct control over the occurrence of A. For example, Mill noted that simple agreement between the occurrences of A and X could lead to the conclusion that night causes day or vice versa, and he knew as well as we do today that this is a simplistic assumption. Thus, if there is no control over the appearance of A, the method of agreement results in a correlation, which by itself is a necessary condition but not a sufficient one for making a causal statement.

A second method of Mill's, called the **method of difference,** shows that if A is not present, then X will not occur. This means that A is a necessary condition for the occurrence of X. The effect (X) never occurs without the cause (A).

The third method combines the previous two into what Mill called the **joint method of agreement and difference.** According to this method, if A occurs then so will X, and if A does not occur then neither will X. This joint method indicates that A is both a necessary and sufficient condition for the occurrence of X. For example, let us consider the atmospheric conditions necessary for rain to occur. The presence of clouds full of rain is a necessary but not a sufficient condition for rain to occur. Without such clouds there will be no rain; however, the cause of rain is clouds plus other conditions (a certain barometric pressure), not clouds alone. So, the necessary and sufficient conditions must be met before rain will occur.

The three methods satisfy Mill's criteria for making causal judgments, and the joint method of agreement and difference also defines the critical ingredients for an experiment. A variable is introduced, the independent variable, and changes in some behavior, the dependent variable, are observed. When the independent variable is not present, the dependent variable does not change in the same way. When that happens, we can say that the independent variable caused the change in the dependent variable, so long as other conditions are held constant, because the independent variable is both necessary and sufficient for producing changes in the dependent variable.

Notice that valid causal statements cannot be made on the basis of a correlation, because only agreement can be demonstrated (the presence or absence of A is not under the control of the researcher). Likewise, observational research can describe whether A precedes X and may give an indication of agreement between the two, but the method of difference and the joint method cannot be invoked. The conclusion is, therefore, that internal validity is, in principle, a characteristic of experiments but not of other research methods. (The qualifier "in principle" means that the experiments have to be conducted appropriately). Internally valid causal statements can be made on the basis of properly conducted experiments by demonstrating that independent variable $A$ produced (caused) changes in dependent variable $X$.

**External validity.**    Just because an experiment can be internally valid does not guarantee that it is valid in other ways. Of course a psychologist, who wants to explain thought and behavior, must do so by conducting experiments. However, as noted in chapter 1, the psychologist also wants the explanations to represent the "real world." **External validity** refers to the validity with which conclusions made on the basis of a research procedure are generalizable across populations of subjects, variables, and settings. By virtue of the fact that experimental situations must be under the control of an experimenter, the setting must be artificial to some degree. If this artificiality promotes artificial behavior, then the experiment would be externally invalid. The experiment would be invalid if the psychological processes produced in the experiment were not the same as those observed outside the experimental setting. Thus, the experiment would not be valid with regard to generality. Usually, external validity is not a serious issue in observational and correlational research, because real behaviors in real settings are being observed or correlated. Although internal validity is lacking in those procedures, external validity is usually assured.

As we noted in chapter 1, experimental settings often appear to have low external validity. (Experiments often lack what is dubbed **face validity,** referring to the fact that they do not appear to be valid at face value.) Pressing buttons under time stress seems unlike the attention demands needed to fly an airplane. However, numerous experimental results, both in and out of airplanes, demonstrate the validity of button-pressing performance as an indicant of attention. The convergence of several measures in several settings is basic to the validity of an experiment. This convergence is the next topic we consider.

**Construct validity.**    To be confident that an experiment has adequate external validity, the results must agree or fit with theoretical expectations. This is usually assessed by conducting many experiments that rule out alternative possible explanations and zero in on a particular one (strong inference; see chapter 1). This technique is also called **converging operations,** which means that the experimental results fit into a theoretical network of ideas in a sensible way. Put another way, converging operations are when several experimental manipulations converge on the same conclusion, as in the button-pressing example mentioned above. When this is done across people and settings, we can be sure that the processes under investigation are not artificially produced by the research, which means that the method has external validity. Furthermore, we can say that the conclusions we can draw from the results have **construct validity** (Cook and Campbell, 1979). If the results of a research procedure allow generalizations about a theory (the results fit in with the larger theory), then we can say that the procedure has construct validity. Note that construct validity is a kind of external validity; it allows a broad generalization. For example, the procedure used by Latané and his colleagues to study social loafing (see chapter 1) fits nicely with the concept of diffusion of responsibility, which therefore gains construct validity.

Correlational procedures are often used to determine construct validity, especially when correlational procedures such as tests have been used to obtain data. The logic and the procedures are straightforward. Suppose we have two tests that purport to measure intelligence and two that are supposed to measure musical ability. If the tests validly assess the traits they are supposed to assess, then an individual's performance on one intelligence test should be related to performance on the other intelligence test. But performance on one of the intelligence tests will not necessarily predict the outcome of the test of musical ability. Of course, if the musical-ability tests are valid, then performance on those two tests should be similar. Thus, if two or more tests yield similar results, they converge on a particular concept—intelligence (or musical ability). We can see in this instance how the name *construct validity* came about: The researcher constructs a name to describe the behaviors that are converged upon by the two tests.

In psychological testing, the kind of validities we have just described are often called **convergent** and **discriminant.** Convergent validity describes a case in which the results of two or more tests are highly correlated with each other (such as our two measures of friendliness), and discriminant validity refers to the fact that tests that are highly correlated with each other are not highly correlated with other tests that are supposed to measure other traits.

Also from the field of psychological testing, we have the notion of **criterion validity,** or what is sometimes called **predictive validity.** This is a check on the internal and external validity of the test. If we have constructed a test to screen applicants to law school, we want the test to do what it is supposed to do—namely, predict success in law school. To determine whether the test is valid, performance on the test is checked against some **criterion** measure. In this instance, a reasonable criterion measure would be some assessment of performance in law school, such as grade point average or class rank. Performance on the screening test should predict law-school performance if it is valid. If it does, then we would say that the test has criterion (predictive) validity.

When our research procedures have internal, external, and construct validity, then we are in a position to make accurate scientific inferences. With regard to laboratory research conducted under highly controlled conditions, Rosnow and Aiken (1973) coined the term **inferential validity** to refer to the case in which the laboratory situation is valid internally, externally, and theoretically. An inferentially valid situation permits the scientist to make valid generalizations and inferences, which is the ideal that the psychologist strives to attain when trying to understand why organisms think and act as they do.

---

| | |
|---|---|
| **CONCEPT** **SUMMARY** | **Internal validity** permits causal conclusions |
| | **External validity** permits broad generalizations |
| | **Construct validity** eliminates alternative explanations |
| | A combination of these validities yields **inferential validity** |

In the final section of this chapter, we will examine the preparation and understanding of tables and graphs. The ability to read the results of a research project is crucial for an evaluation of the project in terms of its reliability, its validity, and its meaning.

#### | | | | INTERPRETING TABLES AND FIGURES

Throughout this text, you will have to examine tables and graphical representations of data (usually called figures) to understand many of the points we intend to make and to understand the results of a piece of research. Since data often appear in a table or figure, you need to understand the mechanics of preparing tables and figures so you can know the important features to look for in them.

### Tables

If you have read the earlier part of this chapter, you already have studied data in a table. In the typical table, such as table 2–1, data and summarized data appear under various headings. Before you look at the data, you should first read the title of the table (the title generally appears immediately under or next to the words Table *n*, where *n* refers to the number of the table). The title of the table should be explicit enough to tell you what sorts of data appear in the table. The title of table 2–1 tells you that it contains frequency of friendliness ratings that are hypothetical. Next, you should examine the headings and subheadings carefully. These will tell you about the conditions or variables that are relevant to the data in the table. For example, in table 2–1 the headings include freshmen and their associated numbers (or name, in the case of Barbara), the seven response categories, and the mean and median. So, you should look for data that show the frequencies with which various categories of friendliness ratings were given to each freshman and the mean and median for each freshman. After you have examined the data in a table, you should read any notes that appear at the bottom of the table. The note at the bottom of table 2–1 tells you how to interpret the entries in the table.

### Figures

You have not yet encountered any figures containing data in this text. Some data are shown in figure 2–1. These are the results of an experiment conducted in one of our classes. The experiment concerned conflict resolution, which was tested by having the students read through a series of questions that asked them to choose between two personal characteristics. The characteristics the students chose from were wealth, health, happiness, intelligence, popularity, talent, and attractiveness. Each characteristic was paired with each other one, and the students read through two series of twenty-one questions. One series had questions such as "Which would you rather

**FIGURE 2–1**

Mean resolution time per conflict in seconds for the approach-approach conflicts and the avoidance-avoidance conflicts. The dependent variable (resolution time) is on the ordinate or vertical axis, and the independent variable (type of conflict) is on the abscissa or horizontal axis. Note that the mean resolution time per avoidance-avoidance conflict (*M* = 8.46) is more than three seconds slower than the mean resolution time per approach-approach conflict (*M* = 5.25).

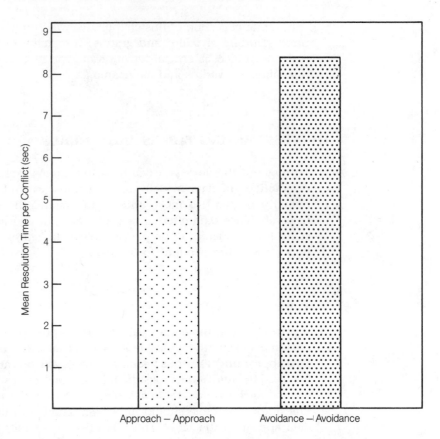

be, more healthy or more wealthy than you are now?" The other series of questions substituted the word *less* for the word *more* (that is, less healthy or less wealthy). The conflict questions containing the word *more* are called approach-approach conflicts, and the conflict questions with the word *less* in them are called avoidance-avoidance conflicts. The students had to circle the characteristic in each pair that they either wanted more of or less of, and their time to go through each set of questions was measured. In figure 2–1, we see the mean resolution time per conflict scaled on the vertical axis in seconds. The vertical axis is called the **ordinate.** On the horizontal axis, which is called the **abscissa,** we have the two types of conflict. Inside the figure are the results of the experiment. Nearly all figures from any type of psychological research have a scale of the dependent variable (what is measured) on the ordinate. In figures from experiments, the independent variable (what is manipulated) is on the abscissa. In correlational research, another dependent variable is on the abscissa. Be sure to examine the labels on the ordinate and abscissa so you know what data are plotted in the figure; then you can examine the data. In figure 2–1 the heights of the bars tell you the mean resolution time per condition, and you can see that it took the students about three seconds longer on average to resolve avoidance-avoidance conflicts than it did to resolve approach-approach conflicts.

Figure 2–1 is a bar graph, and data from an experiment are plotted as bars when the levels of the independent variable are defined at the nominal level. A different way to plot data is shown in figure 2–2. There the data appear as points (circles or triangles) connected by lines (solid or broken). Curves such as these are drawn when the independent variable is measured on a scale other than a nominal scale. In figure 2–2, the abscissa represents the number of steps apart in desirability that two personal traits were for a subject. In the original experiment, students had to choose between all combinations of seven traits: talent, intelligence, wealth, health, happiness, popularity, and attractiveness. The experimenter could have the students rank these traits in importance and then could see if the time to resolve a conflict depended on whether the comparison was between two traits that were close in desirability or between two traits that were very different in desirability. If the traits were ranked in the order in which they are listed here, we might find that the students had more difficulty choosing between less intelligence or less wealth than choosing between less talent and less attractiveness. (As far as we know, precisely that experiment has not been done. The data shown in figure 2–2 are fictitious.)

The abscissa in figure 2–2 is at the ordinal level, so the data are plotted as points within the figure. A line graph like this is used when the independent variable is ordered along a dimension. In the figure, there are two sets of points, one for freshmen and one for seniors. It is conventional to use different symbols for different curves within a graph, as is done with

**FIGURE 2–2**

Mean resolution time per conflict (the dependent variable on the ordinate) as a function of the number of steps apart in the desirability of the trait given up in an avoidance-avoidance conflict (the independent varible on the abscissa) for freshmen (triangles with broken lines) and seniors (filled circles and solid lines). Note that the freshmen and seniors do about the same for the first three steps, but that the freshmen have much more difficulty resolving the conflicts for the final three steps. Thus, the two curves diverge (they are not parallel).

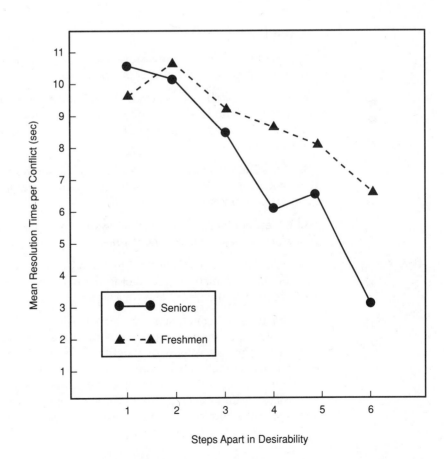

circles and triangles in figure 2–2. It is also conventional to connect data points with straight lines, unless you actually determine the equation for the curve that could pass through those points. After you have examined the ordinate, abscissa, the parameters within the graph (that is, the labels for the different conditions—in this case, freshmen and seniors), and any legend under the figure, you can then study the data. Two aspects of the fictional data in figure 2–2 are noteworthy. First, freshmen take longer to resolve conflicts than do seniors. Second, freshmen and seniors take about the same amount of time to resolve the difficult conflicts (at steps 1 through 3), but the seniors become progressively faster than the freshmen as they go from step 4 to step 5 to step 6. The second feature means that the curves diverge (they are not parallel), and this divergence is called an interaction. Interactions are important aspects of experimental data, and later in the text we will spend a considerable amount of time discussing them.

When you are trying to understand the data in a figure, be sure that you pay close attention to the scale of the dependent variable on the ordinate. Sometimes the scale can be misleading: An abbreviated scale with widely spaced numbers will tend to make differences appear more impressive, and a scale with numbers jammed close together will tend to make differences appear smaller. To see how this works, you might try redrawing figure 2–2 with other scales, in which you alter the spacing.

## |||| SUMMARY

**1.** Reliable research is consistent. Valid research is true or honest in the sense that it is doing what it is meant to do.

**2.** For a research procedure to be reliable, operational definitions that specify the methods and procedures used to produce and measure a concept must be employed. In addition, strict adherence to a protocol will maximize consistency.

**3.** Statistical reliability is determined by the methods of inferential statistics. Statistical reliability generally increases as the size of the sample of observations increases.

**4.** Experimental reliability is determined by replicating the experiment—that is, repeating it one or more times.

**5.** Reliability of a psychological test can be determined by the test-retest method, by administering parallel forms of the test, and by assessing how performance on different halves of a single test agree (the split-half method).

**6.** The types of conclusions we can make about observations is determined by the measurement scale. A ratio scale (such as one that results from counting like weight or height) has a true zero point and permits consideration of ratios between numbers. An interval scale, which does not have a true zero, indicates how great the difference is between two things. An ordinal scale indicates whether one thing is greater than (or less than) another, and a nominal measurement merely names or categorizes objects.

**7.** The rating technique is an indirect way of measuring something in which people assign attributes of objects to particular, experimenter-defined categories. Usually, indirect measurement results in an ordinal scale.

**8.** In the method of magnitude estimation, numbers are assigned directly according to perceived ratios among attributes. Direct measurement can result in a ratio scale.

**9.** Random sampling can lead to a valid, representative sample.

**10.** Internally valid research allows the researcher to reach causal conclusions. According to J. S. Mill, the philosopher, experiments can lead to causal explanation because they rely on what he called the joint method of agreement and difference. In that method, if event *A* occurs, then so will result *X*, and if event *A* does not occur, then neither will result *X*.

**11.** Externally valid research permits generalizations across people, variables, and settings. The external validity of experiments is often suspect.

**12.** Converging operations help ensure construct validity by showing how a set of experimental results agree on an interpretation or construct used to explain behavior.

**13.** In the field of psychological testing, convergent validity refers to a case in which the results of two or more tests are highly correlated with each other, and discriminant validity refers to the fact that test results that are highly correlated are not correlated with the results of other tests that are supposed to measure different psychological traits.

**14.** To determine whether a test is valid, performance on the test is checked against some criterion. If the test can predict the criterion behavior, we say that the test has criterion (or predictive) validity.

**15.** Inferential validity is assured when a research procedure has internal, external, and construct validity.

**16.** Understanding tables and figures is crucial for an understanding of data. The vertical axis of a figure is called the ordinate, on which the dependent variable is scaled. The horizontal axis of a figure is called the abscissa, and in experiments the independent variable appears on the abscissa.


## Key Concepts

| | |
|---|---|
| abscissa | direct measurement |
| confounding | discriminant validity |
| construct validity | external validity |
| convergent validity | face validity |
| converging operations | indirect measurement |
| criterion | inferential validity |
| criterion validity | internal validity |

| | |
|---|---|
| interval scale | protocol |
| joint method of agreement and difference | psychometrics |
| measurement | psychophysics |
| method of agreement | random assignment |
| method of difference | random sampling |
| method of magnitude estimation | rating technique |
| modulus | ratio scale |
| nominal scale | reliability |
| operational definition | replication |
| ordinal scale | sampling |
| ordinate | split-half technique |
| parallel-forms technique | statistical reliability |
| population | test-retest reliability |
| predictive validity | validity |

## Exercises

**1.** Distinguish between reliability and validity.

**2.** Devise an operational definition for each of the following: fatigue, anxiety, personality, and social loafing.

**3.** [*Special Exercise.*] Suppose a researcher finds that students with high intelligence test scores perform better in school than do students with lower test scores. Suppose further that the researcher concluded that high intelligence caused the high grades. What might be wrong with the researcher's conclusion? What would J. S. Mill have to say about the conclusion according to his three criteria for determining causality?

**4.** Suggest two or three ways to determine the criterion validity of an intelligence test. How might you assess the predictive validity of a personality test?

**5.** Identify the type of measurement scale for each of the following attributes: socioeconomic level, height, class rank, basketball jersey number, calendar.

**6.** Devise at least two ways to measure each of the following: attitudes towards premarital intercourse, the severity of crimes, sex appeal (in both men and women), the value of your psychology course.

**7.** For the measurement procedures indicated in question 6, indicate how you would assess their reliability and validity.

## Suggested Readings

Probably the best place to obtain additional information about measurement in psychology is in: Gescheider, G. A. (1976). *Psychophysics: method and theory*. Hillsdale, New Jersey: Lawrence Erlbaum. A good book dealing with all types of psychological research and measurement is: Glenberg, A. M. (1988). *Learning from data*. San Diego: Harcourt Brace Jovanovich.

# APPLICATION
## The Reliability and Validity of the SAT

The College Board Scholastic Aptitude Test (SAT) is one of the most widely used and widely researched tests. Most of you have taken the SAT or a similar test. Is it a good test?

The SAT is a very reliable test. All forms of reliability have been examined, and on all counts the SAT does very well. Generally, reliability is measured by a correlation coefficient (see chapter 9), which tells how two variables relate to each other. A perfectly reliable test, meaning that the two scores are identical at two different times or on alternative forms, would yield a coefficient of +1.0. The usual finding is that the SAT gives reliability coefficients of +.9 or better. Thus, you need not be concerned about the reliability of the SAT.

What about the validity of the SAT? Validity is usually checked by examining the correlation between SAT scores and grades in the freshman year in college. This type of validity check, using grades as the criterion, is called **predictive validity.** The results here are good but not as dramatic as the reliability results. The typical validity coefficient is around +.35. This means that the SAT is a fair predictor of freshman grades. Usually, the high school record is combined with SAT scores for predictive purposes, and this yields a much better prediction of freshman grades (a coefficient of better than +.6).

One area the SAT runs into trouble is in predicting the grades of students who score in the middle ranges (combined scores between 900 and 1200 on the verbal and quantitative components). Within this range other factors, such as motivation and emotional stability, seem to play a very important role in college success. Although the SAT is reliable and has fair validity, college success may be related to factors other than high SAT scores, especially the willingness to work hard and the desire to achieve.

Kaplan, R. M. & Saccuzzo, D. P. (1982). *Psychological testing: Principles, applications, and issues.* Monterey, CA: Brooks/Cole.

# PSYCHOLOGY IN ACTION
## Weber's Law

For this demonstration you will need several empty cardboard milk cartons, a supply of sand, gravel, lead shot, or similar material to partially fill the boxes, and a scale. Fill one of the containers about one-eighth full and add slightly more to another container. Ask a friend to lift them and tell you which weighs more. At first your subject will tell you they are equal in weight. Keep adding material to the heavier container until your subject can tell which is heavier. (Of course, you do not permit your subject to see you filling the heavier container and you randomly place the containers so that the heavier one is not always picked up with the same hand.)

Once the heavier container is determined, it becomes the new standard stimulus. Add material to a new container until it is just noticeably heavier than the standard container. Keep on repeating this procedure until the last container is almost completely filled. Now weigh each of the containers, making careful notes of the differences in weight between adjacent containers. You will find that adding a constant amount of material is not enough to produce a noticeable difference. Imagine that you are holding a three-pound package. You certainly would notice if someone quietly tiptoed up and added another pound. But if you were carrying a 100-pound load, adding another pound would go unobserved. Although x amount is sufficient to allow a subject to distinguish between the first two containers, amounts greater than x are required before the subject is able to tell apart containers later in the series. If you have done your experiment carefully, you will find that a constant percentage of the weight of a container is required before the next container seems heavier. This percentage is called the Weber fraction. Mathematically, Weber's law can be stated as follows: The difference threshold divided by the stimulus magnitude equals a constant (the Weber fraction). Weber's law does not hold for extreme values of stimulus magnitude. Thus, if you repeated your experiment with barbells or paper clips instead of milk containers, you would not get this result.

The Weber fraction also differs for different individuals and for different tasks. You might try repeating your experiment using lines of different length instead of containers of different weight. In this task, your subject would try to determine which of two lines was longer.

The measurement procedure described above is an indirect one because the subjects are required to make judgments about weight or line length according to a small set of categories. How might you undertake the research on line length using the direct-measurement procedure of magnitude estimation?

**ONTOGENY OF A RESEARCH PROJECT**
Research is performed to provide the data base to test theories and hypotheses

**Purposes of Research**

  to provide explanatory data base
  to test theories
  to replicate and extend previous results
  to satisfy curiosity
  to solve problems

**Sources of Research Ideas**

  experts
  journal articles
  textbooks
  curiosity
  practical problems

**Nuts and Bolts of Research**

  get the idea
  formulate a testable hypothesis
  review the pertinent literature
  do pilot work
  design the project
  collect the data

# 3 |||| Ontogeny of a Research Project

In biology, ontogeny refers to the life history of an organism. So in this chapter we will discuss the growth and development of a typical research project. This is essentially a how-to chapter, in which we discuss the purpose of research, where ideas come from, important resources in psychology, and formulating and testing hypotheses.

## |||| PURPOSES OF RESEARCH

The general aim of psychological research is to find out why people and animals think and act as they do. The remainder of this book examines research methods on this topic in detail. Now we want to consider some general elements of the research process.

You may conduct a research project for any one of several good reasons. Ignoring the possibility that you are doing projects solely because of a course requirement, let us consider some purposes behind attempts to answer the fundamental question. *Most basic research is performed to provide the data base for explanations of behavior and to test theories and hypotheses.* With a sufficient data base, derived from the research procedures we have discussed, well-planned experiments (so-called critical experiments) are conducted. These experiments try to pit against each other two theories or hypotheses that make different predictions. One outcome favors theory A and the other theory B. Thus, in principle, the experiment will determine which theory to reject and which to keep. In practice, these critical experiments do not work out so well since supporters of the rejected theory are ingenious in thinking up explanations to discredit the unfavorable interpretation of the experiment.

For example, one theory of animal learning says that reinforcement is necessary for learning to occur. According to this hypothesis, an animal will learn to traverse a complicated maze correctly only if a reward such as food is available at the end of the maze. An alternative hypothesis states that learning can take place in the absence of reinforcement—all a reward does is provide an incentive for making the correct responses that have been learned without reward. A simple, **critical experiment** tests these two hypotheses by first allowing an animal to go through a maze several times without reward, and then introducing the reward to determine whether learning had occurred on the earlier no-reward trials. When this experiment is done, animals show an immediate decrease in errors following the introduction of the reward (Tolman and Honzik, 1930), which seems to reject the position that reinforcement is necessary for learning to take place. However, the reinforcement theorists argue that removing the animals from the maze and handling them provide some reward. If you accept the latter interpretation, our critical experiment is no longer so critical with regard to these two hypotheses. Therefore, the argument about these two positions is still undecided on the basis of this one experiment.

The formulation of a testable hypothesis may be difficult for you. Hypotheses are related to theories (see chapter 1) in that they are usually derived from theories. Thus you may find it easier to state a testable hypothesis if you remember that a hypothesis makes a statement about a presumed (or theoretical) relationship between two or more variables (see Kerlinger, 1986). "Noise disrupts the grades of some people more than others" is an example of a statement that specifies a relationship between variables. To be a good hypothesis, it must be testable. According to Kerlinger, a testable hypothesis either states or implies that the variables are measurable, and it also specifies the nature of the relationship among the variables. In order for the hypothesis about noise disrupting grades to be a testable one, we need to be able to measure grades, noise, and the implied difference among people (the hypothesis asserts that some people are going to be more disrupted by noise than are others). The hypothesis does state the type of relationship to expect (disruption). Note carefully that Kerlinger wants the hypothesis to have variables that can be operationally defined (see chapter 2).

As noted in this chapter, two or more hypotheses or theories are often tested against each other. This is usually done on the basis of the relationship that is predicted. The alternative hypothesis may take the form of a **null hypothesis,** which states that there is no relationship among the variables. A null hypothesis is usually an important component of statistical inference (see appendix B). Regardless of the form of the alternative hypothesis, you should note that hypotheses, as is true of theories, have prediction as one of their important characteristics, and the predictions are what you test in your research.

*A second general purpose of research is to replicate and extend previous findings.* Since we will discuss replication in detail later, we will simply note there that a single observation or experiment is far less convincing than a series of related studies. A network of results provides generality and will converge on an explanation of the phenomenon in question. In this fundamental sense, psychological research is a never-ending (and exciting) enterprise (see chapter 2).

*You may conduct psychological research simply because you are curious.* Although your intuitions and general knowledge may lead to important research, you sometimes will undertake a project just to see what happens. We call this **what-if research.** Students in laboratory courses often come up with what-if experiments, since these projects require no knowledge of theory or the existing data base and can be formulated on the basis of the students' own experience and observations. The main objection to a what-if experiment is its inefficiency. If, as is often the case, nothing much happens—say, the independent variable has no effect—not much is gained from the experiment. But if nothing much happens in a careful experiment where a theory predicts that something will happen, the null results can still be useful. We must admit to having tried what-if experiments. Most of them did not work, but they were fun. Our advice is to check with your instructor before trying a what-if project. More often than not, your instructor can estimate the odds of your coming up with firm results or may even know the results of a similar study that has already been performed. In the latter instance, you would then be able to examine the existing data base.

Research is also done to solve real-life problems. Journals such as *Human Factors, Ergonomics,* and the *Journal of Applied Psychology* contain numerous examples of research directed at achieving practical goals. The relationship between basic and applied research has already been discussed in chapter 1. Here we merely note that if research was not capable of solving real-life problems, there would be no justification for the large sums of money spent each year on research by government agencies and private corporations. The fact that such research programs continue to exist suggests that society believes research to be an effective tool.

## |||| GETTING THE IDEA

After reading the previous section, the thought may have occurred to you that you are still no better off with regard to undertaking your research project. Where do research ideas come from? We mentioned the rather obvious tactic of asking your instructor about what-if research projects. You should seek out a consultant, and within a particular course, your instructor is the obvious choice. Beyond a particular course, on the other hand, you may try to get advice from someone whose competence or interest matches what you are interested in doing. Many faculty members are only too happy to discuss research with you. If you have read an interesting journal article, you can even try writing, or telephoning, the author of the article.

Ideas frequently come from reading journal articles. If you read critically, you will soon have a longer list of possible experiments than you could perform. Every difference of opinion between you and the author leads to a potential experiment. To keep track of ideas generated from your critical reading of journals (textbooks are another source), you should keep records of your research ideas. Most psychologists have some sort of index file containing information about the articles they have read. On your file cards you should have several kinds of information: authors' names, journals, and article titles; and information about the procedure and results. It is probably best to supplement your article file with a file of research ideas. Most psychologists keep a file of such ideas, and you should too. Write down the reference that started you thinking, and a short description of your idea for a project. Many people write down the date the idea occurred, and it is interesting to go back through your files to see how your thinking about some topic has changed over time.

As your idea file gets larger because each article you read suggests at least one additional project to you, you are now confronted with another problem. At first an idea for any project was cause for celebration. Later the problem becomes one of deciding which of several ideas in your file should be tried. Some potential ideas will be eliminated because you do not have access to specialized equipment or special subject populations. Others will be too complicated or will take too long to carry out. After paring down your list, you probably still will have more than one alternative. Assuming that each idea is equally practical and feasible, given your resources, our advice is to tackle the project you think would be most fun.

At this point we would like to remind you of our discussion of curiosity and serendipity in chapter 1. Psychological research is interesting, exciting, and often has important outcomes. For luck to influence your research, you have to do research (follow up on your idea file), and you have to be prepared to do a good job.

If you are unsure about what journals and other resources to examine for research ideas, you can refer to table 3–1 to help you along. The table lists several general sources of information as well as journals with particular topical emphases. Perhaps the most important general resource is *Psychological Abstracts*, which contains brief abstracts of articles from almost all journals that publish psychological research. After you have found an abstract of interest there, you can then read the entire article or send a note to the author, requesting a reprint of the article or additional information. The other resources listed in table 3–1 have a variety of purposes, and we recommend that you familiarize yourself with each of the first seven general-purpose resources and as many of the research journals as seem to be of interest to you. Note that we have included only a small number of research journals in the table, but the ones we have included are among the most widely read in psychological research. Others emphasizing education, clinical problems, sociology, law, and industrial concerns can be ferreted out of your school's library. Many libraries have a **computerized literature search** available. You provide the topic, and the computer scans standard abstracting sources (such as the *Psychological Abstracts*) as well as government documents and technical reports that often are not abstracted. Computer searches can be quick and thorough, but they also can be expensive. However, a computer search is much less costly than the value of time needed to accomplish the same search manually. It is possible for one hour of computer-search time to yield the same number of useful references as three to five days of intensive manual searching. Furthermore, some databases (such as Knowledge Index) have special low rates on nights and weekends that allow even students on tight budgets to afford computer services.

An excellent method for discovering new findings uses the Social Science Citation Index, which can be searched either by computer or manually. By entering a critical or key reference, you can obtain a list of more recent articles that have cited your critical reference. Since these articles contain a discussion of your key reference, it is very likely that they are directly related to your topic of interest. This is an extremely efficient way to bring yourself up to date in some specific content area.

**TABLE 3–1**

Some Important Resources for Psychological Research

| Topic Area | Title of Resource | Comment |
|---|---|---|
| Article Titles<br>Author citations<br>Article abstracts | *Current Contents*<br>*Social Science Citation Index*<br>*Science Citation Index*<br>*Biological Abstracts*<br>*Ergonomics Abstracts*<br>*Index Medicus*<br>*Psychological Abstracts* | Several specialty areas |
| Review articles | *American Psychologist*<br>*Annual Review of Psychology*<br>*Journal of Experimental Psychology: General*<br>*Psychological Bulletin*<br>*Psychological Review* | Book with chapter-length reviews<br>Contains original experiments<br><br>Often contains original studies |
| Laboratory experiments | *American Journal of Psychology*<br>*Animal Learning and Behavior*<br>*Behavior Research Methods, Instrumentation and Computers*<br>*Bulletin of the Psychonomic Society*<br>*Canadian Journal of Psychology*<br>*Cognition*<br>*Cognitive Psychology*<br>*Cognitive Science*<br>*Journal of Comparative and Physiological Psychology*<br>*Journal of Experimental Child Psychology*<br>*Journal of Experimental Psychology: Animal Behavior Processes*<br>*Journal of Experimental Psychology: Learning, Memory, and Cognition*<br>*Journal of Experimental Psychology: Human Perception & Performance*<br>*Journal of Experimental Social Psychology*<br>*Journal of the Experimental Analysis of Behavior*<br>*Journal of Verbal Learning and Verbal Behavior*<br>*Learning and Motivation*<br>*Memory & Cognition*<br>*Perception & Psychophysics*<br>*Physiological Psychology*<br>*Quarterly Journal of Experimental Psychology* | Some field studies<br>Notes on apparatus and computers<br><br><br><br><br><br><br>Now divided into: *Behavioral Neuroscience* and *Journal of Comparative Psychology*<br><br>Some field studies<br><br><br><br><br><br>Small-*n* experiments<br><br>Now called *Journal of Memory and Language* |
| Various research methods | *Applied Ergonomics*<br>*Behavior Therapy*<br>*Child Development*<br>*Developmental Psychology*<br>*Developmental Psychobiology*<br>*Journal of Abnormal Psychology*<br>*Journal of Applied Behavioral Analysis*<br>*Journal of Applied Psychology*<br>*Journal of Educational Psychology*<br>*Journal of Personality and Social Psychology*<br>*Perceptual and Motor Skills*<br>*Psychological Reports* | Case histories, small-*n*<br><br><br><br><br>Small-*n* |

We have tried to design this text to be a source of possible research projects. If you carefully answer the design-related questions that appear at the end of most chapters, the germ of a good research project may be lurking in one or more of your answers. Most of the design questions have been based on actual research, so it is apparent that even experts make errors from time to time. There is no reason why you cannot profit from the mistakes of others. Another source of ideas is the research problem in the "Nuts and Bolts" section of this chapter. We have worked through a problem under the assumption that you could pose and attempt to answer hypotheses about this topic.

The last source of research ideas we wish to mention could be called the **itch of research.** Some particular practical problem is bothering you, and you seem to need an answer. How can I study more effectively? Why do my roommates always go along with the crowd? How can I become a better public speaker? These and related practical concerns are often important goals to good research. To tackle such problems adequately, however, you will probably have to seek the help of a consultant and also examine the relevant data base. Most of the things that are bothering you have probably bothered someone else. Thus, you should review the literature (beginning with *Psychological Abstracts*) relevant to your problem. If you are lucky, you may not have to do much research before you find a solution. However, reasonable solutions to practical problems often take a considerable amount of investigation. This slow progress is one of the things that keeps applied researchers in business.

---

| **CONCEPT SUMMARY** | *Purposes of Research* |
| --- | --- |
| | Provide data base |
| | Test theories |
| | Replication |
| | Curiosity |
| | *Sources of Research* |
| | Experts |
| | Journals |
| | Textbooks |
| | Practical problems |

---

## | | | | NUTS AND BOLTS OF RESEARCH

You have a problem or idea you want to investigate. What next? Well, simply formulate a testable hypothesis, review the literature, conduct preliminary work (pilot research) design the project, and then collect the data. Sounds easy, doesn't it? It isn't. One thing we have noticed (and you may have too, by now) is that students can generate some very interesting ideas for research, but they get bogged down when they try to investigate their problem. The biggest stumbling block seems to be the development of a testable hypothesis and the *general* research plan that goes with the hypothesis. In this section, we work through a problem to show you how people with some experience develop a research project. Three things should be noted: (1) We may have made some inappropriate choices in our analysis of this problem, so you should be alert to the possibility of taking alternative routes to a solution; (2) we deliberately have not included all possible research hypotheses associated with this question, because we want you to think up some of your own; and (3) we have anticipated many of the topics discussed later in the text.

### Dear Folks: I Can't Study . . .

**Problem.**   Where you live is rather noisy, and your grades are not as good as you would like them to be. You are convinced (or, you are trying to convince others such as your parents) that your academic performance is not as good as expected because of the overall noise level of your college residence. Can you demonstrate that noise level inhibits adequate academic work? There are several potential research hypotheses here, and how the hypotheses are posed will determine, in part, your general research plan.

**Hypothesis 1.**   *Students who live in noisy dormitories have lower grade averages than students who live in quiet dorms.* Since this hypothesis suggests a subject variable (where students live) instead of a true independent variable that you can easily manipulate, something other than a laboratory experiment may be most appropriate. The hypothesis suggests that you find some way of assessing "noisiness" and then relate students' grades to the noise level of their residence. You could use a sound-level meter to measure the average sound level. This means you would have to have a sound-level meter. If you don't have access to such a device, noise could be measured by you and some other judges by using a psychophysical scaling procedure. You and the judges could make up a ten-point rating scale on the extent of noise, or you could estimate the magnitude of noise by assigning a number proportional to the noise level. As an alternative, you could have the occupants of a particular dorm rate the noise level. It might be best to have neighbors rate the noise level in some way. In any case, you may have to try out two or three methods to see which is most informative. Such preliminary work is called **pilot research.**
  You may have noticed several difficulties with this general research procedure. When should you measure the noise level? If you take your measures at night, you will be catching people when they should be studying (let's assume that it is a weeknight—Monday through Thursday—because you have a pressing social engagement that prohibits data collection Friday through Sunday). On the other hand, if you just happen to hit a party, you might bias your measures. Thus, you will have to get more than one sample of noise level. Where should you measure the noise level? Getting several samples from all parts of an entire dorm would be very time consuming.

You might have to get samples floor-by-floor or hall-by-hall (it depends on how your dorms are laid out). If you obtain noise samples in this way, you may want to redefine your initial hypothesis as follows: *Students living in noisy areas of a dormitory do more poorly academically than students who live in quiet areas of that dorm.* Now you have to get some measure of academic performance, and this could pose a troublesome ethical problem. Even if your school administration agrees to let you see the grade averages of the students in question, it is possible that those students don't want you to know what their averages are. If you plan to correlate noise and grade average, you need to have each student's grades. Short of breaking into administrative offices, the best thing to do would be to interview each resident, get an estimate of the grade average, and assure the individual that personal data will remain confidential. You would also have to make sure that you received replies from every resident in question, or you would have to devise some way to randomly sample these people. Some of the students in the quiet section might be in the library studying all the time (hence the high grades), or students in the noisy section may have nowhere else to go to throw parties and have a good time.

If you actually do this study or one similar to it, you will probably raise more questions than you answer. Since you are using a correlation design, you will have to be careful about causal statements. Furthermore, there are several questions that remain: You cannot determine whether noisy dorms produce poor grades or whether poor academic performance results in noisy dorms. Why are some dorms noisier than others? Can the noise level be controlled? Are all students equally sensitive to noise?

**Hypothesis 2.**    Let us pursue the last question. After all, your grades are suffering, but your next door neighbor does well despite noisy disruptions on your dorm floor. *Students are differentially disrupted by noise; those who are sensitive to noise perform more poorly than those who are less sensitive to noise.* One way to approach this hypothesis is to develop a survey that reveals the sensitivity to noise. You have an advantage here over Hypothesis 1 because Weinstein (1978) has developed a reliable scale to measure individual differences in sensitivity to noise. Most of this scale is reproduced in table 3–2. Respondents are to circle the appropriate number for each question. Questions marked with an asterisk have the answers reversed before the numerical scores are summed so that a total sensitivity score for a subject can be obtained. Weinstein found that noise-sensitive students have lower scholastic aptitude (as measured by standard tests) than students who are not particularly sensitive to noise. Furthermore, Weinstein correlated noise sensitivity with various personality traits (as measured by other tests) and found the noise-sensitive students had a higher need for privacy than did the less sensitive students. Since Weinstein's work is correlational in nature, some interesting questions arise. Do noise-sensitive students attend fewer parties than noise-insensitive students? What is the relationship between noise sensitivity and the use of stereos, radios, and TVs? What kind of student makes the most noise? What kind of noise is the most disruptive (human noise, music, continuous noise, or sudden noise) and what combinations are important?

**TABLE 3—2**
Some Items on Weinstein's Noise-Sensitivity Scale

|  | Agree Strongly | Maybe | Disagree Strongly |
|---|---|---|---|
| 1. I wouldn't mind living on a noisy street if the apartment I had was nice. | 1 | 2 3 4 | 5 |
| * 2. I am more aware of noise than I used to be. | 1 | 2 3 4 | 5 |
| 3. No one would mind much if someone turns up his stereo full blast once in a while. | 1 | 2 3 4 | 5 |
| * 4. At movies, whispering and crackling candy wrappers disturb me. | 1 | 2 3 4 | 5 |
| * 5. I am easily awakened by noise. | 1 | 2 3 4 | 5 |
| * 6. If it's noisy where I'm studying, I try to close the door or window or move someplace else. | 1 | 2 3 4 | 5 |
| * 7. I get annoyed when my neighbors are noisy. | 1 | 2 3 4 | 5 |
| 8. I get used to most noises without difficulty. | 1 | 2 3 4 | 5 |
| * 9. Sometimes noises get on my nerves and get me irritated. | 1 | 2 3 4 | 5 |
| *10. Even music I normally like will bother me if I'm trying to concentrate. | 1 | 2 3 4 | 5 |
| 11. It wouldn't bother me to hear the sound of everyday living from neighbors (footsteps, running water, etc.) | 1 | 2 3 4 | 5 |
| *12. When I want to be alone, it disturbs me to hear outside noises. | 1 | 2 3 4 | 5 |
| 13. I am good at concentrating no matter what is going on around me. | 1 | 2 3 4 | 5 |
| 14. In a library, I don't mind if people carry on a conversation if they do it quietly. | 1 | 2 3 4 | 5 |
| *15. There are often times when I want complete silence. | 1 | 2 3 4 | 5 |
| *16. Motorcycles ought to be required to have bigger mufflers. | 1 | 2 3 4 | 5 |
| *17. I find it hard to relax in a place that's noisy. | 1 | 2 3 4 | 5 |
| *18. I get mad at people who make noise that keeps me from falling asleep or getting work done. | 1 | 2 3 4 | 5 |
| 19. I wouldn't mind living in an apartment with thin walls. | 1 | 2 3 4 | 5 |
| *20. I am sensitive to noise. | 1 | 2 3 4 | 5 |

Note: on the basis of these questions, the maximum noise-sensitivity score would be 100 points. The points awarded to the subjects' answers to the questions marked with an asterisk are reversed. So, if a subject marked question 20 with a *1*, this would indicate strong agreement with that question—he or she is noise sensitive. To make the scoring of that question compatible with the scoring of question 19, where an answer indicating noise sensitivity would be a circled *5*, we have to assign reverse values to the numbers chosen on question *20: 5* becomes *1*, *4* becomes *2, 2* becomes *4*, and *1* is changed to a *5*. In Weinstein's study, the subjects were also asked about the noise conditions in their dorm. Questions included such things as how often they had to ask neighbors to quiet down and how difficult it was to sleep. (Copyright 1978 by the American Psychological Association. Reprinted by permission of the author.)

**Hypothesis 3.** The lengthy final question in the previous paragraph suggests several hypotheses. *The more annoying a noise is, the greater it will interfere with a complex task.* One way to approach this hypothesis is to survey the students on the degree of annoyance associated with certain types of noises and then relate this to their academic performance. In this instance, a laboratory experiment seems preferable, and there is a substantial data base from which to work (see the end of this section for a list of references). Noises are played (music, party conversations, trucks, aircraft, and so forth) and subjects rate them according to the degree of annoyance. Then the noises are presented while the subjects are engaged in some task. Selecting the levels of your independent variable may be difficult. Do you want to vary it qualitatively (for example, party noise versus trucks versus silence) or quantitatively (vary the intensity of a particular noise)? If you choose the latter, you will probably need a sound-level meter so you can measure the actual intensity of the sound (you could, in the absence of a meter, have judges make preliminary scales of loudness). What task will your subjects perform? What would be a good dependent variable? If you examine the data base for this type of research, you will find that some tasks are more disrupted by noise than others. Thus, a good idea would be to include at least two situations: one task that is likely to be disrupted and another that is unlikely to be disrupted. Some pilot research may be appropriate. Tasks that require listening probably would be more easily disrupted than tasks that did not. After you have selected your independent and dependent variables, you have to worry about subject variables (is the hearing of the subjects equally sensitive?) and your experimental design (should the same or different subjects be in each condition?). Some of the research in the data base suggests that there are carry-over effects from experiencing a particularly annoying noise. If that is the case, (and the issue has not yet been settled—see Moran and Loeb, 1977), then a between-subjects design with different people in each condition may be more appropriate. Alternatively, you could use a within-subjects design, in which the same people are subjected to all levels of the independent variable, and carefully counterbalance the order of presenting the different levels of your independent variable. If you do use a within-subjects design, you may want to assess the carry-over effects of the different levels by examining the effects of order of presenting the levels. This would mean that you would have to perform a fairly complex statistical analysis of your results.

**Hypothesis 4.**   The previous experiment, as is true of any single laboratory experiment, suffers from a potential lack of generality. How do we know that our independent and dependent variables are representative? Should we select additional tasks and types of noises to study? Furthermore, Hypotheses 1 and 2 are restricted in their focus, since they are concerned primarily with college students' reactions to noise. How can we add generality to our research on noise? *Residents of a noisy street will (a) move more frequently and (b) score lower on a rating scale for residential satisfaction than residents of a quiet street.* This hypothesis deals with the long-term effects of permanent residence, so it may avoid some of the problems of generalization associated with the other three hypotheses. However, there are several difficulties associated with doing research on Hypothesis 4. A familiar problem is how to measure sound levels. The experimenter will have to decide whether to measure sound levels only at certain times (for example, during rush hours) or to take 24-hour averages. The independent variable is not completely under the control of the experimenter. Furthermore, it may be confounded with factors such as income, status, population density, and so forth, since persons with lower socioeconomic status are more likely to reside on noisier streets than higher status people who may be able to "get away from it all."

The dependent variables are not entirely satisfactory either. Even if residents of noisy streets more often wish to move, economic factors may prohibit them from doing so. On the other hand, the turnover rate in an area is an objective number that can be reliably measured. The second dependent variable depends a lot on the validity of the rating scale used to assess residential satisfaction. If you used a modification of the scale shown in table 3–2, you could be assured of the reliability of your instrument. However, this scale has not been validated directly, and validation is a time-consuming activity. What can be said for the validity of the scale? In the first place, it looks as if it should measure what it is supposed to measure. In other words, it seems to have face validity—it looks as if it should measure attitudes about noisy living conditions. Also, the scale results fit in fairly sensibly with the other results reported by Weinstein (1978). The scale measures some underlying psychological concept, which indicates that it has construct validity—we actually are measuring something to do with people's attitudes about noise (see chapter 2). To sum up Hypothesis 4: The price of greater ease of generalization in this study is a considerable loss of investigator control.

When we compare the four studies as solutions to the problem posed at the beginning of this section, it is clear that none of them is perfect. This is always true with research. No single piece of research, experiment or otherwise, can completely answer a question. The scientist is forced to focus on a more specific hypothesis, thus answering only a narrow part of the problem. This is a major source of frustration for all psychologists, since no general answers can be found until many tiny pieces, each corresponding to a specific hypothesis, are put together. An environmental psychologist could easily spend an entire career trying to answer the problem of noise and its psychological effects. This also reflects part of the joy and excitement of science. Research is a continuous process, leading to new questions, new modes of attack, and new answers. Have fun in your research!

---

| CONCEPT SUMMMARY | **Steps in the Typical Research Project** |
|---|---|
| | Get the idea |
| | Formulate a testable hypothesis |
| | Review the pertinent literature |
| | Conduct pilot research |
| | Design the project |
| | Collect the data |

---

## References for the Effects of Noise

Broadbent, D. E. (1971). *Decision and stress*. London: Academic Press. This is a good general reference that summarizes a great deal of research on the effects of noise on behavior. Chapter 9 is the most pertinent.

Glass, D. C., & Singer, J. E. (1972). *Urban stress: Experiments on noise and social stressors*. New York: Academic Press. This work includes more than you would ever want to know about noise as a stressor. You might want to read Glass and Singer's article in *American Scientist*, 1972, 60, 457–465, which is also reprinted in *Current trends in psychology: Readings from American Scientist*, edited by I. L. Janis (1977).

The following two articles describe additional research on the effects of noise on behavior. The first contains experiments, the second is a correlational study: Moran, S. L. V., & Loeb, M. (1977). Annoyance and behavioral aftereffects following interfering and noninterfering aircraft noise. *Journal of Applied Psychology, 62,* 719–726. Weinstein, N. D. (1978). Individual differences in reactions to noise: a longitudinal study in a college dormitory. *Journal of Applied Psychology, 63,* 458–466. You should examine the reference lists in these two articles for other papers that seem relevant. *Psychological Abstracts* and *Ergonomics Abstracts* may have abstracts of potentially relevant articles.

## | | | | SUMMARY

**1.** Most research is conducted to provide the data base for explanations and to test theories.

**2.** Research is often conducted to replicate and extend previous results.

**3.** You may conduct psychological research simply because you are curious.

**4.** There are several sources of ideas for research projects: experts, journals, textbooks, and practical problems.

**5.** After getting an idea, you need to formulate a testable hypothesis.

**6.** A thorough literature search should be undertaken before you begin your project. A good initial source is *Psychological Abstracts.*

**7.** You may need to undertake preliminary (pilot) research before you can select the correct values for your variables.

**8.** Finally, you can design your project and collect data. Have fun!

### Key Concepts

| | |
|---|---|
| computerized literature search | nuts and bolts of research |
| construct validity | pilot research |
| critical experiments | purposes of research |
| face validity | sources of ideas |
| itch of research | what-if research |
| null hypothesis | |

### Exercises

**1.** Look up the term *aggression* in the index of a recent issue of *Psychological Abstracts* and read several abstracts listed there. Note how articles with various emphases are organized in the *Abstracts* (for example, animal aggression as opposed to clinical treatment of aggression).

**2.** You might look up *noise* or *human performance: Noise* in the *Abstracts* in order to read about some current research in the area analyzed in this chapter.

**3.** [*Special Exercise.*] Do you listen to music as you are studying? A large percentage of college students do. Many studies have dealt with the effects of music on the ability of people to learn and remember. An interesting controversy has arisen: Some researchers find that listening to music disrupts learning, and others report that music does not disrupt learning. Generate several hypotheses as to why music might or might not have a negative effect on learning. One thing you should consider is the type of music—one of the authors never studied in his dorm room as a freshman because his roommate regularly played Ravel's *Bolero* during the evening.

## Suggested Readings

Additional information about the nuts and bolts of research may be found in: Alsip, J. E., & Chezik, D. D. (1974). *Research guide in psychology.* Morristown, NJ: General Learning Press.

If you are interested in the effects of music on learning, you can find some background information in: Etaugh, C., & Michaels, D. (1975). Effect on reading comprehension of preferred music and frequency of studying to music. *Perceptual and Motor Skills, 41,* 553–554. Wolf, R. H., & Weiner, F. (1972). Effect of four noise conditions on arithmetic performance. *Perceptual and Motor Skills, 35,* 928–930.

---

## APPLICATION
### Skinner on the Scientific Method

B. F. Skinner is one of the most famous psychologists in the world. His early experiments on the effects of reinforcement were excellent, and they have had a profound impact on psychology. Skinner would not be very impressed with chapter 3. In examining his own work, Skinner (1956) emphasized the importance of luck and chance as opposed to a set pattern of data collection. In a somewhat humorous vein, Skinner proposed five principles of the scientific method:

1. When you find something of interest, study it.

2. Some ways of doing research are harder than others. The scientist should enjoy what he or she is doing, so do it the easy way if possible.

3. Many researchers are lucky. By a fortunate choice of equipment, you may hit upon an effective way of studying something, or a lucky accident may lead to an important discovery.

4. Related to the third principle—your equipment may break down. (Skinner began his studies of extinction and schedules of reinforcement because his apparatus failed at an opportune time).

5. You may find one thing while looking for another (serendipity).

None of these principles is incompatible with the guidelines presented in chapter 3. What Skinner's principles emphasize is curiosity. If you are curious and do research, then you will need to be prepared to take advantage of luck and serendipity.

Skinner, B. F. (1956). A case history in scientific method. *American Psychologist, 11,* 221–233.

# PSYCHOLOGY IN ACTION
## Doing Research

This section does not contain a particular project for you to do. Rather, it is a plea to follow some of Skinner's ideas mentioned in the "Application" section of this chapter. Find something you did or read about recently that you considered really interesting. Examine it, study it, and learn about it. Suppose you found in your ethogram of study behavior (see chapter 1) that you were more likely to study in a quiet place. You might ask yourself how that finding relates to the noise and study examples presented in this chapter. Is there a personally relevant research project waiting for you to do?

Have you been lucky or made a serendipitous finding? One thing you may have noticed if you participated in the experiment on reading and naming in the Introduction is that some mismatches between digits and quantity are more likely to slow down your naming time than are others. Is this true for everybody or just you? Does everyone have difficulty with the same mismatches, or do the difficult ones differ from person to person?

Most good scientists are intensely curious about many things. Where others may see commonplace occurrences, scientists may ask why and try to answer the question through research. According to the Nobel prize-winning chemist Albert Szent-Györgyi, "Discovery consists of seeing what everybody has seen and thinking what nobody has thought."

| **ETHICS IN PSYCHOLOGICAL RESEARCH**<br>Follow the APA's guidelines for research with humans and animals | **Ethical Considerations in Research**<br><br>*Is my project designed in accordance with contemporary ethical standards?*<br><br>Will my human subjects be treated in a dignified fashion without having their personal freedom violated or their physical or emotional health damaged?<br><br>Will I treat my animal subjects in a humane fashion?<br><br>Do I understand the ethical principles behind drug research?<br><br>Have I read and understood the ethical principles espoused by the American Psychological Association? |

# 4 ||||| Ethics in Psychological Research

The scientific enterprise creates ethical dilemmas. Scientific knowledge and techniques that can be used for human betterment can be turned to manipulative and exploitative purposes as well. Just as results of research in atomic physics can be used for the treatment of cancer as well as for destructive weapons, so methods discovered to reduce prejudice toward minority groups, to eliminate troublesome behavior problems, or to facilitate learning in school may also be used to manipulate political allegiance, to create artificial wants, or to reconcile the victims of social injustice to their fate. The double-edged potentiality of scientific knowledge poses ethical problems for all scientists. To the extent that psychological research deals with important problems and potent methods, psychologists must recognize and alert others to the fact that the potential for misuse of research increases its potential for constructive application. (American Psychological Association, 1982, p. 16)

## ||||| RESEARCH WITH HUMAN PARTICIPANTS

The quotation in the introduction to this chapter is from a publication of the American Psychological Association. The quote comes from a preamble to a lengthy discussion of ethical principles covering all aspects of psychology and is presented in abbreviated form here to emphasize the ethical obligations of researchers in all areas of science. These obligations are straightforward in principle but difficult to implement. We will examine both the ethical principles and the problems associated with putting them into practice in psychology. Psychologists are concerned with the ethics of research involving both human participants and animals. Although some of this concern is selfish, owing to fear of restriction of research funds and loss of access to subject populations, most psychologists are ethical persons who have no desire to inflict harm on anyone. The mad researcher, who will do anything to obtain data, is largely fictional.

Since it is difficult for an experimenter to be completely impartial and objective in judging the ethical issues concerning his or her own research, most universities and research institutions have peer committees that judge the ethicality of proposed research. Indeed, any federally funded research must be approved by such a committee before any funding is granted.

Let us consider a specific experimental situation to illustrate the implementation of ethical principles. Imagine that you are a psychologist interested in determining to what extent depressive feelings influence how well people remember information. One of the major reasons you want to study this topic is that depression is a fairly common emotional problem among college students, and you would like to have some idea how this problem could affect academic performance. You decide to do a tightly controlled laboratory experiment to determine the effects of depression on memory. Your general strategy is to induce depression in some of your subjects, and then compare their memory to that of other subjects who were not induced to be depressed. The manner in which you induce depression in your subjects follows a procedure devised by Velten (1968). To induce a mood by this procedure, the investigator has the subject read aloud sixty self-referent statements that are associated with the mood in question. In this case, the participant reads statements that are supposed to induce depression, beginning with relatively mild statements such as "Today is neither better nor worse than any other day," and progressing to "I feel so bad that I would like to go to sleep and never wake up." This procedure has been shown to induce a mild, temporary depression; participants report feeling depressed, and their behavior suffers on a variety of tasks.

Even though many details of this experiment have not been specified, it should be obvious that the welfare of the research participants in this study could be jeopardized (for complete details of this experiment, see Elmes, Chapman, and Selig, 1984). Inducing a negative mood (such as depression) in college students could have disastrous effects on their social and intellectual functioning. How can you as an ethical researcher try to preserve and protect the fundamental human rights of your participants? What would you do to protect their welfare and at the same time conduct an internally valid experiment?

In a recent review of research on mood and memory, Blaney (1986) listed a number of studies in which depression was induced in college students. In some experiments, a happy mood was induced in subjects. Do the ethical considerations depend on the kind of mood—happy or sad—that is induced in a subject? Also, researchers have used several different mood-induction procedures in their experiments. Besides the Velten (1968) procedure described above, hypnosis and music have been used to induce a depressed or happy mood. Do ethical considerations depend on the mood-induction technique? These questions concerning mood-induction research illustrate how ethical issues associated with psychological research may vary according to the specific circumstances in the experiment.

The American Psychological Association (1981a, 1987) has provided ethical guidelines for researchers. The association outlined ten general principles governing the conduct of research with human participants. To consider how the welfare of the students was protected in those studies, we will examine the principles that guide research involving human participants. *You should read and understand these ethical principles before you conduct a research project with human participants.*

The decision to undertake research rests upon a considered judgment by the individual psychologist about how best to contribute to psychological science and human welfare. Having made the decision to conduct research, the psychologist considers alternative directions in which research energies and resources might be invested. On the basis of this consideration, the psychologist carries out the investigation with respect and concern for the dignity and welfare of the people who participate and with cognizance of federal and state regulations and professional standards governing the conduct of research with human participants.

**1.** In planning a study, the investigator has the responsibility to make a careful evaluation of its ethical acceptability. To the extent that the weighing of scientific and human values suggests a compromise of any principle, the investigator incurs a correspondingly serious obligation to seek ethical advice and to observe stringent safeguards to protect the rights of human participants.

**2.** Considering whether a participant in a planned study will be a "subject at risk" or a "subject at minimal risk," according to recognized standards, is of primary ethical concern to the investigator.

**3.** The investigator always retains the responsibility for ensuring ethical practice in research. The investigator is also responsible for the ethical treatment of research participants by collaborators, assistants, students, and employees, all of whom, however, incur similar obligations.

**4.** Except in minimal-risk research, the investigator establishes a clear and fair agreement with research participants, prior to their participation, that clarifies the obligations and responsibilities of each. The investigator has the obligation to honor all promises and commitments included in that agreement. The investigator informs the participants of all aspects of the research that might reasonably be expected to influence willingness to participate and explains all other aspects of the research about which the participants inquire. Failure to make full disclosure prior to obtaining informed consent requires additional safeguards to protect the welfare and dignity of the research participants. Research with children or with participants who have impairments that would limit understanding and/or communication requires special safeguarding procedures.

**5.** Methodological requirements of a study may make the use of concealment or deception necessary. Before conducting such a study, the investigator has a special responsibility to (i) determine whether the use of such techniques is justified by the study's prospective scientific, educational, or applied value; (ii) determine whether alternative procedures are available that do not use concealment or deception; and (iii) ensure that the participants are provided with sufficient explanation as soon as possible.

**6.** The investigator respects the individual's freedom to decline to participate in or to withdraw from the research at any time. The obligation to protect this freedom requires careful thought and consideration when the investigator is in a position of authority or influence over the participant. Such positions of authority include, but are not limited to, situations in which research participation is required as part of employment or in which the participant is a student, client, or employee of the investigator.

**7.** The investigator protects the participant from physical and mental discomfort, harm, and danger that may arise from research procedures. If risks of such consequences exist, the investigator informs the participant of that fact. Research procedures likely to cause serious or lasting harm to a participant are not used unless the failure to use these procedures might expose the participant to risk of greater harm, or unless the research has great potential benefit and fully informed and voluntary consent is obtained from each participant. The participant should be informed of procedures for contacting the investigator within a reasonable time period following participation should stress, potential harm, or related questions or concerns arise.

**8.** After the data are collected, the investigator provides the participant with information about the nature of the study and attempts to remove any misconceptions that may have arisen. Where scientific or humane values justify delaying or withholding this information, the investigator incurs a special responsibility to monitor the research and to ensure that there are no damaging consequences for the participant.

**9.** Where research procedures result in undesirable consequences for the individual participant, the investigator has the responsibility to detect and remove or correct these consequences, including long-term effects.

**10.** Information obtained about a research participant during the course of an investigation is confidential unless otherwise agreed upon in advance. When the possibility exists that others may obtain access to such information, this possibility, together with the plans for protecting confidentiality, is explained to the participant as part of the procedure for obtaining informed consent.

Principles 9 and 10 are the ones most relevant to protecting welfare, and they can be summarized by noting that the experimenter has an obligation to minimize harm to the participant. The subject should be warned ahead of time if there is potential harm, the subject should be able to withdraw if he or she chooses, and deception should be used carefully. The experimenter is obligated to undo any harm, and the results should remain confidential with regard to a particular participant unless agreed otherwise. These principles need to be reckoned with in any research project.

## Informed Consent and Deception

The ethical researcher tells the subjects, prior to participation, of "all aspects of the research that might reasonably be expected to influence willingness to participate and explains all other aspects of the research about which participants inquire." This means that the participants must be forewarned about those aspects of the research that may have detrimental effects.

In a simple memory study, in which mode of presentation is the independent variable, probably little more than a general description of the task is required. However, the researcher sometimes must go into more detail when a chance exists that the participant might misinterpret the purpose of the experiment. Often in studies requiring memory or other cognitive abilities, the researcher assures the subjects that the task is not a personality or intelligence test. This is done to reassure the participant and to reduce evaluation apprehension.

In riskier research, such as the depression experiment just outlined, even greater caution is necessary. At the very least, the experimenter should tell the participants that they will be doing something that may make them feel unhappy. This warning allows the potential subject to decide whether to participate in the research. Enough information should be provided so that the person can either withdraw or give informed consent for participation.

There are at least two difficulties in implementing this safeguard. First, many people may not understand the prior information given them (such as children or people with learning disabilities), which puts a special burden on the experimenter to find someone capable of giving informed consent. Second, having to divulge too many details of an experiment could result in an internally invalid research project. Here, there are no easy solutions. If a researcher divulges everything about the study, the possibility of subject reactivity is very strong. For example, Brownell and Stunkard (1982) report that informed consent in medical research can severely hamper the use of a double-blind design. They conducted a study on the effectiveness of an appetite suppressant on overeating. The drug was compared with a placebo in a double-blind design in which neither the attending physician nor the subjects knew who was receiving the drug and who was getting the placebo. So, they attempted to deceive both the participants and the experimenter. The drug, fenfluramine hydrochloride, has many side effects, including drowsiness, diarrhea, dry mouth, and dizziness, which have different degrees of severity for different people. Consequently, prior to the experiment, all subjects were informed of the side effects that could occur if they were given the drug. Brownell and Stunkard found that both the patients and the attending physicians could correctly identify the assignment of medication in 70 percent of the cases. The information given prior to the experiment was enough to sabotage the double-blind design, and the deception did not work. More important, this breakdown in design resulted in unwanted changes in behavior, because correct identification of the medicated group was highly correlated with a favorable outcome of the treatment.

By providing enough information for informed consent, the researcher may undermine the validity of the experimental design. Thus, the ethical researcher is in a dilemma as to how much information should be provided. Obviously, participants should be forewarned of a life-threatening manipulation, and deception about such a variable would be unethical. But the costs and benefits associated with complete disclosure of a less detrimental manipulation are more difficult to assess. In the depression and memory experiment we discussed earlier, the people who signed up to participate were told that some of the things they were going to do in the experiment might make them feel unhappy, and they were given the opportunity to refuse to participate. However, the specific nature of the manipulation, such as the Velten technique and who was going to serve in the experimental group, was not disclosed ahead of time. Complete disclosure might have resulted in reactivity. Since the effects of the manipulation involving depression are temporary, the researchers believed that partial information was enough to permit informed consent.

Since the solution to the informed-consent dilemma is not always apparent, the prudent researcher should seek the advice of others who can be objective about the situation. In the depression and memory study, the following people were consulted prior to the experiment: another experimental psychologist, a dean of student affairs and his assistant, an expert in biomedical ethics, and a counseling psychologist. They commented on deception and the informed-consent issue as well as on other ethical problems, which will be considered next.

## Freedom to Withdraw

Participants should be allowed to decline to participate or to withdraw at any time. Everyone would agree that the mad scientist who straps participants to the chair is unethical. Most also would agree that people who are unhappy about participating should have the right to withdraw. So, what is the ethical dilemma? The major problem revolves around the definition of a willing volunteer participant. Consider the subject pool for the depression and memory experiment: undergraduate students (mostly freshmen and sophomores) taking introductory psychology. They sign up to participate in experiments, and they usually receive some sort of course credit for their service. Are they volunteering when they sign up, or are they under some sort of coercion that they have inferred from the situation? If the students actually receive extra credit, they are likely to be acting on their own volition. If they must participate as part of a course requirement, then the freedom to participate or not is less obvious. When students are required to participate, they should have some optional way of fulfilling the requirement, such as writing a paper or attending a special lecture. The point, then, is to provide freedom to the potential subjects, so that they can participate or not as they choose.

Generally, when the pool of potential participants is a captive audience, such as students, prisoners, military recruits, and employees of the experimenter, then the researcher needs to consider the individual's freedom to withdraw or to participate. In the depression and memory experiment, volunteer students were recruited with the lure of extra credit (participation was not mandatory). When they signed up, they were forewarned about the possibility of unhappiness (they could agree to participate or not). In the instructions at the beginning of the experiment, the students were advised that they had the option of quitting any time they wanted and they would still receive the full extra credit that had been promised (they were free to withdraw).

## Protection from Harm and Debriefing

One additional safeguard to protect research participants from harm is suggested by the American Psychological Association: a way for the subjects to contact the investigator following their participation in the research. Even the most scrupulously ethical project of the minimal-risk sort may have unintended aftereffects. Thus, the participant should be able to receive help or advice from the researcher if problems should arise. We have had participants cry (out of frustration and embarrassment) during what was supposed to be a standard, innocuous memory experiment. Those subjects may have carried away from the experiment a negative self-image or strong feelings of resentment toward the experimenter in particular or research in general.

Because of such unintended effects, the prudent researcher provides for subsequent consultation, or what is called **debriefing.** Debriefing means that the investigator explains the general purposes of the research and the nature of the manipulations so that any questions or misunderstandings the subjects may have are removed.

Let us apply the principles of debriefing and protection from harm to the depression and memory experiment. At the end of that project, the participants were given a list of phone numbers of people who could be contacted in the unlikely event that the subjects felt depressed following the experiment. The list of contacts included the principal investigator, a counselor, and the dean of student affairs and his assistant. Also, the day after participation, each subject who had read the depression-inducing statements was phoned by one of the experimenters, who tried to determine whether the participant was having any negative aftereffects.

The participants were also thoroughly debriefed. They were told about the mood-induction procedure, and how its effects were temporary. In addition, other details of the experimental design and rationale were outlined, and any questions the participants had were answered.

## Removing Harmful Consequences

Debriefing subjects and giving them phone numbers may not be sufficient in a risky project. If a participant could indeed suffer long-term consequences as a result of serving in a research project, the investigator has the responsibility to remove those consequences. It may be difficult to reverse the feelings of resentful subjects, because the resentment may be unintended and undetected. However, where the risks are known, the ethical investigator must take steps to minimize them.

Prior to the debriefing in the depression and memory experiment, the participants read a series of self-referent statements designed to induce elation. This exercise was supposed to counteract the effects of the negative mood induced earlier. Then the participants were questioned about their current feelings, and they were also asked to sign a statement which said they left the experiment feeling no worse than when they began it. All participants signed the statement, but had they not, a contingent plan was to keep them in the laboratory under the supervision of one of the experimenters until they felt better.

## Confidentiality

What a subject does in an experiment should be confidential unless otherwise agreed. An ethical researcher does not run around saying things like: "Bobby Freshman is stupid; he did more poorly than anyone else in my experiment." Also, personal information about particular participants, such as their attitudes toward premarital sex or their family income, should not be revealed without the subjects' permission. The principle of confidentiality seems straightforward, but a researcher can be faced with an ethical dilemma when trying to uphold confidentiality.

This dilemma arose in the depression and memory experiment. The experimenter was confronted with an ethical problem, because he believed it was necessary to violate the principle of confidentiality in order to uphold the principle of protection from harm. Let us see how this problem developed. One of the first tasks of the participants was to answer some questions concerning their mental health. They were to indicate whether they were currently seeking professional help for a personal problem, and to give some details about the problem and the therapeutic procedure. The participants were assured that their answers were confidential. Then the subjects completed a clinical test that assessed their current level of depression. If a participant indicated that he or she was being treated for depression and scored high on the test, the experiment was discontinued at that point. Confidentiality was promised so that honest responses could be obtained, and the test was administered to prevent a depressed person from becoming even more depressed by the mood-induction procedure. Thus, the intent was to minimize harm. In the course of the experiment, two students scored very high on the depression test, and one of them was not undergoing therapy. Since the test was known to be a reliable and valid predictor of clinically serious depression, the principal investigator believed that it was necessary to warn one of the college's counselors about the two students who appeared to have very high levels of depression. Then, under the guise or a routine interview, the counselor talked to these students.

This type of dilemma occurs frequently in research. The researcher may find it necessary to violate one ethical principle in order to adhere to another. There are no easy choices when this happens. If the highly depressed students had suspected that the investigator had betrayed their confidence, permanent resentment and mistrust could have resulted. On the other hand, had the one student who was not undergoing therapy committed suicide, the investigator would have been responsible for an awful tragedy. At that time, preventing such a tragedy seemed much more important than upholding the participants' right to confidentiality.

Thus, ethical decisions rarely are made on the basis of empirical facts. Rather, the decisions usually are based on the pragmatic criterion. This criterion focuses on how to best protect the participants and at the same time conduct a meaningful, valid project. Imagine that you are on an ethics committee, and you must decide whether to allow the following examples of proposed research:

**1.** An environmental psychologist sits in a crowded library and keeps detailed records of seating patterns.

**2.** An environmental psychologist takes videotapes of seating patterns in a library. These tapes are maintained indefinitely, and library patrons do not know they have been filmed.

**3.** An experimental psychologist tells students that he is interested in their reading comprehension when in reality he is recording the speed of their responses rather than their comprehension.

**4.** A social psychologist is studying bystander intervention in a liquor store. Permission has been obtained from the store manager. In clear view of a patron, an experimenter "steals" a bottle of liquor. A second experimenter approaches the patron and asks, "Did you see him steal that bottle?"

**5.** A social psychologist connects surface electrodes to male participants, with their prior approval. These subjects are told that the electrodes are connected to a meter in front of them that measures sexual arousal. In reality, the meter is controlled by the experimenter. Participants are then shown slides of nude males and females. The meter gives high readings for pictures of males, leading the participants to believe that they have latent homosexual tendencies.

Since it is difficult to gain agreement on ethical issues, we cannot make definitive judgments about these examples. However, informal discussions with our colleagues reveal that only the first example was unequivocally considered ethical. Since the psychologist was merely observing and did not know the people, informed consent was not deemed necessary. Any individual, psychologist or not, could easily observe these same people in the library. The potential harm to participants was small.

You may be surprised that objections were raised to every other example. Number 2 was thought to invade personal privacy since the tapes were not erased after the data had been abstracted. Number 3 would be acceptable only if the experimenter carefully debriefed participants by explaining the nature and reasons for this minor deception. Subjects may get upset over what they think is poor performance even in a harmless laboratory test of reading speed. Potential psychological damage may result from any task. As mentioned previously, we have had subjects cry, cheat, and swear in standard laboratory tests of learning and memory. Number 4 was actually performed; a patron denied seeing the theft and then called the police as soon as she left the store. The investigator had to go down to the police station to bail out the experimenters. Number 5 was also performed, and it too was considered unethical, even with debriefing. It is not clear whether the potential psychological harm of leading the participant to think he had hidden homosexual tendencies could be removed by even immediate extensive debriefing. This would especially be the case if the person did indeed have latent homosexual tendencies.

These examples show that there is no clear answer as to what is ethical. The responsibility rests on the researcher, review committees, and also journal editors who review research for publication. Although deception and concealment may be justified in limited instances, great caution is demanded in such research. One of the first things to do when designing a project is to consider the ethics of your procedure. Seek advice from your friends and instructor. Deceit and danger are not prerequisites of good research; they should be avoided as much as possible.

## |||| ETHICS IN RESEARCH WITH ANIMALS

Animals are used extensively in psychological research, to answer questions that would be impossible or impractical to answer by using human beings. However, some people believe that animals should not be used in various kinds of research, on ethical grounds (Bowd, 1980). For example, Rollin (1985) has argued that if the concept of legal and moral rights can be applied to human research, it can also be applied in the same way to animal research. He suggested that the status of research animals needs to be elevated to that of human subjects, with many of the same rules that currently govern human research applied to animals. Recently, many sensational reports in the media have discussed the purported mistreatment of laboratory animals and the attempts of animal-rights advocates to limit the use of animals in research. Therefore, a consideration of why animals are used in research is important, and an understanding of the ethical safeguards for animals is necessary.

Animals are often the subjects of research because they are interesting and because they form an important part of the natural world. The number of bird-watchers and other amateur naturalists, as well as the numerous comparative psychologists and ethologists, readily attest to the interest. More important in terms of ethical concerns, however, is that animals serve as convenient, highly controlled models for humans *and* other animals.

Ethics prohibit experimentally induced brain damage in human beings, preclude deliberate separation of a human infant from its parents, forbid testing of unknown drugs on human beings, and generally exclude dangerous, irreversible, and immoral manipulations of human beings. Animal-rights advocates believe that research on animals should have the same prohibitions. According to the animal-rights advocates, researchers need to uphold the rights of both human beings and animals, because, for example, they believe that experimental destruction of a monkey's brain is as ethically reprehensible as the destruction of the brain of a human being. Three points summarize the animal advocates' position: (1) animals feel pain and their lives can be destroyed, as is true of humans (Roberts, 1971); (2) destroying or harming any living thing is dehumanizing to the human scientist (Roberts, 1971); and (3) claims about scientific progress being helped by animal research are a form of racism, called **speciesism** by Singer (1978), and, like interracial bigotry, are completely unwarranted and unethical. Most experimental psychologists, especially psychobiologists, have strong reservations about the validity of these points. Let us consider each in turn.

Surely animals feel pain and suffering. However, ethical standards exist in all scientific fields that use animals as research subjects. A major portion of these principles concerns the proscription of undue pain and inhumane treatment. No ethical psychologist would deliberately mistreat research animals, nor would an ethical psychologist deliberately inflict undue harm on an animal. Again, the vision of the mad scientist is merely that—a vision, and not a reality. A second reservation about pain and suffering as a deterrent to using animals should be mentioned. Many scientists believe that the disruptive effects of harm deliberately produced during a scientific investigation are much less tragic for animals than for human beings. Hoff

(1980) argues that an animal stricken by blindness suffers less than a person stricken by blindness. Hoff does not advocate cruelty. Rather, her point is that harmful outcomes of research, though unpleasant and, perhaps, morally wrong, affect animals less than they do human beings.

Of course, Hoff's position is arguable. Roberts (1971) would consider Hoff's position as supporting her argument that many forms of animal research dehumanize the human investigator. Only a bloodless and unethical monster would remove the brain from a monkey and then keep the brain alive through a variety of ghastly means. To us, this argument seems specious for two reasons. In the first place, most animal-rights advocates exploit living things in one way or another. Even if they do not eat the flesh of animals (and most do), they do eat other living things, such as vegetables and fruits. Is it dehumanizing to kill a radish? If animal life is different from plant life, then it may be reasonable to argue that human life is different from animal life, as Hoff believes. In the second place, a substantial amount of animal research is undertaken to understand and help animals. Consider your favorite dog or other domestic pet. You may feel uneasy about the fact that many psychologists, physiologists, and veterinarians conduct experiments on dogs—experiments that we all agree would be unethical to conduct on human beings. However, there is a serious pragmatic and ethical dilemma here. If we love dogs and if we want them to be as happy and as healthy as possible, some kinds of dangerous research must be done on these animals so that humane care can be given to them. It seems ironic to us that those who appear to love animals the most would advocate measures that could be disastrous for those animals.

As a model for human behavior, animal research is essential for scientific progress. This may be a form of speciesism, but given the validity of our previous arguments, speciesism may not be so bad. Consider these two quotes from Robert J. White, an eminent neuroscientist and neurosurgeon, who conducted the brain-removal studies alluded to earlier: "As I write this article, I relive my vivid experiences yesterday when I removed at operation a large tumor from the cerebellum and brain stem of a small child. This was a surgical undertaking that would have been impossible a few decades ago, highly dangerous a few years ago, but is today thanks to extensive experimentation on the brains of lower animals, routinely accomplished with a high degree of safety" (1971, p. 504). "I consider the employment of animals in biological and medical research so critical to continued human existence and survival as to be beyond logical challenge" (p 512).

Gallup and Suarez (1985) reviewed the rationale, extent, and use of animals in psychological research. They considered the possible alternatives and concluded that in many cases there is no viable alternative to the use of animals in psychological research.

The American Psychological Association (1981a) has provided guidelines governing animal research. As a general principle,

> An investigator of animal behavior strives to advance understanding of basic behavioral principles and/or to contribute to the improvement of human health and welfare. In seeking these ends, the investigator ensures the welfare of animals and treats them humanely. Laws and regulations notwithstanding, an animal's immediate protection depends upon the scientist's own conscience.

The five primary considerations for researchers using animal subjects are listed below.

**1.** The acquisition, care, use, and disposal of all animals are in compliance with current federal, state or provincial, and local laws and regulations.

**2.** A psychologist trained in research methods and experienced in the care of laboratory animals closely supervises all procedures involving animals and is responsible for ensuring appropriate consideration of their comfort, health, and humane treatment.

**3.** Psychologists ensure that all individuals using animals under their supervision have received explicit instruction in experimental methods and in the care, maintenance, and handling of the species being used. Responsibilities and activities of individuals participating in a research project are consistent with their respective competencies.

**4.** Psychologists make every effort to minimize discomfort, illness, and pain of animals. A procedure subjecting animals to pain, stress, or privation is used only when an alternative procedure is unavailable and the goal is justified by its prospective scientific, educational, or applied value. Surgical procedures are performed under appropriate anesthesia; techniques to avoid infection and minimize pain are followed during and after surgery.

**5.** When it is appropriate that the animal's life be terminated, it is done rapidly and painlessly.

The above guidelines were designed for experienced researchers. The APA (1981b) has also provided guidelines for the student researcher. These are presented in appendix 4A of this chapter.

Both sets of guidelines emphasize decent care and treatment. Both also mention additional regulations. Before using animal subjects, you should understand the contents of both sets of guidelines, and you should become familiar with relevant state and local humane regulations. *An ethical psychologist does not mistreat animal subjects, nor does an ethical psychologist submit animal subjects to undue pain or harm.*

## |||| ETHICS IN DRUG RESEARCH

Guidelines for the use of drugs in research involving both humans and animals are printed in Appendix 4B of this chapter. The primary purpose for reprinting these guidelines is to discourage most undergraduate research on drugs, especially projects using human beings. Special government permits are required for research with controlled substances (including marijuana), and most student projects neglect to include appropriate **aftercare** for their human participants. You are responsible for accidents, antisocial behavior, and worse yet, addiction that could result from an experimentally induced high. If you are compelled to engage in drug research, use animals as your subjects and use legal substances. If you do, be sure you understand the rules in Appendix 4B as well as the other legal documents that are mentioned therein.

#### | | | | **MONITORING ETHICAL PRACTICES**

The American Psychological Association provides ethical guidelines for psychological research. Acceptance of membership in the Association commits the member to adherence to these principles. The principles are also intended for nonmembers, including students of psychology and others who work on psychological research under the supervision of a psychologist.

The American Psychological Association established an Ethics Committee that fulfills a number of purposes. Through publications, educational meetings and convention activities, the Ethics Committee educates psychologists and the public about ethical issues related to psychological research. The Committee also investigates and adjudicates complaints concerning unethical research practices. Examples of these cases can be found in an APA (1987) publication titled, *Casebook on ethical issues.* The Ethics Committee also publishes an annual report in *American Psychologist.*

Most institutions involved in psychological research have guidelines regarding research with animals and humans in addition to the APA ethical guidelines. Many universities have a special committee that monitors the use of human and animal subjects. Researchers must submit a detailed outline of the planned research to the committee. The committee evaluates the types and levels of risk involved in the research and considers the potential value of the research. They often propose additional or alternative procedures that will reduce the level of risk to the subject.

In addition to the above guidelines, there are federal government regulations concerned with the protection of human and animal subjects. These regulations require that any individual or institution that applies for federal grants must follow certain research practices designed to minimize the level of risk to the subject. These regulations also require that institutions monitor research in order to protect the rights of the subjects of such research.

---

**CONCEPT SUMMARY**

*An ethical researcher*
Protects the welfare of human participants
Treats animal subjects humanely
Does drug research with caution

---

#### | | | | **SUMMARY**

**1.** As ethical investigator protects the welfare of research participants by following the ethical standards of the American Psychological Association.

**2.** Minimal use of deception on the part of the investigator as well as informed consent permit the participant to make a reasoned judgment about whether to participate.

**3.** The ethical investigator respects the participant's right to decline to serve in the research or to withdraw at any time.

**4.** In an ethical investigation, the participant is protected from physical and mental harm.

**5.** After the data have been collected, participants should be debriefed to remove any misconceptions that may have arisen.

**6.** An ethical investigator will attempt to remove any harmful consequences that resulted from the research.

**7.** Unless otherwise agreed, information about a research participant is confidential.

**8.** Attempts to uphold these ethical principles sometimes lead to a dilemma in that adherence to one principle may violate another.

**9.** An ethical investigator treats animal subjects in a humane fashion.

**10.** Research with drugs poses special welfare problems, especially those concerned with the aftercare of the participants.

## Key Concepts

| | |
|---|---|
| aftercare | freedom to withdraw |
| confidentiality | informed consent |
| debriefing | protection from harm |
| deception | removing harmful consequences |
| ethical principles of the American Psychological Association | speciesism |

## Exercises

Reconsider the ethical principles presented in this chapter and read the list of ethical principles published by American Psychologist Association (1981, 1987).

**1.** Read selections from the *Casebook on Ethical Issues* published by the American Psychological Association (1987), which is probably available in your library. This book describes the background of different ethical complaints, how the complaints came to be sent to the Ethics Committee, and how the cases were adjudicated. Select two cases and consider the ethical principles involved in the case. Describe why you agree or disagree with the adjudication of the Ethics Committee.

**2.** Read two of the articles listed below. These articles describe the ethical issues associated with different types of psychological research. Consider the general ethical principles that apply in both cases. Describe how the ethical issues differ between the two types of research discussed in the articles.

## Suggested Readings

Bowd, A. D. (1980). Ethical reservations about psychological research with animals. *Psychological Record, 30,* 201–210.

Imber, S. D., Glanz, L. M., Elkin, I., Sotsky, S. M., Boyer, J. L., & Leber, W. R. (1986). Ethical issues in psychotherapy research: Problems in a collaborative clinical study. *American Psychologist, 41,* 137–146.

Melton, G., & Gray, J. (1988). Ethical dilemmas in AIDS research: Individual privacy and public health. *American Psychologist, 43,* 60–64.

Milgram, S. (1977). Ethical issues in the study of obedience. In S. Milgram (Ed.), *The individual in a social world* (pp. 188–199). Reading, MA: Addison-Wesley.

Scarr, S. (1988). Race and gender as psychological variables: Social and ethical issues. *American Psychologist, 43,* 56–59.

Sieber, J. E., & Stanley, B. (1988). Ethical and professional dimensions of socially sensitive research. *American Psychologist, 43,* 49–55.

Smith, C. P. (1983). Ethical issues: Research on deception, informed consent, and debriefing. In L. Wheeler & P. Shaver (Eds.), *Review of personality and social psychology* (Vol. 4, pp. 297–328). Beverly Hills, CA: Sage.

---

## Appendix 4A: Guidelines for the Use of Animals in School Science Behavior Projects

1. In the selection of science behavior projects, students should be urged to select animals that are small and easy to maintain as subjects for research.

2. All projects *must* be preplanned and conducted with humane considerations and respect for animal life. Projects intended for science fair exhibition must comply with these guidelines as well as with additional requirements of the sponsor.

3. Each student undertaking a school science project using animals *must have a qualified supervisor.* Such a supervisor shall be a person who has had training and experience in the proper care of the species and the research techniques to be used in the project. The supervisor *must* assume the primary responsibility for all conditions of the project and must ensure that the student is trained in the care and handling of the animals as well as in the methods to be used.

4. The student shall do relevant reading about previous work in the area. The student's specific purpose, plan of action, justification of the methodology, and anticipated outcome for the science project shall be submitted to and approved by a qualified person. Teachers shall maintain these on file for future reference.

5. No student shall inflict pain, severe deprivation, or high stress levels or use invasive procedures such as surgery, the administration of drugs, ionizing radiation, or toxic agents *unless* facilities are suitable both for the study and for the care and housing of the animals and *unless* the research is carried out under the extremely close and rigorous supervision of a person with training in the specific area of study. These projects must be conducted in accordance with the APA *Principles for the Care and Use of Animals.*

6. Students, teachers, and supervisors *must* be cognizant of current federal and state legislation and guidelines for specific care and handling of their animals (e.g., the Animal Welfare Act). Copies of humane laws are available from local or national humane organizations. A recommended reference is the *Guide for the Care and Use of Laboratory Animals,* available from the Superintendent of Documents, U.S. Government Printing Office, Washington, D.C. 20402, Stock Number 017-040-00427-3.

7. The basic daily needs of each animal shall be of prime concern. Students *must* ensure the proper housing, food, water, exercise, cleanliness, and gentle handling of their animals. Special arrangements *must* be made for care during weekends, holidays, and vacations. Students must protect their animals from sources of disturbance or harm, including teasing by other students.

8. When the research project has been completed, the supervisor is responsible for proper disposition of the animals. If it is appropriate that the animal's life be terminated, it shall be rapid and painless. *Under no circumstances should students be allowed to experiment with such procedures.*

9. Teachers and students are encouraged to consult with the Committee on Animal Research and Experimentation of the American Psychological Association for advice on adherence to the guidelines. In cases where facilities for advanced research by qualified students are not available, the Committee on Animal Research and Experimentation will try to make suitable arrangements for the students.

10. A copy of these guidelines shall be posted conspicuously wherever animals are kept and projects carried out, including displays at science fairs.

From *American Psychologist,* Vol. 36, 1981. Copyright 1981 by the American Psychological Association. Reprinted by permission of the publisher.

### Appendix 4B: APA Guidelines for Psychologists on the Use of Drugs in Research

General Principle: A psychologist or psychology student who performs research involving the use of drugs shall have adequate knowledge and experience of each drug's action or shall work in collaboration with or under the supervision of a qualified researcher. Any psychologist or psychology student doing research with drugs must comply with the procedural guidelines below. Any supervisor or collaborator has the responsibility to see that the individual he supervises or collaborates with complies with the procedural guidelines.

#### Definition of a Qualified Researcher

1. A qualified researcher possesses a Ph.D. degree based in part upon a dissertation that is experimental in nature and in part upon training in psychology, pharmacology, physiology, and related areas, and that is conferred by a graduate school of recognized standing (listed by the United States Office of Education as having been accredited by a recognized regional or national accrediting organization).

2. A qualified researcher has demonstrated competence as defined by research involving the use of drugs which has been published in scientific journals; or continuing education; or equivalent experience ensuring that the researcher has adequate knowledge of the drugs, their actions, and of experimental design.

#### Definition of a Drug

In these Guidelines, the term drug includes (a) all substances as defined by the term drug in the "Federal Food, Drug, and Cosmetic Act" (21 USC 321) and (b) all substances, Schedules I–V, as listed in the "Comprehensive Drug Abuse Prevention and Control Act of 1970" (21 USC 812; PL 91-513, Sec. 202) in its present form or as amended (Federal Food, Drug and Cosmetic Act, 21 USC, Sec. 201 (g), Appendix A). Copies of these acts are available from the Superintendent of Documents, United States Government Printing Office, Washington, DC 20402.

#### Procedural Guidelines

1. All drugs must be legally obtained and used under conditions specified by state and federal laws. Information concerning these laws should be obtained from federal or state authorities.

2. Proper precautions must be taken so that drugs and drug paraphernalia that are potentially harmful are available only to authorized personnel. All such drugs used in experiments should be kept in locked cabinets and under any additional security prescribed by law.

3. All individuals using or supervising the use of drugs in research must be familiar with PL 91-513, the "Comprehensive Drug Abuse Prevention and Control Act of 1970," and its implementing regulations as well as all amendments to the act and other drug laws relevant to their research.

4. The use of drugs must be justified scientifically.

5. All individuals using or supervising the use of drugs in research must familiarize themselves with available information concerning the mode of action, toxicity, and methods of administration of the drugs they are using.

6. In any experiment involving animals, the welfare of the animal should be considered as specified in APA's "Precautions and Standards for the Care and Use of Animals."

7. Research involving human subjects is governed by additional guidelines as set forth in APA's "Ethical Standards for Psychological Research."

8. The present Guidelines should be brought to the attention of all individuals conducting research with drugs.

9. The present Guidelines should be posted conspicuously in every laboratory in which psychologists use drugs.

Source: American Psychological Association Ad Hoc Committee on Guidelines for the Use of Drugs and Other Chemical Agents in Research. From *American Psychologist*, Vol 27, 1972. Copyright 1972 by the American Psychological Association. Reprinted by permission of the publisher.

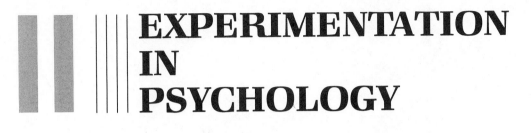

# EXPERIMENTATION IN PSYCHOLOGY

| **BASES OF EXPERIMEN- TATION** The researcher produces a comparison by letting one or more variables change while holding other variables constant | **Independent Variables**  At least two levels of a variable are manipulated to provide a standard of comparison. Interactions may occur when there are two or more independent variables.  **Dependent Variables**  Specific behaviors are measured in an experiment.  **Control Variables**  In the ideal experiment, all other variables are held constant.  **Experimental Group or Condition**  The treatment group or condition that receives the level interest of the independent variable.  **Control Group or Condition**  The group or condition that is untreated or receives a comparison (baseline) level of the independent variable. |
| --- | --- |

# 5 ||| Bases of Experimentation

*A tightly designed, well-conducted experiment is the goal of psychologists who attempt to answer the question of why we think and act as we do. In this chapter we will consider the basic characteristics of a good experiment. The essential ingredient of an experiment is production of a comparison while holding other variables constant.*

## |||| EXPERIMENTATION: AN EXAMPLE

The experimental analysis of mother-infant love provides insight into the value of experimentation as a way of fixing belief. Let us consider an experiment by Harry F. Harlow (1905–1981), the eminent psychologist whose work has been among the most frequently cited in contemporary psychology.

Most mothers love their babies and most babies love their mothers. How does this attachment develop? When we observe human mothers and their babies interact, a very obvious fact about their relationship is that the baby is dependent on the mother for care—especially for food. Mothers handle and cuddle their babies often every day, and much of this interaction is associated with feeding or its aftermath (for example, burping and diaper changing). On the basis of such observation, Freud developed an elaborate theory of child development, a part of which assumed that babies have innate oral tendencies, which the mother satisfies by means of feeding. Thus, Freud and many psychologists assumed that the development of mother-infant love occurred because the feeding function performed by the mother satisfied the infant's needs. Harlow (1958) noted that physical contact was highly correlated with feeding, and he wondered whether the feeding was the important variable in attachment or whether it was the contact that was confounded with the feeding. Of course, numerous other stimulating conditions occur during feeding (sight, smell, and warmth, among others), but Harlow had noticed that baby monkeys that were raised in the laboratory became very attached to soft, cuddly cloth pads. So he decided to do an experiment to determine whether feeding or contact was more important in the development of affection.

For obvious ethical and practical reasons, Harlow did not try to have human mothers interact with their children without feeding them, nor did he try to have feeding without touching. Rather, he used macaque monkeys, which are more mature at birth than human beings and which grow more rapidly than we do. Since these monkeys are physically mature enough at birth to move around and find food, their behavior can be measured easily. To determine the relative importance of feeding and contact in attachment, Harlow developed the testing situation illustrated in figure 5–1. An infant monkey living in a cage had two surrogate (artificial replacement) mothers: One was covered with terry cloth, like the one on the right, and one consisted of bare wire, like the one on the left. For some monkeys, the wire mother had a milk-filled, baby-bottle "breast" and the cloth mother did not. For other monkeys, the feeding mother was the cloth mother, and the wire mother did not have a breast.

Harlow measured the time the monkeys spent each day clinging to the wire and cloth mothers, and he found the results shown in figure 5–2.

In the two graphs, we see mean hours per day plotted on the ordinate, and the age of the monkeys plotted on the abscissa. The data in the left-hand panel are for the monkeys that were fed on the cloth mother, and the data in the right-hand panel are for those fed on the wire mother. Notice that regardless of the source of food, more time was spent on the cloth mother than on the wire mother. Harlow found that this preference for the cloth mother persisted throughout the entire experiment, which lasted 165 days.

Harlow concluded that contact comfort is a more basic variable in attachment than is feeding. He argued that the dramatic preference that

**FIGURE 5–1**
Wire and cloth mother surrogates. Courtesy of Harlow Primate Lab, University of Wisconsin.

**FIGURE 5–2**
Time spent on cloth and wire mother surrogates. (Harlow, 1958. Copyright 1958 by the American Psychological Association.)

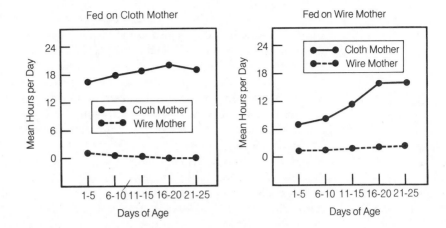

persisted for cloth mothers even when the wire mothers provided food indicates that the purpose of nursing is to guarantee that the infant and mother have contact. In more general terms, we can say that Harlow explained infant-mother love as being caused by the contact comfort, not the feeding, that the mother provides. Harlow's conclusion is contrary to the results of less systematic observation that seemed to show that feeding is of primary importance. In essence, such casual observation focused on a correlation, and we cannot infer causation on the basis of a correlation (see chapter 2). How do experiments permit us to make causal statements?

## | | | | WHAT IS AN EXPERIMENT?

**Experiments** are tests designed to arrive at a causal explanation (see Cook and Campbell, 1979). We noted in chapter 2 that the conditions necessary for arriving at explanations were set forth in the nineteenth century by the philosopher John Stuart Mill (1843/1930). The conditions he outlined provide a good definition of an experiment.

Mill argued that causation can be inferred if some result, X, follows an event, A, if A and X vary together and if it can be shown that event A produces result X. For these conditions to be met, the *joint method of agreement and difference* must be used. In the joint method, if A occurs then so will X, and if A does not occur, then neither will X. Let us apply this reasoning to the work on attachment done by Freud and Harlow.

Freud thought that feeding causes attachment, because the two vary together in natural settings. In Mill's terminology Freud observed the agreement between feeding and attachment and nothing else. Since the joint method of agreement and difference was not used by Freud, we cannot say that feeding causes attachment. Rather we can merely note that the two vary together; they agree (that is, they correlate).

In contrast to Freud, Harlow applied the joint method of agreement and difference to the attachment setting by allowing baby monkeys access to either a soft, cloth-covered surrogate or to a hard, wire one. For some animals the soft mother was associated with food, and for others the hard mother was associated with food. Thus, we have the makings for a causal analysis of attachment: To what do baby monkeys cling—soft mothers or feeding mothers? As we have just seen, Harlow showed that babies preferred to cling to the soft mothers, regardless of feeding site, and he concluded that contact comfort is a crucial component of the attachment process.

Note well what Harlow did by applying the joint method of agreement and difference. He provided the conditions for a basis of comparison by having the babies fed in the absence of comfort or by having comfort in the absence of feeding. Thus, a true test was implemented that permitted a causal explanation of the results.

The hallmark of an experiment is the production of a comparison by controlling the occurrence or nonoccurrence of a variable and observing the outcome. Boring (1954) noted that the concept of **control** in experimentation derives from Mill's methods. One way we can view control is in terms of direct manipulation (*A* occurs or does not occur), which, according to the joint method of agreement and difference, leads to a basis for comparison (hence, the term *control group*, as explained later). Control also suggests that we can eliminate alternative explanations of our results. Usually control in experimentation is thought of in three ways: (1) there is a control condition for purposes of *comparison*; (2) the levels or values of the independent variable can be *produced*; and (3) the experimental setting can be controlled by holding certain aspects *constant* (for example, type of apparatus or method of measurement). These three types of control—comparison, production, and constancy—are crucial to the conduct of an experiment that will yield an explanation of why people and animals think and act as they do. In fact, comparison, production, and constancy provide us with a definition of an experiment (see the Concept Summary).

---

| **CONCEPT SUMMARY** | An experiment occurs when a particular *comparison* is *produced* while other aspects of the situation are held *constant*. |
|---|---|

---

In summary, producing comparisons, as Harlow did, can allow us to rule out the possibility of a mere correlation between variables. Correct use of Mill's procedure can lead to causal statements.

## | | | | ADVANTAGES OF EXPERIMENTATION

Let us examine another research problem to illustrate the advantages of experimentation. One characteristic of modern life is that many of us are subjected to changes in atmospheric pressure during air travel. Furthermore, a substantial portion of the world's population lives at elevations between 2,000 and 10,000 feet. What this means is that many people are subjected to mild decompressions in barometric pressure. Are these decompressions hazardous, as are so many other things in the world today (such as pollution, pesticides, and food additives)? This question was the impetus for experiments conducted by Graessle, Ahbel, and Porges (1978). Early research indicated that greatly reduced barometric pressure (as occurs in altitudes greater than 10,000 feet) can retard both fetal and newborn development. Graessle and colleagues wanted to see whether lesser decompressions, more like those experienced during air travel, also affected the development of infants.

To study this problem, the researchers experimented with pregnant rats. The general procedure was to subject the rats to a series of mild decompressions similar to those experienced during air travel (around 6,000 feet), and then compare the growth and behavior of rats born to the mothers that experienced decompression to the growth and behavior of rats born to mothers kept at ground level (728 feet, in this instance).

Now for some particulars of their research. Pregnant rats were randomly divided into two groups: One group received seven daily decompressions for twenty days during pregnancy, and the second group of mothers was kept at ground level. Changes in pressure for the one group (up to a pressure equaling an altitude of 6,000 feet) lasted about twenty minutes. These changes in pressure were gradual, simulating the sorts of changes that occur during air travel. Following birth, all infant rats were weighed daily and received periodic testing of their ability to grasp a thin wire, turn over (the righting reflex), move on an inclined plane, and climb (pull themselves up a thin wall when suspended by their forepaws).

The *independent variable* (what was varied) was atmospheric pressure, and the *dependent variables* (the things observed and measured) included the weight of the babies and the various behaviors just described. One way to view Harlow's experiments on love is that the independent variable was locus of food—on a hard or soft surrogate. What was Harlow's dependent variable? At this point we need to mention a third class of variables, the **control variables,** which the experimenter holds constant. In the decompression experiment, control variables included similar housing and feeding conditions for all rats at all times, identical testing procedures, and the fact that the treated and untreated mothers were of the same strain of rats. Species, housing, age, and health were among the control variables in Harlow's work.

Ordinarily we call the group of subjects that receives the independent variable the **experimental group;** the designation for the untreated subjects is the **control group.** (Note that a control group is not the same as a control variable. The meaning of "control group" will become clear momentarily.) In the decompression experiment, the decompressed mother rats and their babies represent the experimental group. The mothers and infants that were kept at ground level as a comparison or baseline group make up the control group. Note that these labels (experimental or control group) make some sense; that is, the control group receives a different treatment, and an examination of this group's behavior serves to indicate changes that would occur in the absence of the independent variable. Thus, the control group *controls* for changes that may occur whether or not any particular variable is introduced into the situation. The experimental group, of course, defines the experiment for us. The experimental group is the one that receives the treatment of interest—decompression, in this case. (Note that we are using Mill's procedure to arrive at an explanation.) Graessle and colleagues found that rats given decompressions before birth began to climb at a later age than the control animals and that the prenatally decompressed rats gained weight more slowly than the controls.

The experimental/control distinction is less obvious in Harlow's experiments because he pitted the effects of softness and feeding against each other. He had softness and feeding combined for one group and separated for another.

The results of the decompression experiment are intriguing and may have important practical implications. If you were interested in this topic, you might have considered the possibility of doing this experiment with pregnant human beings. The ethics of that tactic would be questionable without knowing in advance the effects of mild decompressions. That is why we do many types of experiments, especially preliminary ones and ones like Harlow's, on animals. An alternative approach to the decompression problem might be to do the research **ex post facto** which means selecting our subjects after the fact. Thus, we could do a quasi-experiment (see chapter 1). We would find infants whose mothers had flown on airplanes during pregnancy. Then we would compare their development to that of infants whose mothers had remained at ground level during pregnancy. Other than the tedious job of identifying the subjects in the first place (imagine trying to identify human subjects ex post facto for a Harlow-type study), the major drawback to the research done ex post facto is a loss of control. As we will discuss in chapter 9, it is very difficult to hold potentially relevant variables constant after the fact. In particular, we would be hard put to find two groups of subjects whose only difference was that some had flown on planes prenatally and some had not.

We can conclude, therefore, that, like the Harlow work, this animal study about the effects of mild decompression is more ethical, more economical, and better controlled than alternative research procedures. This experiment is not problem free, however. You might find it worthwhile to consider some of the difficulties associated with the experiments just described. One obvious problem concerns generalizing from rat or monkey development to human development.

| | |
|---|---|
| **CONCEPT SUMMARY** | ***Experiment***<br>A particular comparison is produced while other variables are held constant.<br>***Experimental Group***<br>Receives the important level of the independent variable.<br>***Control Group***<br>Serves as the untreated comparison group or receives a comparison level of the independent variable. |

#### | | | | **VARIABLES IN EXPERIMENTATION**

Variables are what make experiments run. Effective selection and manipulation of variables make the difference between a good experiment and a poor one. This section covers the three kinds of variables that must be carefully considered before starting an experiment: independent, dependent, and control variables. We conclude by discussing experiments that have more than one independent or dependent variable.

### Independent Variables

Independent variables are manipulated by the experimenter. The brightness of a lamp, the loudness of a tone, the number of decompressions given to a rat are all independent variables, since the experimenter determines their amount. Independent variables are selected because an experimenter thinks they will cause changes in behavior. Increasing the intensity of a tone should increase the speed with which people respond to the tone. Increasing the number of decompressions given to a mother rat may change the rate of development of her babies. When a change in the level (amount) of an independent variable causes a change in behavior, we say that the behavior is under control of the independent variable. Failure of an independent variable to control behavior, often called a *null result*, can have more than one interpretation. First, the experimenter may have incorrectly guessed that the independent variable was important, and the null results may be correct. Most scientists will accept this interpretation only reluctantly, and thus the following alternative explanations of null results are common.

The experimenter may not have created a valid manipulation of the independent variable. Let us say you are conducting an experiment on second-grade children and your independent variable is the number of small treats (chocolates, peanuts, or whatever) the children get after each correct response in some task. Some children get only one, whereas others get two. You find no difference in behavior between the two groups. Perhaps if your independent variable had involved a greater range—that is, if it went from one piece of candy to ten pieces of candy—you would have obtained a difference. Your manipulation was not sufficient to reveal any effect of the independent variable. Or perhaps, unknown to you, the class had a birthday party just before the experiment started and your subjects' stomachs were filled with ice cream and birthday cake. In this case, maybe even ten pieces of candy would not have shown any effect. That is why, in studies of animal learning in which food is used as a reward, the animals are deprived of food before the experiment starts. Thus experimenters are careful to produce a strong manipulation of the independent variable. Failure to do so is a common cause of null results. Other common causes of null results are related to dependent and control variables, to which we now turn.

### Dependent Variables

The dependent variable is observed and recorded by the experimenter. It depends on the behavior of the subject, which, in turn, is supposed to depend on the independent variable. The time it takes to press a switch, the speed of a worm crawling through a maze, the age when a rat climbs are all dependent variables, since they are observed and recorded by the experimenter.

One criterion for a good dependent variable is reliability (see chapter 2 for a discussion of reliability in testing and measurement). When an experiment is repeated exactly—same subject, same levels of independent variable, and so on—the dependent variable should yield about the same score as it did previously. Unreliability can occur if there is some deficit in the way we measure the dependent variable. Let us say we want to measure the weight in grams of a candle before and after it has been lit for fifteen minutes. We use a scale that has a spring which moves a pointer. The spring contracts when it is cold and expands when it is hot. As long as our weight measurements are taken at constant temperatures, they will be reliable. But if temperature varies while objects are being weighed, the same object will yield different readings. Our dependent variable is then unreliable. Generally, we want our measuring devices to be consistent, just as it is crucial for the observer to be consistent (as in following a protocol, see chapter 2).

Null results can often be caused by deficits in the dependent variable even if it is reliable. The most common cause is a restricted or limited range of the dependent variable so that it gets "stuck" at the top or bottom of its scale. Imagine you are teaching a rather uncoordinated friend how to bowl for the first time. Since you know from introductory psychology that reward improves performance, you offer to buy your friend a beer every time he or she gets a strike. Your friend gets all gutter balls so you drink the beer yourself. Thus you can no longer offer a reward, which means that the unrewarded performance should decrease. But since it is impossible to do any worse than all gutter balls, you cannot observe any decrement. Your friend is already at the bottom of the scale. This is called a **floor effect.** The opposite problem, that of getting 100 percent correct, is called a **ceiling effect.** Ceiling and floor effects prevent the influence of an independent variable from being accurately reflected in a dependent variable (these effects are discussed in detail later).

A final source of null results is one associated with inferential statistics. The results of a statistical test (see appendix B) may fail to reject the hypothesis that the experimental and control groups do not differ when, in fact, they do. This failure to reject the null hypothesis when it should be rejected is called a **type 2 error.** The likelihood of committing a type 2 error increases as we lower the level of statistical significance, but the likelihood can be decreased by increasing the power (sensitivity) of the experiment (see appendix B).

### Control Variables

A control variable is a potential independent variable that is held constant during an experiment. It does not vary, because it is controlled by the experimenter. For any one experiment, there are more desirable control variables than can ever be controlled in practice. In even a relatively simple experiment (for example, requiring people to memorize three-letter syllables), many variables should be controlled. Time of day (diurnal cycle) changes a person's efficiency, and ideally this should be controlled. Temperature could be important since your subject might fall asleep if the testing room were too warm. The time that has elapsed since a person's last meal might also affect memory performance. Intelligence is also related. The list could go on. An experimenter tries to control as many salient variables as possible, hoping that the effect of uncontrolled factors will be small relative to the effect of the independent variable. The smaller the size of the effect produced by the independent variable, the more important it is to carefully control other extraneous factors. Holding a variable constant is not the only way to remove extraneous variation. Design techniques, which we shall discuss in the next chapter, also control extraneous variables. However, holding a variable constant is the most direct experimental technique for controlling extraneous factors, and so we shall limit our definition of control variables to this technique. Null results often occur in an experiment because there is insufficient control of these other factors— that is, they have been left to vary unsystematically. This is especially true in studies outside of laboratories where the ability to hold control variables constant is greatly decreased. Remember, we call these unintended effects **confoundings,** since their influence confounds (or confuses) the proper interpretation of the results.

| | |
|---|---|
| **CONCEPT SUMMARY** | *Independent* variable is *manipulated* <br> *Dependent* variable is *observed* <br> *Control* variable is held *constant* |

### Name the Variables

Because independent, dependent, and control variables are so important, we have included some examples here for you to check your understanding of these terms. For each situation, name the three kinds of variables. Answers are provided at the end of this section.

**1.** An automobile manufacturer wants to know how bright brake lights should be, in order to minimize the time required for the driver of a following car to realize that the car in front is stopping. An experiment is conducted to answer this. Name the variables.

**2.** A pigeon is trained to peck a key if a green light is illuminated but not if a red light is one. Correct pecks get rewarded by access to grain. Name the variables.

**3.** A therapist tries to improve a patient's self-image. Every time the patient says something positive about himself or herself, the therapist rewards this by nodding, smiling, and being extra attentive. Name the variables.

**4.** A social psychologist does an experiment to discover if men or women give lower ratings of discomfort when they are one of six people crowded into a telephone booth. Name the variables.

## Answers

**1.** Independent (manipulated) variable

Intensity (brightness) of brake light.

Dependent (observed) variable

Time from onset of brake light until depression of brake pedal by following driver.

Control (constant) variables

Color of brake light, shape of brake pedal, force needed to depress brake pedal, external illumination, and so on.

**2.** Independent variable

Color of light (red or green).

Dependent variable

Number of key pecks.

Control variables

Hours of food deprivation, size of key, intensity of red and green lights, and so on.

**3.** Independent variable

Actually, this is not an experiment because there is only one level of the independent variable. To make this an experiment, we need another level (say, rewarding positive statements about the patient's mother-in-law). Then the independent variable would be kind of statement rewarded.

Dependent variable

Number (or frequency) of positive statements about self.

Control variables

None. This is a poor experiment.

**4.** Independent variable

Sex of the participant. Note: This is not a true independent variable, because the experimenter did not manipulate it. This is a quasi-experiment.

Dependent variable

Rating of discomfort.

Control variables

Size of telephone booth, number of persons (6) crowded into the booth, and so on.

## More Than One Independent Variable

It is unusual in a psychology journal to find an experiment in which only one independent (manipulated) variable was used. The typical experiment manipulates from two to four independent variables simultaneously. There are several advantages to this procedure. First, it is often more efficient to conduct one experiment with, say, three independent variables than to conduct three separate experiments. Second, experimental control is often better, since with a single experiment some control variables—for example, time of day, temperature, and humidity—are more likely to be held constant than would be the case with three separate experiments. Third, and most important, results generalized across several independent variables—that is, shown to be valid in several situations—are more valuable than data that have yet to be generalized. Fourth, just as it is important to establish generality of results across different types of experimental subjects and settings, we also need to discover whether some result is valid across levels of independent variables.

Let us say we wish to find out which of two rewards facilitates learning geometry by high school students. The first reward is an outright cash payment for problems correctly solved, and the second is early dismissal from class—that is, each correct solution entitles the student to leave class five minutes early. Assume that the results of this hypothetical experiment showed early dismissal to be better. Before we make early dismissal a universal rule in high school, we should first establish its generality by comparing the two kinds of reward in other classes, such as history and biology. Here, subject matter of the class would be a second independent variable. It would be better to put these two variables into a single experiment than to conduct two successive experiments. This would avoid problems of control, such as one class being tested the week of the big football game (when no reward would improve learning) and the other class being tested the week after the game was won (when students felt better about learning).

When the effects produced by one independent variable are not the same across the levels of a second independent variable, we have an **interaction.** The search for interactions is a major reason for using more than one independent variable per experiment. This can be best demonstrated by example.

Piliavin, Piliavin, and Rodin (1975) were interested in discovering under what conditions a bystander would help someone in an emergency. The emergency was faked on a New York City subway car (the F train, appropriately enough). A white male carrying a cane stumbled and fell to the floor. Would other passengers aid this "victim"?

The experiment had two independent variables. In half of the trial, victims had an ugly red birthmark placed on their face with theatrical makeup. The presence or absence of this birthmark was the first independent variable. An observer wearing a white medical jacket (identifying him as a physician or a medical intern) was present in half the trials. The same observer was present without the white jacket for the other trials. So, the presence or absence of the supposed physician was the second independent variable. The combination of the two independent variables yields four conditions: (1) birthmark and intern; (2) birthmark and no intern; (3) no birthmark and intern; (4) no birthmark and no intern. The dependent variable was the percentage of trials in which passengers came to the aid of the victim by either touching the victim or asking him if he needed help.

Results of this experiment are shown in figure 5–3, with each independent variable plotted alone. People were more willing to help victims who lacked an ugly birthmark. They were also more willing to help when no medical intern was present.

Figure 5–4 shows, however, that this interpretation of the results can be misleading. If, as figure 5–3 implies, both independent variables have their own unique effect, the results should look like the two parallel lines plotted in figure 5–5. Instead, the lines in figure 5–4 are not parallel, which indicates an interaction between the two independent variables. The percentage of trials in which help was given depends on the levels of each independent variable. If the victim had no birthmark, then the presence or absence of an intern had little effect on helping. But when the victim had a birthmark, passengers were far less willing to help when an intern was present.

Now let us imagine that this experiment had been performed in two separate parts. In the first part, only the birthmark was varied. The experimenter would not have known that the presence of an intern would have reduced helping. In the second part, only the presence of the intern was varied. Results would have been quite different, depending on whether the victim had a birthmark. You can see that by doing the experiment in two parts, we would have lost a great deal of information.

Figure 5–4, which contains the actual results, shows an interaction. The effects of one indepéndent variable depend on the level of the other independent variable. The least amount of help was given when the victim had a birthmark and the intern was present.

In summary, an interaction occurs when the effects of one independent variable are determined by the levels of other independent variables. When

**FIGURE 5–3**

Effects on helping of two independent variables. Each variable is plotted separately. (Data from Piliavin et al., 1975. Copyright 1975 by the American Psychological Association. Adapted by permission of the author.)

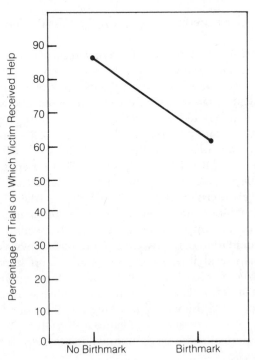
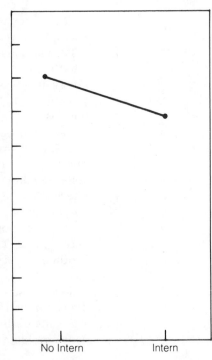

**FIGURE 5–4**

Effects of two independent variables on helping behavior. (Data from Piliavin et al., 1975. Copyright 1975 by the American Psychological Association. Adapted by permission of the author.)

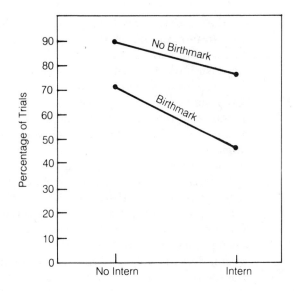

interactions are present, we do not discuss the effects of each independent variable separately. Because the effects of one variable depend upon the levels of the other variables, we are forced to discuss interacting variables together. Interactions are an extremely important topic, so they will receive additional discussion in chapter 7.

## More Than One Dependent Variable

The dependent (observed) variable is used as an index of behavior. The experimenter must decide which aspects of behavior are relevant to the experiment at hand. Some variables are traditional, but this does not mean they are the only, or even the best, index of behavior. Take, for example, the behavior of a rat pressing a bar or a pigeon pecking a key. The most common dependent variable is the number of presses or pecks observed.

**FIGURE 5–5**

Fictitious data showing no interaction between the two independent variables.

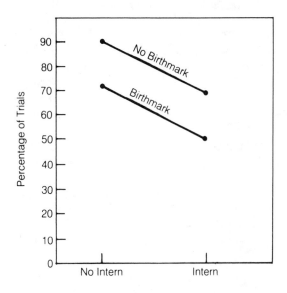

But the force with which a key is pecked can also lead to interesting findings (see Notterman and Mintz, 1965), as can the latency or time to respond. Researchers can usually come up with several dependent variables that may be appropriate. Let us say we wish to study the legibility of the typeface that you are now reading. We cannot observe legibility, of course. What dependent variables might we observe? Here are some that have been used in the past: retention of meaningful information after reading text, time needed to read a fixed number of words, number of errors in recognizing single letters, speed in transcribing or retyping text, heart rate during reading, and muscular tension during reading. This list is far from complete.

Reasons of economy argue for obtaining as many dependent measures at the same time as is feasible. Nevertheless, the typical experiment uses only one or at most two dependent variables simultaneously. This is unfortunate since, just as the generality of an experiment is expanded by having more than one independent variable, it is also expanded by having several dependent variables. One reason for not using several measures is that the results may be hard to interpret. Sometimes it may not be possible to determine whether the dependent variables are measuring the same thing or different things. Another reason more dependent variables are not used is that it is statistically difficult to analyze several dependent variables at once. Modern computer techniques make the calculations feasible, but many experimental psychologists have not been well trained in these multivariate statistical procedures and thus hesitate to use them. Although separate analyses could be conducted for each dependent variable, this loses information in much the same way that separate analysis of independent variables ignores interactions. Because multivariate analysis is complex, we will not discuss it here. Nevertheless, you should be aware that it is often advantageous to use more than one dependent variable in an experiment.

---

**CONCEPT SUMMARY**

**Variables in Experiments**

| Type | Operation | Example |
|---|---|---|
| Independent variables | At least two levels of a variable are *manipulated* | Hard and soft surrogates; decompression |
| Dependent variables | Particular behaviors are *measured* | Time spent clinging; infant growth and movement |
| Control variables | Other variables are *held constant* | Strain of animals; general test environment |

Multiple independent and dependent variables are important. An interaction occurs when the effects of one independent variable depend on the level of another independent variable.

| | | | **SUMMARY**

**1.** The joint method of agreement and difference permits causal explanation by showing that result $X$ occurs when event $A$ occurs, and that result $X$ does not occur when event $A$ does not occur.

**2.** An experiment can be defined as the production of a particular comparison while other aspects of the situation are held constant. Thus, comparison, production, and constancy are the hallmarks of control in experimentation.

**3.** Independent variables are those manipulated by the experimenter. It is important to select appropriate levels of the independent variable to avoid null results.

**4.** The dependent variable is the behavior observed and recorded by the experimenter. A reliable dependent variable is consistent. You need to guard against the possibility of ceiling and floor effects on your dependent variable by making sure that it does not have a restricted range of values.

**5.** A control variable is a potential independent variable that is held constant during an experiment. It is controlled to minimize confounding.

**6.** Using more than one independent variable is important in ensuring general results. When the effects produced by one independent variable are not the same across the levels of a second independent variable, we have an interaction.

**7.** Obtaining measures on more than one dependent variable can provide important information and increase the generality of the results of the experiment.

## Exercises

**1.** [*Special Exercise.*] An experimenter examined the effects of LSD on complex learning of rats. One group of rats was given a very small dose of LSD, so small a dose that it was unlikely to have any behavioral effects. A second group was given a large dose. Then, both groups ran through a complex maze several times. The dependent variable was the number of errors the rats made before obtaining the food reward at the end of the maze. The large-dose group made 4.5 times as many errors as the small-dose group, and the experimenter concluded that LSD can negatively affect complex learning. Comment on the levels of the independent variable that were used. What other dependent variables could be recorded? Comment on the conclusion by the experimenter.

**2.** Define what an experiment entails. Your definition should include mention of independent, dependent, and control variables.

**3.** Design an experiment to determine the effect of warmth on mother-infant attachment (assume an experimental setup similar to Harlow's). Specify the levels of your independent variable, describe your dependent variable, and note important control variables.

## Key Concepts

| | |
|---|---|
| ceiling effect | ex post facto |
| confounding | floor effect |
| control | independent variable |
| control group | interaction |
| control variable | joint method of agreement and difference |
| dependent variable | null results |
| experiment | type 2 error |
| experimental group | |

## Suggested Readings

Numerous experiments on a variety of topics can be found in Elmes, D. G. (1978). *Readings in experimental psychology.* Chicago: Rand McNally.

Harlow has published many articles on love. Two accounts worth examining are Harlow, H. F. (1959, June). Love in infant monkeys. *Scientific American,* 200(6), 68–74; and Harlow, H. F., & Harlow, M. K. (1966). Learning to love. *American Scientist,* 54, 244–272.

---

## APPLICATION
### Confounded Experiments in Advertising

A major value of a tightly controlled experiment is that the results are unambiguous: You can be confident that the independent variable led to changes in the dependent variable. Your conclusion about the effectiveness of the independent variable depends on minimal effects of extraneous factors—confounding variables. A recent advertising campaign presented an incorrect conclusion because the intended independent variable (Pepsi versus Coke) was confounded with another variable.

In the advertisement, people were asked to choose between the two cola drinks. In one series Pepsi was in a cup labeled *S* and Coke in a cup marked *L*. Most people chose the drink in the *S* cup (Pepsi), so the conclusion was that cola drinkers prefer Pepsi. Is this a legitimate conclusion?

An experiment by Woolfolk, Castellan, and Brooks (1983) calls the advertising results into question. These authors reason that the labels on the cups may have had some influence on the choices made by the people in the advertisement. This supposition is based on the knowledge that labeling of various kinds can have a strong effect on consumer behavior. As a first step in their research, Woolfolk and her associates determined that college students like the letter *S* better than the letter *L*. Then the researchers had other students choose between the colas presented in cups labeled *L* and *S*. In this experiment, unlike in the advertisement, the letters were the only independent variable, because the type of cola in the cups was held constant. For half the subjects, both cups contained Pepsi; and for the other half, both cups contained Coke. Regardless of the type of cola in the cups, the students preferred cola *S* to cola *L* in 85 percent of the cases.

Thus, it is possible that the conclusion in the advertisement was confounded by the preference for certain letters and did not result just from the preference for different colas. Let the viewer beware!

Woolfolk, M. E., Castellan, W., & Brooks, C. I. (1983). Pepsi versus Coke: Labels, not tastes, prevail. *Psychological Reports, 52,* 185–186.

## PSYCHOLOGY IN ACTION
### Preference for Cola Drinks

A good follow-up to the findings of Woolfolk and associates (1983) would be to do the taste-test experiment appropriately. Perform the experiment with unmarked cups (or at least cups that do not have markings that are visible to your subjects). You will need some small paper cups and a supply of beverages (say, Pepsi and Coke, or perhaps Sprite and 7-Up). Allow each person to taste a small amount of each beverage and then indicate his or her preference. Make sure that your subjects do not know the brand names of your drinks (and, of course, make sure they do not see you pouring the drinks into the cups). A rating-scale procedure or a magnitude-estimation procedure (see chapter 2) could be used as an alternative dependent variable. If you use one of these dependent variables, you will probably want to have your subjects make judgments about each drink separately along some dimension (say, a goodness-of-taste dimension).

One thing you should try to do in this experiment is to make sure that half your subjects taste Coke first, then Pepsi, and that the other half of your subjects taste the beverages in the reverse order. This reversal of order is called **counterbalancing** and is used to guard against the possibility that the order of tasting the drinks has an effect on the dependent variable. Counterbalancing is discussed in chapter 6.

| EXPERIMENTAL DESIGN<br>Variables should be selected to maximize internal validity | **Between-Subjects Design**<br><br>In the simplest case, the experimental group receives the independent variable and the control group does not.<br><br>To minimize the confounding of subject characteristics with group membership, randomly assign participants to conditions or match their characteristics between groups.<br><br>**Within-Subject Design**<br><br>Each participant receives all levels of the independent variable.<br><br>To minimize confounding caused by carry-over effects, the order of testing each level of the independent variable must be counterbalanced or randomized. |
| --- | --- |

# 6 ||||  Experimental Design

A carefully designed experiment will permit valid conclusions to be drawn about the effects of the independent variable on the dependent variable. In this chapter, we consider how to design experiments with a between-subjects configuration, where independent groups of subjects receive the different levels of the independent variable. We also consider a within-subjects configuration, in which all subjects receive all levels of the independent variable. A threat to validity for the between-subjects case has to do with the initial equality of the subjects in the different groups. In within-subjects experiments, the effects of one treatment may carry over to another, which could confound the effect of the independent variable.

## |||| INTERNAL VALIDITY IN EXPERIMENTS

In a properly conducted experiment, the situation is controlled so that changes in dependent variables result solely from changes in independent variables. In a good experiment, we can make valid causal statements about the results. A valid observation, as noted in chapter 2, is one that is sound or genuine because it reveals a true effect. A properly designed experiment can have valid results, and experiments that lead to valid results are said to be **internally valid** (see Cook and Campbell, 1979). By means of control, (such as the joint method), the researcher rules out inadvertent confounding, and the results reflect the effects of the intended variables. As discussed in chapter 5, Harlow (1958) was able to assert that contact comfort was more important for attachment than was feeding. He designed his experiment to maximize the effects of comfort versus feeding and to minimize the effects of extraneous variables, which means that Harlow's work was internally valid.

Experiments are internally valid in principle. Internal validity does not occur automatically, but rather through a careful selection of variables and an adequate experimental design. Underwood has noted that there is one basic principle of research design: "design the experiment so that the effects of the independent variables can be evaluated unambiguously" (1957, p. 86). In this chapter, we will discuss features of experimental design that help provide internal validity. To illustrate how experimental design is related to validity, we will first consider two situations in which design flaws could prevent valid causal statements.

## Executive Monkeys

The topic of stress-induced ulcers, especially among high-powered executives, is a common one in the popular press. Early laboratory experiments by Brady (1958) and his colleagues (Brady, Porter, Conrad, and Mason, 1958) demonstrated the development of stress ulcers in "executive" monkeys. Brady initially tested monkeys to see whether they could learn to respond quickly by pressing a button to avoid electric shock. Monkeys that responded at a high rate during this test were allowed to be executives in a second phase of the experiment. In the second part of the experiment, an executive monkey and a "co-worker" received strong electric shocks periodically over long periods of time (usually a four-hour session). This was considered to be a highly stressful work situation for the monkeys. The executive monkeys could press a button that would postpone the shock. In this avoidance task, the co-worker of the executive received a shock every time the executive received one, but the co-worker did not have any control over the occurrence of the shocks. The executive had control over the presentation of the shocks by being able to avoid them. If the executive did not press the button often enough, both he and his helpless co-worker would get shocked. Brady found that the executives developed severe gastrointestinal ulcers and died, whereas the helpless co-workers did not develop any obvious disorders. This finding led Brady, along with many other psychologists, to conclude that the stress of management could produce ulcers under controlled conditions.

Brady's conclusion was considered to be a valid one for quite some time. But then a number of laboratory reports began to appear that seemed to indicate greater production of stress ulcers in helpless animals than in those who had control over electric shock (for example, Weiss, 1968). Were the earlier findings the result of poor design, or were the later results a fluke? Subsequent work by Weiss (1971) confirmed the fact that helpless animals were indeed more affected than those who had control, and his work suggested why the original studies about executive monkeys were flawed and, thereby, invalid. Weiss noted that Brady's executives responded at a high rate at the beginning of the experiment. Then Weiss demonstrated that animals which respond at high rates in a stressful avoidance task are likely to get ulcers, regardless of whether they are helpless or in control. Because the tendency to respond at high rates was confounded with the independent variable (helplessness or executive control) in Brady's work, some psychologists made the invalid conclusion that control under stressful situations leads to ulcers. The critical design flaw underlying the invalid conclusion was assignment of the highly responsive monkeys to the executive condition. Later we will consider some general rules for ensuring that the characteristics of the subjects do not have a confounding influence on the effects of the independent variable. Without such rules it would be difficult, if not impossible, to have an internally valid experiment.

## Experiments with LSD

Lysergic acid diethylamide (LSD) is a hallucinogenic substance that was a popular and dangerous drug used to induce a "high" in the drug culture of the late 1960s and early 1970s. Because LSD was so popular and also seemed to produce some of the symptoms associated with schizophrenia, a severe mental disorder, psychologists tried to determine the effects of LSD on behavior in the controlled environment of the laboratory.

Laboratory research on the effects of LSD began in the early 1960s, and some of those studies provide useful lessons in designing internally valid experiments. We shall examine an early study by Jarrard (1963) that illustrates an experimental design in which each subject receives all levels of the independent variables (several different-sized doses of LSD, in this case). This type of design is called a **within-subjects design** and differs from the **between-subjects design** used by Weiss, in which different subjects received the various levels of the independent variable (the animals were either helpless or executives, but not both).

Jarrard wanted to determine the effects of several different doses of LSD on well-established behavior. Initially, he trained rats to press a lever to obtain a food reward. When the behavior of the rats stabilized and they were performing well, Jarrard began testing the effects of LSD on the rate of lever pressing. His experiment involved six levels of the independent variable. The baseline or control amount of LSD was zero—the rats were injected with a saltwater solution that matched the salinity of their body fluids. The remaining five doses of LSD represented a proportion of each rat's body weight and were .05, .10, .20, .40, and .80 milligrams of LSD per kilogram of body weight. The general procedure involved placing the rats in the lever box immediately after injection for a two-hour test period. Several days separated each test of the injections.

At this point we need to consider several problems that could prevent Jarrard from having an internally valid experiment. Suppose Jarrard tested all his animals in the same order, going from the control dose to the largest dose. Such a design could lead to problems, because the susceptibility to LSD could change across successive administrations. The rats could become more tolerant of LSD (less affected by it) or they could become sensitized (more affected by it). In either case, tolerance or sensitization, the effects of later doses of LSD would be influenced by the rats' having received the earlier doses. This confounding effect also could occur if testing began with the largest dose and ended with the smallest.

Because Jarrard did not know whether LSD had long-term carryover effects such as tolerance and sensitization, he needed to find a way to administer doses so he could determine the effects of a particular dose independent of the other doses. He chose to counterbalance the order of doses across subjects. To **counterbalance** means to offset some contrary influence. The possible confounding effect of carryover from one dose to another was counterbalanced by having each dose appear equally often at each ordinal position in the test sequence. For example, one subject might have received the following sequence: control, .05, .40, .10, .80, .20. Another subject might have received .40, control, .10, .20, .05, .80. The remaining four rats would then receive different orders of treatments so that for all six rats, each dose was tested first, second, third, fourth, fifth, and sixth. This procedure should balance across doses any tolerance or sensitization that could occur as a result of repeated administration of LSD. On the average, each condition occurs at each ordinal position.

Jarrard found that the pressing of a bar for food was slightly enhanced by the two smallest doses of LSD and severely impaired by the two largest doses, compared with the effects of the saltwater injection (the control condition). These are internally valid results because they are not confounded by carryover effects caused by repeated testing of the independent variable. A major topic of this chapter is prevention of carryover effects in within-subjects designs.

## |||| EXPERIMENTAL DESIGN

The work of Weiss and Jarrard that we have just discussed illustrates the purpose of good experimental design: to minimize extraneous or uncontrolled variation in order to increase the likelihood that an experiment will produce internally valid results. Here we will cover some common techniques used to improve the design of experiments. This discussion should provide you with an understanding of the aims of the psychologist designing a particular experiment.

The first design decision an experimenter must make is how to assign subjects to the various levels of independent variables. The two main possibilities are (1) to assign only some subjects to each level, as Weiss did, or (2) to assign each subject to every level, as Jarrard did. As mentioned earlier, the first possibility is called a between-subjects design and the second a within-subjects design. Let us reconsider Weiss's study from the standpoint of the two types of design and pretend that we are going to repeat his work. The two main conditions in that experiment were the executive condition, in which the animals had control over the shocks, and the helpless condition, in which the animals received shocks regardless of what they did. Let us assume that we have ten rats available for our study. A between-subjects design and a within-subjects design for the experiment are illustrated in table 6–1. The between-subjects design calls for you to divide your subjects in half (into two groups of five rats each), with one group receiving the executive treatment and the other the helpless treatment. (The proper method for assigning subjects to each group will be discussed shortly.) The within-subjects design has all ten rats tested with both levels of the independent variable; that is, each rat is tested in the executive condition and in the helpless condition. (The proper method to determine the order in which each subject gets these two treatments will also be discussed later.) Before reading on, consider which design you would use and provide reasons. The factors involved in this sort of decision are considered below.

### Between-Subjects Designs

The between-subjects design is conservative (safe) because there is no chance of one treatment contaminating the other, since the same subject never receives both treatments. However, the between-subjects design must contend with the possibility that the subjects in the two groups are different enough to influence the effects of the treatments. Any between-subjects

**TABLE 6-1**
Between-Subjects and
Within-Subjects Designs
for Weiss' Experiment,
with Ten Rats as the
Subjects (numbered 1 to
10)

BETWEEN-SUBJECTS DESIGN

| | Independent Variable | | |
| Individual subjects | Executive Condition | Helpless Condition | |
|---|---|---|---|
| | 1 | 6 | Half of the subjects are in |
| | 2 | 7 | the executive group and |
| | 3 | 8 | half are in the helpless |
| | 4 | 9 | group. |
| | 5 | 10 | |

WITHIN-SUBJECTS DESIGN

| | Independent Variable | | |
| Individual subjects | Executive Condition | Helpless Condition | |
|---|---|---|---|
| | 1 | 1 | All subjects receive both the |
| | 2 | 2 | executive and the |
| | 3 | 3 | helpless treatments. |
| | 4 | 4 | |
| | 5 | 5 | |
| | . | . | |
| | . | . | |
| | . | . | |
| | 10 | 10 | |

experiment has the potential for being confounded because of differences among the subjects in the two groups. For example, the results of Brady's experiment were confounded by putting the highly responsive animals in the executive condition.

**Randomization and matching.**   In any between-subjects experiment, the researcher must somehow guarantee that as few differences as possible exist among the subjects in the various treatment groups. Clearly, if we took the five animals most susceptible to stomach ulcers and put them into the executive group, and we put the five least susceptible into the helpless condition, we might arrive at results that mask the true effects; we would have an internally *in*valid experiment. This is exactly what happened in the original executive-monkey experiment, since we now know that highly responsive animals are likely to ulcerate under stress. To prevent this kind of outcome, the experimenter tries to have groups that are equivalent at the beginning of the experiment.

One possible technique to use is called **matching,** in which important subject characteristics are matched in the various treatment conditions. In this experiment, one way to match subjects would be to administer a pretest to the animals to determine their response rates. Then subjects that had equal or very similar rates of response could be paired up. Unlike the procedure Brady used to assign subjects, this procedure calls for one member of each pair being randomly assigned to one group and the other member being assigned to the second group. One difficulty with matching is that an experimenter cannot match for everything. Indeed, the experimenter may not know what characteristics should be matched. Even though matched on some characteristics, the groups may differ on some other potentially relevant dimension. Thus, matching is done on the basis of the most likely confounding variables. Even so, matching on one variable could cause a mismatch on another.

In addition to the problems mentioned, another difficulty—**subject attrition**—can make matching an ineffective way to try to equate groups. Subject attrition means that one or more of the subjects in an experiment do not complete participation, or their behavior changes for reasons other than the independent variable. Attrition can occur for any number of reasons. For example, a subject might get sick and fail to continue. An animal subject might die or perform so poorly that the data are uninterpretable. A human subject in the experiment might refuse to continue to participate. In a long-term experiment, the subjects might mature, which means that their characteristics change during the course of the experiment. If we carefully match our subjects across conditions in order to equate our groups, then subject attrition in one group will make our groups unequal and our matching will have been in vain. This may be true even if just one subject is lost from a particular group.

If group characteristics are determined by an unbiased procedure (random assignment), attrition will have a less detrimental effect. However, attrition can still pose problems, with regard to both the reliability and the validity of our observations. If some form of attrition is likely, matching should not be used.

*Randomization* is a more common technique to ensure the formation of equivalent groups of subjects. One way to form two groups by randomization would be to assign arbitrary numbers to the subjects and then pull numbered slips of paper out of a hat or some other container. Similarly, when we are ready to assign a particular subject to a condition, we could throw a die, with even throws being assigned to one group and odd throws to the other. If we do not have any dice, a table of random numbers could be used to generate odd and even digits.

A table of random numbers is provided in table C-7 in the appendix. Random-number tables are very easy to use. To generate odd and even numbers, select a row of numbers in the table. Proceed across the row, noting whether each number is odd or even. If you reach the end of a row, simply select a different row of numbers and continue the procedure.

Each of these methods of randomization ignores the characteristics of the subjects and leads to a random, unbiased assignment to conditions. Randomization means that each subject has an equal and unbiased opportunity to be in any of the conditions of the experiment. Randomization is how Weiss improved the design of the executive-monkey experiment. However, randomization does not guarantee that your groups will always be equal. By chance, more of the highly responsive animals might be assigned to one of the groups. The odds of this rare occurrence can be calculated by the methods of statistics. This is one reason experimental design and statistics are often treated as the same topic. However, experimental design has to do with the logic of arranging experiments, whereas statistics deals with calculating odds, probabilities, and other mathematical quantities. Although matching may be preferable to randomization, in some cases we may not be sure about the basis of matching so that randomization is the preferred assignment procedure.

| CONCEPT SUMMARY | **Between-Subjects Design** |
|---|---|
| | Separate groups of subjects receive different levels of the independent variable. To control for individual differences: |
| | Randomly assign subjects to conditions, or |
| | Match subject characteristics in each group. |

## Within-Subjects Designs

Many experimental psychologists prefer the within-subjects design to the between-subjects design. The within-subjects design is generally more efficient, because each subject is compared with himself or herself in the different experimental conditions. In our experiment, this means that any differences resulting from the executive and helpless treatments would not be caused by differences between the animals in the two conditions (as could be true of the between-subjects design), since all subjects receive all treatments.

As indicated in the earlier discussion of Jarrard's experiment, the efficient within-subjects design brings with it the serious risk of **carryover effects** from one treatment to the next, which could result in an invalid experiment. That is, the effects of one treatment may carry over to another condition. These are particularly serious if the conditions affect each other (or carryover) in different ways (e.g., the experimental condition affects the control differently than the control condition affects the experimental condition). Imagine that ten rats first underwent the helpless condition and then were placed in the executive condition in Brady's experiment with executive monkeys. As a result of their earlier experience with being helpless, the animals may react poorly to the executive condition, where they now have control over the shocks. This would destroy any true differences between the two levels of the independent variable. In any within-subjects experiment, there is the danger that experience in an early part of the experiment might change behavior in a later part of the experiment, because the effects of one treatment might carry over to the other treatment. This can be caused even by routine factors, such as practice or fatigue. How do we reduce this source of invalidity?

**Randomization.**   One way to minimize carryover among treatments is to randomly determine the order of their application. A random order can be established by using a table of random numbers or by writing the treatments on slips of paper and drawing them out of a hat. The logic is the same as that just described for assigning subjects to conditions in between-subjects designs. However, although randomization produces equivalent treatment orders in the long run, it is less likely to be suitable when there is only a small number of treatments. In most experiments, the number of subjects exceeds the number of treatments, so randomization is a good technique for assigning subjects to conditions but not for determining the order of treatments.

**Counterbalancing.** As mentioned earlier, Jarrard used a technique called counterbalancing to balance the order of treatments across stages of his experiment. By balancing the effects of order of treatments across subjects, Jarrard was able to minimize carryover effects. In counterbalancing, each treatment occurs in each time period of the experiment. This means that every treatment has the same chance of being influenced by confounding variables. In other words, we *counter* the effects of potential confounding variables by *balancing* them over the periods when the treatments are administered.

Complete counterbalancing ensures that all possible treatment orders are used. In the executive-monkey experiment this is easy, because there are only two orders of treatments: helpless then executive, executive then helpless. As the numbers of conditions increase, the numbers of orders get larger. Three treatments have six different orders, four treatments have twenty-four different orders, five conditions have one hundred and twenty different orders, and so on. So, as the levels of the independent variable increase, complete counterbalancing soon becomes impractical. Instead, experimenters must settle for incomplete counterbalancing, in which each treatment occurs equally often in each portion of the experiment. In other words, condition A occurs first, second, and third equally often, as do conditions B and C. This arrangement is called a *Latin-square design*.

The order of treatments within a Latin square could be determined randomly, in which case we would have a **block randomization** procedure. Usually, however, when the number of treatments is greater than two, but not much greater than seven or eight, the **balanced Latin-square** design is the most appropriate. Some Latin squares are shown in figure 6–1. The middle and right-hand squares are balanced, which means that when each condition is tested it will, across subjects, be preceded and followed in equal frequency by every other condition. This last feature is very useful in minimizing carryover effects among conditions and makes the balanced Latin square preferable to other incomplete counterbalancing schemes.

Constructing a balanced Latin square is easy, especially if there is an even number of treatments. Let us label the four conditions in an experiment from *A* to *D*. A balanced Latin square can be thought of as a two-dimensional matrix in which the columns (extending vertically) represent conditions tested and the rows (extending horizontally) represent subjects. In the right most square of figure 6–1, subjects are labeled *1* through *4*, and the order in which they receive treatments is determined by reading across the row. Thus, in this example, subject 1 receives the conditions in the order *A, B, D, C*. The general formula for constructing the first row of a balanced Latin square is *A, B, X, C, X − 1, D, X − 2*, and so forth, where *X* stands for the final or total numbers of conditions (in this case *D* is the last treatment). After the first row is in place, then go down the columns with the successively designated treatments, starting over when you get to *X*. (Note how this procedure was followed in the third square in figure 6–1). When a balanced Latin-square design is used, subjects must be run in multiples of the number of treatments (in this case, four), in order to appropriately counterbalance conditions against carryover effects.

When an experiment contains an odd number of conditions, it becomes a bit more complicated to use a balanced Latin square. Two squares must

**Figure 6–1**

*Three Latin squares for counterbalancing the order of four treatments. Letters represent treatments. Thus, the first subject receives treatment A first, B second, and then C followed by D. Note that each treatment occurs only once in each row and each column. In the second and third squares, the* order *of treatments is balanced; each treatment precedes and follows every other treatment equally often.*

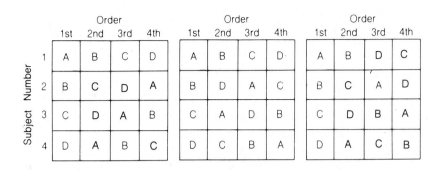

be used, the second of which is the reverse of the first. A balanced Latin square for five conditions is shown in figure 6–2. Once again numbers indicate subjects, and letters stand for conditions in the experiment. When a balanced Latin square is used with an odd number of treatments, each subject must be tested in each condition twice. In general, the first square is constructed in exactly the same manner as when there is an even number of conditions, and then the second square is an exact reversal of the first. The balanced Latin square is an optimal counterbalancing system for many purposes, since each condition occurs, on the average, at the same stage of practice, and each condition precedes and follows every other equally often.

Counterbalancing is useful not only for assigning treatment orders, but also for determining the order of testing when there is more than one dependent variable. The primary concern is to balance any potential carryover effects for any given subject. To illustrate, let us reconsider the decompression study described in chapter 5. In that study, baby rats received several tests so that the experimenter could determine whether prenatal decompression had affected them. Suppose there is reason to believe that the infant rats' performance on one test, such as climbing, could influence their behavior on another test, such as grasping. So, even though the different measures are not independent variables in the usual sense, the order in which they are administered may affect what is measured. One test might make the infant rats tired or could, conceivably, enhance their muscle tone. If we have two measures, A and B, we can completely counterbalance the order of assessment across subjects so that the average effect will be balanced.

**Figure 6–2**

*Balanced Latin square for five experimental conditions (A–E). Rows indicate the order in which subjects 1–5 are to experience conditions. When there is an odd number of treatments, each one must be given to each subject twice, in order to obtain a balanced Latin square.*

Order of Testing

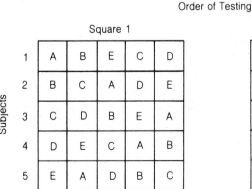

What do we do for an individual subject? One solution to this problem, and the one most psychologists would pick, would be to use **intrasubject counterbalancing** (an **ABBA design**). This would eliminate the confounding of each assessment with time of assessment, because each measure would occur at the same time on the average (1 + 4 = 5 for A and 2 + 3 = 5 for B, where the numbers refer to the order of test). But perhaps the specific order of testing might also matter. If $A$ is the grasping test and $B$ the climbing test, it is possible that climbing is so fatiguing that the results of the grasping test are biased.

Two solutions to differential order effects are possible. One would be simply to increase the number of subjects and just administer one test to each subject. Of course, this would defeat the purpose of multiple testing and using the subject as its own control. Another solution would be to use more than one within-subjects counterbalancing scheme. For example, half the subjects might get the reverse of the scheme that the other half receives. So half the subjects would be tested in the ABBA order and the other half would be tested in the order BAAB. Across subjects, as well as within subjects, therefore, we would balance the testing of the subjects.

These counterbalancing procedures are useful in a variety of ways. They can be used to assign subjects to treatments, to determine the order of testing, to determine when certain materials are given to particular subjects, and, in general, to minimize the effects of one aspect of an experiment on another. Applying counterbalancing techniques helps us toward achieving an internally valid experiment.

---

| **CONCEPT SUMMARY** | **Within-Subjects Design** |
|---|---|
| | All subjects receive all levels of the independent variable. To control for carryover effects: |
| | Randomize the order of treatments or |
| | Counterbalance the order of treatments. |

---

## ⅠⅠⅠⅠ CONTROL CONDITIONS

Most experiments contain some **control group** (between-subjects design) or *control condition* (within-subjects design). In its simplest form, the control group is the group that does not receive the levels of interest of the independent variable. It is misleading to say that the control group does not receive the independent variable, because independent variables must by definition have at least two levels, one of which may be the control level. For example, say we are interested in analyzing the effect of noise on studying. Using a between-subjects design, we would expose one group of subjects to loud noise for half an hour while they were studying; this is the level of interest of the independent variable. A control group would study the same material for half an hour, but in a quiet setting. Then we would test both groups on the material. Any difference in test performance between the two groups would be attributed to the effect of noise.

In the experiment just described, the control group did not receive any treatment (no noise was introduced). This is not always the case. As you will recall from chapter 5, we described a study on decompression in which the control condition was ground-level pressure at 728 feet. Another control condition could have been sea level (zero altitude). In another part of the country, 1,000 feet might have been the appropriate control altitude. The important characteristic of a control condition is that it provides a **baseline** against which some variable of the experiment can be compared. Sometimes the best baseline is no particular treatment, but many times the best baseline requires some activity. This problem occurs sometimes in memory research.

Let us say that a group of subjects is required to learn two different lists of words (Table 6–2); the experimenter is interested in how learning one list interferes with learning the other. The experimental group (receiving the level of interest of the independent variable) first learns list A, then learns list B, and then is tested again on list A. The experimenter would like to show that learning list B interferes with learning list A. But before any conclusion of this sort can be reached, a comparison control condition is required. Merely comparing the results of the final test of list A with the results of the first test is insufficient, because subjects might do less well on the last list-A test simply because they are tired, or do better because of extra practice. If a control condition with no treatment were used, a control group would learn list A, then would sit around for the time it takes the experimental group to learn list B, and then would be tested again on list A. But this would be a poor control condition because subjects might practice or rehearse list A while they are sitting around. Practicing would improve their final performance on the last list-A test and incorrectly make the experimental group look as if learning list B interfered with learning list A more than it really did. A proper baseline condition would occupy the control group during the time the experimental group was learning list B. Perhaps these subjects would be instructed to do arithmetic or some other busywork that would prevent rehearsal. An example of such an experimental design is shown in Table 6–2. Another example is the baseline condition used by Jarrard in the LSD study. He used a placebo injection of saline instead of no injection at all. The reason for this injection baseline is that the injection itself could have disrupted the behavior of the rats. Without this comparison, there may have been an inappropriate assessment of the effects of LSD.

Sometimes the control condition is contained implicitly within the experiment. Suppose we want to study learning in rats, and our independent variable is the number of food pellets (one or five) we give the rats when they make the correct response. No experimenter would bother to include

**TABLE 6–2**

Examples of experimental and control groups for list learning.

| | First Period | Second Period | Third Period |
|---|---|---|---|
| Experimental group | Learn list A | Learn list B | Test list A |
| Control group | Learn list A | Do arithmetic | Test list A |

a control group or condition with zero pellets, because no learning could occur under this odd circumstance. The control condition is implicit, in that five pellets can be compared with one, and vice versa. Since the experimenter might well be as interested in effects of a single pellet as in five, we probably would not explicitly call the one-pellet level a control condition. But it does provide a baseline for comparison—and so, for that matter, does the five-pellet condition, since the one-pellet results can be compared with it.

## Mixed Designs

Experiments need not be exclusively of within-subjects design or between-subjects design. It is often convenient and prudent to have some independent variables treated as between-subjects and others as within-subjects in the same experiment (assuming the experiment has more than one independent variable, of course). If one variable seems likely to cause transfer or carryover effects (for example, administering a drug), it can be made a between-subjects variable while the rest of the variables are within-subjects. This compromise design is not as efficient as a pure within-subjects design, but it often is safer. Mixed designs are described in more detail in the next chapter.

## |||| CHOOSING AN EXPERIMENTAL DESIGN

We have noted that the between-subjects design precludes carryover effects from one treatment to another, and that the within-subjects design does not confound subjects with conditions. Furthermore, we have suggested that the within-subjects design is usually more efficient than the between-subjects design, so obtaining repeated observations from the same subjects may be preferable to using independent groups. In this section, we will consider some rules of thumb for selecting an experimental design, regardless of the particular research topic. At the end of this section, there are several experimental problems for which you are to choose a design.

## Carryover Effects

If your independent variable is likely to have a permanent effect on the subject and would prevent subsequent unconfounded testing, then a between-subjects design should be used. What sorts of independent variables would operate in this way? Independent variables that permanently alter the state or development of the subject would certainly have carryover effects. These might include effects of prenatal compression, prenatal nutrition, nearly all kinds of physiological damage (brain lesions, some drugs, toxic chemicals, and so on), most time-dependent variables (the effect of persuasion on later consumer behavior or the effects of a particular reading technique on second-grade achievement), and any other variable whose effects are likely to be irreversible. Most subject variables (sex, age, ethnic group, and so on) require a between-subjects design, but these variables are not true independent variables. The special problems associated with research involving subject variables will be examined in chapter 10.

If you are interested in changes in behavior over time, such as improvements in learning, changes of strategy in a particular task, or optimal performance on a task, then you will want to use some variant of a within-subjects design. You either will need to expose your subjects to repeated measures, (for example, you might place rats in a maze twice each day for a month), or you will need to give each subject several treatments over time. In effect, you are looking for a carryover effect, which is really what a great deal of learning research is all about.

## Individual Differences

You might think it trivial of us to say that people differ from each other. However, **individual differences** among subjects are not a trivial problem when it comes to designing a good experiment. If your subject pool contains individuals who are markedly different from each other or if you expect that large individual differences in thought or behavior are likely to show up in your experiment, you may be better off using a within-subjects design rather than a between-subjects design. The within-subjects design automatically takes care of differences among your subjects. As long as you counterbalance appropriately (and carryover effects are not a problem), you can control for these individual differences in a within-subjects design.

A case in point is testing the effectiveness of drugs. Drug manufacturers know that people and animals differ in their sensitivity to drugs, which is one of the reasons Jarrard used a within-subjects design to test the effects of LSD. Once the drug is marketed, many different types of people will be taking the drugs. Therefore, it is imperative that many different types of people be tested and that several drugs be tested on the same person. Within-subjects administration of several levels of a drug compared with a placebo will also control for individual differences that may appear on the behavioral or attitudinal task used to assess drug effects. For example, if the effects of a drug on pain tolerance are being tested, it is important to do this study within-subjects, because we know ahead of time that there are tremendous individual differences in reaction to pain in the absence of any externally administered substance.

Obviously, if a drug is likely to have long-term effects, a between-subjects design must be used. Another reason that many clinical tests of drug effectiveness use between-subjects designs is that subjects with certain diseases are selected. The experimental group of subjects is given the drug, and a control group with the same disease is given a placebo or another drug. If one of the drugs is effective, then for humanitarian reasons all patients in the study receive it after the experimental comparison is completed.

Many research problems pose a particular dilemma: You must balance carryover effects against the possible contaminating effects of large individual differences. There is no easy solution to this problem. Sometimes the easiest way out is to do the study one way (for example, within-subjects) and then do it the other way (between-subjects). Although such a tactic may seem inefficient, in the long run it will add to the generality of the results.

### Design Problems

For each of the following problems, decide upon a within- or between-subjects design. If you think the situation warrants it, set up your experiment with both types of design. For practice, you should indicate the independent, dependent, and control variables. If you choose a within-subjects design, specify the counterbalancing procedures, and if you use a between-subjects design, indicate how subjects will be assigned to conditions. Regardless of your design, indicate your reasons for selecting either the within- or between-subjects configuration.

**1.** A researcher wants to see which is easier to learn: hard-to-pronounce syllables (such as WMH, JBT, SJK) or easy-to-pronounce syllables (such as LEJ, NAM, HEK). Two lists, containing either twenty pronounceable syllables or twenty hard-to-pronounce syllables, will be prepared. Each element in a list will be shown for two seconds. At the end of the series, the subjects will try to write down the syllables from memory.

**2.** A cleanser manufacturer is interested in the effects of package color on the sales of Scrubbo super cleanser. Cartons of Scrubbo that are identical except for the background color of the label (maroon, pink, or aqua) will be prepared. Sales will be monitored for the next four months.

**3.** A child psychologist wants to determine the effects of cloth versus paper diapers on toilet training. Day-old infants will be used to begin in the project. The age at which diapers are no longer needed (to the nearest week) will be determined.

**4.** A researcher wants to determine whether rats learn a complex maze more quickly when practice is spaced (spread out in time) rather than massed. The effects of massing practice trials (one trial every ten seconds) will be compared to the effects of distributing practice trials (one every ten minutes). The dependent variable will be the number of trials the rats need to learn the maze perfectly.

**5.** The Burpo beer company is test-marketing flavored light beers. It wants to see whether consumers prefer strawberry-, licorice-, or avocado-flavored Burpo. Several bottles of each flavor will be made. Consumers will fill out a questionnaire on how much they like the flavor, body, and aroma of the various flavors.

| CONCEPT SUMMARY | **Summary of Control Techniques for Between- and Within-Subjects Designs** | | |
|---|---|---|---|
| | *To Control for* | *Between-Subjects Design* | *Within-Subject Design* |
| | Individual differences (sex, age, I.Q.) | Randomized assignment—unbiased assignment of subjects to groups | Individual differences automatically controlled |
| | | Matched assignment Hold variable constant across groups (test only females) Equate variables across groups (use equal numbers of right-handed and left-handed subjects) | |
| | Situational differences (time of day the data are collected, room temperature) | Randomize the effects of these variables Hold constant or equate these variables | Same as between-subjects |
| | Carryover effects (order of testing, assignment of materials) | Usually carryover effects do not occur. If they do, same techniques as in within-subjects | Intrasubject counterbalancing (ABBA) Intragroup counterbalancing Randomized order Complete counterbalancing Incomplete counterbalancing (Latin-square designs) |

|||| **SUMMARY**

**1.** Experiments with well-chosen variables and clean designs permit accurate conclusions to be drawn from the results. Such experiments are said to have internal validity.

**2.** In a between-subjects design, different subjects are assigned to the different levels of the independent variable.

**3.** In a within-subjects design, each subject receives all levels of the independent variable.

**4.** With a between-subjects design, there is no chance for the effects of one treatment to contaminate the effects of another. However, the differences between the people in the different groups may confound the effects of the independent variable.

**5.** The within-subjects design is more efficient than the between-subjects design, and we do not have to be concerned about differences between subjects contaminating the results. However, we do have to worry about the carryover of one treatment to another.

**6.** To ensure that the individual differences between subjects in various groups are not confounding a between-subjects experiment, we should assign the subjects to conditions on a random basis. Alternatively, the subjects' characteristics can be matched across groups.

**7.** By varying the order of presenting the treatments, we can minimize the carryover effects in the within-subjects design. The order can be randomized or completely counterbalanced. When there is a large number of treatments or levels of the independent variable, we can achieve incomplete counterbalancing by using a balanced Latin square.

**8.** A control group or control condition provides a baseline against which some variable of an experiment can be compared.

**9.** If the independent variable is likely to have a permanent effect on the subject and would prevent subsequent unconfounded testing, then a between-subjects design should be used.

**10.** If large individual differences in thought or behavior are likely to occur, a within-subjects design may be preferable to a between-subjects design.

## Key Concepts

| | |
|---|---|
| balanced Latin square | internal validity |
| baseline | intrasubject counterbalancing (ABBA) |
| between-subjects design | Latin-square design |
| block randomization | matching |
| carryover effects | randomization |
| control condition | subject attrition |
| counterbalancing | within-subjects design |
| individual differences | |

## Exercises

**1.** *[Special Exercise.]* What is wrong with the following experimental design? To study how the creation of mental images affects retention, an experimenter used a within-subjects design. A long list of unrelated words was presented to the subjects, with each word being presented one at a time. Half the words were printed in black ink and the other half in red ink. The subjects were told to create a vivid mental image of the red words and to simply say the black words over and over to themselves until the next word was shown. After all the words were presented, the subjects had to write down as many of the words as they could, in any order they wished.

**2.** *[Special Exercise.]* Find the problem in this between-subjects experiment. An experimenter wanted to determine how a monetary payment affected attitude change.

The first twenty-two subjects to appear at the laboratory were offered fifteen dollars if they agreed to publicly endorse an unpopular political candidate. The next twenty-two subjects to appear at the laboratory were offered one dollar if they agreed to endorse the same candidate. The percentage of people who agreed to the request in each group was the dependent variable.

## Suggested Readings

A complete discussion of the advantages and disadvantages of between- and within-subjects designs can be found in Kerlinger, F. N. (1986). *Foundations of behavioral research.* New York: Holt.

For a discussion of subtle biases that can occur with the use of within-subjects designs, see the following article: Poulton, E. C. (1982). Influential companions: Effects of one strategy on another in the within-subjects designs of cognitive psychology. *Psychological Bulletin, 91,* 673–690.

An interesting historical perspective of the use of control conditions in the design of experiments can be found in Boring, E. (1954). The nature and history of experimental control. *American Journal of Psychology, 67,* 573–589.

## APPLICATION
### Counterbalancing in the Wild

Saari and Latham (1982) wanted to determine the effect of payment schedule on the performance and attitudes of beaver trappers in southwestern Washington. The trappers worked for a forest-products company and were paid an hourly wage during the course of the following experiment.

After a baseline measure of trapping performance under the hourly payment scheme, two incentive conditions were introduced in a within-subjects design. When trappers were under a continuous reinforcement schedule, they received an additional dollar for each beaver that was trapped. When the trappers were under a variable ratio schedule of four, they received four dollars when they brought in a beaver, if they correctly predicted twice whether the roll of a die would yield an odd or an even number (by chance alone, the trapper could pick the correct solution one out of four times). Thus, in one condition there was always a one-dollar payment, whereas in the other the payment was on the average given once every four times. Counterbalancing of the order of treatments was accomplished in the following way: The trappers were randomly split into two groups, and then the groups alternated weekly stints under either the continuous or the variable payment schedule. The alternating schedule continued for the entire trapping season.

Saari and Latham found that the number of beavers trapped increased under both payment schedules, but the increase was much larger under the variable ratio schedule than under the continuous one. Furthermore, they found that the trappers preferred the ratio schedule to the continuous schedule.

These results are very similar to those found when rats or pigeons are put under variable ratio schedules of reinforcement. Generally, behavior is more persistent under variable schedules of reinforcement than under continuous ones.

Saari, L. M., & Latham, G. P. (1982). Employee reactions to continuous and variable ratio reinforcement schedules involving a monetary incentive. *Journal of Applied Psychology, 67,* 506–508.

# PSYCHOLOGY IN ACTION
## The Stroop Effect

An interesting within-subjects experiment is a follow-up to the one in which you participated in the introduction to this book. That experiment used a within-subjects design, and the three conditions were reading digits, naming the number of pluses, and naming the number of digits, where the name of the digits was incongruent with the number of digits (for example, you read "3 3," and you were to say "2"). Your follow-up could include a fourth condition in which the name of a digit and its quantity were congruent (for example, 4 4 4 4). You could use the three series from the original experiment and devise your own congruent fourth series. There are thirty-two items in a series, and the numbers (or quantities) 1 through 4 are counterbalanced in the sequence via a Latin square. You will need a stopwatch or clock to determine the time it takes to read through each series.

To design this experiment appropriately, set up a counterbalancing scheme to determine the order with which a subject receives each condition. A balanced Latin square is the best way to do this, so that across subjects each condition occurs first, second, third, and fourth equally often, and each treatment precedes and follows every other treatment equally often (see figure 6–1).

Additional information on reading and naming can be found in chapter 12 under the heading "Stroop Effect." This effect is named after a scientist named Stroop who first used conflicting reading and naming stimuli to study these processes (Stroop, 1935). In its use of conflicting and congruent quantities of digits, your follow-up experiment is similar to one done by Windes (1968), who used a between-subjects design. Your experiment is also similar to one done by Hintzman and associates (1972), who, using a within-subjects design, printed names of colors in congruent or incongruent ink colors, and then asked the subjects to name the ink color.

You might want to combine your results with those of your classmates. Each member of the class could test four subjects. Each set of four subjects would complete a single balanced Latin square used to determine the order of conditions. Your interest should focus on the differences among the three naming conditions: neutral (+ +), incongruent (3 3), and congruent (2 2). If your results follow those of Hintzman and coworkers, you should find that the congruent is faster than the neutral, which serves as the control condition, and the incongruent is slower than the neutral.

Hintzman, D. L., Carre, F. A., Eskridge, V. L., Owens, A. M., Shaff, S. S., & Sparks, M. E. (1972). "Stroop" effect: Input or output phenomenon? *Journal of Experimental Psychology, 95,* 458–459.
Windes, J. D. (1968). Reaction time for numerical coding and naming of numerals. *Journal of Experimental Psychology, 78,* 318–322.

# COMPLEX EXPERIMENTATION
Interactions between independent variables

## Between-Subjects Experiments

| Description | Features | Problems |
|---|---|---|
| 2 × 2 factorial design: 2 independent variables, each with 2 levels yielding 4 independent groups | 2 main effects and an interaction of the 2 variables | Confounding of subjects with groups |

## Within-Subjects Experiments

| Description | Features | Problems |
|---|---|---|
| 2 × 2 within factorial design (treatments × treatments × subjects). Each subject receives each level of each independent variable (4 treatments in a 2 × 2) | More efficient than between designs; each subject is its own control; main effects and interactions can be determined | Confounding via carry-over effects must be minimized—counterbalance or randomize; use several observations in each condition to increase reliability |

## Mixed Designs

| Description | Features | Problems |
|---|---|---|
| A combination of independent variables manipulated both between and within subjects. Each subject receives each level of the within-subjects variable, and separate groups are determined by the levels (and types) of between-subjects variables | Has virtues of the above; very good for looking at interaction of practice (trials) with another independent variable | All controls above must be considered, but carryover is usually a variable, so its effects are measured |

# 7 |||| Complex Experimentation

The purpose of this chapter is to discuss the design and interpretation of experiments that have more than one independent variable. Such multifactor experiments emphasize the interaction between independent variables. Multifactor experiments can be viewed as extensions of one-variable experiments. Some designs vary the independent variables between subjects and others vary them within subjects. It is also possible to have a mixture of a between-subjects and within-subjects manipulation of the independent variables. We will consider all three of these possibilities here.

## |||| FACTORIAL DESIGNS

Why perform complex experiments? Later we will see that increased control in quasi-experiments comes about by including both subject variables and true (externally manipulated) independent variables in the study. However, increased control is not the primary reason for conducting laboratory experiments with more than one independent variable. Rather, the major reason has to do with the complexity of thought and behavior. Limiting experimental analysis to a one-at-a-time variable manipulation cannot mirror the numerous, intertwined forces that influence people outside the laboratory. Therefore, multifactor experiments are likely to have better ecological validity than single-factor experiments. The topic of ecological validity—whether an experiment has external as opposed to internal validity—will be discussed later. We can increase the generality of our results by doing experiments that attempt to match the complexity of forces that combine to influence our thought and behavior. In addition, complex causal statements can be made, which should increase internal validity.

Does this mean that what we have said before about analysis is invalid? No. In any research problem, the basic factors need to be determined before we can make more complex observations. In much the same way that naturalistic observation and correlational studies often precede basic experimentation, simple experiments often provide the groundwork for more complex ones. Scientific maturity occurs gradually. The data base grows slowly, and the theories gradually develop. We begin with description and prediction, and we end with explanation. Explanation itself goes through a developmental process—from simple experiments to complex ones.

## A 2 × 2 Experiment in Social Psychology: The Sleeper Effect

An extremely common finding in memory research is that information fades over time. When new information is presented you can easily remember it immediately. But as time passes, your ability to recall this information decreases. However, there is an interesting finding in social psychology in which the passage of time improves the effect of a persuasive message. This interesting quirk is called the **sleeper effect.** Imagine that you have just watched a TV commercial for a new food product: Bulimia diet pizza. You can indicate how persuasive this message was by rating how likely you are to run to your local grocery store and purchase this new food. Let's pretend that, on a scale of one to ten, your rating was five. If you are asked to rate this food again at a later time, and you give a rating that is higher than five, you have just demonstrated the sleeper effect: The impact of the persuasive message has increased over time.

To obtain the sleeper effect, the persuasive message must be accompanied by a **discounting cue.** This is a message that causes you to distrust the accuracy or credibility of a persuasive message. For example, imagine that you have just read a one-page rave review of a new sports car manufactured by General Motors. If you were then told that the review came from the pages of *Car and Driver* magazine, your reaction would be different than if you were told that the review was written by the General Motors press department. *Car and Driver* would be a confirming cue that improves your belief in the message, whereas the General Motors press department would be regarded as a biased source of information. The sleeper effect is most likely to be obtained when the cue—a discounting cue—casts a doubt on the source of the message.

Although many explanations of the sleeper effect have been offered, those that focus upon the role of memory have been the most popular (Pratkanis, Greenwald, Leippe, & Baumgardner, 1988). One such explanation is called the dissociation hypothesis. At the time of presentation, the persuasive message and the discounting cue are strongly attached. Thus, they tend to cancel one another out, and little opinion change occurs. After time has passed, the link between the message and the cue gets weaker. In particular, while the message is remembered, the discounting cue is forgotten. The discounting cue is not retrieved because the link between message and cue has weakened over time. This causes a net positive change in opinion, resulting in the sleeper effect.

To explain the logic behind a 2 × 2 experimental design, we shall consider a portion of recent results on the sleeper effect reported by Pratkanis and co-workers (1988). In a 2 × 2 factorial design, there are two independent variables, each with two levels, or values. The word *factorial* indicates that all possible combinations of all levels of each independent variable are examined. Thus as shown in figure 7–1(a) a 2 × 2 factorial design contains four combinations of conditions: {1A,2A}, {1B,2A}, {1A,2B}, {1B,2B}. In the Pratkanis experiment, two independent variables were (1) whether the discounting cue was presented before or after the persuasive message, and (2) the length of the delay (either 0 or 6 weeks) between the message and the opinion rating. Thus, there were four combinations of interest: {before-none}, {after-none}, {before-6 weeks}, {after-6 weeks}. The design of the experiment is shown in figure 7–1(b).

**FIGURE 7–1**

(a) The four treatment combinations in a 2 × 2 factorial design, in which separate groups of subjects receive each combination. (b) The 2 × 2 factorial design of the experiment by Pratkanis and co-workers (1988).

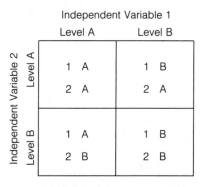

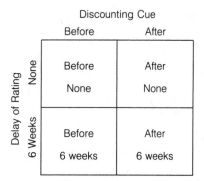

(a) The four treatment combinations in a 2 × 2 factorial design, in which separate groups of subjects receive each combination.

(b) The 2 × 2 factorial design of the experiment by Pratkanis and co-workers (1988).

Figure 7–2 shows the effects of cue presentation on the opinion rating. The line is almost flat, indicating little effect. On the basis of figure 7–2, we would conclude that cue presentation does not alter the sleeper effect. The effect of a single independent variable in a factorial experiment is called a **main effect.** Figure 7–2 shows that the main effect of cue presentation is almost zero because there is almost no difference between the ratings for level A (before) and for level B (after) for cue presentation.

**FIGURE 7–2**

Effects of cue presentation on the sleeper effect. Adapted from Pratkanis and co-workers (1988). (Copyright 1988 by the American Psychological Association. Reprinted by permission of the author.)

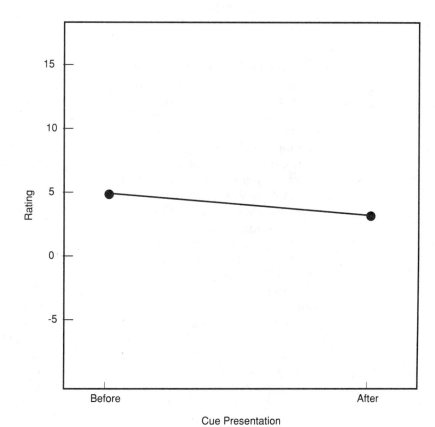

**FIGURE 7–3**
*Effects of delay on the
sleeper effect. Adapted
from Pratkanis and co-
workers (1988).
(Copyright 1988 by the
American Psychological
Association. Reprinted by
permission of the
author.)*

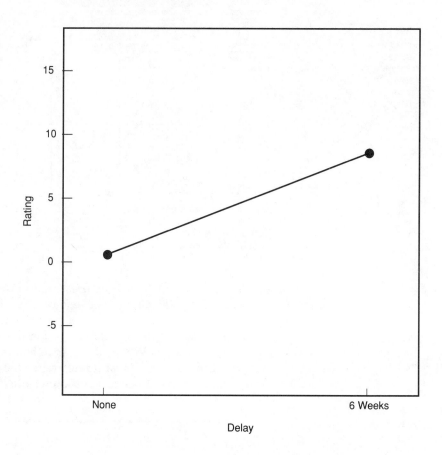

Now look at figure 7–3, which shows the effects of delay on the opinion rating. Here there is a main effect. The rating is higher, indicating greater persuasion, at the six-week delay. This result is, of course, the sleeper effect. However, based only on figures 7–2 and 7–3, which show only main effects, we would conclude that the sleeper effect and effects of cue presentation are unrelated. Although the experiment reveals a sleeper effect, it appears that the effect has nothing to do with whether the discounting cue comes before or after the persuasive message.

However, this conclusion is wrong. Figure 7–4 shows results for all four combinations in the 2 × 2 factorial design. The interpretation of results here is quite different. When the cue comes before the message, there is no sleeper effect. When the cue comes after the message, there is a large sleeper effect. So, contrary to the wrong conclusion drawn from figures 7–2 and 7–3, the timing of the discounting cue is absolutely crucial. An accurate interpretation of these results requires knowledge of all four combinations of independent variables. This outcome is called an **interaction.** An interaction occurs when the effects of one independent variable depend upon the level of another independent variable. In Figure 7–4 the effects of delay depend upon the presentation of the discounting cue. Thus, there is an interaction between delay and presentation.

According to Pratkanis and colleagues, the results of figure 7–4 cast doubt on the dissociation explanation of the sleeper effect because the dissocia-

**FIGURE 7–4**
The interaction of delay and cue presentation and their influence on the sleeper effect. Adapted from Pratkanis et al. (1988). (Copyright 1988 by the American Psychologist Association. Reprinted by permission of the author.)

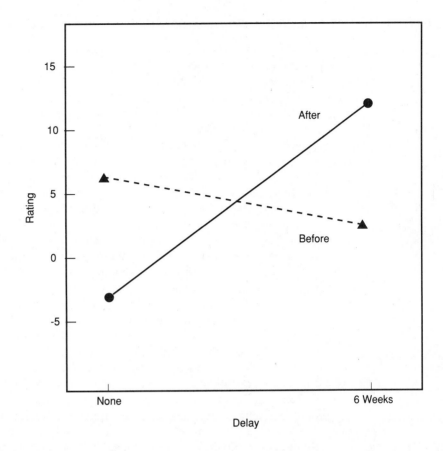

tion explanation predicts a sleeper effect regardless of when the cue is presented. A better explanation is called *differential decay*. It states that the impact of the cue decays more rapidly than that of the message (Pratkanis et al., 1988). Presenting the cue before the message eliminates the sleeper effect by weakening the persuasive impact of the message. However, as is the case with most critical experiments, a firm believer in the dissociation explanation might also adopt this latter explanation and argue that postulating a second factor—persuasive impact to explain the lack of a sleeper effect—applies equally to the dissociation hypothesis. While Pratkanis and co-workers offer other arguments for differential decay, especially those that relate the sleeper effect to other findings in memory research, it is clear that more research is required to pin down this interesting quirk. In the words of Pratkanis and colleagues: "Long live the sleeper effect."

---

**CONCEPT SUMMARY**

**Interactions**

In multifactor experiments, an interaction occurs when the effects of one independent variable depend on the level of other independent variables.

### Control in Between-Subject Factorial Designs

In a between-subjects design, each combination of independent variables is administered to a separate group of subjects. We want to make sure that the characteristics of the subjects are not confounded with group membership. In the ideal case, we would randomly select our subjects and then randomly assign them to our conditions. We are usually unable to have total random selection of our subjects because we do not have the procedures available to select, in an unbiased fashion, from *all* rats or *all* college students. It is therefore essential that we assign our subjects to conditions in a way that minimizes the possibility of confounding subject traits with our manipulations. When there are many groups in a factorial design, unbiased assignment is crucial. (Recall that chapter 6 outlines ways to randomly assign subjects.)

Another way to make unbiased assignments of subjects to groups is to use a balanced Latin square to determine group membership. Chapter 6 details the procedures for constructing balanced Latin squares. The way to use this counterbalancing technique for subject assignment in a 2 × 2 design is as follows: Label the four groups (for example A, B, C, and D) and then make a balanced square for those symbols. Use the order of conditions in the rows of the resulting Latin square to determine assignment. The first subject to appear in the laboratory is assigned to condition A, the second to B, the third to D, and the fourth to C. Then use the next row to assign the next four subjects, and so on until all subjects are tested. You may have to construct many squares or use the same square repeatedly if you have more subjects than cells in your square. Note that the purpose of this procedure is the same as random assignment to conditions: to make sure there is little relation between the subject's characteristics and assignment to a particular group. One advantage of the Latin-square technique is that in a large experiment that takes a long time to conduct, the order in which the treatments are conducted is known well in advance and also balanced across time. Thus, any historical factors that might be confounded here are balanced across groups.

In general, randomization, counterbalancing, and other control techniques help prevent potential confounding variables from interacting with the independent variables. In your design, you should try to reduce the possibility of such unwanted interactions. There are no hard-and-fast rules for choosing a control technique. The ones used are often chosen pragmatically. The particular control procedure you use is up to you: Make sure that you minimize confoundings and that you use controls that are easy to implement.

We limited the discussion of between-subjects designs to what is often called a **random-groups design,** which refers to unbiased assignment of subjects to conditions. An alternative method of assignment is matching (see chapter 6). In a **matched-groups design,** the experimenter tries to reduce the variability of observations between groups resulting from subject differences by matching the subjects on other variables. Thus, in the sleeper-effect experiment we just described, subjects could be matched on the basis of IQ before randomly assigning them to conditions. (Each subgroup of matched subjects is randomly assigned to the groups.) In our earlier discussions, we pointed out the difficulty of matching on relevant variables. Some subject variables, such as sex and age, can be matched across groups, or they can serve as quasi-independent variables. If matching is going to be difficult, you might want to use a complex within-subjects design, which we will discuss next.

---

| **CONCEPT SUMMARY** | **Factorial Designs** |
|---|---|

All possible combinations of each level of each independent variable are examined. For example, a $3 \times 3$ case having independent variable A with levels A1, A2, and A3 and independent variable B with levels B1, B2, and B3 yields nine groups:

| | | |
|---|---|---|
| A1B1 | A1B2 | A1B3 |
| A2B1 | A2B2 | A2B3 |
| A3B1 | A3B2 | A3B3 |

---

## | | | | COMPLEX WITHIN-SUBJECTS DESIGNS

The within-subjects design is often used instead of a between-subjects design, because within-subjects manipulation is more economical (requires fewer subjects) and automatically controls for individual differences. Of course, if permanent carryover effects are likely, a within-subjects design may be inappropriate.

Using a within-subjects design can result in a substantial reduction in the number of subjects needed for testing. However, the reduced number of subjects may require that you increase the number of observations per subject in each condition to ensure that your data are reliable. We should obtain numerous samples of a subject's behavior (just as is done in small-$n$ experiments: see chapter 8). By doing so, we reduce the likelihood that some extraneous factor has influenced the results. For instance, in many learning, memory, perception, and reaction-time experiments, events occur rapidly, placing great demands on the subject. If the subject coughs or blinks at an inappropriate time, we may incorrectly underestimate performance on that trial.

Thus, whereas in a between-subjects design we test a large number of subjects, in a within-subjects design we obtain several observations on a small number of subjects. Even with numerous observations per subject, the within-subjects design is usually more efficient than the between-subjects one.

### A Complex Within-Subjects Experiment

Do you like to solve puzzles? Many people do. One kind of popular puzzle is the anagram, which consists of a word in which the letters have been rearranged. The solver tries to recreate the word from the anagram. Psychologists have examined many of the factors involved in anagram solution, because these puzzles seem to represent a relatively simple sort of problem-solving task. (Many psychologists probably study anagram solution because they like to solve them themselves.) One important variable in anagram solution is the frequency of the solution word. The higher the frequency of the word in written English, the easier people can solve an anagram of the word (Mayzner and Tresselt, 1966). One hypothesis suggests that the effects of solution-word frequency occur because people generate words as they are attempting to solve anagrams, and they are more likely to generate high-frequency words than low-frequency ones.

Dewing and Hetherington (1974) noted that the imagery of a word is associated with ease of learning and remembering. They predicted that if high noun imagery (a word such as *chair*) leads to greater availability than does low noun imagery (a word such as *truth*), then anagrams whose solution words have high imagery should be easier to solve than those whose solution words have low imagery. It should be easier to solve AHICR than URTTH. The researchers also wanted to determine the effects of hints on the ease with which subjects solved the anagrams. They presented a structural hint (the first and last letter of the solution word), a semantic hint (the title of the category to which the solution word belonged), or no hint. They hypothesized that if availability is important, the structural hint would help more when there were low-imagery solution words than when there were high ones because the structural hint would delimit the number of possible solutions. However, if the subjects did not generate low-frequency words as solutions to the anagram, then semantic clues would not help them solve low-imagery anagrams. Therefore, Dewing and Hetherington examined the effects of two independent variables on anagram solution: the imagery value of the solution word (high versus low) and the type of hint (none, structural, or semantic).

If this were a between-subjects experiment, we would call this a 2 × 3 factorial design. However, Dewing and Hetherington used a within-subjects design in which all levels of each independent variable were experienced by all subjects, and thus we have what is usually called a **treatments × treatments × subjects design.** This designation derives from the type of statistical analysis associated with the design (see appendix B). Since in this experiment all combinations of variables were tested (as in a between-subjects design), within-subjects factorial is a good shorthand label. In this experiment, there were six conditions (2 × 3), representing all combinations of the levels of each independent variable: Anagrams with low-imagery solution words were solved with three different hints, and anagrams with high-imagery solution words were solved with the same three types of hint. Dewing and Hetherington chose to use a within-subjects design rather than a between-subjects one because individuals differ markedly in their ability to solve anagrams. By using a within-subjects design, the researchers were assured that each subject served as his or her own comparison across conditions, which eliminated individual differences as a confounding factor in the experiment.

Before considering the results of this experiment, let us examine some additional details of the procedure. Every subject had to solve two anagrams under each of the six (2 × 3) conditions. The high- and low-imagery words were chosen carefully: They were all five-letter nouns, they were all of about the same frequency of occurrence in written English, and different anagrams were developed for each word and administered to different subgroups of subjects. The time taken to solve each anagram was the dependent variable.

The results of the experiment by Dewing and Hetherington are shown in figure 7–5. As is true of a multifactor between-subjects design, you need to examine the results for both main effects and interactions. When there are two independent variables, you need to look for two main effects and one interaction. Note in figure 7–5 that much faster solution times occurred for the high-imagery solution words than for the low-imagery ones. Note also the striking effects of the hints: Performance was much slower when no hint was given. Since the lines of the functions are not parallel, you should expect an interaction. The effects of the hints depended on the imagery value of the solution word. For the high-imagery words, the semantic clue aided solution more than the structural hint did, but for the low-imagery words, the opposite was the case. Statistical analyses by Dew-

**FIGURE 7–5**

Anagram solution times in seconds as a function of the imagery of the solution word for the three hint conditions. (Copyright 1974 by the American Psychological Association.)

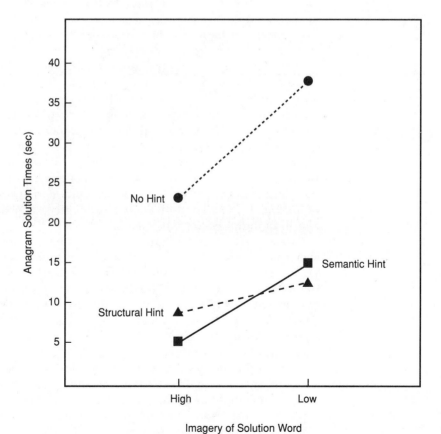

ing and Hetherington confirmed that both main effects were reliable, and there was a statistically significant interaction.

## Control in Complex Within-Subjects Designs

When a complex within-subjects design is used, you need to be concerned about carryover effects just as you do when only one independent variable is varied within subjects. Furthermore, you need to guard against many kinds of confounding that can occur in any multifactor experiment.

How did Dewing and Hetherington avoid the possibility of carryover effects from one treatment to another? They needed to be sure that having solved one type of anagram with a specific hint (say, a high-imagery solution word with a structural hint) did not influence the ability to solve another type of anagram with a different clue. Another potential carryover they had to consider was practice, because each subject had two tries on each type of anagram, and the subjects might have gotten better at solving anagrams during the course of the experiment. Dewing and Hetherington minimized carryover effects by having a different random order of the twelve anagrams for each subject. Presumably, the cards on which the anagrams and hints were written were shuffled before testing began. Thus, each condition had an unbiased chance of being tested in any of the twelve test orders, and each condition had an unbiased chance of being preceded and followed by every other condition. Since there are seventy-two subjects, Dewing and Hetherington had seventy-two random orders of presenting the twelve conditions, and it is unlikely that any inadvertent carryover occurred to confound the results.

The use of a random order should guard against both types of carryover (effects from condition-to-condition, and practice effects). However, Dewing and Hetherington did not have to worry much about differential practice effects, because earlier research had shown that practice effects are minimal unless the subjects receive several weeks of practice. Nevertheless, it would have been dangerous for them to have confounded conditions with order of testing. A small amount of confounding could occur, and there is no reason to tempt fate.

Two alternative procedures for controlling carryover in the anagram experiment are block randomization and counterbalancing (see chapter 6). The major difference between block randomization and complete randomization is that the order of treatments is randomized twice in the block-randomization technique. Each of the six conditions appear once in a random order in the first six trials, and then each treatment is tested again in a random order in the second block of six trials. One advantage of block randomization over complete randomization is that the blocking procedure guarantees that every condition will be tested before a particular condition is tested again. Across test trials, therefore, block randomization is less likely than complete randomization to confound test order and condition. Typically, block randomization is determined for each subject, just as a different random order was determined for each subject by Dewing and Hetherington.

Counterbalancing could minimize carryover effects as well. One way to counterbalance would be to generate 6 × 6 balanced Latin squares for the six treatments and assign two rows to each subject to determine the order of presenting the conditions. An advantage of this procedure over randomization (either blocked or complete) is that balanced Latin squares ensure that each treatment precedes and follows every other treatment equally often. A disadvantage might be that the researchers would have to test subjects in multiples of six to be sure that all sequences in the Latin squares were administered.

Some additional aspects of the design used by Dewing and Hetherington are noteworthy. Since the high-imagery and low-imagery solution words came from different semantic categories, Dewing and Hetherington wanted to be sure that the semantic hints they used were not better for one class of solution word than the other. Prior to conducting the anagram experiment, they conducted pilot work (see chapter 3) in which they had ten other subjects rate the degree of association (on a five-point scale) between each solution word and its semantic clue. The raters, who did not know the purpose of the anagram experiment, determined that the degree of association between semantic hints and solution words was about the same for the high- and low-imagery words. Alternatively, Dewing and Hetherington could have attempted to find high- and low-imagery words that belonged to the same semantic categories so that the same semantic clue could be given to each. This would have been difficult, because it is hard to conceive of a low-imagery piece of furniture to pair with the high-imagery word *chair*. Other matches for high- and low-imagery words are also unlikely.

Another variable that could have been controlled but was not, is the spelling of the solution words. The high- and low-imagery solution words had different first and last letters, and this may be an important confounding. However, finding words with the same first and last letters that differed only in imagery would be very difficult. One thing Dewing and Hetherington did to account for different spellings was to consider the frequency with which successive letter pairs in the solution word occurred in the English language. This is known as bigram frequency. Earlier research had noted that the bigram frequency of the solution word interacted with the bigram frequency of the anagram. Solution times were fastest for anagrams whose bigram frequency matched the bigram frequency of the solution word. This was true for both high and low bigram frequencies. In Dewing and Hetherington's experiment, solution-word bigram frequency was similar for the high- and low-imagery words, and, as noted previously, the experimenters used three different anagrams for each solution word.

Finally, we should note that Dewing and Hetherington completely counterbalanced clue conditions across the three anagrams generated for a particular word. In other words, the three sets of anagrams were combined factorially with the three hint conditions. In the nine lists of anagrams generated by this 3 × 3 combination, each of the treatment conditions was assigned to each anagram. This procedure probably was effective in eliminating a confounding of materials with conditions, which means that a particular anagram could not account for the differential effect of the hints.

CONCEPT
SUMMARY

**Complex Within-Subjects Designs**

Every subject receives all combinations of each level of the independent variables.

For example, Dewing and Hetherington's (1974) experiment had the following conditions: an independent variable for solution-word imagery (high imagery or low imagery) and an independent variable for type of hint (semantic, structural, or none). A factorial combination of the 2 × 3 conditions yields high, semantic; high, structural; high, none; low semantic; low, structural; and low, none.

## |||| MIXED DESIGNS

Since there are advantages and disadvantages to both pure within- and pure between-subjects designs, it is not surprising that many researchers use **mixed designs.** Mixed designs have one or more between-subjects independent variables and one or more within-subjects conditions. Mixed designs are very common in learning and physiological research, in which the interest is in the effects of some variable over time or practice. Usually the variable of primary interest has strong carryover effects (such as brain damage), so it is manipulated between subjects. Practice or time is necessarily a within-subjects variable in this case, because the same organism is repeatedly measured. You will sometimes see within-subjects designs, especially those involving large numbers of practice trials, called **repeated-measures design.** The experimenter using this kind of mixed design is often interested in an interaction between the two variables. Does behavior under the different levels of the between-subjects factor differ across trials (or whatever the within-subjects factor may be)?

To illustrate a mixed design, we will consider an experiment dealing with a classic problem in the psychology of learning: the partial-reinforcement effect. We will examine only one aspect of this phenomenon; namely, behavior is usually more persistent following intermittent presentation of reinforcement than after continuous presentation. This means that when a reinforcement is withheld, responding persists longer if partial reinforcement has been used than if continuous reinforcement has been presented. One way to study this phenomenon is to reinforce some animals in a maze on every trial, and to reinforce others less than 100 percent of the time. After the animals have learned, we withdraw all reinforcement and see how long the behavior of running the maze lasts, or, in the jargon of learning, how long it takes the behavior to extinguish.

The simplest sort of maze is the straight alley, which is composed of a start box in which the animal is placed, an alley through which the animal runs when the start-box door is opened, and the goal box where the animal is reinforced. The reinforcement is generally food, and usually the animal has been deprived of food prior to the experiment. The dependent variable is the running speed, or the time it takes the animal to run the straight-alley maze. Often the animal's speed in each section of the runway is measured, and we determine a speed for leaving the start box, for traversing the alley, and for approaching the goal. Learning is indicated by the fact that after a number of trials, the rat's speed increases (the latency decreases). At first the rat dawdles along, but on later trials it goes through the maze quickly.

Suppose we now wanted to ask a straightforward question about learning in this situation: How is learning affected by the amount of reinforcement? Intuitively you might expect learning to increase as the amount of rein-forcement increases. You should realize that this depends on how the "amount of reinforcement" and "learning" are defined. We could vary the amount of reinforcement by varying the percentage of trials on which sub-jects receive reward, or by varying the magnitude of reward after each trial. We could also measure learning in at least two ways—one might be running speed, the other resistance to extinction. The latter measure is found by seeing how long after training an animal will continue running a maze when it no longer receives reinforcement. Let us confine our interest to varying the percentage of rewarded trials. The experiment that is needed to answer our question has now become more manageable. We vary the percentage of trials on which the animals receive a reward for running the maze (the independent variable), and we measure the time it takes the animals to run the maze and their resistance to extinction (or running speeds during extinction training).

If subjects are rewarded only on some percentage of trials and we want to see how this affects extinction of maze running, should we use a within-subjects or a between-subjects design? If we use a within-subjects design, we would need fewer subjects and the variability within conditions would be less. However, in using a within-subjects design we would have to be concerned with the effects of one training schedule on the others used. Once an animal has learned a task under one reinforcement schedule, the animal will not approach the task as though it were new when the task is relearned under a new schedule of reinforcement, even if there has been extinction of the response after it was first learned. (Extinction does not eliminate the memory of the training; it simply stops the animals from responding.) Because of the danger of such carryover effects from one condition to another in this situation, it would probably be better to use a between-subjects design. Weinstock (1958) conducted an experiment in which the percentage of trials on which subjects received reinforcement was varied between subjects. Since Weinstock was interested in the effects of reward percentage on changes in behavior across trials, part of his ex-periment included repeated measures within subjects. Thus, the complete design is a mixed one: Trials is the within-subjects variable, and percentage of reward the between-subjects variable.

Weinstock tested female rats under six conditions of reinforcement in a simple maze. The rats were tested after twenty-two hours of water depri-vation, and access to water in the goal box was the reinforcer. Each rat was given only one trial a day. If more than one trial a day had been given, then rats that had received water on the early trials would have been less mo-tivated to run on later trials than rats that had not received water on the early trials. Having rats run only one trial per day at a constant twenty-two hours of water deprivation eliminated this problem, but it made the experiment quite lengthy and onerous for the experimenter. It took Weinstock about half a year, testing rats eight hours a day, to complete this experiment.

For the first twelve trials, all rats received continuous reinforcement (CRF), and were rewarded with water after each trial. On trials 13 to 108, the subjects were tested on one of six reinforcement schedules in a between-subjects design. It is easiest to think of these ninety-six trials as being composed of eight blocks of twelve trials, with the partial-reinforcement schedule as the number of reinforced and nonreinforced trials in each block of twelve. One group of subjects received continuous reinforcement (twelve reinforced and zero nonreinforced, or 12–0), and five other groups received partial reinforcement. One group received ten reinforced and two nonreinforced trials in each block of twelve; other groups can be labeled 8–4, 6–6, 4–8, and 2–10, according to the number of reinforced and non-reinforced trials in a block of twelve. It was randomly determined within a block of twelve trials which trials would be reinforced and which not for each condition. After ninety-six trials under one of these six schedules of reinforcement, all rats were given sixty more trials during which they received no reinforcement. Thus these are extinction trials. Weinstock's experiment is outlined in table 7–1.

The extinction running speeds from Weinstock's experiment are shown in figure 7–6. Running speeds during extinction declined with increases in the percentage of trials for which the subjects received reward during acquisition. The continuously reinforced subjects ran the slowest during extinction, and the groups that received the fewest rewarded trials ran the fastest. Thus, learning produced by partial-reinforcement schedules does not extinguish as rapidly as learning produced by continuous-reinforcement schedules. This result is called the partial-reinforcement extinction effect.

The results in figure 7–6 show an interaction. The effects of one variable depend on the level of the other. Performance decreases in extinction (across nonreinforced trials), but it extinguishes more rapidly in some conditions (group 12–0) than in others (group 2–10). In general, when one of the variables in a mixed design involves repeated measures, one of the things to look for is an interaction indicating a differential effect of the between-subjects variable over trials.

**TABLE 7–1**

An outline of Weinstock's (1958) experiment on the effects of partial reinforcement on maze running speed.

| | | Days | | | |
|---|---|---|---|---|---|
| 1–7 | 8–19 Trials 1–12 | 20–115 Trials 13–108 | RF–NRF[a] | | 116–176 Trials 109–169 |
| All rats were handled 6–8 minutes per day. | All rats received continuous reinforcement for 12 trials. | Rats received reinforcement according to six schedules of reinforcement for 96 trials in blocks of 12 trials. | 12–0 10–2 8–4 6–6 4–8 2–10 | | All rats received nonreinforced (or extinction) trials. |

[a]The number of trials in each block of 12 trials for which subjects received reinforcement (RF) or nonreinforcement (NRF).

**FIGURE 7–6**

Mean reciprocal latency (speed) of maze running as a function of trials (in blocks of five, with one trial occurring each day) during extinction in Weinstock's experiment. The less reinforcement the rats received during acquisition (the fewer trials on which they were reinforced), the greater their speed during extinction, or the more slowly the behavior extinguished. This is the partial-reinforcement extinction effect. (Copyright 1958 by the American Psychological Association.)

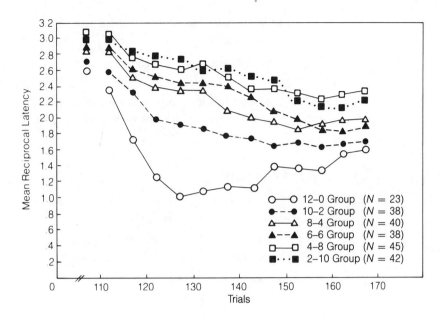

In most mixed designs, the control procedures we have already discussed will be applicable. Obviously, when trials or practice is an independent variable, you will have carryover effects. In that instance, you need to observe or measure these effects rather than eliminate them, as would be the case when trials or practice simply covaries with the independent variable under investigation.

|||| **SUMMARY**

**1.** Multifactor experiments have more than one independent variable, and these variables may have more than two levels.

**2.** When more than two independent variables are varied, we have a factorial design in which all possible combinations of the levels of the independent variables are examined. In a 2 × 2 factorial design, there are four combinations of levels of independent variables.

**3.** The primary reason for using multifactor designs is to look for interactions. An interaction is when the effects of one independent variable depend on the level of other independent variables.

**4.** When there are two independent variables, there are two main effects (one associated with each variable), and there can be an interaction.

**5.** Treatments × treatments × subjects is the designation usually given to factorial designs in which the variables are manipulated within subjects.

**6.** The control procedures used in multifactor experiments can be complicated, but they are similar in principle to the procedures (randomization, counterbalancing, and so on) used in experiments that have just one independent variable.

**7.** The within-subjects design is sometimes called a repeated-measures design when trials or practice is the variable of interest.

**8.** In a mixed design, one or more variables are varied between subjects and one or more variables are varied within subjects.

## Key Concepts

interaction

main effects

matched-groups design

mixed designs

random-groups design

repeated-measures designs

sleeper effect

treatments × treatments × subjects design

2 × 2 factorial design

## Exercises

**1.** Discuss the advantages of using complex within-subjects designs as opposed to complex between-subjects designs.

**2.** [*Special Exercise.*] A researcher varied the size (large or small) of the food reinforcement that was given to rats in a straight-alley maze. The time it took the rats to run down the alley was the dependent variable, and the mean time in seconds for each block of ten trials was as follows:

|  | Block 1 | Block 2 | Block 3 | Block 4 |
|---|---|---|---|---|
| Large reward | 38 | 30 | 20 | 15 |
| Small reward | 52 | 32 | 16 | 12 |

The experimenter concluded that since the overall time was slower in the small-reward group, large rewards lead to more rapid learning. What other conclusions can be drawn from the data in the table? Draw a figure showing these results.

**3.** [*Special Exercise.*] An experimenter is interested in studying the effects of practice on retention. If a within-subjects design is used and the independent variables are types of rehearsal (rote and elaborative) and number of presentations (1, 2, 3, and 4), indicate how the words to be remembered could be counterbalanced over the four different numbers of presentations. What are some additional confoundings that must be eliminated?

## Suggested Readings

Several complex experiments are reprinted in Elmes, D. G. (1978). *Readings in experimental psychology.* Chicago: Rand McNally. See especially articles 14 and 25.

# APPLICATION
## Improving the Learning of Foreign-Language Vocabulary

Many laboratory experiments indicate that imagery and the type of rehearsal can improve retention. Do these kinds of results also occur in more practical situations?

Atkinson (1975) indicates that certain kinds of rehearsal techniques can dramatically improve the learning and retention of foreign-language vocabulary. One procedure that has been successful is called the keyword method. We will outline how this method is appropriate for learning Russian vocabulary, although it has worked in the learning of other languages as well. The keyword method splits vocabulary learning into two parts. In the first part, the subject associates a spoken foreign word with the keyword. This is easily done because the keyword sounds very much like the foreign word. In the second part, the subject tries to form a mental image of the keyword and the English translation interacting in some way. So, first the foreign word is connected to the keyword and then the keyword is connected to the English translation.

In Russian, the word *dym* (as spelled in our alphabet) sounds similar to the English word *dim* and means smoke. If we use the English word *dim* as the keyword, *dim* and *dym* are first linked together. Then we might form a mental image of a dim picture that has been clouded by smoke. In Atkinson's experiments, subjects hear the foreign words and are given the keyword and the English translation. The subjects provide their own mental image linking the keyword to the translation.

Learning is much faster with the keyword technique than without it—control subjects take about one-third longer to learn the same number of translations as do similar subjects who use keywords. Tests of retention up to about six weeks later indicate that the subjects using keywords recall about 65 percent more than the controls. Use of memory techniques in many situations can lead to superior retention.

Atkinson, R. C. (1975). Mnemotechnics in second-language learning. *American Psychologist, 30,* 821–828.

# PSYCHOLOGY IN ACTION
## Distraction and Difficulty in Letter Detection

Detection of various kinds of targets (for example, planes on a radar screen) usually deteriorates when the observer is distracted or is under stress of some sort (Broadbent, 1971). The purpose of this experiment is to see whether distraction interacts with the difficulty of the detection task.

The subject's task will be to read through a newspaper article at a rapid rate, crossing out certain letters as he or she is reading. Half of the detection periods will occur in a quiet setting and the other half will take place where moderately loud music is playing. Thus you will need a newspaper and a radio (or some other source of music).

The difficulty of the task will be determined by the particular letters that the subjects are to cross out. Half the time the subjects should cancel out all the *u*'s they can find, and on the rest of the trials they should cancel out all the *f*'s. The letter *f* was chosen because people generally make a substantial number of errors when they try to detect *f* (Read, 1983). This occurs because the letter *f* is often pronounced as a *v* (as in the word *of*), and people usually do not cancel out those *f*'s. The letter *u* was chosen because it occurs with about the same frequency as the letter *f*, and only occasionally is it pronounced in an unusual fashion (as a *w* in words beginning with a *q*, which means you might want to select newspaper passages that do not contain the letter *q*).

You should probably use a within-subjects design in this experiment, so you will have to figure out some sort of counterbalancing scheme (see chapter 6) for the four conditions: detecting the letter *u* in a quiet setting, detecting the letter *f* in a quiet setting, detecting the letter *u* with music playing, and detecting the letter *f* with music playing.

Subjects should be tested in each condition once. Allow each subject to read for thirty seconds. After testing, you can calculate the error rate by dividing the number of correct detections (*f* or *u*) by the total number of *f*'s or *u*'s in the passage. (Be sure that you detect all the *f*'s when you are scoring the data.) You should combine your results with those of other students to increase the stability of your data.

Look for an interaction in your results. Usually, the most difficult detection task is the one most affected by the distraction.

Broadbent, D. E. (1971). *Decision and stress*. New York: Academic Press.
Read, J. D. (1983). Detection of Fs in a single statement: The role of phonetic recoding. *Memory & Cognition, 11*, 390–399.

| **SMALL-*N* EXPERIMENTS** Numerous observations on small numbers of subjects | **Psychophysical Problems** *Adaptation level:* usual within-subjects control procedures *Thresholds:* method of limits staircase method *Sensitivity and decision criteria:* signal-detection methods ROC curves **Operant Conditioning Designs** *Reversal design* (ABA): used when behavior can return to baseline *Multiple-baseline design:* used within subjects when behavior does not reverse; used between subjects when behaviors altered are not independent |
| --- | --- |

# 8 |||| Small-*N* Experiments

In this chapter, we will examine slightly different ways of applying Mill's **joint method of agreement and difference.** Small-*n* designs present levels of the independent variable numerous times to a small number of subjects. Such experiments are common in psychophysical research and in operant-conditioning research.

The control-group (between-subjects) and control-condition (within-subjects) designs discussed in the previous three chapters represent the major types of experimentation in psychology. In the past, however, studies of behavior usually involved experiments on single subjects or a small number of subjects. Fechner, the first psychophysicist (see chapter 2), studied himself and a relative in his pioneering work of the 1850s. Later in the 1880s, the first laboratory experiments on memory examined the retention of a single subject, Hermann Ebbinghaus, the man who devised and conducted the experiments. Even Pavlov, the pioneer in the study of classical conditioning, focused his attention on a small number of dogs.

Today, these **small-*n* designs** (*small* refers to the number of subjects) are used in many areas of psychological research, as well as in many areas of applied psychology. Rather than having a few observations on large groups of subjects, small-*n* experiments entail a substantial number of observations on a small number of subjects. During the course of an experiment, various levels of the independent variable(s) are introduced, and the resulting changes in behavior are measured. Since small numbers of subjects take part in small-*n* experiments, economy and control usually are imposed through the use of variants of the within-subjects procedures. Thus, each subject typically receives each level of the independent variables several times. As we shall see, versions of between-subjects designs also have been used.

Some small-*n* experiments require special control procedures, which we will consider here. Our treatment will focus on two substantive areas of psychology, psychophysics and operant conditioning, which best represent modern uses of small-*n* experiments. We will have to detail some of the specific content and theories associated with these two fields. Since psychophysics and operant conditioning both have broad general concerns, however, you should not be misled into thinking that the use of small-$n$ experiments is limited to these areas. Small-$n$ experiments are powerful tools for determining why people and animals think and act as they do.

## |||| PSYCHOPHYSICAL EXPERIMENTS

Psychophysics, you will remember from chapter 2, refers to the branch of psychology that attempts to relate psychological judgment to the characteristics of physical stimuli. In the typical psychophysical experiment, a small number of subjects may make a number of judgments about a large number of stimuli. Very often a subject will be required to rate or otherwise judge the same event several times. The reason that a small number of subjects usually participate in psychophysical studies has to do with economy. If we want to determine the subject's sensitivity to flashes of dim light, we might present test flashes of varying intensities as many as 7,000 times. Obviously doing this with twenty to thirty subjects would be extremely time consuming. The general tactic is to get reliable measures from a few subjects, and, if we are examining rather simple psychophysical judgments, we may not have to worry too much about individual differences. Where individual differences may play a more important role (say, in judging the degree of abstractness of common English nouns), then a larger number of subjects may need to be tested. Spreen and Schulz (1966), for example, had fifty-eight college students rate 329 nouns for concreteness, specificity, and pronounceability.

What sorts of control procedures should be instituted in a psychophysical study? Regardless of whether a small or large number of subjects are tested, carryover effects from one judgment to the next must be balanced across subjects. In the Spreen and Schulz study, carryover effects were handled by presenting the 329 words in a different random order to each subject.

One particular carryover problem that occurs in psychophysical scaling tasks involves changes in adaptation level (Helson, 1964). **Adaptation level** refers to the context or reference level for making a particular psychophysical judgment. The context within which a particular judgment is made can influence how an observer responds. Suppose you are given the task of rating these acts for seriousness: treason, running a red light, failing to signal a turn, and keeping excess change at the grocery. You might have some difficulty deciding which of the last three crimes is bad relative to each other and the awful crime of treason. Compare your rating of that series with the following: child abuse, rape/murder, treason, arson, and keeping excess change at the grocery. In this instance, keeping excess change is relatively "good," and you may have some difficulty rating the other crimes. A considerable amount of research has been concerned with adaptation level and its effects on psychophysical judgment (for example, Parducci, 1968). You should watch for adaptational effects and present your stimuli in such a way as to minimize these effects. In addition to random presentation of the stimuli (Spreen and Schulz, 1966), other forms of counterbalancing may help to minimize carryover effects from one judgment to the next.

In addition to adaptation level, another problem confronting the psychophysicist has to do with individual differences among subjects. Consider the problem of sensitivity to stimuli, which was a major concern of the early psychophysicists in the mid-nineteenth century. Suppose we determined that Betty seems more sensitive to tones of low intensity than Bill. This difference could be owing to something in Bill's hearing apparatus that makes him less sensitive to sound intensity than Betty, and this would be an important individual difference to know about (especially if a hearing aid were indicated). However, another individual difference could account for Bill's apparently low sensitivity, and this has to do with differences among people in their willingness to respond, "Yes, I detected it" in a psychophysical test of sensitivity. Bill might be more cautious than Betty and might have to be very sure he heard something before responding Yes. Thus, the difference between Betty and Bill could have been caused either by differences in sensitivity or by differences in willingness to say Yes. We have, therefore, the possibility of confounding; we do not know whether our dependent variable (responding to tones) was influenced by the independent variable (tonal intensity) or to some other factor such as response bias.

To determine differences in sensitivity, we need procedures that rule out or measure the confounding effects introduced by individual differences in willingness to respond. Since the determination of sensitivity is crucial to a basic understanding of sensory processes and their everyday use (such as taste sensitivity for substances in foods or beverages), we will spend some time considering the classical methods of measuring sensitivity, and then we will examine a more modern technique.

## Measuring Sensitivity: Thresholds

In everyday language, a **threshold** is the part of a doorway you step through or over to enter a room. Classical psychophysicists believed that stimuli had to cross such a hypothetical barrier to enter the brain or the mind. If a stimulus were strong, it could easily jump over the threshold. A feeble stimulus might not be able to make it across the threshold. The question, then, is: How strong must a stimulus be to cross the threshold?

At first, the answer may seem obvious. All we have to do is slowly increase the intensity of a stimulus, such as a tone or a dim light, until the observer responds, "Yes, I detect it." However, a problem arises when we try to repeat this process, because the point at which an observer suddenly detects the stimulus often changes from trial to trial. The early psychophysicists thought that this variability in detection resulted from momentary changes in sensitivity and response bias, so they developed several experimental procedures and statistical methods to estimate the best value for the threshold. We will discuss only one such method, invented by Fechner in the mid-1800s, known as the **method of limits.**

If we performed an experiment using the method of limits to determine the threshold for a tone, results would look like those shown in table 8–1. Each column represents data from one block of trials. The first block starts with a clearly audible tone to which the observer responds Yes. The tone is lowered in successive steps until the observer reports No, which ends that trial block. The next block starts with an intensity so low that the observer cannot hear the tone and thus responds No. On successive trials, the intensity is gradually increased until the observer reports hearing the tone. The process of alternating trial blocks continues until table 8–1 is complete. The experimenter starts each block at a different intensity to avoid extra cues that might mislead the observer, and usually administers a large number of trial blocks to get an accurate assessment of the threshold.

If the observer were a perfect stimulus detector, the point at which responses switch from Yes to No (or vice versa) would always be the same. This ideal point would be the threshold. Stimuli less intense than this value would never be detected, and stimuli that were greater or equal to this ideal threshold would always be detected. Real data from real people do not have this ideal characteristic and therefore resemble the data in table 8–1.

Observers are often influenced by their expectations as to when it is time to change their response from Yes to No, or vice versa. For example, if a series requires several Yes responses before the threshold is reached, some observers may decide that they are giving too many Yes responses and thus may prematurely respond No. Other observers may be very cautious about changing their responses (like Bill) and so may delay too long. Indeed, the same observer at different times may commit both of these errors. So that this variability is accounted for, the threshold is operationally defined: We determine the mean (average) of the points in each trial block where the

**TABLE 8–1**

Using the Method of Limits to Determine an Absolute Threshold

| Stimulus Intensity | Response | | | | |
|---|---|---|---|---|---|
|  | ↓ | | ↓ | | |
| 200 |  |  | Yes |  |  |
| 180 | Yes |  | Yes |  |  |
| 160 | Yes |  | Yes |  |  |
| 140 | Yes | Yes | Yes |  |  |
| 120 | Yes | No | No | Yes |  |
| 100 | Yes | No |  | No |  |
| 80 | No | No |  | No |  |
| 60 |  | No |  | No |  |
| 40 |  | No |  | ↑ |  |
| 20 |  | No |  |  |  |
|  |  | ↑ |  |  | Mean |
| Threshold | 90 | 130 | 130 | 110 | 115 |

Note: In the first series of trials, the experimenter starts with a strong stimulus and decreases its itensity until the observer can no longer detect it. The threshold is the mean of the stimulus intensities that yielded the first "no" response and the last "yes" response. In the next series of trials, a weak stimulus was increased in intensity until it was detected. It is customary to start each series at a different stimulus intensity so that it is less likely that the observer's responses will be influenced by the length of a series. Stimuli are in arbitrary units—that is, the intensities ranging from 20 to 200 could represent weight or anything else that might vary in intensity.

observer switches from Yes to No (or No to Yes), and the mean of these means is the threshold, which is, of course, a statistical definition. A threshold defined this way is called an **absolute threshold,** since the Yes-No judgments are not based on a comparison of two stimuli but instead are absolute judgments about the detection of a single stimulus.

Since the absolute threshold is a statistical concept, much like the Average Taxpayer, it has other statistical properties in addition to the mean. These will be illustrated by computing a **difference threshold** as shown in table 8–2. Difference thresholds are based on relative judgments, where a constant, unchanging comparison stimulus is judged relative to a series of changing stimuli. The question is: How different must two stimuli be before they can be reliably distinguished?

The traditional example of a difference threshold involves a subject lifting pairs of weights, one of which is always the same, and judging whether the new weight is heavier than, lighter than, or equal to the standard weight. Several series of ascending and descending trials are given. The upper threshold is the average point at which the subject changes from responding "Heavier" to responding "Equal." The lower threshold is the point at which "Equal" responses give way to "Lighter" responses. The difference between these two values is called the **interval of uncertainty.** The difference threshold is operationally defined as half the interval of uncertainty. Thus in table 8–2, the difference threshold is 25 grams. The mean of upper and lower thresholds is called the **point of subjective equality** (285 grams in table 8–2).

You may think that the method of limits is inefficient, since each trial block in table 8–1 contains many successive responses (Yes or No) that do not change. A newer version of the method of limits, called the **staircase**

**TABLE 8–2**
Using the Method of Limits to Determine a Difference Threshold.

| Comparison Stimulus (grams) | Response | | | |
|---|---|---|---|---|
| | ↓ | | ↓ | |
| 400 | | | | |
| 380 | | | Heavier | |
| 360 | Heavier | | Heavier | |
| 340 | Heavier | | Heavier | |
| 320 | Heavier | | Equal | Heavier |
| 300 | Equal | Heavier | Equal | Equal |
| 280 | Equal | Equal | Equal | Equal |
| 260 | Lighter | Equal | Lighter | Lighter |
| 240 | | Equal | | Lighter |
| 220 | | Lighter | | |
| 200 | | Lighter | | |
| | | ↑ | | ↑ |

Standard stimulus }

| | | | | | Mean |
|---|---|---|---|---|---|
| Upper threshold | 310 | 290 | 330 | 310 | 310 |
| Lower threshold | 270 | 230 | 270 | 270 | 260 |

Interval of uncertainty = 310 − 260 = 50 grams

Note: For descending series, the upper threshold is the mean of stimulus values corresponding to the last "Heavier" response and the first "Equal" response. The lower threshold is the mean of the last "Equal" response and the first "Lighter" response. The standard stimulus is always 300 grams.

**TABLE 8–3**

Using the Staircase Method to Determine an Absolute Threshold

| Stimulus Intensity | Response | | | |
|---|---|---|---|---|
| | ↓ | | | |
| 180 | Yes | | | |
| 160 | Yes | | | |
| 140 | Yes | Yes | ↓ | Yes |
| 120 | Yes | No | No | ↑ |
| 100 | Yes | No | | |
| 80 | No | ↑ | | |
| | Threshold = 124 | | | |

**method** (Cornsweet, 1962), concentrates on presenting stimuli around the threshold. For the first trial, the method is similar to the method of limits. However, once an estimate of the threshold is obtained, the staircase method never presents stimuli that are far from the estimate. This is shown in table 8–3. As soon as the threshold estimate is crossed, the direction of stimulus intensity reverses (the intensity values go up and down, like a staircase). Thus the efficiency is improved by keeping the stimuli much closer to the threshold than is the case for the method of limits. The threshold is calculated as the mean value of all stimuli presented, beginning with the second trial block (the second column of responses in table 8–3).

In using the method of limits and its variants, classical psychophycisists assumed that they were measuring a person's sensitivity. Any momentary differences in willingness to respond were supposed to be eliminated by obtaining substantial numbers of observations from highly trained observers. Thus, it was believed that pure measures of sensitivity were obtained. About twenty years ago, a new method was devised to measure sensitivity. This procedure, which was derived from the **theory of signal detection,** became the dominant psychophysical method. Signal-detection theory assumes that response bias is always present, and the method provides an estimate of this bias instead of trying to average it out as in the method of limits. In an exciting contradiction to earlier work, signal-detection theory denies the very concept of a threshold.

## No Thresholds: The Theory of Signal Detection

According to signal-detection theory, two basic internal processes control our detection of signals. Arrival of a signal or stimulus at a receptor creates a (hypothetical) **sensory impression** that on the average depends on the intensity of the signal. However, this impression is not sufficient to cause a Yes response even for strong signals. Instead, a subsequent **decision process** evaluates the magnitude of this sensory impression. Both sensory and decision processes must be involved in order for an observer to report sensing a signal. We will consider an everyday example of these two processes.

Any decision you make depends on the costs and benefits associated with it. Imagine that a friend has set up a blind date for you. The costs of accepting the blind date (a wasted evening) are probably less than the possible benefits (an enjoyable evening now and more enjoyment in the future), which means many of us would accept a blind date even though we know nothing about the person we will be dating. Since we lack information about the stimulus (the person who is our date), a Yes response is based mostly on our decision about costs and benefits. Now imagine a situation in which the costs are high: accepting or offering a proposal of marriage. Those of us who eagerly accept blind dates would not get married if we were offered only the information needed for us to decide whether to go on a blind date. The costs of an unsatisfactory marriage are much greater than of a miserable blind date. In terms of decision theory, we are conservative decision makers when considering marriage but liberal decision makers when considering a blind date. This decision bias does not depend on the characteristics of the stimulus; indeed the same stimulus (person) could be involved in both instances, but only on the costs and benefits of our decision.

We have just presented a situation in which decision processes played a primary role. Let us now consider how sensory information enters into signal detection. The sensory process transmits a value to the decision process. If this value is high, the decision process is more likely to yield a Yes response, once costs and benefits are evaluated. If the sensory value is low, the decision process is more likely to yield a No response, even if costs and benefits favor a Yes decision. How does the sensory process find a value to send?

Signal-detection theory assumes that **noise,** a random disturbance that can be confused with signals, is always present in the human observer. (A typical auditory signal-detection experiment will have, in addition to signals, white noise—a hissing sound you can hear by turning your television to an unoccupied channel.) Imagine sitting in a soundproof booth and wearing headphones. On each trial you must decide whether you heard a faint tone combined with white noise or only the white noise by itself. Signal-detection theory assumes that any stimulus, even noise, produces an **internal distribution** of sensory impressions. The sensory impression on each trial provides only one point, and the distributions develop from the many sensory impressions that occur during an experiment (see the discussion of distributions in appendix A). Since sensory impressions are not directly observed, the distributions for stimulus trials and for noise trials are hypothetical. The sensory impression arising when only noise occurs will tend to be small, so over many trials a (hypothetical) distribution with a small mean will be established. When a signal and noise occur, the sensory impression will tend to be larger, so a distribution with a greater mean will be formed over many trials.

Therefore, during an experiment two distributions will develop—one for noise only and one for signal plus noise. Two hypothetical distributions of sensory impression are shown in figure 8–1. Since the two distributions overlap in the middle, some values of sensory impression are ambiguous; they could have occurred as a result of noise or the signal. Ambiguity would be minimized if the two distributions were very far apart. But even in the laboratory, life is usually not that simple because the decision process needs to be considered. A *criterion*, shown as a vertical line in figure 8–1, must

**FIGURE 8–1**

*Hypothetical distributions along a sensory continuum. Once a particular sensory impression occurs, the criterion determines whether a Yes or No response will be made. Large impressions to the right of the criterion lead to Yes responses, and small impressions to the left lead to No responses. The distance between the means of the two distributions is called d'.*

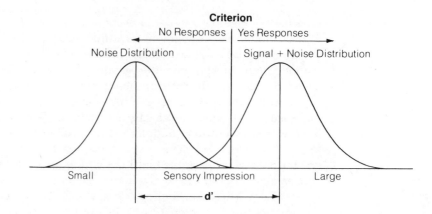

be set to determine whether a response will be Yes or No. The decision process sets the position of the criterion. If costs and benefits favor a liberal decision policy, the criterion will be set far to the left so that most responses will be Yes. If a conservative policy is used, the criterion moves to the right, which will yield mostly No responses. In either case, some errors will be made.

Correctly detecting a signal when it is presented is called a **hit.** Incorrectly responding Yes when only noise is presented is called a **false alarm.** With a liberal decision strategy (criterion set to the left), hits will be high, but since there are numerous Yes responses, the number of false alarms will also be high. (Imagine someone who said Yes on every trial. The hit rate would be 100 percent and so would the false-alarm rate.) With a conservative decision strategy, false alarms will be low but so will hits. (If someone said No on every trial, the false-alarm rate would be 0 percent, as would the hit rate.) If we plot hits as a function of false alarms, as the decision criterion moves from conservative to liberal we get the representation depicted in figure 8–2. The curve in this figure is called a **receiver-operating-characteristic** (or ROC) function. Both hits and false alarms are infrequent (conservative criterion) at the lower left of the curve. As the criterion becomes more liberal, hits and false alarms become more likely, and the ROC

**FIGURE 8–2**

*A receiver-operating-characteristic function. The distance from the diagonal to the center of the curve is proportional to d'. The diagonal represents chance performance; the observer guesses about the presence or absence of a signal. Thus, the percentage of hits equals the percentage of false alarms along this "guessing" diagonal.*

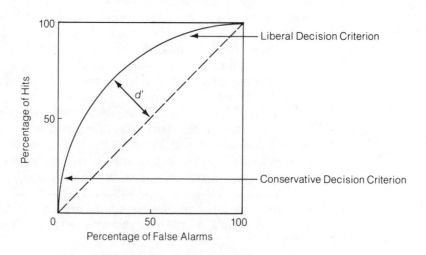

curve moves upward to the right. The slope of the ROC curve tells us the criterion. Flat slopes reveal a liberal decision criterion (generally, the upper right of the curve) and steep slopes a conservative criterion—generally, the lower left of the curve. (The slope of curves like ROC functions is determined by the slope of a line that is drawn tangent to a particular point on the function and intersects one of the axes of the graph.) The distance from the diagonal tells us how far apart the noise and signal-plus-noise distributions of figure 8–1 lie. When they are far apart, indicating a more discernible signal, the ROC curve moves upward to the left, away from the diagonal. When the signal is less detectable and the two distributions are closer together, the ROC curve moves closer to the diagonal. Thus, the ROC function tells us about both the sensory process (distance between signal-plus-noise and noise-only distributions) and the decision process (slope). Since an experimental condition generates only a single point on the ROC curve, many conditions are needed to alter the hit and false-alarm rates. Usually, hit and false-alarm rates are manipulated by altering the payoff associated with them. (If a hit were worth two dollars and a false alarm penalized you fifty cents, would you be more liberal or more conservative than if a hit were valued at fifty cents and a false alarm penalized you two dollars?) Another way of manipulating the rate of hits and false alarms is to vary how often the signal occurs. If, over a series of trials, a signal occurred 90 percent of the time, you would be more likely to say Yes on any trial than when the signal occurred very infrequently on the previous trials.

By now you may be wondering what all this has to do with thresholds. Nowhere does the ROC curve have a label that reads "threshold." Whether an observer will respond Yes or No depends on the sensory impression and the decision criterion. Signal intensity may be held constant, but since there are varying payoffs for hits and false alarms, you can generate an ROC curve showing $d'$ (sensitivity) and the slope of the curve at various points. There is no operational definition of a threshold. Instead, two quantities are operationally defined. The sensitivity of the observer is called $d'$ and is defined as the distance between signal and noise distributions in figure 8–1, or as the maximum distance between the ROC curve and the diagonal in figure 8–2. The criterion of the decision processes is often called **beta** and is the slope of the ROC function at the point of interest, for example, a hit rate of 55 percent. Together these two quantities determine what a classical psychophysicist would call a threshold.

A major advantage of signal-detection methods over a classical procedure such as the method of limits is the ability to measure both sensitivity and response bias. In many areas of applied psychology, being able to assess these two perceptual processes is very important. Let us consider just one example.

Most people do not like pain, so anything that decreases pain is of interest. Many reports from China have indicated that the insertion of needles into parts of the body can reduce pain; the procedure is called acupuncture. A reasonable question to ask is whether the reduction in pain after acupuncture treatment results from a lowering of sensitivity to pain or from a higher, more conservative criterion for reporting the presence of pain. Clark and Yang (1974) tried to determine how acupuncture works on the perception of pain.

In Clark and Yang's experiment, observers had one arm treated with acupuncture needles, and one arm untreated. On signal trials, each arm was then stimulated with intensely painful radiant heat. The acupuncture worked: The perception of pain in the acupunctured arm was lower than in the untreated arm. A signal-detection analysis revealed that $d'$ (sensitivity to pain) was about the same in the two arms. However, acupuncture did raise the criterion for making a pain response. This means that the control of pain by acupuncture did not result from changes in sensitivity, but rather from changes in response bias. Note that acupuncture worked to reduce the perception of pain and, therefore, should be a useful clinical tool for managing pain. The way it did so (by influencing response bias) may tell us something about how acupuncture works in general.

To recapitulate, psychophysical procedures, both classical and modern, obtain substantial numbers of observations from a small number of subjects. Typical independent variables include stimulus intensity, stimulus frequency, and response payoff. Several levels of these variables are presented many times, and changes in behavior, such as detection or hits and false alarms, are observed.

Reliable and valid measurement is an important part of understanding psychological processes, and the psychophysical techniques outlined above are important measurement techniques. Although determining people's judgments of weights and tones may seem esoteric, psychophysical procedures have many important practical and theoretical uses. As indicated by the work of Clark and Yang on acupuncture, and as shown in the "Application" section at the end of this chapter, psychophysical techniques have been used successfully in many applied settings. An understanding of the methodological principles underlying accurate psychological measure is a crucial tool for the psychologist who desires to determine why people and animals think and act as they do.

---

| CONCEPT SUMMARY | Psychophysics Problems and Solutions | |
|---|---|---|
| | **Problem** | **Solution** |
| | Adaptation level | Randomization, counterbalancing |
| | Determining sensitivity | Measure threshold via method of limits or staircase method |
| | Determining sensitivity | Measure criterion and sensitivity via signal-detection methods |

---

## | | | | OPERANT-CONDITIONING EXPERIMENTS

The work of Skinner (1938) and his associates (Sidman, 1960) is classified as small-$n$ because most of the experiments involve the conditioning of a small number of subjects under a number of tightly controlled conditions.

The general approach has been dubbed the *experimental analysis of behavior*, and a journal, *Journal of the Experimental Analysis of Behavior*, is devoted to such small-*n* experimentation. In operant-conditioning experiments, the argument for using few subjects does not have to do with economy, as it does in psychophysical research. Proponents of this approach argue that by very carefully controlling the experimental setting and by taking numerous and continuous measures of the dependent variable, powerful control can be obtained and valid conclusions can be reached. In contrast to standard experimental procedures in which conclusions are based on average performance of large numbers of subjects randomly assigned to conditions, this small-*n* approach relies on a detailed examination of the behavior of a small number of organisms.

## The Reversal Design

The logic behind the **reversal design** is straightforward: First obtain a baseline measure of the subject's behavior, then see how that behavior changes when an independent variable is introduced, and finally reverse the conditions back to the original and measure the behavior again under this second baseline. In its basic form, this design is labeled the **ABA design,** where A and B refer to the different phases of the experiment. Use of an AB design does not allow an experimenter to make definite statements about the effects of the variable introduced during the B phase. If there is a change in the dependent variable when the treatment is administered in the B phase, the experimenter cannot conclusively establish that it is owing to the independent variable, because there is a lack of control comparisons (we are using a form of Mill's method of agreement). The change in the dependent variable might have occurred anyway, without the treatment variable being applied, as a result of confounding from some uncontrolled variable the experimenter might not have observed. Note that in the AB design there is always a time confounding with the introduction of B following A. The third phase in the ABA design, the reintroduction of a baseline, serves to rule out the effects of confounding by returning the conditions of the experiment to their original, baseline level, with the independent variable no longer applied. If behavior in the second A phase returns to its baseline level, an experimenter can conclude that it was the independent variable that affected the change during the B phase. The only time this generalization does not apply is when a secondary variable, not detected by the experimenter, happens to be perfectly correlated with the independent variable. Such situations are unlikely.

The results of an applied reversal design are shown in figure 8–3. In this interesting experiment, Hart, Allen, Buell, Harris, and Wolf (1964) wanted to decrease the excessive crying of Bill, a nursery school student. During the A phases, the nursery school teacher simply counted the number of Bill's crying episodes and tried to comfort him. During the B phases, the teacher attempted to decrease crying by extinguishing it. The teacher ignored his crying episodes and rewarded Bill with attention every time he responded to minor calamities (such as falls or pushes) in a more mature

**FIGURE 8–3**

*The number of crying episodes exhibited by Bill, a nursery school student, during the four phases of an ABAB experiment initiated to control his crying problem. (After Hart et al., 1964, from Wolf and Risley, 1971. Reprinted by permission of the author and publisher.)*

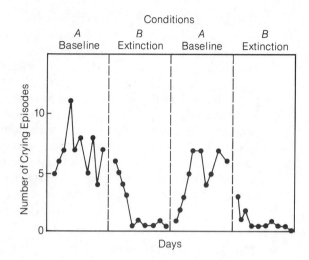

way. Usually the teacher paid attention to Bill's crying in the A phases. Since it would be counter to the purpose of the experiment to leave Bill in an A phase (crying excessively), a second B phase was instituted to reduce crying. As shown in figure 8–3, the number of crying episodes decreased markedly in the first B phase, which completes the AB phase of the design. But we cannot be certain that the combination of extinction and reward of appropriate behavior was responsible for Bill's improved behavior. Perhaps he was getting along better with his classmates, his parents were treating him better at home, or there was some other factor that improved his disposition. Thus, the A phase was reintroduced; that is, Bill was again reinforced via attention for crying. As shown in the third panel of figure 8–3, it took only four days to reestablish the baseline level of crying, which led the experimenters to conclude that reward (paying attention to appropriate behavior) and extinction (ignoring crying) were responsible for the termination of crying in the first B phase. Since the second B phase also resulted in the extinction of crying, the reward hypothesis is supported.

The reversal design is commonly used in applied settings (as in the case of Bill), and it is also frequently used in basic experiments. Boe and Winokur (1978) used a reversal design to study what controls a person's choice of words in conversations. The subject's task was to orally answer three questions during each of three sessions that occurred at weekly intervals. The questions contained target words that the experimenters thought the subjects would echo in the course of answering each question. The first and last sessions (the A phases) had the following target words: *changes, feel, society, employment, wages,* and *training.* The target words in the questions of the B phase were synonyms of those used in the A phases: *effects, believe, culture, hiring, salaries,* and *preparation.* All of the questions were about the women's liberation movement, and Boe and Winokur expected that answers concerned with job payment would include *wages* in the A phases and *salaries* in the B phase if the subjects were echoing the wording of the questions. The results followed expectation: More B words were emitted during the B phase than during the A phases, and vice versa for the A words. Use of the ABA design allows us to conclude that the specific content of the questions exerted some control over the content of the answers. Use of the AB design would not have permitted that conclusion.

**Extensions of the Reversal Design.**   As in the standard within-subjects experiments, small-*n* experiments often include carryover effects that prohibit using the reversal design. If the treatment introduced in the B phase has long-term effects on the dependent variable, then reversal is impractical. Furthermore, the experimenter may want to obtain several samples of the subjects' behavior under the same independent variable or under several independent variables. There are a number of ways to solve these problems, but we will consider just two.

Rose (1978) used what could be called an ACABCBCB design, where A phases refer to baseline conditions, and B and C phases include different independent variables. Rose was interested in the effects of artificial food coloring on hyperactivity in children. Two hyperactive eight-year-old girls were subjects. They had been on a strict diet, the K-P diet (Feingold, 1975), which does not allow foods containing artificial flavors and colors and foods containing natural salicylates (many fruits and meats). On the basis of uncontrolled case studies (AB designs), Feingold reported that the K-P diet reduced hyperactivity.

Rose's A phase was the behavior of the two girls under the ordinary K-P diet. The B phase was another type of baseline. It involved the introduction of an oatmeal cookie that contained no artificial coloring. The C phase included the independent variable of interest: oatmeal cookies containing an artificial yellow dye. This artificial color was chosen because it is commonly used in the manufacture of foods, and it had the additional benefit that it did not change the taste or appearance of the cookies. (When asked to sort the cookies on the basis of color, judges were unable to do so systematically with regard to the presence of the dye.) The subjects, their parents, and the observers were blind to when the children ate the dye-laced cookie. Various aspects of the two girls' behavior were recorded during school by several different observers.

All measures are in agreement for both subjects, so we show in figure 8–4 the percentage of time one of the girls was out of her seat (that is, when she was overactive). Notice that hyperactivity occurred only in the C phase, when the child had ingested a cookie with artificial coloring in it. There was no placebo effect (B phase), since the behavior during the A and B phases is essentially the same. Thus, Rose concluded that artificial colors can lead to hyperactivity in some children.

## Multiple-Baseline Design

Rose's extension of the reversal design allows an experimenter to examine the effects of more than two levels of the independent variable. However, the extension does not permit experiments involving independent variables that are likely to have strong carryover effects. The **multiple-baseline design,** illustrated in figure 8–5, is suitable for situations in which the behavior of interest may not reverse to baseline levels (that is, when there are permanent carryover effects).

**FIGURE 8–4**

Percentage of time out of seat during baseline (A), placebo cookie (B), and artificially colored cookie (C) phases. Asterisk indicates a C phase resulting from a violation of the diet, but one that was inadvertent, not experimentally introduced. (After Rose, 1978, in *Journal of Applied Behavior Analysis*, vol. 11, p. 444. Copyright 1978 by the Society for the Experimental Analysis of Behavior, Inc. Reprinted by permission of the publisher and author.)

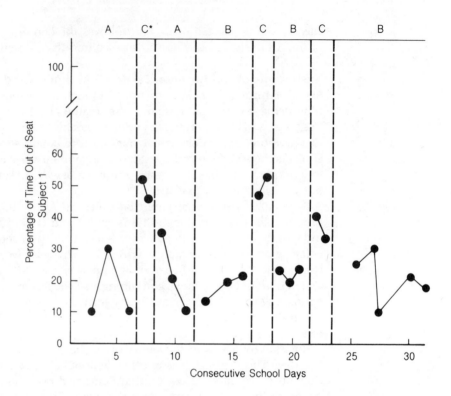

Two features of the multiple-baseline design are noteworthy. First, notice that different behaviors (or different subjects) have baseline periods of different lengths prior to the introduction of the independent variable. The baseline periods are to the left of the vertical lines, and the treatment periods, in which the independent variable has been introduced, are to the right of the vertical lines. Using such a design in the case of Bill (described earlier) might involve a continual baseline monitoring of some other unwanted behavior (say, picking fights) when the extinction period for crying was introduced. Then after several days perhaps, the extinction procedure could be applied to the fighting behavior. The design and results of this

**FIGURE 8–5**

An outline of the multiple-baseline design. Different people (between-subjects) or different behaviors (within-subjects) have baseline periods of different lengths. The vertical lines indicate when the independent variable (the treatment) was introduced.

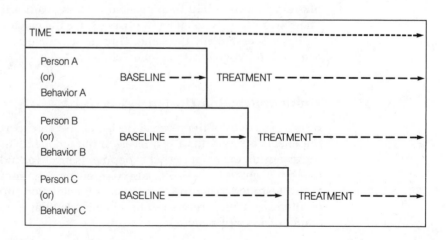

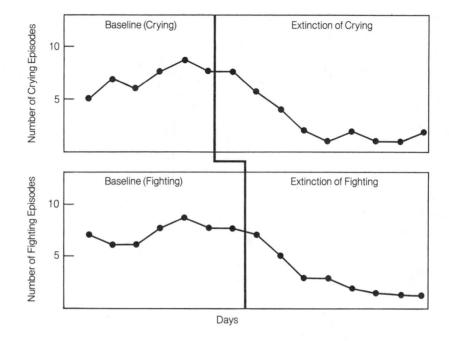

**FIGURE 8–6**

Hypothetical results of a multiple-baseline experiment on Bill. Two behaviors, crying and fighting, are extinguished after different baseline periods.

hypothetical experiment are shown in figure 8–6. Notice that, in general, one behavior is allowed to occur under baseline conditions while the other behavior is being treated. If the untreated behavior holds steady prior to the introduction of the independent variable, and then changes afterward, the assumption is that it is the independent variable that alters the behavior and not some other change taking place over time. However, if the target behaviors are not independent—that is, if the treatment of one influences the occurrence of the other (Bill's fighting decreases when crying is extinguished), then the changes in behavior can not be attributed to the independent variable. This problem leads us to the second important feature of the multiple-baseline design illustrated in figure 8–5.

The multiple-baseline design can be used as a small-*n* equivalent of the between-subjects design. As shown in figure 8–5, instead of several behaviors being monitored as in a within-subjects design, different people can be monitored for different periods prior to the introduction of the independent variable. This type of multiple-baseline design, as is true of the ordinary between-subjects design, should be appropriate for situations in which the independent variable will have strong carryover effects. The between-subjects multiple-baseline procedure is also appropriate for cases where target behaviors are likely to be influenced by each other, such as could have occurred in our hypothetical experiment concerning Bill.

An experiment by Schreibman, O'Neill, and Koegel (1983) nicely illustrates the between-subjects form of the multiple-baseline design. Schreibman and her co-workers were interested in teaching behavior-modification procedures to the normal siblings of autistic children so that the normals could become effective teachers of their autistic siblings. Autism is a behavior disorder of unknown origin. It is characterized by impoverished social behavior, minimal language use, and self-stimulation of various kinds. For

**FIGURE 8–7**

*The normal siblings' use of correct behavior-modification procedures, and the autistic children's appropriate responses. The baseline period is to the left of the vertical line for each pair of children. The pluses and bull's-eyes show behavior in a generalization setting. (From Schreibman et al., 1983, in* Journal of Applied Behavior Analysis, *vol. 16, p. 135. Copyright 1983 by the Society for the Experimental Analysis of Behavior, Inc. Reprinted by permission of the publisher and author.)*

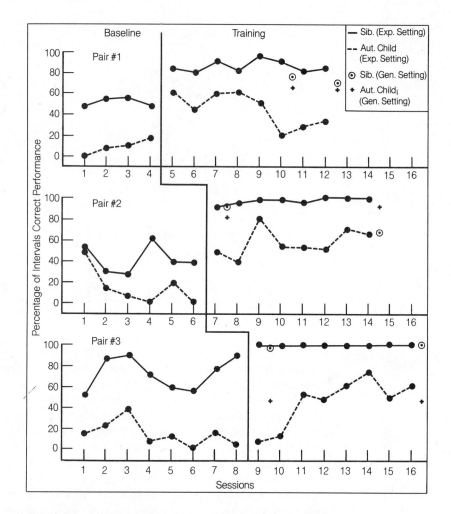

each of three pairs of siblings—one normal (mean age was 10 years) and one autistic (mean age was 7 years)—several target behaviors, such as counting, identification of letters, and learning about money, were chosen for the normal sibling to teach the autistic sibling. Since the normal siblings had to learn correct behavior-modification techniques, such as reinforcement for appropriate responding, the experimenters first recorded baseline measures of the normal siblings' use of correct behavior-modification techniques, and the correct performance of the target behaviors by the autistic children. The baseline data for each pair of children are shown to the left of the vertical lines in figure 8–7. Since learning behavior-modification techniques is likely to influence a wide variety of behaviors of both the teacher and pupil (the normal and autistic, respectively), a multiple-baseline design across pairs of children was used. Changes in the behavior of normal and autistic children after the normals were trained to use behavior-modification procedures are shown to the right of the vertical lines in figure 8–7. Note that correct performance by both children in each pair increased after the beginning of training. Schreibman, O'Neill, and Koegel concluded that the training, and not some other confounding factor (such as changes resulting from being observed), altered the behavior.

Another interesting feature in figure 8–7 are the data points represented by plus signs and bull's-eyes. These symbols show the children's behavior in a setting that was entirely different from the training room, one in which the children did not know they were being monitored by the experimenters. Behavior in this generalization setting was very similar to the behavior in the training room, so the treatment program was effective in making general changes in the children's behavior.

The operant conditioning research designs described above are representative of the powerful research techniques developed by Skinner and his followers. Careful control and the application of Mill's joint method of agreement and difference have provided an enormously valuable data base for psychology. Furthermore, as we have seen, the procedures have been used in applied settings with substantial success. The small-*n* procedures of operant analysis are important tools for psychologists who wish to understand thought and behavior.

---

| CONCEPT SUMMARY | **Small-*N* Designs in Operant-Conditioning Research** |
|---|---|
| | ***Reversal Design (ABA or ABAB)*** |
| | Interspersed between baseline periods (*A*) are independent-variable phases (*B*). If the behavior reverses to baseline levels, we assume that the independent variable caused the changes that occurred during the B periods. |
| | ***Extensions of the Reversal Design*** |
| | More than one independent variable is used, and there are numerous baseline periods. |
| | ***Multiple-Baseline Design*** |
| | Several behaviors (within-subjects) or several people (between-subjects) receive baseline periods of varying length, and then the independent variable is introduced. Both forms of the multiple-baseline design are useful when behaviors will not reverse after the introduction of the independent variable. The between-subjects type is useful when the behaviors being studied are not independent of each other. |

## | | | | SUMMARY

**1.** Small-*n* experiments, in contrast to most control-group and control-condition designs, involve numerous observations on small numbers of subjects.

**2.** One carryover problem in psychophysical experiments is adaptation level, the context or reference level for making a particular judgment.

**3.** The method of limits, in which stimuli are presented in ascending and descending orders of intensity, is the traditional way of measuring thresholds.

**4.** The absolute threshold is the average point at which an observer switches from detection (Yes responses) to nondetection (No responses).

**5.** When the method of limits is used, variability in responding is handled by averaging the results of large numbers of ascending and descending trial blocks.

**6.** The difference threshold in the method of limits involves heavier, lighter, and equal stimuli being compared with a constant stimulus. The difference threshold is defined as one-half the interval of uncertainty, which is the difference between the upper and lower threshold.

**7.** The staircase method is a modification of the method of limits. Stimuli close to an estimated threshold are presented in abbreviated ascending and descending series.

**8.** The theory of signal detection assumes that perception is composed of a sensory impression, which is then evaluated by a decision process.

**9.** Signal-detection experiments involve some trials that have a signal embedded in noise, and other trials that have noise only. The observer's tasks is to respond Yes on signal-plus-noise trials.

**10.** According to signal-detection theory, hypothetical internal distributions of sensory impressions develop across a series of trials. The difference between the means of the noise distribution and the signal-plus-noise distribution represents signal strength ($d'$), and a decision criterion set within these distributions determines whether a response is Yes or No.

**11.** A hit occurs when a subject correctly detects a signal that is presented. A false alarm occurs when the subjects incorrectly report a signal when only noise is presented.

**12.** A plot of hits against false alarms yields a receiver-operating-characteristic (ROC) function.

**13.** Flat slopes on the ROC function indicate a liberal decision criterion leading to numerous hits and false alarms. Steep slopes show a conservative criterion with fewer hits and fewer false alarms. The criterion measured this way is often called beta. The distance of the ROC curve from the "guessing" diagonal is a measure of sensitivity ($d'$), which varies with signal strength.

**14.** Hit and false-alarm rates are varied by the payoff associated with each kind of response and by the probability of signal-plus-noise trials.

**15.** Signal-detection methods are useful in determining whether a particular perception is influenced by sensitivity or the decision criterion.

**16.** Operant-conditioning experiments in the tradition of Skinner use small-$n$ designs, on the assumption that valid conclusions can be reached by making large numbers of observations on a few subjects in a carefully controlled experimental setting.

**17.** The reversal design (*ABA* design) is a common within-subjects design that involves independent-variable periods (*B* phases) interspersed among baseline periods (*A* phases).

**18.** The major assumption underlying the reversal design is that if the behavior reverses to baseline levels in the second *A* phase after removal of the independent variable, then the independent variable caused the changes in behavior.

**19.** One extension of the reversal design involves numerous baseline periods and more than two levels of the independent variable.

**20.** The multiple-baseline design involves assessing different behaviors (within-subjects) or different people (between-subjects) for baseline periods of different length, prior to introducing the independent variable.

**21.** If, when the multiple-baseline design is used, behavior changes only when the independent variable is introduced, then we assume that the independent variable caused those changes.

**22.** The multiple-baseline design is useful when the independent variable has strong carryover effects that limit reversal of behavior to baseline levels.

**23.** The between-subjects version of the multiple-baseline design is appropriate when the behaviors to be altered are not independent of each other.

## Key Concepts

absolute threshold

adaptation level

beta

criterion

*d'*

decision process

difference threshold

extensions of the reversal design

false alarm

hit

internal distribution

interval of uncertainty

method of adjustment (see "Application" section)

method of limits

multiple-baseline design

noise

point of subjective equality

receiver-operating-characteristic (ROC)

reversal design (*ABA*)

sensory impression

small-*n* designs

staircase method

theory of signal detection

threshold

## Exercises

**1.** Relate the presentation of signals in the method of limits and the signal-detection method to the occurrence of the independent variable in the reversal design used in operant conditioning.

**2.** Discuss the differences between the method of limits and signal-detection methods. How might each be used to test whether a placebo pill (a pill that is inert, such as a sugar pill) alters sensitivity to pain.

**3.** Discuss the logic underlying the use of the reversal design and the multiple baseline design. How do these relate to Mill's joint method of agreement and difference?

**4.** [*Special Exercise.*] For each of the following topics, indicate whether a reversal design, a multiple-baseline design, or both designs is appropriate:

The effects of reward and punishment on vocabulary learning by autistic children.

The effects of brain damage on operant responding by rats.

The effects of praise on the amount of homework done by high-school students.

The effects of monetary rewards on learning how to ski.

The effects of rewards on using a seat belt to and from work.

## Suggested Readings

A good, general reference for psychophysics is Gescheider, G. A. (1976). *Psychophysics: Method and theory.* Hillsdale, NJ: Erlbaum.

You will find that the following book discusses both the design of small-*n* experiments and the application of behavior modification techniques to your own problems: Williams, R. D., & Long, J. D. (1979). *Toward a self-managed life style* (2d ed.). Boston: Houghton-Mifflin.

---

## APPLICATION
### Designing a Better Toilet Seat

Psychophysics and psychological measurement are not just esoteric procedures used in research. Many areas of applied psychology regularly use them. This is particularly so in the field of *human-factors engineering* (also called *ergonomics*). Human-factors psychologists are concerned with developing devices of one sort or another to fit the human user. Dental chairs, automobile dashboards, and snow shovels, for example, have been redesigned with the human user in mind. Let us see how the method of limits and rating scales (see chapter 2) were used to try to improve the design of toilet seats.

McClelland and Ward (1982), using the method of limits, had subjects adjust the height and angle of toilet seats. Subjects began at a particular height or angle, then moved the height or angle by means of a control switch which regulated a motor that moved the toilet seat appropriately up or down (for height) or off the horizontal (for angular adjustment). Two sequences were run starting from below the standard height, and two were run starting from above. (Note that this is a modification of the standard method of limits; it is very similar to what the psychophysicists call the **method of adjustment,** in which a variable stimulus is adjusted by the observer until it matches a standard.) The dependent variable was the average height that was preferred on all four runs. The preferred seat angle was similarly determined. McClelland and Ward used rating scales to find out the preferred shape of the toilet seat. Five seats of various shapes were rated— a standard seat and four that differed in terms of aperture and the amount of support supplied to the buttocks.

The researchers found that the preferred seat angle was very close to the horizontal for both men and women. As for height, the men preferred a seat about two inches higher than that preferred by women. The preferred height by men was identical to the current British standard for seat heights (this research was conducted in England) and about the same as standards in the United States. However, McClelland and Ward recommended that the standard be lowered by about one and one-half inches. They made this recommendation for two reasons: They wanted women and children to be better accommodated than they are with the current (higher) standard; and medical research has indicated that a much lower seat has some physiological benefits.

As far as seat shape is concerned, McClelland and Ward discovered that seats with a more elongated opening than is standard were preferred by both men and women. Furthermore, the researchers found that their subjects liked seats that offered more thigh and buttock support than is provided by the standard seat.

Very little change has occurred in the human factors of toilets since they were first designed. Perhaps the work of McClelland and Ward will allow us all to be seated with more comfort.

McClelland, I. L., & Ward, J. S. (1982). The ergonomics of toilet seats. *Human Factors, 24,* 713–725.

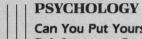

## PSYCHOLOGY IN ACTION
### Can You Put Yourself on a Better Schedule of Reinforcement?

All of us have habits we would like to break, and other habits we would like to develop. Smoking, drinking, nail-biting, watching too much TV, and not studying enough are some of the bad habits that college students often say they would like to alter. Failure to control these behaviors is often blamed on laziness or a defective personality. However, a behavioral analysis of such problems suggests a simple alternative to these interpretations: bad habits are being reinforced, and to change them we must alter the schedule of reinforcement by which we live. If all these bad habits are learned, then they can be altered by learning, too. The general aim is to alter the reinforcements in our lives so that they occur after desirable behavior and not after undesirable behavior.

Suppose you are in danger of flunking out of school because you study too little and, being addicted to the movies, you attend them too often. You know you have a problem, but you are in a rut and you don't know how to get out. What can you do to modify your behavior?

The first step is to set a goal for yourself. It is not enough to say that you want to study more; you must have a concrete, measurable goal. Say you decide to study six hours a day outside of class. Your second step would be to institute some means of carefully monitoring your study behavior. How much do you already study, on the average? You should carry a notebook and record every studying episode as it occurs each day, and then total these episodes at the end of the day. You can also get a weekly average. Say you discover at the end of a week that you are averaging fifty-nine minutes of studying per day; obviously you are a long way from your target of six hours a day.

The next step is to set yourself a realistic goal in your first attempt. It might be too much of a shock to your system to go directly from one to six hours of studying per day; worse, you might give up early on, deciding it is impossible. So let us assume that you plan to increase your studying to two hours a day at first. But how? You should analyze the situation and see what activities prevent you from studying. The main deterrent is your going to the movies, but surely other activities also intrude. You might set up an activity schedule to monitor your behavior, as shown in the table below.

| Time | Monday | Tuesday | Wednesday | Thursday | Friday | Saturday | Sunday |
|---|---|---|---|---|---|---|---|
| 7:00 | | | | | | | |
| 8:00 | | | | | | | |
| 9:00 | | | | | | | |
| 10:00 | | | | | | | |
| 11:00 | | | | | | | |
| 12:00 | | | | | | | |
| 1:00 | | | | | | | |
| 2:00 | | | | | | | |
| 3:00 | | | | | | | |
| 4:00 | | | | | | | |
| 5:00 | | | | | | | |
| 6:00 | | | | | | | |
| 7:00 | | | | | | | |
| 8:00 | | | | | | | |
| 9:00 | | | | | | | |
| 10:00 | | | | | | | |
| 11:00 | | | | | | | |

You should then try to change your environment so that it is more conducive to study. Try to avoid those friends who might encourage you to go to the movies. Don't avoid them entirely, of course, but plan to spend more time at the place where you study. Analyze your study area—are there many distractions? (These might include roommates, magazines, radios, and televisions.) If there are many distractions, abandon your room as a place of study and find a quiet hideaway where only you and your books will be present. Studies have shown that if you can associate a particular place exclusively with study behavior and then force yourself to go to this place, you can increase studying dramatically. Finally—and this is one of the most important steps—you must figure out a reward for yourself for successfully studying the allotted amount of time. For example, you could promise yourself that if you have studied two hours each day during the first week, you can go to the movies with your friends. Thus one of the main reinforcers in your life—going to the movies—is made contingent on other behavior. In essence, you are reinforcing yourself for studying.

During the next week, try studying three hours a day, continuing to carefully monitor your time and study habits. In each successive week, increase your amount of study per day, until you reach your goal in a few weeks. Technically, you are *shaping* study behavior in yourself by reinforcing successive approximations to the target behavior, just as animals are taught complicated tricks by being reinforced for gradual approximations to them. If you can keep the reinforcement contingencies in place, you will have dramatically changed your behavior.

The case we have used here may not apply directly to your situation, but in all likelihood you have habits you would like to break or change. You can do so by applying the rules specified here: Set a concrete target goal and by reinforcing yourself for each step taken, gradually alter your behavior to approximate that goal. R. D. Williams and J. D. Long have written a book, *Toward a Self-Managed Life Style*, that explores the possibility of changing many areas of our lives by effectively reinforcing positive behavior and not rewarding negative behavior. Besides methods for improving study habits, they discuss behavioral self-management programs for losing weight, increasing exercise, managing time, controlling smoking and drinking, and becoming more assertive.

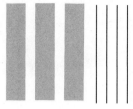

# QUASI-EXPERIMENTAL AND EX POST FACTO RESEARCH

| OBSERVATION AND CORRELATION | Observation |
|---|---|
| Internal validity is suspect in research without independent variables | Limit ranges of observations and guard against reactivity. |
| | Use unobtrusive observations, participant observation, or unobtrusive measures. |
| | **Correlation** |
| | Source and direction of causality may be impossible to determine. |
| | Truncated range may be a problem. |
| | Using more than one correlation may help to increase validity. |

# 9 |||| Observation and Correlation

Observation and correlation are research techniques that do not include an independent variable. As such, these procedures often are not internally valid—sound causal statements cannot be made on the basis of observation or correlation—because an independent variable has not been varied by the researcher. This does not mean that observation and correlation have little value. In psychology, these techniques add to the data base necessary for performing subsequent controlled experiments, and observation often is an end in itself. Furthermore, since observation and correlation generally involve dependent variables of high intrinsic interest, these research tools are likley to be externally valid.

#### |||| EX POST FACTO RESEARCH

In this chapter and the next, we will examine research procedures that lack a true independent variable. Such techniques are called *ex post facto* (see chapter 1) in the case of observation and correlation because the variables are selected after the fact. Quasi-experiments have independent variables that are selected by the experimenter. Those types of research, unlike a true experiment, do not involve the manipulation of one or more independent variables. Rather, in observation and correlation there are no independent variables, only dependent variables, and in quasi-experiments the independent variables are not manipulated directly by the experimenter. Because the researcher does not directly control the variables, ex post facto research and quasi-experiments have been called passive research (for example, Cook and Campbell, 1979) to highlight the fact that variables are selected rather than manipulated for some persons. The term *passive* has a somewhat negative connotation, because it implies that the researcher is not doing very much. As we shall see, ex post facto research and quasi-experiments are not necessarily passive in the sense of laziness. It may be true that the researcher does not manipulate independent variables, but it is not true that such researchers are lazy or that their findings are unimportant or uninteresting. Indeed, many central problems in psychology must be studied by such techniques.

What are the consequences of not having direct control over the variables in ex post facto research and quasi-experiments? One important consequence has to do with *internal validity* (see chapter 2). A carefully designed experiment, you will remember, is internally valid because you can make valid causal statements about the results. One is able to infer causality because changes in the dependent variable result from manipulation of the independent variable. Since independent variables are missing in ex post facto research and are not varied directly in quasi-experiments, internally valid causal statements are going to be much more difficult to make than in the case of a true experiment. One of the major themes of this chapter and the next on quasi-experiments is how a researcher makes these kinds of research procedures as internally valid as possible.

A second consequence of doing ex post facto research and quasi-experiments concerns another kind of validity—*external validity*. Externally valid research has generality, is representative of the so-called real world, and does not distort the question under investigation. By their very nature, experiments are artificial (that is, they are highly controlled), which means that a single experiment may be unrepresentative in terms of its subjects, setting, and variables. We may have to conduct several interrelated experiments to converge on a generalizable explanation. The issue of external validity is a complex one and is examined in detail in chapter 10. For now, you should note that although ex post facto research and quasi-experiments are usually internally invalid, they are often externally valid. When we select or observe what nature has given us, we study real behaviors in real situations. When we observe mother-infant interactions or correlate the effects of violent television on aggression, we may not be able to make internally valid causal statements even if the variables are real and extremely interesting. Now we will examine some of the threats to internal validity in ex post facto research and some ways to minimize those threats.

| **CONCEPT SUMMARY** | In research without a true independent variable, internal validity is suspect. |
| --- | --- |

## Naturalistic Observation

Miller (1977) has enumerated several important roles that naturalistic observation can play in psychology. One way to summarize Miller's thinking is to say that observation provides a major part of the data base which can lead to subsequent, more highly controlled research. Naturalistic observation describes the thoughts and behaviors of organisms, which is a necessary first step in understanding. A familiar example is Harlow's work on mother-love in infant monkeys. Prior to his experiments, Harlow needed to know what behaviors infant monkeys exhibited, and he needed to know some of the things infant monkeys seemed to like (their soft blankets) and dislike (the wire floor of the cage). With this background information, Harlow could attempt to determine causal relationships via experimentation. Thus, we should not view observation as somehow secondary or subordinate to experimentation because it lacks control. Observation may be valuable in its own right and provide important information for later experiments.

In making naturalistic observations, we confront two basic problems that threaten the validity of the observations. One problem has to do with delimiting the choice of behaviors to observe. Human observers have a finite capacity to perceive and think about events. Although most of us may be able to walk and chew gum at the same time, most of us cannot attend to and remember twenty different behaviors occurring over short periods of time. Thus, there has to be some boundary on the range of behaviors that we plan to observe. The second problem concerns the participant's reaction to being observed. We will discuss reactivity in general terms in a later chapter, but here we will detail this problem in observation, because it is a fundamental threat to the validity of the procedure.

## What Do We Observe?

How do we delimit the range of behaviors to be studied? Part of this answer seems straightforward. If we are interested in human nonverbal communication, we observe human nonverbal communication. However, this is not necessarily easy to do. In the first place, nonverbal communication is highly complex, so that an observer may still have difficulties limiting the boundaries of observation. In the second place, examining nonverbal behaviors presupposes that we already know some of the behaviors to observe. Obviously, we do not enter a research project devoid of all knowledge, but neither do we start out with all the answers. What usually happens is that we begin a series of observational studies, in which successive projects rely on previous data to refine and delimit the field of inquiry. Let us consider two examples to illustrate the refinement procedure.

**Flashing eyebrows.** The famous ethologist of human behavior Eibl-Eibesfeldt (1970, 1972) has done a substantial amount of field research on human facial expressions. He and his colleagues traveled around the world taking pictures of facial expressions in a variety of contexts. Careful examination of the expressions indicated that many are similar across cultures, and some are not. In the process of examining facial expressions associated with people greeting each other, Eibl-Eibesfeldt discovered that most humans give a brief eyebrow flash. He went on to examine this phenomenon in detail. Generally, the eyebrow flash is a brief (one-sixth of a second) raising of the eyebrows, accompanied by a slight smile and a quick nod of the head. The eyebrow flash has been observed in people of many cultures, including Bushmen, Balinese, and Europeans. However, some cultures seem to differ in their use of the eyebrow flash. The Japanese do not use the flash, because in Japan it is considered suggestive or indecent. Furthermore, Eibl-Eibesfeldt found that the flash occurred in other circumstances, such as in flirting and acknowledging a gift or service (that is, as a kind of thank you), in addition to greeting. Thus, previous observations suggested additional ones for Eibl-Eibesfeldt, and by delimiting his range of inquiry he was able to garner substantial information about a common human behavior.

**Testing neonates.**    Our second example of refinement comes from studies of newborn humans (neonates). What do neonates do, and what can we look for in their behavior? Most people think of neonates as being limited in their behavior. However, neonates can do more than eat, sleep, eliminate, and cry. All their senses are operative, and they possess a number of complex reflexes. Brazelton and his associates (for example, Lester and Brazelton, 1982) have spent many years refining a scale to assess the optimal performance of neonates on a variety of behaviors. Initially, the scale assessed reflexes (squeezing, blinking) and a few behaviors. Repeated observations of neonates from a variety of cultures and in a variety of situations led to changes, which, in turn, caused more changes. The resulting Brazelton Neonatal Behavioral Assessment Scale contains measurements of sixteen reflexes and twenty-six behaviors. The reflexes are rated on a three-point scale (low, medium, and high), and the behavioral items, such as responses to a pinprick and hand-to-mouth activity, are rated on nine-point scales. Earlier observations had suggested that the level of arousal was very important with respect to the appearance and magnitude of certain behaviors, so the current scale indicates when the neonate should be assessed on the various behaviors. For example, responses to a pinprick are assessed when the neonate is asleep or quiet, but not when the neonate is alert or crying. Hand-to-mouth behaviors can be assessed during any state. Brazelton and his co-workers have been particularly concerned with individual and cultural differences in development, and they have conducted numerous quasi-experiments to examine these differences. The quasi-experiments would not have been possible had they not made the exhaustive series of observations that led to the development of the assessment scale.

## Reactivity

There are two general ways to guard against the participants' reactions ruining observations: (1) we can make **unobtrusive observations,** or (2) we can take **unobtrusive measures** (Webb, Campbell, Schwartz, and Sechrist, 1981). We will consider these in turn.

**Unobtrusive observations.**    Imagine that you are walking down a street in your hometown. Occasionally you greet a friend (perhaps with a handshake, perhaps with an eyebrow flash). As your walk continues, a man with a large camera approaches and proceeds to take moving pictures of you every time you greet one of your friends. How are you likely to react to this attention? Quite likely, your mode of greeting people would change dramatically. (Have you ever noticed how spectators behave at sporting events when they know the television camera is on them?) Eibl-Eibesfeldt guarded against participant reactivity in his research by using a camera with a special sideways lens. This lens permitted him to aim the camera 90 degrees from the subject; presumably, the subject would think that Eibl-Eibesfeldt was photographing something else. Thus, the subject would not react abnormally to the presence of the observer and his camera; instead, the subject would act naturally, which is what Eibl-Eibesfeldt intended. The special camera lens allowed the researcher to observe without intruding on the subject, which means that Eibl-Eibesfeldt used an unobtrusive observation technique.

In general, unobtrusive observations of subjects are likely to reveal more natural behavior than if the subjects are aware of being observed. In studying animals, researchers use unobtrusive observations whenever possible so that the behavior of interest will not be affected by the observer's presence.

Sometimes, however, either the subjects themselves, the terrain, or some other aspect of the project demands close contact. In these situations, **participant observation** often provides a solution. For example, Fossey (1972) spent a great amount of time observing the mountain gorilla. The mountain gorilla lives in central Africa, and its habitat is threatened by human beings who are moving into that area. The mountain gorilla's natural habitat is in the mountainous rain forest, which makes long-range unobtrusive spying out of the question. Fossey was particularly concerned with the free-ranging behavior of the gorillas, so she decided to become a participant observer. This was difficult, because the gorillas are not tame. She had to mimic the gorillas so that they would become accustomed to her presence. She mimicked aspects of the animal's behavior, such as eating, grooming, and making weird gorillalike vocalizations. As she said, "one feels like a fool thumping one's chest rhythmically or sitting about pretending to munch on a stalk of wild celery as though it were the most delectable morsel in the world. But the gorillas have responded favorably" (p. 211). It took several months for Fossey to gain the confidence of the gorillas, and she continued to live with and study the gorillas until her death in 1986. How would you like to act like a gorilla for ten or fifteen years?

**Unobtrusive measures.** Unobtrusive measures, in contrast to unobtrusive observations, are usually indirect observations of behavior. Unobtrusive measures are indirect because it is the result of behavior, not the behavior itself, that is being studied. Thus, instead of measuring behavior directly, we examine it áfter the fact by looking at what the behavior accomplished. Instead of observing a student's studying activities, we examine his or her transcript. Instead of living with the gorillas, we look at their effect on the environment. Obviously, unobtrusive measures are not suitable for all questions being investigated (an unobtrusive measure of an eyebrow flash might be difficult), but for some these measures are not merely good, they are the only ones that are feasible. Consider the question of graffiti in public restrooms. Who does it? What does the graffiti usually concern? A number of serious ethical questions (ethics are discussed in chapter 4) would be raised if a researcher stood around in restrooms observing the patrons. However, the graffiti topics can be examined and can provide substantial information. Kinsey, Pomeroy, and Martin (1953) discovered that graffiti in men's restrooms was more erotic than graffiti in women's restrooms. Furthermore, they found more graffiti in men's rooms than in women's rooms.

Using unobtrusive measures is akin to a hunter following animal tracks or a police officer examining clues such as fingerprints. Tracks and clues are left behind and often allow us to infer things about the behavior that caused them. Recently, a popular psychological and anthropological unobtrusive measure has been to examine the garbage and other refuse that people discard. From the characteristics of the discarded objects, the observer attempts to understand some aspect of the behavior behind that refuse (for example, a discarded liquor bottle or love letter that has been thrown away could reveal information about behavior).

---

**CONCEPT SUMMARY**     To increase the validity of naturalistic observation, use

*Unobtrusive observations*

*Participant observation*

*Unobtrusive measures*

---

## |||| CORRELATIONAL RESEARCH

In correlational research, as mentioned in chapter 1, investigators attempt to determine how two or more dependent variables covary, and from that covariation, they make predictions and selections. Since correlational research involves two or more observations, the sources of invalidity associated with naturalistic observation are likely to be present. Thus, we may want to use such things as unobtrusive observations in doing correlational studies. Before discussing some unique problems of correlational research, we will consider a statistical way in which correlations are determined.

### A Correlation Coefficient

There are several different types of correlation coefficients, and the type used depends on the characteristics of the variables being correlated. As an example of how to calculate a correlation coefficient, we shall consider one commonly used by psychologists, the Pearson product-moment correlation coefficient, or **Pearson r.** You should remember that this is only one of several; if you need to compute a correlation on some data, you should consult a statistics text to determine which one is appropriate for your particular case.

Let us imagine that we are one of the bevy of psychologists who devote their careers to the study of intelligence. One of these psychologists hits upon a simple, intuitive idea concerning head size and intelligence, which goes like this: An analogy can be made between the head (where information is stored) and other physical vessels, such as boxes, where all kinds of things can be stored. On the basis of such analogical reasoning, which is common in science, we can make the following prediction about the properties of physical containers: As head size of a person increases, so should the person's capacity for intellect. More things can be stored in bigger boxes than in smaller ones, and similarly, more information should be stored in larger heads than in smaller heads.

This "theory" proposes a simple relation between head size and intelligence; as head size increases, so should intelligence. A positive correlation between these two variables is predicted. This theory can be tested in the following manner. A random sample of the population could be taken and the persons chosen could be measured on two dimensions: head size and their performance on a brief intelligence test. Three hypothetical sets of results from ten subjects are presented in table 9–1. Notice that for each individual there are two measures, one of head size and the other of intelligence. Also notice that in order for the two types of measures to be correlated, they need not be similar in any way. They do not have to be on the same scale. Just as we can correlate head size with intelligence, we could also correlate memory ability with street address or with any two sets of numbers.

The mathematical assessment of correlation coefficients is discussed in appendix A. If you are unfamiliar with this material, you might review pages 318–321, where the mathematical formula for $r$ is presented. Pearson $r$ is calculated for the data presented in (a) column of table 9–1. Working through this example will help you better understand the basis of correlation coefficients. Researchers seldom use the mathematical formula to calculate $r$ by hand. Most researchers now rely on calculators or computers to calculate correlation coefficients for them.

**Scatter diagrams.**  So that you get a better idea of the graphic representation of correlations, the data in table 9–1 are presented in figure 9–1,

**TABLE 9–1**
Three hypothetical examples of data taken on head size and intelligence-test scores representing (a) a positive correlation, (b) a low (near-zero) correlation, and (c) a negative correlation.

| (A) POSITIVE CORRELATION | | | (B) ZERO CORRELATION | | | (C) NEGATIVE CORRELATION | | |
|---|---|---|---|---|---|---|---|---|
| Subject | Head size (cm.) | Test score | Subject | Head size (cm.) | Test score | Subject | Head size (cm.) | Test score |
| 1 | 50.8 | 17 | 1 | 50.8 | 23 | 1 | 50.8 | 12 |
| 2 | 63.5 | 21 | 2 | 63.5 | 12 | 2 | 63.5 | 9 |
| 3 | 45.7 | 16 | 3 | 45.7 | 13 | 3 | 45.7 | 13 |
| 4 | 25.4 | 11 | 4 | 25.4 | 21 | 4 | 25.4 | 23 |
| 5 | 29.2 | 9 | 5 | 29.2 | 9 | 5 | 29.2 | 21 |
| 6 | 49.5 | 15 | 6 | 49.5 | 14 | 6 | 49.5 | 16 |
| 7 | 38.1 | 13 | 7 | 38.1 | 16 | 7 | 38.1 | 14 |
| 8 | 30.5 | 12 | 8 | 30.5 | 15 | 8 | 30.5 | 17 |
| 9 | 35.6 | 14 | 9 | 35.6 | 11 | 9 | 35.6 | 15 |
| 10 | 58.4 | 23 | 10 | 58.4 | 16 | 10 | 58.4 | 11 |
| | $r = +.93$ | | | $r = -.01$ | | | $r = -.89$ | |

**FIGURE 9–1**

Graphic representation of the data from table 9–1, showing the characteristic pattern of (a) a high positive correlation, (b) an essentially zero correlation, and (c) a strong negative correlation.

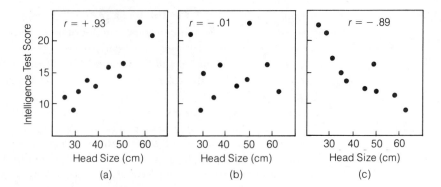

where head size is plotted along the horizontal $x$-axis (the abscissa) and test score is plotted along the vertical $y$-axis (the ordinate). Such graphs are usually called **scatter diagrams** because they show how two sets of scores scatter when plotted against each other. Notice that the high positive correlation between head size and intelligence in the (a) column of table 9–1 is translated into a visual representation that tilts upward to the right in figure 9–1(a) with intelligence test scores increasing as head size increases. The negative correlation in the (c) column of the table is depicted as sloping downward to the right in figure 9–1(c), with intelligence scores decreasing with increases in head size. You can see how knowing a person's score on one variable helps us predict (though not perfectly in these cases) the level of performance on the other. In regard to the hypothetical data in the (a) and (c) panels of figure 9–1, knowing a person's head size would help predict his or her intelligence, and vice versa. This is the primary reason correlations are useful: They specify the amount of relation and allow predictions to be made. Notice that this last statement cannot be made about the data in panel (b), where there is essentially a zero correlation. The points are just scattered about and there is no consistent relation between test score and head size, which is just what a low Pearson $r$ reflects. Even in cases in which the size of the correlation is rather large, we will not be able to predict perfectly an individual's score on one variable, given his or her performance on the other. Even with $r = +.75$ between head size and test score, it is still quite possible for a person with a large head size to have low intelligence, and vice versa. Unless the correlation is perfect ($+1.00$ or $-1.00$), our prediction of one score when we are given the other will not be perfect, either.

What do you think the real correlation would be between head size and intelligence of a random sample of the population at large? Although we have not actually done such a study, we think it quite likely that it would be rather large and positive (perhaps $+.60$ to $+.70$), in support of our theory of intelligence based on head size. What can we conclude from this? How can correlation coefficients be interpreted? We turn to this issue next.

**Interpreting correlation coefficients.** An important warning is always given in any discussion of correlation: The existence of even a sizable correlation implies nothing about the existence of a causal relation between the two variables under consideration. On the basis of just a correlation, we cannot say whether factor $X$ causes factor $Y$, factor $Y$ causes factor $X$, some underlying third factor causes both, or the two are completely unrelated. *Correlation does not necessarily imply causation.* Let us consider some examples. Suppose we have found a correlation of $+.70$ between head size and intelligence. This is in general agreement with our theory that larger heads hold more information, but certainly there are other interpretations of this relationship. It could be argued that the high positive correlation between head size and high scores on an intelligence test is mediated or produced by some third factor underlying both, such as age. We know that heads grow as people age and that intelligence improves with age. Therefore age (or one of its correlates) might actually be responsible for the large positive correlation we have found between head size and high scores on the intelligence test.

In correlational studies we cannot conclude that any one factor produced or caused another, since a number of factors are likely to have varied simultaneously with those of interest. In performing an experiment, we attempt to avoid this problem by directly manipulating one factor while holding all the others constant. Then the influence of the manipulated factor on whatever it is we are measuring can be directly attributed to the factor of interest. When two factors (or more) are varied at the same time so that we cannot know whether one factor, the other factor, or both operating together produce some effect, we say that the factors are confounded. *Confounding* is inherent in correlational research and leads to difficulties in interpreting data. In the example of the correlation between head size and intellect, we cannot say that variations in head size produced or caused differences in test scores, since head size was confounded with at least one other factor—age. We have relied just on the method of agreement (chapter 5), and we have not produced a comparison by the method of differences.

In other cases the relation between two factors may seem to allow a causal interpretation, but again, strictly speaking, this is not permitted. Some studies have shown a positive correlation between the number of handguns in a geographic area and the number of murders in that area. Proponents of gun control might use this evidence to support the contention that an increased number of guns leads to (causes, produces) more murders, but again this is not the only plausible interpretation. People in high-crime neighborhoods may buy handguns to protect themselves. Or some third factor, such as socioeconomic class, may mediate both. Thus, no conclusion is justified simply on the basis of a moderate or even high correlation.

Since correlations can be calculated between any two sets of scores, even high correlations often are accidental and not linked to one another. There may be a very high correlation between the number of preachers and the number of pornographic movies produced each year since 1950, with both being on the increase. But it would take an unusual theory to relate these two in a causal manner.

A high degree of correlation is given greater weight in cases in which obvious competing explanations (from confounding factors) seem less plausible. Most of the early evidence linking cigarette smoking to lung cancer was correlational, yet the conclusion was drawn (over the protests of the cigarette manufacturers) by the 1964 Surgeon General's report that cigarettes were likely to lead to or cause cancer. This eventually led to warnings on cigarette packages and a ban on advertising cigarettes on television, among other things. Thus the correlation was taken as indicative of a causal relation, probably because competing hypotheses seemed implausible. It seems unlikely, for example, that having lung cancer causes one to smoke more cigarettes (to soothe the lungs?). More plausible, perhaps, is that some underlying third factor (such as anxiety) produces the relationship or that it is accidental. We should mention, by the way, that experimental studies with animals (typically beagles) have established that there is a link between cigarette smoking and lung cancer.

As a final example of the pitfalls of the correlational approach, consider the negative relation between cigarette smoking and grades mentioned previously (chapter 1). Heavy smoking has been related to poorer grades. But does smoking cause poorer grades? It seems unlikely, and certainly there are obvious alternative interpretations. Students with poor grades may be more anxious and thus smoke more. Or very sociable students may smoke more and study less, and so on. Once again, no firm conclusions on the causal direction of a relation between two variables can be established simply because the variables are correlated, even if the correlation is perfect. As is true of the observational method, the correlational method is very useful for suggesting possible relations and directing further inquiry, but it is not useful for establishing direct causal relations. The correlational method is superior to the observational method because the degree of relation between two variables can be precisely stated, and thus predictions can be made about the approximate value of one variable if the value of the other is known. Once again, the greater the correlation (nearer $+1.00$ or $-1.00$), the better the prediction.

**Low correlations: A caution.**   If high correlations cannot be interpreted as evidence of some sort of causal relation, we might think that we should at least be able to rule out a causative relationship between two variables if their correlation is very low, approaching zero. If the correlation between head size and test scores had been $-.02$, would this have ruled out our theory that greater head size leads to higher intelligence? Of if the correlation between smoking and lung cancer had been $+.08$, should we have abandoned the idea that smoking and lung cancer are causally related? The answer: sometimes, under certain conditions. But other factors can cause low or zero correlations and may mask an actual relationship.

One common problem is that of **truncated range.** If we are to calculate a meaningful correlation coefficient, the scores in each of the variables of interest must differ to some extent. A certain amount of spread or variability in the numbers must exist. If in the panels of table 9–1 all the head sizes were the same and the test scores varied, the correlation between the two would be zero. Work it out yourself. If we looked at the correlation between head size and intellect only in college students, it might be quite low because the differences between the two variables evident in this group of subjects may not be very great compared with the population at large. This could happen even though there might be a positive (or negative) correlation between the two variables if head size were sampled over a wider range. So, the problem of restricted range can produce a low correlation even when an actual correlation exists between two variables.

You might think that everyone would recognize this problem and avoid it, but it is often more subtle. Consider the problem of trying to predict success on the basis of Scholastic Aptitude Test (SAT) scores at a college with very high admission standards. The scores on the verbal and quantitative subtests can range from 200 to 800, with average (mean) performance of just below 500. Imagine that mean scores at our hypothetical college are 700 on each subtest. The admissions officer computes a correlation between combined SAT scores and freshman grades and finds it to be + .10, very small indeed. Her conclusion: SAT scores cannot be used to predict grades in college. The problem, however, is that only scores from a very restricted range were considered, specifically very high ones. People with low scores were not admitted to the college. Thus, the truncated-range problem is very likely to be a factor here. If the college had randomly admitted people and then after the fact had determined the correlation between SAT scores and grades, the correlation might have been much higher. Psychologists often use homogeneous populations such as college students, so the restricted-range problem must be carefully considered in interpreting correlations.

A final problem in interpreting low correlations concerns whether certain assumptions underlying the use of a particular correlation coefficient have been met. If critical assumptions are not met, its use may be inappropriate and lead to spuriously low estimates of relationship. These assumptions have not been discussed here, but you should check on them in a statistics book before employing Pearson $r$ or any other correlation coefficient. For example, one assumption underlying Pearson $r$ is that the relationship between the two variables is linear (can be described by a straight line) rather than curvilinear, as in the hypothetical (but plausible) relationship between age and long-term memory shown in figure 9–2. At very young ages the line is flat, then it increases between ages 3 and 16, where it again levels off until late middle age, where it drops slightly, until very old age, where it decreases at a greater rate (Craik, 1977). Thus we can predict recall of words from age fairly well, but Pearson $r$ will be rather low since the relation between the two variables is not linear. The presence of a nonlinear relation could be checked by plotting a scatter diagram as in figure 9–1 or 9–2. Low correlations, then, might not reflect an absence of relationship, but only that the assumptions of the particular coefficient employed were not met.

## Internal Validity in Correlational Research

Does watching violent TV programs cause aggressive behavior? Eron, Huesman, Lefkowitz, and Walder (1972) measured children's preference for violent programs and how aggressive the children were as rated by their peers. For these third-graders, Eron and co-workers found a small positive

**FIGURE 9–2**

*A hypothetical figure depicting the curvilinear relation between memory and age. Although memory is related to age in a systematic fashion and we could predict recall by knowing age, Pearson r would be quite low since the relation is not linear.*

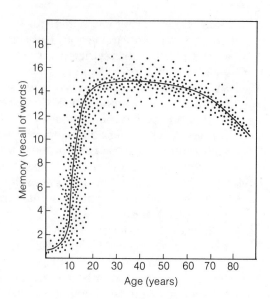

correlation, $r = +.21$, indicating that children who were more aggressive tended to watch more violent TV (and less aggressive children tended to watch less violent programs). How are we to interpret this positive correlation? Can we say that watching violent programs causes aggressiveness? The answer is no, and to see why this is the case, all we have to do is turn our causal statement around and assert that being aggressive causes a preference for violent TV. We have no reasonable way to decide upon the possible direction of causality, based on this one correlation coefficient.

As noted earlier, when we do not know the direction of causality (violent TV causes aggression versus aggressive traits cause a preference for violent programs), there is a strong possibility that some third, confounded variable is the cause of the obtained relation. In this example, researchers did not control either the programs watched or the initial aggressiveness, so they cannot rule out other variables, such as genetic differences in aggressiveness or differences in home life. Internally valid causal statements are difficult if not impossible to make on the basis of a single correlation coefficient.

The internal validity of correlational research may be enhanced by examining patterns of correlations. One technique is called the **cross-lagged-panel correlation** procedure. Eron and co-workers used it in a ten-year follow-up study of the same children in the "thirteenth" grade. The results are summarized in figure 9–3. The correlation between a preference for violent TV and aggression was essentially zero ($r = -.05$) in the thirteenth grade. Similarly, they found a negligible relation between preference for violent TV in the third and thirteenth grades ($r = +.05$), but they obtained a moderate relation between aggressiveness in the two grades ($r = +.38$), indicating that it is a somewhat stable trait. Of more interest are the cross-lagged correlations (the ones along the diagonals of the figure) in assessing the direction of the relationship. Do aggressive people watch violent TV, or does watching violent TV produce aggressiveness? We can determine which of these two possibilities is most likely by examining the diagonal correlations. Essentially no relationship exists between aggressiveness in the

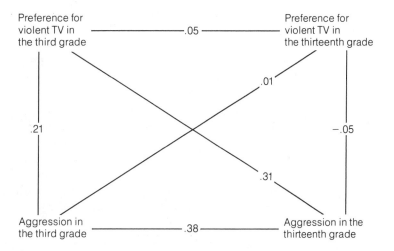

**FIGURE 9–3**

Correlations between a preference for violent television programs and aggression as rated by peers for 211 males over a 10-year period. The important cross-lagged correlations are on the diagonals. (After Eron, Huesman, Lefkowitz, and Walder, 1972. Copyright 1972 by the American Psychological Association. Reprinted by permission of the author.)

third grade and watching violent TV in the thirteenth ($r = +.01$). However, a fairly substantial correlation exists between a preference for watching violent TV in the third grade and exhibiting aggressiveness in the thirteenth ($r = +.31$). In fact, the relation is even greater than the relationship between these two variables shown in the earlier study when the subjects were third-graders. Thus the direction of relation seems to be that watching violent TV programs in the third grade may produce aggressiveness later. The underlying assumption is that if one variable causes the other, the first (watching violent TV programs) should be more strongly related to the second (aggressiveness) later in time than when the second (effect) variable is measured at the same time as to the first (cause). In other words, causes should take some time to produce their effects (see figure 9–3).

Using these cross-lagged panel correlations and other complex analyses, Eron and colleagues concluded that watching violent TV programs early in life probably causes, in part, aggressive behavior later in life. Recent research by Eron (1982) supports this conclusion. Of course, many other factors contribute to aggressiveness, but this is one example of how cross-lagged panel correlations can aid in increasing internal validity in correlational research. Note, however, that our causal statements cannot be as strong as those which come from experiments because the method of differences was not used.

The general strategy of the cross-lagged procedure, then, is to obtain several correlations over time, and then, on the basis of the size and direction of the $r$s, determine what leads to what. The cross-lagged technique is fairly new to psychological research and has the obvious drawback that the research project may be very time consuming. Nevertheless, this method for enhancing the internal validity of correlational research has been used in several problem areas, such as showing that a large vocabulary enhances the ability to spell (rather than the other way around) and that air pollution is an important cause of death in large cities rather than death being a cause of pollution (Cook and Campbell, 1979).

In addition to cross-lagged-panel correlations, there are several other statistical procedures used to try to gain a better understanding of causation in correlational research. Some of these include partial correlation, multiple-regression analysis, and path analysis. As is true of the cross-lagged procedure, these other techniques involve an examination of several relations and not just a single correlation. These statistical techniques are described in numerous texts (see especially Cook and Campbell, 1979). Although this book is not concerned primarily with statistical techniques, we should note that these additional techniques are important aids to interpreting correlational research. As a general rule, remember that internal validity is always suspect in correlational research because of possible third-variable confounding. Cook and Campbell, as well as others (for example, Rogosa, 1980), have noted that many of the assumptions underlying complex correlational research are questionable. Thus, we have additional reasons to suspect causal statements made on the basis of correlational evidence.

---

**CONCEPT SUMMARY**     Sources of invalidity in correlational research:

   *The third-variable problem*

   *Direction of causation*

   *Truncated range*

---

#### | | | | SUMMARY

**1.** Ex post facto research does not use a true independent variable, which means that internal validity is suspect, even though external validity is present.

**2.** In naturalistic observation it is necessary to delimit the range of behaviors that are observed. Usually a sequence of observational studies is conducted, with succeeding studies relying on earlier observations to refine and limit the observational focus.

**3.** Reactivity of the participants to being observed is a major source of invalidity in naturalistic observation.

**4.** Reactivity can be minimized by unobtrusive measures and unobtrusive observations. Participant observation may also reduce reactivity.

**5.** The Pearson product-moment correlation coefficient ($r$) gives an indication of the strength and direction of a correlation.

**6.** Scatter diagrams are a convenient way to represent how two variables covary.

**7.** Confounding is inherent in correlational research, because the direction of causation is usually difficult to determine, and a third (or many other) unknown variable(s) may underlie the observed relation.

**8.** A low correlation may be misinterpreted to indicate the absence of a relationship, when actually the low correlation is owing to a truncated range of scores on one or both variables.

**9.** Attempts to increase the internal validity of correlational research usually involve an examination of more than one correlation.

**10.** The cross-lagged-panel correlation procedure looks at patterns of correlations across time.

**11.** Although multiple correlations are more informative than a single one, you should use extreme caution when making causal statements on the basis of correlations, since the method of differences has not been employed.

## Key Concepts

confounding

cross-lagged-panel correlation procedure

delimiting observations

ex post facto

external validity

internal validity

participant observation

Pearson product-moment correlation coefficient (Pearson *r*)

reactivity

scatter diagrams

truncated range

unobtrusive measures

unobtrusive observations

## Exercises

**1.** [*Special Exercise.*] Suppose you have a theory that very handsome or beautiful people spend more time grooming in front of mirrors than people who are less attractive. Devise a way of examining this hypothesis by means of unobtrusive observations. Can you think of some unobtrusive measures that might be used?

**2.** [*Special Exercise.*] A psychologist studied the remote memory of college graduates by seeing how many names of old television programs they could correctly recognize. The results indicated that there was no correlation between the subjects' intelligence-test scores and their ability to recognize the names of old programs (*r* = +.07). Assuming that the procedure of memory testing was valid and that the age of the subjects was not a problem, can you think of some problems in this research that would prevent you from making a valid conclusion about the small *r*?

**3.** An illustration of how Pearson *r* is calculated for the data in (a) column of Table 9–1 is presented in appendix B. Work through this example, and then calculate *r* values for the data in (b) and (c) columns of table 9–1. Make sure that your *r* values are the same as those values given at the bottom of table 9–1.

**4.** The table here shows some fictitious data from a college admissions office. For ten students, we have the scores from the verbal portion of their Scholastic Aptitude Test (SAT) as well as their freshman grade-point average (GPA). The GPA is on a four-point scale, where F = 0, D = 1, C = 2, B = 3, and A = 4 points. Calculate the correlation coefficient between these two sets of scores. What might you conclude?

| Student | Verbal SAT | Freshman GPA |
|---|---|---|
| 1 | 471 | 2.00 |
| 2 | 403 | 1.50 |
| 3 | 510 | 2.25 |
| 4 | 485 | 2.00 |
| 5 | 575 | 2.25 |
| 6 | 445 | 1.75 |
| 7 | 400 | 2.50 |
| 8 | 590 | 3.25 |
| 9 | 560 | 2.50 |
| 10 | 555 | 2.75 |

**5.** [*Special Exercise.*] There are a number of potential methodological problems associated with observational research. Some of them are discussed in this chapter. What are these methodological problems and how are they overcome? For a more detailed discussion of these problems and others, see the suggested readings listed below.

## Suggested Readings

An extensive discussion of correlational techniques and methods of observation can be found in Kerlinger, F. N. (1985). *Foundations of behavioral research.* New York: Holt. 3d ed.

An interesting article on the use and development of observational skills is Boice, R. (1983). Observational skills. *Psychological Bulletin, 93,* 3–29.

A detailed discussion of methodological problems and considerations in observational research can be found in the following two articles: Woolfolk, A. E. (1981). The eye of the beholder: Methodological considerations when observers assess nonverbal communication, *Journal of Nonverbal Behavior, 5,* 199–204; and Wildman, B. G., & Erickson, M. T. (1977). Methodological problems in behavioral observation. In J. D. Cone and R. P. Hawkins (Eds.). *Behavioral assessment.* New York: Brunner/Mazel.

An extensive discussion of current research relating aggression to watching violent television can be found in Eron, L. D. (1982). Parent-child interaction, television violence, and aggression of children. *American Psychologist, 37,* 197–211.

## APPLICATION
### Difficulties of Observation

Direct observation may seem a straightforward and simple process: we open our eyes, look hard, and see what is there. But the history of science is replete with examples of phenomena which have eventually turned out to be radically different from the way they were initially perceived We consider two examples here, one from psychology and one from physics, to show that scientists must be continually vigilant for errors in their own observations.

Ivan P. Pavlov (1849–1936) was a Russian physiologist who won the Nobel Prize for medicine in 1904 for his work on how gastric juices operate during digestion. Pavlov also made important contributions to psychology by identifying and studying classical (or Pavlovian) conditioning. When Pavlov began studying learning in dogs, he and his co-workers discovered they had a problem that had not been apparent when they had previously been concerned only with the digestive system. The difficulty lay in how to describe the behaviors they were observing. Pavlov describes the problem of studying conditioned reflexes:

But how is this to be studied? Taking the dog when he eats rapidly, snatches something in his mouth, chews for a long time, it seems clear that at such a time the animal strongly desires to eat, and so rushes to the food, seizes it, and falls to eating. He longs to eat. .   . . When he eats, you see the work of the muscles alone, striving in every way to seize the food in the mouth, to chew and to swallow it. From all this we can say that he derives pleasure from it. .   . . Now when we proceeded to explain and analyze this, we readily adopted this trite point of view. We had to deal with the feelings, wishes, conceptions, etc., of our animal. The results were astounding, extraordinary; I and one of my colleagues came to irreconcilable opinions. We could not agree, could not prove to one another which was right. .   . . After this we had to deliberate carefully. It seemed probable we were not on the right track. The more we thought about the matter, the greater grew our conviction that it was necessary to choose another exit. The first steps were very difficult, but along the way of persistent, intense, concentrated thinking I finally reached the firm ground of pure objectivity. We absolutely prohibited ourselves (in the laboratory there was an actual fine imposed) the use of such psychological expressions as the dog guessed, wanted, wished, etc. (Pavlov, reprinted 1963, pp. 263–264).

A second problem is relevant to observation in all types of research. This is the issue of how much our conceptual schemes determine and bias what we "see." Pavlov's statement is eloquent testimony to the difficulty of establishing objective methods that would enable us all to see things in the same way. He had found it initially "astounding" and "extraordinary" that this difficulty existed, and was surprised at the elaborate pre-cautions needed to ensure objectivity. Philosophers of science have pointed out that our observations are always influenced by our conceptions of the world—if in no other way, at least by the particular observations we make (see, for example, Hanson, 1958, chapter 2). "Pure objectivity," to use Pavlov's phrase, is quite elusive, if not impossible. Objective and repeatable observation in science is an ideal to be approximated, but we may never be completely confident that we have achieved it. Nevertheless, we must make every possible step toward this ideal, which is what much of the technical paraphernalia of science is designed to help us with.

The problem of observations being unduly influenced by expectations is not, however, automatically overcome by the use of sophisticated equipment, as is evident in an illus-tration cited by Hyman (1964, p. 38). In 1902, shortly after X rays were discovered, the eminent French physicist Blondlot reported the discovery of "N rays." Other French sci-entists quickly repeated and confirmed Blondlot's discovery; in 1904, no fewer than 77 publications appeared on the topic. However, the discovery became controversial when American, German, and Italian scientists failed to replicate Blondlot's findings.

The American physicist R. W. Wood, failing to find N rays in his own lab at Johns Hopkins University, visited Blondlot. Blondlot displayed a card to Wood with luminous circles painted on it. Then he turned down the room light, fixed N rays on the card, and pointed out to Wood that the circles increased in luminosity. When Wood said he could see no change, Blondlot argued that this must be because Wood's eyes were too insen-sitive. Next, Wood asked if he could perform some simple tests, to which Blondlot con-sented. In one case, Wood moved a lead screen repeatedly between the N rays and the cards, while Blondlot reported the corresponding changes in luminosity of the circles on the card. (The lead shield was to prevent passage of the N rays.) Blondlot was consistently in error, and often reported a change in luminosity when the screen had not been moved. This and other tests clearly indicated that there was no evidence for the existence of N rays, despite their "confirmation" by other French scientists.

After 1909, there were no further publications on N rays. The mistake was too much for Blondlot. He never recovered, and he died in disgrace some years later. We can see from this dramatic example that even with the sophisticated apparatus of physicists, errors of observation are possible, and must be guarded against.

Hanson, N. R. (1958). *Patterns of discovery.* Cambridge: Cambridge University Press.
Hyman, R. (1964). *The nature of psychological inquiry.* Englewood Cliffs, N.J.: Prentice-Hall.
Pavlov, I. P. (1963). *Lectures on conditioned reflexes.* New York: International Publishers.

---

# ‖‖ PSYCHOLOGY IN ACTION
## Amount of Sleep and Tension Headaches

This project is a variation of a research procedure used by Hicks and Kilcourse (1983). These researchers were interested in the relationship between the number of hours of sleep subjects got and the frequency of tension or migraine headaches the subjects experienced. In a health survey, the researchers asked college students: (1) Estimate the number of hours of sleep you usually get each night, and (2) Do you have tension or migraine headaches often? _____ Sometimes? _____ Never? _____. Hicks and Kilcourse found an inverse relationship between these two variables; that is, people with more headaches slept less than those with fewer headaches. However, the researchers' mode of categorizing the frequency of headaches did not allow them to calculate a product-moment correlation coefficient.

You can modify their second question by asking: "Estimate the number of tension or migraine headaches you have each month." Ask twenty or so of your college acquaintances the modified question and the one concerning the estimated number of hours of sleep. Survey enough people so that you do not have a truncated range on one of your variables. Then calculate the *r* between these two variables.

You can enhance the reliability of your results by combining your data with those of classmates. If you pool your data, make sure that you and the others doing the project are surveying different people. When your data are combined, you may wind up with a large number of subjects, so you will find that MINITAB or some other statistical package will be helpful in calculating *r*.

To anticipate a later Psychology in Action project (chapter 10), you should collect some additional demographic data on your subjects, such as age, sex, and year in school.

Hicks, R. A., & Kilcourse, J. (1983). Habitual sleep duration and the incidence of headaches in college students. *Bulletin of the Psychonomic Society, 21,* 119.

| QUASI-EXPERIMENTAL RESEARCH Increasing internal validity when the variables are selected, not manipulated | *Sources of invalidity in quasi-experiments* |  |
|---|---|---|
|  | history<br>maturation<br>selection bias<br>mortality<br>delayed effects<br>regression artifacts |  |
|  | *How does one make valid causal statements in* |  |
|  | **Case Studies?** | Use *deviant-case analysis* (a nonequivalent control group); examine several dependent variables |
|  | **Interrupted Time Series?** | Use *nonequivalent control group;* study several dependent variables; search for additional natural treatments |
|  | **Subject-Variable Research?** | Use matching on potentially relevant characteristics; beware of regression artifacts |
|  | **Developmental Research (Age)?** | Use *cross-sequential design* to minimize generation and time-of-test confoundings; include *true independent variable* and look for interactions |

# 10 |||| Quasi-Experimental Research

*In this chapter, we consider research that includes independent variables that are selected rather than manipulated by the researcher. Many experiments done in the field, and laboratory experiments that have subject variables as the independent variables, use manipulations that occur naturally and either are selected by the investigator for subsequent observation or are actually investigated ex post facto. These natural treatments represent a form of correlation (they are, in essence, dependent variables), which poses many difficult control and interpretive problems.*

## |||| INTERNAL VALIDITY IN QUASI-EXPERIMENTS

*Quasi-experiments* refer to experimental situations in which the experimenter does not directly manipulate variables as in a typical laboratory experiment. In a quasi-experiment, some or all of the variables are selected, which means that they are not under direct control of the experimenter. Either the effects of natural "treatments" (such as disasters) are observed, or particular subject variables (such as age, sex, weight) are of interest. In either case, we must be wary of internal validity, because the experimenter does not manipulate the variables. In other words, the joint method of agreement and difference is not under direct control. In chapter 1 we noted that quasi-experiments have the advantage of being intrinsically interesting, and they also allow researchers to examine variables that would be unethical to manipulate directly. In this chapter, we will consider the pitfalls of quasi-experiments and how to minimize those problems.

### Natural Treatments

Ex post facto analyses of the effects of some naturally occurring event, such as a disaster or a change in school curricula, are usually interesting and important but are often difficult to interpret in a causal fashion. Most quasi-experiments involving naturally occurring treatments have a structure that is similar to some of the small-*n* experiments *(ABA)* discussed in chapter 8. We might, for example, have records of third-grade achievement before and after (the $A$ phases) the introduction of a new method for teaching reading (the $B$ phase). Note carefully: This example does not represent a true reversal design, because there is not a removal of the treatment to allow a return to the original baseline. In fact, most quasi-experiments of the general form **observation-treatment-observation** cannot be true reversal designs for two reasons: (1) the treatment is not under the experimenter's control; and (2) most natural treatments, such as curriculum revision, are likely to have long-term carryover effects. Not only must we be concerned with carryover effects, but we must also worry about the changes in the subjects themselves. If we examine the effects of a new reading program on third-grade achievement, one thing that is confounded with the introduction of our treatment is a change in the age of our subjects. Although age itself does not cause anything, many important changes correlate with age: more experience in school, better test taking, improved linguistic skills, better social adjustment, biological maturation, and the like. These changes, which are called **maturation,** nearly always can confound the results of research concerned with natural treatments. Furthermore in a classroom setting, numerous outside influences could affect the results. Since the researcher does not have direct control over the setting, the subjects are not insulated from numerous possible distractions as they are in a true experiment. This source of confounding is called **history** by Cook and Campbell (1979).

Thus, two particular threats to internal validity with naturally occurring treatments are the history of the subject and any changes in the subject that occur over time. Either or both of these factors could vary directly, inversely, or not at all with the intended treatment. In addition, the effects of history and change could interact in several different ways. Ways to minimize these difficulties (for example, matching) generally involve more active participation on the part of the experimenter. One thing that could be done in ex post facto analysis of the effects of reading techniques is to find a control-group third-grade class that did not have this new technique imposed upon it, which would result in a quasi-experimental design similar to the one shown in table 10–1. This looks like an ordinary experimental design, but remember—we have no direct control over the situation, and, as we shall soon see, by adding a matched control group we have incurred additional threats to internal validity. This type of design is sometimes called a **nonequivalent control group** design because random assignment to conditions is not used, and matching is attempted after the fact. Because the subjects are not randomly assigned to groups, we have the possible problem of **selection bias.** As discussed in chapters 2 and 6, random

**TABLE 10–1**

A hypothetical quasi-experimental design for examining curricula changes on third-grade achievement scores.

| | | | Time |
|---|---|---|---|
| Experimental Third Grade | Observe Achievement ⟶ | Change Reading Method ⟶ | Observe Achievement |
| Control Third Grade | Observe Achievement ⟶ | (no change) ⟶ | Observe Achievement |

Note: The third-grade classes are assumed to be very similar, differing only in terms of the imposed curriculum change. There was not random assignment to the two groups, and usually the control group is determined ex post facto. Thus, this design includes a nonequivalent control group.

assignment to conditions generally equates the subject characteristics in the various conditions of the experiment. With natural treatments, on the other hand, we select our subjects, not assign them, and we have no guarantee that our selection will be as unbiased as randomization in a true experiment.

We will now consider two quasi-experimental designs that appear in the psychological literature: the one-shot case study and the interrupted-time-series design.

## One-Shot Case Studies

We can view the one-shot case study in the following way: We have a long-term treatment on an individual and after the fact we obtain some measurements of that individual's thought and action. If we use the same notation that we used for the reversal design, we can call this an *AB* design (where *A* is the history and *B* is the current behavior). Treatments occur and then we observe their effects. Note that the treatments do not allow baseline observations. Viewing the one-shot case study as an *AB* design immediately points to the threat to internal validity: There is no baseline or control condition. **Deviant case analysis** is one way to obtain a control group in case-study research. In deviant case analysis, we take an individual as similar as possible to our case except for a crucial missing treatment (a drunkard for a father, a disabling illness, and so forth) and determine how the individuals are different from each other. The similar individual is a nonequivalent control, not a true control.

In a sense, therefore, interpreting a case history is similar to doing detective work. The typical case study involves a large number of dependent variables. Thus, the researcher who wishes to make causal statements on the basis of a case study has to look for important clues and then interpret the meaning of those clues in the context of all the other observations. Consider the case of Ruth L., who had a severe compulsion to clean everything. Her early experience with extremely fussy governesses and a desire to please her mother by being very neat and clean may have combined to later make her anxious in the presence of dirt.

Be careful how you interpret this discussion. As a laboratory research design, the one-shot case study with only one or two dependent variables would be sloppy and internally invalid. It is simply a terrible experimental design. However, in the typical case study, in which a great deal of information is available, causal "detective" work is often more reasonable and more likely to lead to internally valid conclusions. The researcher gains control by increasing the number and complexity of the observations. Remember that case studies involve retrospective reports, which means that the life-history "facts" may be forgotten or distorted. A cautious investigator might tentatively accept the reports as internally valid.

## Interrupted-Time-Series Design

The **interrupted-time-series design** is often encountered in quasi-experimental research, and it represents the logical extension of the general observation-treatment-observation design (see table 10–1). In the simplest time-series design, we have a single experimental group for which we have multiple observations before and after a naturally occurring treatment. Instead of examining just one or two third-grade classes, we could observe third-grade classes over several years. Or we could follow the achievement of the pupils across their entire school career. We need to know when the time series is interrupted by some treatment. Then we compare observations before and after the treatment to see whether it had any effect. Suppose we had records of public-school achievement for a city that added fluoride to its water one year. We would plot achievement against time and look for changes in achievement subsequent to fluoridation.

Such a hypothetical time-series analysis is shown in figure 10–1. What we look for in a time-series analysis are changes following interruption by the treatment. Note the rather dramatic increase in achievement following the introduction of fluoride. Can we assert that fluoride causes better achievement? No—for the same reason that we have difficulty interpreting a single correlation coefficient. Possibly, fluoride had an indirect effect, which means that some confounding factor is the principal cause. Perhaps fluoride reduced absenteeism resulting from dental appointments, and it was the reduced absences that permitted higher achievement. The possibility of such indirect effects makes it difficult for researchers to arrive at internally valid conclusions.

In our example, we could examine the absence rate before and after the introduction of fluoride. This could be done by plotting absence rate as well as achievement over time. Or we could try to find a control group that was similar to our experimental group but was untreated with fluoride.

**FIGURE 10–1**

A hypothetical example of a time-series analysis of the effects of fluoride on school achievement scores.

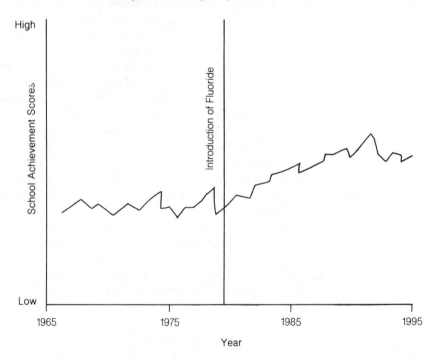

Finding a satisfactory control group might be difficult (imagine trying to find a town that differed from yours on only one dimension). Furthermore, such a control group would be nonequivalent and would leave us open to the problems of matching. Of course, our control group would have to have an absence rate similar to that of the experimental group, but it would still be nonequivalent because random assignment was not used.

Although a no-treatment control is often desirable, there are other things to look for in a time-series analysis that may be helpful (back to the detective's clues). We can use several dependent variables, such as absenteeism and the number of extracurricular activities, but we also can examine other treatments in much the same way that a case study is combed for additional hints. Since time series often involve a long time period, the researcher has to rely on the availability of complete and accurate records. In our example, we would need to have detailed records of every student, the administration, and the faculty in order to make internally valid statements. Without these records, we could not rule out plausible alternative explanations.

Even with the records, there may be difficulties. The innumerable other changes that can take place mean that confounding is always a threat to internal validity. Over a thirty-year period, performance in school could change for several reasons, and these natural treatments could operate independently or they could interact. Teachers and administrators change, curriculum changes, and economic changes occur, which could all lead to internal invalidity. A major source of confounding in a long-term time series is what is called **mortality.** Pupils graduate and move away, or they may die. Such changes in the group of subjects would lead to a special form of selection bias (Cook and Campbell, 1979), because the same subjects would not be studied before and after the introduction of the treatment.

The difficulties of the interrupted-time-series design are magnified when the effect of the treatment is delayed or masked by other variables (Cook and Campbell, 1979). The effects of fluoride are unlikely to be immediate. Fluoride reduces dental problems, such as cavities. If absenteeism changes because of a reduction in cavities, then we might have additional interpretive problems. Cavities take time to develop, and fluoride does not eliminate cavities once they have taken hold. Thus, the effects of fluoride might be delayed, and we would not be in a position to interpret what caused the changes in achievement. Furthermore, the effects of fluoride could be masked by the intrusion of some variable that counteracts its effects, such as a bubble-gum factory moving to town.

These cautions notwithstanding, the interrupted-time-series design is very useful, especially in applied research. A good example of a time-series analysis is a study by McSweeny (1978) who showed that the introduction of a small fee for directory assistance (the "Information" operator) dramatically reduced the number of directory-assistance calls. Since most such calls were for numbers and addresses that were published, the telephone company wanted to eliminate these nonessential calls in order to keep the lines open for essential assistance. The number of daily calls in Cincinnati dropped by about 70,000 following the introduction of the 20-cent fee, showing that the strategy was an effective one.

Phillips used time-series analyses to investigate some of the psychological reasons leading to death. In an extensive and interesting series of papers, Phillips examined some of the causes of natural death (1972), the precipitants of suicide (1977, 1978), and the causes of homicides (1983). His general strategy involves determining the number of deaths before and after a particular event. Thus, death rate is the dependent variable, and the quasi-independent variable is the event that interrupts the time span over which Phillips makes his observations. Let us examine how he used an interrupted-time-series analysis to investigate the effects of mass-media violence on homicide rates in the United States.

Phillips began his study of the effects of media violence on homicides by carefully examining the literature on television violence and aggression (see the discussion in chapter 9 about the work by Eron and associates). From this literature, he concluded that aggression was most likely to occur following a story in which violence appeared to be (1) justified, (2) exciting, (3) real, and (4) rewarded. A natural violent event that fits these characteristics is a heavyweight-boxing match. Using an interrupted-time-series analysis, Phillips determined the number of homicides that occurred before and after boxing matches that received wide media presentation over the period 1973–1978.

Phillips found a remarkable 12.4 percent increase in homicide rates following the publicized boxing matches. He also found that this increase could not be attributed to extraneous variables such as the season of the year or the day of the week. If there is a causal relationship here, how did Phillips determine the aspects of prize fighting that lead to increase in homicides? Phillips became a detective. First, he determined that boxing matches do not simply precipitate a homicide that would have occurred in the absence of the match. He arrived at this conclusion by showing that the number of homicides did not go down before boxing matches, which they would have to do if the homicide rate is roughly constant over time and is merely pushed into reality by the match. Second, Phillips ruled out the possibility that the homicide rate increased because boxing matches are associated with gambling. He found that other major sporting events usually associated with gambling, such as the Super Bowl and the World Series, do not lead to an increase in the homicide rate.

Phillips concluded that the relationship between boxing and homicide rate is probably a result of modeling; that is, social learning processes that induce people to model or imitate others seem to account for the increase in homicides following the major prize fights. Phillip's reasoning went like this: If imitation or modeling is important, then the victims of homicides should be similar to the victim in the boxing match. This means that if a young white male loses a boxing match, for example, then the murders of young white males should increase, but the murders of young black males should not. Phillips found substantial evidence to support his modeling idea: The increase in homicide rate following a boxing match mostly includes murders of people who are very similar to the losers of the match.

Phillip's use of the interrupted-time-series analysis has been a valuable way to determine the effects of media violence on homicide rate. His use of detective work in trying to arrive at a causal analysis of his findings is a good lesson in probing for answers and rejecting alternative explanations.

| | |
|---|---|
| **CONCEPT SUMMARY** | **Increasing Internal Validity** |
| | *In case studies, use* |
| | Deviant-case analysis |
| | Nonequivalent control |
| | Multiple dependent variables |
| | *In interrupted-time-series studies, use* |
| | Nonequivalent control |
| | Multiple dependent variables |
| | **(Beware of confounding caused by lack of control.)** |

|||| **DESIGNS EMPLOYING SUBJECT VARIABLES**

Much research in psychology is concerned with differences in the way various groups of people behave. A **subject variable** is some measurable characteristic of people. Examples are numerous and include intelligence (IQ), weight, anxiety, sex, age, need for achievement, attractiveness, race, ability to recall dreams, as well as many types of pathological conditions (schizophrenia, alcoholism, brain damage, and so on). Subject variables are often used in psychological research, but their use demands special consideration since investigation or selection of them is made after the fact. Thus, because the subject variables are not manipulated directly, designs using subject variables represent one more type of quasi-experimental research.

In experiments, an investigator has control over manipulation of the independent variable; it can be manipulated while all else is held constant. If we are interested in the effect of pornographic movies on physiological arousal and later sexual excitement, we can take two statistically equivalent groups of people (or the same people at different times), show them a movie with pornographic scenes included or omitted (while we hold other variables constant), and measure their responses. We can then be confident (but never certain) that the difference between the movies produced any observed differential effect in arousal. The case is very different with subject variables, though. An experimenter cannot manipulate a subject variable while holding other factors constant; he or she can only select subjects who already have the characteristic to some degree, and then compare them on the behavior of interest. If the subjects in the different groups (say, high, medium, and low IQ) differ on the behavior, we cannot conclude that the subject-variable difference produced or is responsible for the difference in behavior. The reason is that other factors may vary with the subject variable and thus be confounded with it. So if high-IQ subjects perform some task better than low-IQ subjects, we cannot say that IQ produced or caused the difference, because the different groups of subjects are likely to vary on other relevant dimensions such as motivation, education, and the like. When subject variables are investigated, we cannot safely attribute differences in behavior to them, as we can with true experimental variables. Such designs, then, essentially produce correlations between variables, and we should beware of the same types of confounding that occur in correlational research. We can say that the variables are related, but we cannot say that one variable produced or caused the effect in the other variable.

This is a very important point, so let us consider an example. Suppose an investigator is interested in the intellectual functioning of people suffering from schizophrenia. People diagnosed as belonging to this group are given numerous tests meant to measure various mental abilities. The researcher also gives these tests to another group of people, so-called normals, as a control measure. He or she discovers that schizophrenics do especially poorly (relative to normals) in tests involving semantic aspects of language, such as understanding the meaning of words or comprehending prose passages. The investigator concludes that the schizophrenics perform these tests more poorly *because* they are schizophrenics and that their inability to use language well in communication is a likely contributing cause of schizophrenia.

Studies like this are common in some areas of psychology. Conclusions similar to those just mentioned are often drawn, but they are completely unjustifiable. Both conclusions are based on correlations, and other factors could well be the critical ones. Schizophrenics may do more poorly than normals for any number of reasons. They may not be as intelligent, as motivated, as educated, or as wise at taking tests. Possibly, the fact that they have been institutionalized for a long time with resulting poverty of social and intellectual intercourse accounts for the differences. We cannot conclude that the reason the two groups differ on verbal tests is schizophrenia or its absence in the two groups. Even if we could, it would certainly not imply the other conclusion, that language problems are involved in causing schizophrenia. Again, all we would have is a correlation between these two variables, with no idea of whether or how the two are causally related.

Use of subject variables is very common in all psychological research, but it is absolutely crucial in areas such as clinical and developmental psychology, so the problems with making inferences from such research should be carefully considered. A primary variable in developmental psychology is age, a subject variable, which means that much research in this field is correlational in nature. In general, the problem of individual differences among subjects in psychology is often ignored, though there are often appeals to consider the problem as crucial (for example, Underwood, 1975). Let us look at some ways to make more sound inferences from experiments that use subject variables.

## Matching

The basic problem in the investigation of subject variables, and in other quasi-experimental research, is that whatever differences are observed in behavior may be caused by other confounded variables. One way to try to avoid this problem is by **matching** subjects on the other relevant variables. In the comparison of schizophrenics and normals we noted that the two groups were also likely to differ on other characteristics, such as IQ, education, motivation, institutionalization, medication, and perhaps even age. Rather than simply comparing the schizophrenics to normals, we might try to compare them to another group more closely matched on these other dimensions so that the main difference between the groups is in the presence or absence or schizophrenia. For example, we might use a group of neurotics who, on the average, are similar to the schizophrenics in terms of age, IQ, length of time institutionalized, sex, and some measure of motivation. When the two groups have been matched on all these characteristics, then we can more confidently attribute any difference in performance between them to the factor of interest, namely, schizophrenia. By matching, we attempt to introduce the crucial characteristic of experimentation— being able to hold extraneous factors constant to avoid confoundings— into what is essentially a correlational observation. Our goal is to be able to infer that the variable of interest (schizophrenia) produced the observed effect.

There are several rather serious problems associated with matching. For one thing, matching often requires a great deal of effort because some of the relevant variables may be difficult to measure. Even when we go to the trouble of taking the needed additional measures, we may still be unable to match the groups, especially if few subjects are involved before matching is attempted (for example, research on an unusual type of brain damage or other medical disorder). Even when matching is successful, it often greatly reduces the size of the sample on which the observations are made. Thus, we then are less confident that our observations are reliable (stable and repeatable).

Matching is often difficult because crucial differences among subjects may have subtle effects. In addition, the effects of one difference may interact with another. Thus, subtle *interactions* among matched variables may confound the results. To illustrate these difficulties, let us reconsider some of the work done by Brazelton and associates on neonatal behavior mentioned in the previous chapter (Lester and Brazelton, 1982).

Brazelton's primary interest is in cultural differences in neonatal behavior as measured by the Brazelton Neonatal Behavioral Assessment Scale. The general strategy is to compare neonates from various cultures and ethnic groups with neonates from the United States. In these quasi-experiments, culture or ethnic group, which is a subject variable, is the quasi-independent variable. Attempts are usually made to match the neonates from different cultures along various dimensions such as birth weight, birth length, and obstetrical risk (including whether the mother received medication during birth, whether the baby was premature, and so on). Lester and Brazelton show that there is a synergistic relationship among these factors. **Synergism** in a medical context means that the combined effects of two or more variables are not additive—the combined effect is greater than the sum of the individual components—which means that the variables interact. The way in which neonatal characteristics and obstetrical risk interact is as follows. Studies have shown that the behavior (as measured by the Brazelton scale) of slightly underweight infants is more strongly influenced (negatively) by small amounts of medication taken by the mother than is the behavior of neonates who are closer to the average in weight. So it is very difficult to match subjects appropriately because low birth weight has additional subtle effects on the behavior of the children. Even though the neonates are carefully selected, subtle and interactive effects of the matched variables can influence the results. This is an especially difficult problem in Brazelton's work, because much of his research has examined neonates from impoverished cultures, where birth weight is low and obstetrical risk is very high. Generally, you should remember that matched variables are rarely under direct control, which means that the possibility of confounding is always present.

Another problem with matching involves the introduction of the dreaded **regression artifact.** This is discussed in chapter 12, but we will explain it briefly here. Under certain conditions in many types of measurements a statistical phenomenon known as **regression to the mean** occurs. The mean of a group of scores is what most people think of as the average—the total of all observations divided by the number of observations. For example, mean intelligence in a sample of sixty people is the sum of all their intelligence-test scores divided by 60 (see appendix A). Generally, if people who received extreme scores (that is, very high or very low) on some characteristic are retested, their second scores will be closer to the mean of the entire group than were their original scores. Consider an example. We give 200 people a standard test of mathematical reasoning for which there are two equivalent forms, or two versions of the test that are equivalent. The average (mean) score on the test is 60 of 100 possible points. We take the fifteen people who score highest and the fifteen who score lowest. The means of these groups are 95 and 30, respectively. Then we test them again on the other form of the test. We might find that the means of the two groups are 87 and 35. On the second test, the scores of the two extreme groups regressed toward the mean; the high-scoring group scored more poorly, whereas the low-scoring group had somewhat better scores. This sequence of events is illustrated in figure 10–2. In the high-scoring group, some people whose true scores are somewhat lower than the scores they received were simply lucky on the first test and scored higher than they should have. When retested, these subjects tended to score lower, nearer their true score. The situation is reversed for the low-scoring group.

This regression toward the mean is always observed when there is a less-than-perfect correlation between the two measures. The more extreme the selection of scores, the greater the regression toward the mean. It also occurs in all types of measurement situations. If abnormally tall or short parents have a child, its adult height will probably be closer to the population mean than to the height of the parents. As with most statistical phenomena, regression to the mean is true of groups of observations and is probabilistic (that is, it may not occur every time). For example, in the second test of mathematical reasoning, a few individual subjects may regress away from the mean, but the group tendency will be toward the mean. In any event, if we had selected subjects on the basis of their reasoning scores and then matched them in two groups, subsequent differences may have been caused by some treatment or may have been the result of regression to the mean. If we do not have the true scores, and if we do not use random assignment, then regression to the mean may be a confounding factor leading to changes in behavior.

**Figure 10-2**

Hypothetical changes in IQ scores resulting from regression to the mean. The high-scoring and low-scoring subgroups regressed toward the mean of the entire group when they were retested.

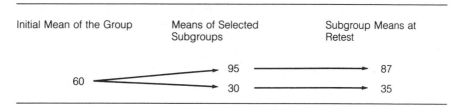

Ex post facto research and quasi-experiments with subject variables are conducted often to evaluate educational programs, so those who practice such research need to be aware of the many thorny problems associated with it. Without matching, an investigator may not be able to say much about the results. Matching helps alleviate the problem of confoundings in some cases, but then the possibility of regression artifacts arises. And many researchers seem unaware of this problem.

When matching is a practical possibility, and when regression artifacts are evaluated, we can be somewhat more confident of conclusions from our results. But we still have only a correlation, albeit a very carefully controlled one. Matching is useful, but it is not a cure-all. In our example involving schizophrenics, if the schizophrenics perform worse than the new matched control group of neurotics, can we then conclude that schizophrenia *produces* inferiority in language usage? No, we cannot. There could be something else, some other difference between the two groups. We can never be sure that we matched on the relevant variables. Perhaps neurotics are superior in their use of language!

| **CONCEPT SUMMARY** | **Matching** |
| --- | --- |
| | Be alert for |
| | **Subtle interactions** |
| | **Regression artifacts** |

## Age as a Variable

One subject variable, age, deserves its own discussion for two reasons. In the first place, developmental psychology is a popular and important part of scientific psychology. In the second place, age as a variable poses very difficult confoundings that have generated some interesting and powerful research designs.

Suppose we are interested in determining the effects of age on the ability to use two types of learning strategies. One type of strategy might improve recall (Tversky and Teiffer, 1976), because when our subjects use this strategy correctly they will be able to associate one thing with another. In remembering the names of simple objects (for example, *knife*, *tree*, and *cat*), subjects recall one object which helps them recall another object (for example, recalling *cat* reminds them of *tree*, because cats climb trees and trees make them think of *knife*, because they carve their initials in a tree with a knife). We will call this the recall strategy. The other strategy might help your subjects recognize things (as in a multiple-choice test). In this recognize strategy, subjects look for minute differences among objects so that they can later specify which of several similar objects was actually shown to them.

We decide to see how children of different ages utilize these two strategies. How are we going to design our project? The most straightforward (and most likely) design is the **cross-sectional design.** Using this method, we would select children of different ages (for example, ages 5, 8, and 12) and then randomly assign half of each age group to one of the strategy conditions. Or we could use the more time-consuming **longitudinal method.** Here, we would test a subject when he or she was 5, then at 8, and then again at age 12. In the cross-sectional method, we figuratively cut through the age dimension, and in the longitudinal method we follow a particular individual along the age dimension. These two developmental methods are quite often used in studies in which age is a variable, yet they both contain serious confoundings that could make the internal validity of the research highly suspect.

What are some of these serious confoundings? Before we can discuss them, we need to discuss age itself. Since age is a subject variable, it cannot be considered a true independent variable. Age is a dimension; in particular, it is a time dimension along which we can study behavior. Some developmental psychologists have suggested that we consider age as a dependent variable because it is a variable that varies with other subject characteristics from birth to death (Wohwill, 1970).

In any event, we cannot directly vary age, so we must be wary of any concomitant variables associated with it. Different research designs have different confoundings. In the cross-sectional method, age is confounded with the generation of birth. Not only is one of the authors of this textbook twenty-two years older than his son, he and his son also differ in terms of the generations in which they were born, and generation itself is a complex variable. In this sense the generation gap is real—someone born in 1942 is not just twenty-two years older than someone born in 1964. The older person was born into a different world populated by different people who had different attitudes and education than the counterparts (what the developmental psychologists call cohorts) of the younger person.

When we use the longitudinal method, we follow a particular individual who will maintain the same cohorts. With this method, therefore, we do not have to worry about the generation/age confounding. However, the longitudinal method confounds age with time of treatment or testing. If you test the memory of a child at age 5 and then at age 12, not only is the person seven years older on the second test, but the world has changed in the interim. Using the longitudinal method, we might find that college students' attitudes about energy conservation in 1985 have changed since the subjects were 5 years old in 1971. Is the change in attitude owing to a change in age or to a change in the world?

Figure 10–3 shows some research designs that can be used when age is a variable. Note that the **time-lag design** (the design indicated along the

**FIGURE 10–3**

*Some quasi-experimental designs used when age is a variable at the time of testing.*

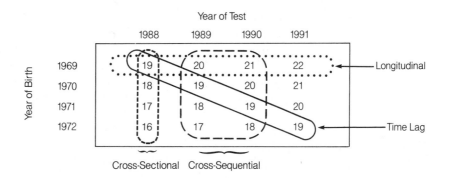

diagonal) aims at determining the effects of time of testing while holding age constant (only 19-year-olds are tested in this example). As is true of the cross-sectional design, the time-lag design confounds cohorts of the subjects with the target variable.

Schaie (1977) has outlined many sophisticated designs to overcome the confoundings we have just described. One of these designs is illustrated in figure 10–3. The **cross-sequential design,** indicated by the central box, involves testing two or more age groups at two or more time periods. Note that this design includes features of the other three designs we have mentioned. Subjects of different ages are tested at the same time as in the cross-sectional method; an individual is tested successively as in the longitudinal method; and different subjects of the same age are tested at different times as in the time-lag design. In the cross-sequential design, therefore, the researcher can determine the effects of most of the potential confoundings. Consider just one example from figure 10–3—the 20-year-old who was born in 1969. The effects of age are tested both longitudinally and sectionally (a 20-year-old is compared with subjects of different ages in 1989 and that 20-year-old is tested again in 1990). If the effects of age are the same in both of these comparisons, then we can rule out cohorts and time of testing as important confoundings.

The cross-sequential design is cumbersome. Many subjects have to be tested over a period of time, which may make a research project impractical. Therefore, this design is not used as often as it probably should be. Most developmental researchers use the more manageable cross-sectional design.

A typical cross-sectional experiment has age as a quasi-independent variable as well as another true independent variable. In the Tversky and Teiffer (1976) study outlined earlier, three age groups were tested on their ability to use the recall strategy and the recognize strategy. The recall strategy improved retention at all ages (5, 8, and 12), but the recognize strategy proved beneficial only to the oldest children. Such results are an example of an *interaction* (see chapters 4 and 6), which means that the effects of one variable are dependent on the level of the other variable—the effects of type of strategy depended on the age of the subjects.

The tactic of using age and a true independent variable in developmental research means that the researcher expects an interaction. Whatever variables are confounded with age (in the Tversky and Teiffer study, age was confounded with grade in school in addition to the usual confoundings associated with a cross-sectional design) might be differentially affected by a true independent variable. The clever psychologist tries to pinpoint what components of age determine thought and behavior, and the search for particular interactions may help. Note that the purpose of both the cross-sequential design and the search for interactions is to enhance the internal validity of developmental research. Age is a complex variable, and we must simplify it in order to have a valid analysis.

A final way that the internal validity of research with subject variables can be enhanced is to use construct validity as a mode of converging operation (see chapters 2 and 12). Instead of searching for interactions to try to tease apart the true effects of a subject variable from those effects owing to variables that are correlated with it, we could coordinate the results with a particular theory. Highly-refined theories of personality and child development use this technique. For example, Piaget developed a comprehensive theory of child development that makes particular predictions about the kinds of behavior exhibited by children at different stages of cognitive development (Piaget and Inhelder, 1969). Although these stages are partially associated with chronological age, they are presumed to be a function of maturation and experience. Thus, the stage of development, as shown in certain kinds of behaviors, and not age, is viewed as the causal factor. Piaget's theory specifies how and when these stages will occur, so that age-related behavioral differences should fit into the network of the theory. When the predicted changes do occur (that is, when they agree with Piaget's theory), we say that there is construct validity for the theory. The theory permits one to rule out the effects of a correlated variable (age in this case) and converge on an explanation of why certain behaviors are observed.

| CONCEPT SUMMARY | Threats to Internal Validity in Quasi-Experimental Research With Some Solutions | | |
|---|---|---|---|
| | *Research Procedure* | *Threat to Internal Validity* | *Ways to Enhance Internal Validity* |
| | Case studies | Source of causation; baseline "condition" maturation; history; selection bias | Deviant case analysis (a nonequivalent control); detective work |
| | Interrupted time series | Changes in subjects and environment; delayed effects | Nonequivalent control group; detective work |
| | Subject variables | Dimensions on which to match; regression artifacts | Matching; include true independent variable and seek interactions |
| | Age as a variable | Confoundings with: time of testing, generation of birth | Cross-sequential design; include a true independent variable and seek an interaction; converging operations |

| | | | **SUMMARY**

**1.** In research that is internally valid, it is possible to make straightforward statements about cause and effect. In quasi-experimental research, in which there is no direct control over the independent variables (they are examined after the fact) causal statements may not be possible because of confoundings.

**2.** Quasi-experiments have one or more ex post facto components: either naturally occurring variables or subject variables (or both).

**3.** When there are natural treatments, problems such as history, maturation, selection bias, and nonequivalent control groups may confound the results.

**4.** One-shot case studies and the interrupted-time-series design are two quasi-experimental procedures with low internal validity. The researcher must be a good detective to determine the causal agents in these procedures, because mortality and delayed effects are threats to internal validity.

**5.** Likewise, the researcher needs to be a good detective when he or she tries to handle subject variables by matching subjects on the basis of particular characteristics. Just what characteristics are to be matched often poses a difficult problem, and those characteristics may regress toward the mean in many instances, and subtle interactions among the matched variables may occur.

**6.** Age as a subject variable provides many real threats to internal validity because it is confounded with numerous other factors.

**7.** Using the cross-sequential design and looking for interactions of age with true independent variables are two ways to enhance the internal validity of developmental research.

## Key Concepts

| | |
|---|---|
| age | nonequivalent control group |
| cross-sectional method | observation-treatment-observation |
| cross-sequential design | one-shot case study |
| deviant-case analysis | quasi-experiment |
| history | regression artifact |
| interaction | regression to the mean |
| interrupted time series | selection bias |
| longitudinal method | subject variable |
| matching | subtle interactions |
| maturation | synergism |
| mortality | time-lag design |

## Exercises

**1.** [*Special Exercise.*] A considerable amount of evidence indicates there is an inverse relationship between birth order and intelligence (Zajonc and Marcus, 1975). Birth order refers to the order in which children enter the family unit (first born, second born, and so on). Intelligence tends to be lower for later-born children than for the earlier ones. List as many factors as you can that might be confounded with birth order. How might you determine which of these factors is important in influencing intelligence? In other words, how do we enhance internal validity when birth order is the variable? What quasi-experiments can be done?

**2.** The *Journal of Applied Psychology* often reports studies that used an interrupted-time-series design. Examine several recent issues and note, in particular, any control conditions that are included.

**3.** Age as a variable in geriatric research (the study of old age) is often more difficult to analyze than in child development studies. Why?

**4.** Discuss the ways in which mortality, selection bias, history, and maturation can threaten the internal validity of quasi-experiments.

## Suggested Readings

Donald T. Campbell has written a great deal about quasi-experimental research. The best place to begin is with the first book listed here. More detail is presented in the second one. Campbell, D. T., & Stanley, J. C. (1963). *Experimental and quasi-experimental designs for research*. Chicago: Rand McNally. Cook, T. D. and Campbell, D. T. (1979). *Quasi experimentation: Design and analysis issues for field settings*. Chicago: Rand McNally.

---

## ‖‖‖ APPLICATION
### Predicting Behavior from Case Studies

Case studies provide substantial information about an individual, and clinical psychologists often rely on them to determine the causes of current behavior. We pointed out in this chapter that such an endeavor may be difficult, and we also noted that valid causal statements from case studies may be impossible. Are case studies good for predicting future behavior? You know that prediction on the basis of correlations can be successful. Can the information from a case study be used in the same way?

Given that you are a psychology major taking a college-level course in research methods, can we predict that you will be a research psychologist? Based just on your case, our prediction is likely to be inaccurate. If we examine the case histories of some psychologists, it is easy for us to see that prediction can be poor.

John B. Watson (1878–1958), founder of the school of behaviorism in psychology and pioneer in the field of learning, was a philosophy major as an undergraduate. After he was forced out of academic psychology because of an adulterous affair with a graduate student, he became an executive in a large advertising agency.

Probably none of his classmates or teachers would have predicted that B. F. Skinner would become an influential and famous psychologist. Skinner was an English major as an undergraduate, and after graduation he spent some time leading a bohemian life as an aspiring writer of fiction.

As a more contemporary example, consider Gordon H. Bower, the distinguished investigator of learning and memory. Bower, who wanted to be a psychiatrist, attended college on a baseball scholarship. He had received offers of professional baseball contracts, but a fortunate experience in an experimental psychology course and a desire to avoid the military draft led him to choose experimental psychology over baseball.

Each of these vignettes indicates that accurate predictions from case studies can be difficult. This difficulty is very obvious in the field of criminal law, where it is often necessary to predict whether convicted felons will continue their criminal behavior or be law-abiding citizens following their release. There is considerable controversy in psychology and psychiatry concerning attempts to predict the future actions of a dangerous criminal, such as a murderer or a rapist. Accurate predictions about rapists and murderers are crucial, but difficult. Usually only a weak probabilistic statement can be made: "The chances are that this criminal will not rape again." Most people do not consider this a strong enough prediction. To generate more accurate predictions, we need more detailed information than a simple case study can provide. At the very least, a substantial number of correlations among various kinds of behavior patterns must be made before reasonable predictions are possible. An important area of research awaits you.

## PSYCHOLOGY IN ACTION
### A Quasi-Experiment

Try these quasi-experiments as a follow-up to the correlational research described in "Psychology in Action" for chapter 9. The project there dealt with the relationship between amount of sleep and tension or migraine headaches.

If you recorded demographic data (age, sex, year in school) for each of your subjects in the sleep/headache research, you can do a quasi-experiment using one of your demographic variables to define your independent variable. For example, you could compare the number of headaches reported by men and women. Another quasi-experiment could examine the amount of sleep obtained by freshmen, sophomores, juniors, and seniors. There are other possibilities, which we will allow you to figure out.

Although these quasi-experiments may look like ordinary between-subjects experiments, do not forget that you have not manipulated an independent variable—your groups here are determined by selection, not manipulation. Thus, you need to be cautious about making causal statements.

# IV PRAGMATIC ASPECTS OF RESEARCH

| THREATS TO VALIDITY Reactions of participants, researcher bias, and problems in communication | Questions to Answer |
|---|---|
| | *How will the participants in my project react?* Is my naturalistic observation unobtrusive? Can I assess normal and motivated forgetting in my case study by corroborating evidence? Is my test able to counteract the problem of response styles? Does my experimental plan contain "blinding" or other procedures to ensure that the subjects react appropriately to the independent variable? |
| | *How will I, the researcher, influence the results of my project?* Will my personal characteristics influence the behavior or the subjects? Have I defined a research plan that permits me to treat all participants the same (except for deliberate variation)? Do I have to be blind to certain aspects of the research in order to be unbiased? Am I aware of my own biases and preconceptions? Am I an objective researcher? |
| | *Do other scientists understand what I am investigating?* Are my terms operationally defined? |
| | *Does my project represent an externally valid attempt to determine why people think and act as they do?* Are my subjects representative? Have I selected meaningful variables to examine and vary? Is the setting I plan to use ecologically valid? |

# 11 ||| Threats to Validity in the Research Procedure

Conducting a good research project is difficult because there are numerous problems awaiting you. The purpose of this chapter is to forewarn you about many of these difficulties, most of which have to be confronted before all the details of your research plan have been determined. Other pitfalls can influence how you interpret the *results* of research; these will be examined in a later chapter. In this chapter we will discuss (1) how the researcher and subject react to being involved in research; (2) how to ensure accurate communication among scientists; and (3) how to try to determine the validity of your research procedure.

## ||| PITFALLS RESULTING FROM REACTIONS OF ||| PARTICIPANTS

Good research requires careful planning and careful interpretation. Several pitfalls can hurt both the conduct of research and its interpretation. In this chapter, we are concerned with those problems that can arise while you are conducting your research. We will tell you about several problems you can avoid by carefully planning ahead.

In many areas of psychological research, we can view the reactions of the participants not only in terms of the project itself, but also in terms of everyday social interaction. Suppose you are responding to a survey that asks you to estimate the number of times a day you think about sex. Go ahead and make a guess. Now, suppose you are asked the same question in a personal interview. Would your answer in the interview be the same as the one given in the survey? You might be reluctant to say "I think about sex at least fifteen times a day." On the other hand, writing "15" in response to a question on an anonymous survey might not bother you at all. In general, ordinary social interaction may put demands on a research participant that changes the way he or she reacts.

Weber and Cook (1972) used the phrase **subject roles** to highlight the important social and psychological factors that occur in research and may influence the results. As used here, *role* refers to how the participants perceive the research setting and how they then react to it. Since the perceived role may determine how the subjects respond, unnatural responding, **reactivity,** could occur and confound the results. We will consider several examples of reactivity and some possible solutions.

The term **demand characteristics** was at one time the standard way to refer to subject reactivity. The phrase was coined by Orne (1962) to highlight the pressure put on people participating in research. Orne emphasized the obedience of the subject to the researcher's demands. We believe that reactivity is a more general term to describe the roles that subjects may adopt than is the phrase *demand characteristics.*

## Reactivity in Descriptive Research

**Naturalistic observation.**     The effects of subject reactivity in observational research were discussed in chapter 9. Here, we will remind you that unobtrusive observations and unobtrusive measures are the primary means of countering reactivity in an observational setting. As we shall see, variations of such procedures may be valuable in other settings.

**Case studies.**     Case studies are individual histories, which means that much of the evidence in these studies is **retrospective** in nature (that is, it comes from looking back into the past). Looking backward often causes problems. One difficulty is that the evidence may be inaccurate as a result of ordinary forgetting. We may not remember what our thoughts and actions were in nursery school because what has happened since then interferes with our memory of early events. A second problem has to do with reactivity—**motivated forgetting** may occur. This refers to the active way in which humans reconstruct their past experiences. People often distort unpleasant events, which results in "remembering" the wrong things. The bad things are forgotten (the shoplifting episodes we took part in as 9-year-olds), and the good things are remembered and sometimes made even better (the stellar piano recital or the forty-seven merit badges earned in scouts). Research has shown that mothers and fathers often misremember events about their own children's early years (Robbins, 1963). This distorted remembering often has to do with emotionally related phenomena, such as when the child began toilet training and weaning. It is interesting that the errors in remembering tended to err toward what is recommended or expected by child-rearing experts (for example the noted pediatrician Dr. Benjamin Spock). One way around this problem is to get corroborating evidence from other individuals. This may be difficult to do, and the corroboration is also subject to both kinds of forgetting.

**Surveys, interviews, and tests.**     Demands that lead to motivated forgetting are also present in other forms of descriptive research. Since many of the responses on tests and surveys are not retrospective, we talk about the possible contamination as **response style** or *response sets.* Different people may have habitual ways of answering questions. These habits may result from how they view themselves or from the expectations of the researcher and society (more on this later). In general, there are three kinds of response styles: yea-saying or **response acquiescence,** naysaying or **response deviation,** and **social desirability.** College-bound high school graduates respond "no" to the question "Do you use marijuana daily?" Does this answer reflect the true behavior of these people, or does the answer reflect the habitual tendency to say no (response deviation)? Or the answer could be a socially desirable one because marijuana is a controlled substance and many authorities frown upon its use. The high school graduates not heading for college tended to answer yes to this question twice as often as the college-bound (Bachman and Johnston, 1979). Is this answer a true one, or does the "yes" simply indicate that these people are likely to acquiesce and say yes regardless of what the question is? Based on the answer to this one question, we cannot determine whether the answer is a true one or the result of a particular response style.

Edwards (1953, 1957) has developed an interesting solution to the response-style problem. The respondent is presented with a question that demands a **forced choice** between equally desirable and undesirable alternatives. On Edwards's test, called the Personal Preference Schedule, the respondent has to select one of two activities or indicate which of two thoughts or feelings better reflects the characteristics of the respondent. For example, the respondent might have to choose between painting a picture or writing a play. This forced-choice technique is designed to minimize contamination caused by response styles.

Associated with the problem of response styles is a problem more difficult to cope with, the **volunteer problem.** Volunteer subjects differ in a number of ways from potential participants who do not volunteer (Rosnow and Rosenthal, 1970). Volunteers tend to be more intelligent, better educated, more cooperative, better adjusted, and in greater need of social approval than nonvolunteers. These characteristics of volunteers could strongly influence participant reaction. A volunteer has somewhat of a super response style: Everything about the subject plays a role in determining the sorts of responses he or she gives. The volunteer problem might also limit the generality of results in an experiment.

What the volunteer problem means in terms of your own research is that you have to be careful in sampling from the population of participants available to you. If your test or survey is boring and requires that the respondent go to extreme lengths to be cooperative (trudging through a blizzard at 11:00 P.M. to the psychology building), then the answers you get may be based on a biased sample of opinion (this is an example of selection bias; see chapter 10). The problem is also serious, as Rosnow and Rosenthal point out, in opinion surveys that rely on volunteer mailings or phone-ins. What are we to make of the results of a magazine survey that relies on voluntary compliance of the readers? Or, how about the radio survey that solicits calls from its listeners? In both cases we do not know anything about the people who did not respond, nor do we know anything about the people who do not read that magazine or listen to that station. We can find out about the nonrespondents by expending a great deal of time and effort. Usually, this effort is not made.

There are three solutions to the nonrespondent problem. First, you can get a **random sample** of the entire population that is available to you. This means that every potential respondent has an equal chance of being questioned. Second, you could give the nonrespondents some kind of extra incentive to participate in your project. They could be offered money or be given detailed information about the research project. The extra inducements might bias the results of the experiment, however, by treating some subjects differently from others prior to participation in the project. Third, you could replicate your research with additional samples of subjects. This would be a good solution if the problems associated with volunteers and nonrespondents were not likely to recur in your replications.

## Correlational Research

Since test results and survey data often provide the bases for correlations, the problems just mentioned are applicable here. Demands on participants might be magnified in correlational research that involves two measures of the people that are taken at the same time. Participants do not usually react passively to the inquiries of the researcher. Instead, they often try to figure out what is going on and respond according to their perceptions of the project and in ways that will make themselves look good to the researcher (Weber and Cook, 1972). For example, suppose you surveyed a college population about their sexual and religious attitudes. Simultaneously (or a little later) you also asked them about their use of drugs. Most college students could figure out at least some purposes of the project.

## Experimentation

Walk up to a stranger and say, "Please do me a favor by doing ten push-ups." Repeat your request to several others. Then, repeat the procedure, but this time say, "I'm doing a psychology experiment. Please do me a favor by doing ten push-ups." The odds are that you will get very little compliance from the first group of people and very few refusals from the second group. People sometimes will do things in the name of science and experimentation that they will not ordinarily do (Orne, 1962). In other words, experiments may not only examine behavior, they may produce it! Reactivity can be an important source of contamination of experimental data.

Orne (1962, 1969) noted that subjects entering an experiment have some general notions of what to expect and are usually trying to figure out the specific purpose of the experiment. They are likely to believe that reasonable care will be taken for their well-being and that whatever the experimenter asks them to do will serve a useful purpose. Because many psychological experiments would provide uninteresting results if the true purpose were known, elaborate deceptions are often used to mask the goal of the experiment. But, as Orne points out, these might sometimes be rather transparent. At any rate, the general problem exists as to how the subject's expectations affect or determine her or his behavior in an experiment. Orne notes:

> Insofar as the subject cares about the outcome, his perception of his role and of
> the hypothesis being tested will become a significant determinant of his behavior.

The cues which govern his behavior—which communicate what is expected of him and what the experimenter hopes to find—can therefore be crucial variables. Some time ago I proposed that these cues be called "*demand characteristics* of an experiment." . . . They include the scuttlebutt about the experiment, its setting, implicit and explicit instructions, the person of the experimenter, subtle cues provided by him, and, of particular importance, the experimental procedure (Orne, 1969, p. 146, italics added).

Participant reaction may limit the generality of the results of an experiment because, if the results are produced by just the participants' perception of the experimental situation, they will not generalize to other situations. Frequently, when people know they are being observed, their behavior is greatly affected. One famous case of this is the **Hawthorne effect,** named after the Western Electric Company plant at which an experiment was conducted on factors affecting worker productivity (Homans, 1965). Six average women workers participated in a longitudinal study of factors affecting the rate at which they assembled telephone relays. First, the baseline rate of producing relays was measured. Then the women were placed in a special test room, and, after a period of adjustment to their new circumstances, they experienced a number of changes in their daily routine that were supposed to affect productivity. During one period of the study, rest pauses were inserted into their schedule, and later the frequency of pauses was increased. During another period, their method of payment was changed, and during yet another, a light lunch was provided, and so on. The experiment lasted for more than a year and the results were quite surprising. With few exceptions, no matter what changes were made—whether there were many or few rest periods, whether the workday was made longer or shorter, and so on—the women tended to produce more and more telephone relays. Although the reason for this change is difficult to determine (since a number of variables were confounded), the fact that the women knew they were in an experiment, felt the special attention, and wanted to cooperate are likely candidates. The workers knew that the experimenters expected the changes in the working conditions to affect them, so they did. The women kept working harder and harder. (For a different interpretation, see Parsons, 1974.)

Since the changes in behavior apparently resulted from the fact that the workers were in an experiment and not because of the independent variables that were manipulated, we can say that the Hawthorne effect represents one kind of reactivity. Orne argues that to some extent experiments with humans always have this feature built in. The subject is an active participant interested in what is happening and is usually eager to help. Orne and his associates have done a great deal of research on demand characteristics in experimentation. Some of the most interesting studies deal with reactivity in hypnosis research.

Investigators have asked subjects under hypnosis to do all sorts of things, often with notable success. One apparently well-established finding is that subjects under hypnosis can be led to perform various antisocial and destructive acts, such as throwing acid in someone's face and handling venomous snakes (Rowland, 1939; Young, 1952). Orne and Evans (1965) suspected that this might have been owing more to the demand characteristics of the situation than to the effects of hypnosis. They asked subjects to perform a series of dangerous acts such as grasping a venomous snake, taking a coin from fuming acid, and throwing nitric acid in the experimenter's face. There were several treatment conditions: (1) subjects who were under deep hypnosis, (2) subjects who were told to simulate being hypnotized, (3) awake control subjects who were not asked to simulate hypnosis but who were pressed by the experimenter to comply with the requests, (4) awake control subjects who were not pressed to comply, and (5) people who were asked to perform the task without being made part of an experiment. The experimenter did not know which condition the subjects were in, so as to minimize bias. The results are summarized in table 11–1. As would be expected, people not in the experimental setting refused to carry out the antisocial tasks, but as other investigators had reported, a high percentage of hypnotized subjects did carry out the tasks as instructed. However, *all* simulating control subjects also performed the tasks and even the nonsimulating controls, if pressed to comply, performed them to a large extent, which demonstrates the power of the experimental situation. Thus, hypnosis is not necessarily responsible for subjects performing the antisocial acts. Rather, reactivity to the experimental situation, including the setting, the instructions, and the way subjects think they are supposed to behave while under hypnosis, is sufficient to produce the antisocial acts. Perhaps people can be induced to perform antisocial acts under deep hypnosis, but current studies do not offer reliable evidence to support this idea.

Weber and Cook (1972) described various social roles that could influence behavior in a laboratory setting. These roles are similar to the response styles we discussed. Subjects might adopt a **good-subject role** in accordance with the theory of demand characteristics put forth by Orne. A subject acting in a good-subject manner will do anything necessary to validate the experimental hypothesis. The **faithful-subject role** is one in which the participant attempts to be honest and faithful, even if he or she has some idea about the experimental hypothesis. The participant who exhibits a **negativistic-subject role** will attempt to sabotage or otherwise mess up the experiment (Masling, 1966, has called this the "screw you effect").

In an extensive review of the literature, Weber and Cook did not find much evidence that these roles played a significant part in the confounding of laboratory experiments. However, they did find some evidence for the importance of a fourth role—the **apprehensive-subject role** (also see Rosenberg, 1969). The apprehensive subject feels uncomfortable about being evaluated in an experiment, and because of this **evaluation apprehension** the participant tries to respond in a socially desirable way. Weber and Cook summarized a number of studies that point to evaluation apprehension as an important potential confounding in experiments. Unfortunately, predicting exactly what kinds of behaviors will be elicited by evaluation apprehension is very difficult. For example, Weber and Cook report that in conformity studies, subjects who have some idea about the purpose of the experiment tend to conform less than unaware subjects (because of apprehension, the aware subjects do not want to appear to be "sheep"). On the other hand, in learning studies in which better performance signifies a "better" subject, aware participants often perform better than unaware

**TABLE 11–1**

Percentage of Subjects Who Performed Dangerous Tasks in Response to Requests by the Experimenter (Adapted from Orne & Evans, 1965. Copyright 1965 by the American Psychological Association. Adapted by permission of the author.)

| Subject group | Grasp venomous snake | Take coin from acid | Throw acid at experimenter |
|---|---|---|---|
| Real hypnosis | 83 | 83 | 83 |
| Simulating hypnosis | 100 | 100 | 100 |
| Waking control— pressure to comply | 50 | 83 | 83 |
| Waking control— without pressure to comply | 50 | 17 | 17 |
| Nonexperimental | 0 | 0 | 0 |

ones. Thus, it is hard to predict what changes in behavior may occur as a result of apprehension.

Countering the effects of reactivity in experimentation is often very difficult. Unobtrusive measures and observations may not work in a laboratory setting, because most people know they are in an experiment. Consequently, many psychologists do their experiments in a natural setting. This **field research** is similar to naturalistic observation, except field experiments have a real or ex post facto independent variable. Going into the field, where people may be unaware that they are being experimented upon, poses additional problems: Loss of control that is characteristic of laboratory experiments may exist; and unobtrusive measures may violate some of the ethical standards of research. Furthermore, field studies are not necessarily more externally valid than laboratory experiments. Dipboye and Flanagan (1979) found that field studies in industrial and organizational psychology generally involve a narrow range of subjects, settings, and dependent variables.

One way to insert unobtrusive measures into a laboratory experiment is to use **deception.** Deception can push reactivity in a particular direction, so that the subject will respond naturally to the true independent variable. In a famous example of deception by Milgram (1963), participants were led to believe they were giving shocks to a "learner" in order to improve the rate of learning. In fact, the shock apparatus was fake and the learner just pretended to receive strong shocks. Many people regard this sort of deception as unethical. However, deception by omission may sometimes be acceptable. Typical behavior may be elicited without *necessarily* violating ethical standards when certain facts about the study are not mentioned. For example, let us say that half the subjects in a memory experiment receive special instructions on how to learn and remember. The control group does not receive these instructions; this group serves as a baseline for "natural" memorizing. Whenever deception by omission is used, we must be careful to maintain the dignity of the person being studied (see chapter 4).

When we withhold some pertinent information from the participant, we say we are running a **blind experiment.** A good example is a study by Carver, Coleman, and Glass (1976), who examined the suppression of fatigue by Type A and Type B men. Type A's are aggressive people who really strive to win in competitive situations, and they are supposed to be prone to coronary heart disease (Wright, 1988). Type B's are less aggressive and competitive, and they are less likely to have heart problems. Types A's and B's were put on an exercise treadmill to see how long they would exercise relative to their maximum capacity. Carver and associates also got subjective estimates of fatigue from the participants. During the course of the experiment, the researchers made every attempt to remove any hint of competition—both against the clock and against other people's performance on the treadmill. In fact, the subjects were told they would be removed from the treadmill after a predetermined time. In actuality, the time on the treadmill was determined by the participant, who indicated when he had had enough. Confronting the Type A's with evidence of competition might have enhanced their competitive drive, and the experimenters wanted the A's to become fatigued in the absence of any apparent competition. So, making the subject blind to the nature of the experiment seemed important. In this instance, the deception does not seem unethical. Carver and co-workers found that the Type A's worked longer on the treadmill than B's. Despite the extra effort, the A's reported less fatigue than the B's.

Another way to control reactivity is to perform a **simulated experiment,** as Orne and Evans (1965) did in their hypnosis study. As mentioned earlier, they used people who simulated being hypnotized as well as subjects who were hypnotized. The logic here is straightforward. The demands of the situation are assumed to be the same for subjects in both the experimental condition and the simulating control condition. If the experimental manipulation (hypnosis) is truly effective, then the behavior of the experimental group should differ reliably from that of the simulating group. A simulated experiment is sometimes called a **thought experiment** (Richman, Mitchell, and Reznick, 1979). In general, the approach is to test an independent variable on the experimental group. Simulating subjects were told about the independent variable and are asked to indicate what they would do in that situation. If the results of the thought experiment are highly similar to the results owing to the independent variable, we can conclude that there are important reactivity factors contaminating the effects of the independent variable.

---

| CONCEPT SUMMARY | **Subject Reactivity: Pitfalls and Their Solutions** | | |
|---|---|---|---|
| | *Research Procedure* | *Pitfall* | *Possible Solution* |
| | Observation (chapter 9) | Reactivity | Unobtrusive measures and observations |
| | Case study | Motivated forgetting | Corroborating evidence |
| | Surveys, tests, and correlation | Response styles | Forced-choice responding |
| | | Volunteer problem | Random sample, extra incentives, replications |
| | Experimentation | Reactivity (Hawthorne effect) | Deception ("blind") |
| | | | Simulated experiments |

## | | | | **RESEARCHER BIAS**

While you are carefully watching your subjects to make sure there are no disruptive reactivity effects in your project, you should be spying on someone else—yourself. Barber (1976) makes a distinction between the investigator, the person responsible for designing, analyzing, and interpreting research, and the experimenter, the person actually conducting the study. He has presented an extensive and valuable discussion of ten investigator and experimenter effects. Since you are likely to be both investigator and experimenter in your research, we combine our discussion of these problems under one heading—**researcher bias.**

The researcher, just like the subject, is fallible. Thus, we need to know where and when the researcher can have detrimental effects on the outcome of an experiment. Pitfalls associated with the researcher can occur either deliberately or inadvertently. We hope that there are few deliberate effects, because they can be very costly.

### Deliberate Researcher Bias

When scientists engage in research, they expend substantial time and effort. Therefore, instances of deliberate fabrication are not surprising. A researcher who is enamored of a particular theory may fudge the data enough to support the theory. A researcher with strong political or social beliefs may report some results and suppress others. For the same reasons, these biased scientists may design their projects such that negative or ideologically bad results will be unlikely. Surely there is no place in scientific psychology for such insidious practices.

How do we guard against deliberate bias? We have to assume that scientific training emphasizes objectivity and the acquisition of knowledge. The goal of scientific psychology is to find out why people and animals think and act as they do—it is not to support particular theories or political credos. Scientists must be as objective as possible, especially when data conflict with personal interest.

How do we detect deliberate bias? Science is self-correcting; truth will win out. Unfortunately, it may take a long time for fakery to be discovered. A sure way to speed up detection is to increase the number of direct replications (Barber, 1976). Direct replications are exact repetitions of an experiment (see chapter 12). If important pieces of research are not directly repeatable, then the scientifically valid data will make their appearance in the literature by replacing the bogus findings.

### Inadvertent Researcher Bias

Inadvertent effects are probably more widespread and harder to detect than deliberate researcher bias. Just how often they occur is difficult to determine, because many parts of the research process may be inadvertently contaminated. A scientist's political beliefs, for example, could result in an incomplete survey that assesses some attitudes and not others. This does not necessarily indicate deliberate bias, but may merely represent the fallibility of the scientist. The scientist can think about only a limited number of things at a time, so the research designs will partially reflect his or her preferences. This sort of problem can have very subtle manifestations. For example, animal learning is not a politically sensitive research area. However, the research design, apparatus, and species of animal can be determined by the researcher's preconceptions of animal learning (Barber, 1976). Thus, the questions asked by the researcher and the answers that are obtained may be the result of the researcher's preconceptions. There are two solutions to this problem: (1) Researchers should be aware of their own underlying preconceptions (these preexisting notions are what philosophers of science call "paradigms"; Kuhn, 1962); and (2) many scientists should undertake a variety of attacks on a problem.

Another source of researcher bias derives from treating participants in a project differently over and above any *planned* differences in treatment. A substantial amount of evidence indicates that how the researcher treats the subjects can have a profound effect on the results of the experiment. (Barber, 1976). What measures can be taken to prevent a researcher from inadvertently influencing the outcome? Suppose you were the researcher in the study by Carver, Coleman, and Glass (1976) about fatigue suppression in Type A's and Type B's. You know ahead of time that half your subjects (the A's) might be prone to coronary heart disease. You record the exercise time on the treadmill as the subjects are working at or beyond their maximum oxygen consumption. Would you treat Type A's and Type B's differently? Would subtle body movements or the tone of your voice clue the Type A's to take it easy so they do not overstress their hearts? (This is unlikely, since the Type A's were young—they supposedly had the *potential* for coronary problems later in life.)

There are two ways to minimize this type of researcher bias. In the first place, the researcher must conduct the project as uniformly as possible for all participants (see chapter 2). The only differences in treatment should be those which are introduced deliberately—independent variables, different questions in a survey, different observing times, and so on. Type A's must be treated exactly like Type B's. This was done by Carver and coworkers, who even went so far as to eliminate the data on a subject who was acquainted with one of the data collectors.

A second way to minimize inadvertent differential treatment is to make the researcher *blind* with respect to potentially important attributes of the participants or the task. The experimenters in the study by Carver and associates did not know whether a subject was a Type A or a Type B, which diminished the chances of treating the Type A's differently on the treadmill. When subjects' behaviors are recorded in some way for later analysis, the people who score the recorded behavior often are blind to the treatment administered to a particular subject. In this instance, being blind to the treatment condition increases the likelihood that the scorer of the results will be objective and not be biased by his or her expectations of what the results should be. The tactic of making the researcher blind is the other side of the coin of making the subjects blind to aspects of the task. If both the subject and the researcher are blind, we have what is called a **double-blind** design.

Double-blind designs are common in medical experiments that test the effectiveness of drugs. The experimental group is given the drug, and the control group is given a placebo substance. A **placebo** (the word is derived from a Middle English word meaning *to be pleased*) is a pharmacologically inert substance (a "sugar pill") given to control subjects to deceive them. The controls, along with the experimental group, assume they are receiving a real drug, so the expectations are the same for the two groups. Not only are the placebo subjects blind, so is the researcher. The researcher does not know who is receiving the placebo and who is getting the real drug. In the typical drug experiment, the substances have code numbers that cannot be deciphered by the person administering the drugs. However, someone knows who received the placebo and who received the drug. These precautions decrease the possibility of the control subjects being treated differently than the experimental subjects (except, of course, one group receives the independent variable and the other does not). The double-blind design is not always foolproof (see chapter 4).

The personal attributes of a researcher may bias the actions of the participants. The age, sex, race, and authority of the researcher may determine how the subjects react. For example, a subject in an interview is more likely to report sexual thoughts when the interviewer is of the same sex (Walters, Shurley, and Parsons, 1962). This kind of problem is solved if there is more than one researcher and each one follows the research protocol exactly. In your own research, you may not be able to enlist assistance from others. Therefore, you should try to treat each subject identically.

We have emphasized strict adherence to procedure as one way to minimize inadvertent researcher bias. This is especially important for minimizing the possibility of recording data incorrectly. In every condition for every subject, we must record data in the same way. This means that before the project begins, we have to define exactly what an acceptable datum is. Furthermore, in animal research we must guard against **anthropomorphizing.** This refers to the tendency to attribute human characteristics, especially thoughts and feelings, to animals. Anthropomorphism is sometimes obvious, as in "The dog loved and respected its master," and sometimes not so obvious as in, "The rat was hungry so it ate a lot." A similar problem arises in describing the thoughts and feelings of primitive tribes. An observer might attribute standard western thought to primitives, as in "Their love of individual liberty conflicted with the socialist ideology of the tribal council." All of these examples are actually theoretical statements that may not be warranted on the basis of the data. How do we define "love" in a dog? Does it mean that the dog wagged its tail or came when it was called? What is hunger for a rat? These sorts of issues are examined in the next section.

| | |
|---|---|
| **CONCEPT SUMMARY** | **Controlling Researcher Effects** |
| | *Deliberate Effects* |
| | Objectivity; Direct replications |
| | *Inadvertent Effects* |
| | Uniform treatment; Double-blind design |

#### | | | | **RELIABILITY OF COMMUNICATION**

No serious discussion, scientific or otherwise, can progress very far unless the participants agree to define the terms they are using. Imagine that you and your date are having a friendly argument about who is the best athlete of the year. How do you define athlete? You both would agree about such common sports as tennis, swimming, and gymnastics. But what about more esoteric sports like frisbee throwing, hang-gliding, and hopping cross-country on a pogo stick? Should practitioners of these activities be considered for your athlete-of-the-year award? Until this question of definition is answered, your discussion may just go around in circles.

Similar problems can arise in scientific discussions. Let us imagine that scientists in psychophysical laboratories in West Lafayette, Indiana, and Clayton Corners, Arkansas, are studying tail-flicking responses of the horseshoe crab to flashes of light. One laboratory finds that crabs give tremendous tail flicks, whereas the other lab finds that crabs hardly move their tails at all. The scientists are very concerned and they exchange terse letters and autographed pictures of their respective crabs. Eventually they discover the reason for the discrepancy. They were each defining the flash of light differently (since their flashes were of different durations), even though the brightness of the two flashes was similar. When they adjusted their flashes to be the same, both labs obtained the same results. This example is a little farfetched since, as we all know, crabs cannot autograph their pictures. Furthermore, all good psychologists know the importance of defining the stimulus exactly, so this confusion would probably not have occurred in the first place. But this example does show what *could* happen if scientists were not very careful about defining their terms.

Although social conservation and scientific discourse both require definitions, the requirements for scientific definition are more stringent. Terms that are perfectly adequate for ordinary conversation are usually too vague for scientific purposes. When you state that someone has a pleasant personality, other people have a good idea of what you mean. But when a psychologist uses the term *personality* in a technical sense, a great deal of precision is necessary. This important distinction between technical usage and common usage occurs frequently in psychology. It is all too easy to slip and use technical language imprecisely, especially in psychology. Words like *information, anxiety,* and *threshold* have broad everyday meanings, but they must be precisely limited when they are used in a technical sense. The most common way of providing such technical meaning is by using an **operational definition** (chapter 2).

An operational definition is a formula for building a construct in a way that other scientists can duplicate. "Take the eye of a newt, the leg of a frog, three oyster shells, and shake twice" is an operational definition, although we may not know what is being defined. This recipe can be duplicated and so meets the major criterion for an operational definition. You can tell from this example that an operational definition does not have to make any sense, as long as it is clear and can be copied. In general terms, something is operationally defined when the procedures or operations used

**FIGURE 11–1**

*A schematic diagram of the apparatus used by Morin and Grant (1954). Stimulus lights and response buttons are not linked in any obvious relationship. For example, pressing the leftmost response button does not control the leftmost light, but instead turns off the third light from the left.*

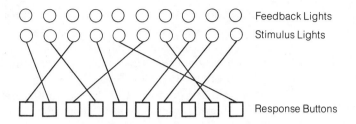

Feedback Lights

Stimulus Lights

Response Buttons

to produce and measure it are clearly specified. For instance, we might operationally define a construct called *centigrams* as the product of your height in centimeters and your weight in grams. Since any scientist can easily determine the centigram score, this is an operational definition. Of course, it probably could not be used for any important scientific purpose, but the potential utility of an operational definition is a separate issue from its clarity.

The major virtue of operational definitions is that they help prevent us from confusing technical concepts with their equivalents in common language. Let us look at an experiment where participants were faced with two rows of ten lights and one row of ten buttons (Morin and Grant, 1954), as shown in figure 11–1. A stimulus lamp went on, and a correct button press would extinguish it and present the next stimulus lamp, and so forth. This task would be simple if each light were connected to the button directly underneath it. However, lights and buttons were haphazardly joined. This was why the top row of feedback lights was used. Pressing any button lit up a feedback light showing which stimulus light (that is, the one directly below the feedback light) was controlled by that button. After several days of practice, the experimenters tested participants to see whether they had learned the light-button relationships. All participants could correctly draw a diagram linking lights and buttons, so the experimenters disconnected the feedback lights. The time taken to press the buttons went up dramatically. A similar effect occurs when we learn to operate a typewriter. It does not take long to be able to diagram the relationship between keys and letters. But even though we know where each letter is on the keyboard, we need a fair amount of practice before we can type equally well with our eyes opened or closed. This seems like a contradiction. On the one hand, the ability to draw the diagram correctly is evidence that the light-button relationships were learned. On the other hand, the increase in time is evidence that the relationships were not learned.

This apparent contradiction stems from using the term *learning* in its common-language sense. Technically, learning can never be observed directly. Instead, it is inferred from a change in behavior—that is, we need at least two measures of behavior before we can state that learning occurred. In the light-button experiment, one measure of learning was the decrease in time needed to press the buttons with succeeding days of practice. However, this measure was taken when the feedback lights were connected, so the fact that subjects performed differently (needed more time) when conditions were changed by removing feedback lights is not really astonishing. The other measure of learning—the ability to accurately draw a diagram—assumes that no one could have drawn the diagram before the experiment began, since participants would have had no experience with the arbitrary connections between lights and buttons. Thus there was no need to obtain two drawings (before and after); and only one (after) was requested. This showed learning. Note that the two operational definitions of learning are quite different. The first uses time as a measure, and the second uses ability to draw a diagram. Since these definitions differ, we should not think it odd that the results of two different measures of learning also differ. The confusion arises from the common-language habit of calling both of these measures indices of learning. Since they have separate operational definitions, we could call them by different names, for example, learning (time) and learning (drawing). Thus, measurement of any process that cannot be directly observed, but must instead be inferred, should be tied to operational definitions.

The way in which terms are operationally defined is illustrated in table 11–2. In this example, the concept, learning, is defined by the operation used to produce it (practice on the button-pressing task) and the operations used to measure it (drawing a diagram versus time to perform the task). Since learning was examined in an experimental situation, we can specify both the causes of learning (changes in the independent variable) and the results of those causes (changes in the dependent variables). If we simply measured or assessed learning by means of observation or test (or survey), we could define our concept only in terms of dependent variables. The additional operational specification that results from experimental manipulation indicates another advantage of experimentation over other forms of research. When independent variables are varied, both "sides" of a concept can be tied to the operations that are performed. When there are no independent variables, the operations that produced the concept under investigation may be indeterminate.

The problem with having a few dozen varieties of learning, each with its own operational definition, is that so many definitions can make it difficult for us to get any kind of theoretical integration. Considerable economy or parsimony exists when we have to discuss just one kind of learning. Psychology, like any science, strives for general concepts that unify data. Thus, undue preoccupation with operational definitions might seem to be pushing us in the wrong direction. The solution is to seek operational definitions that come together upon common theoretical constructs. (This notion of converging operations is so important that it is discussed at length in chapter 12.) Since giving up operational definitions entirely, as some phi-

**TABLE 11–2**
Operational definitions of learning in the Morin and Grant experiment.

| Operation Producing Concept | Concept Defined | Measurements |
|---|---|---|
| Button-pressing practice | Learning | Time to perform |
| Button-pressing practice | Learning | Drawing accuracy |

Note: Practice, the antecedent condition, produces learning, which is reflected in the behaviors that were measured (the dependent variables). Since antecedent conditions are rarely manipulated directly in nonexperimental research (such as tests, surveys, and naturalistic observation), we usually have to guess at or infer the conditions that produced what we are studying.

losophers of science have suggested, is too risky—it would lead to difficulties as in the earlier example of the light flashes and horseshoe crabs—we must aim for a theoretical framework that pulls our operational definitions together.

When we link our operational terms, we make them valid. In other words, our concepts become useful, reasonable explanations, not just clear, reliable ones. In a very real sense, then, the goal of scientific psychology is to provide valid explanations (concepts) for why we think and act as we do.

## EXTERNAL VALIDITY OF THE RESEARCH PROCEDURE

Does our research have anything to do with why people and animals think and act as they do? Have we selected an object of study that is representative? Is our research setting one that will yield a valid answer to our fundamental question? In sum, is our research externally valid?

We alluded to some of these issues in chapters 1 and 2. Several problems associated with external validity must be dealt with before a project is begun. In this section, we will detail the problems of subject representativeness, variable representativeness, and setting representativeness. We will also present some ways in which these problems can be handled.

### Subject Representativeness

Basic research in psychology relies heavily on two subject populations: white rats and college students. Are these organisms representative? Are data from these organisms pertinent to general statements about psychological processes?

One way to answer these questions is to say that rats and college students *have* to be representative. Rats and other animals are often used because the scientist can control the heredity and environment of animals more easily (and more ethically) than that of humans. Also rats and college students are readily available to most researchers. The justifications for using rats and college students (some might claim that they are being overused) are control, convenience, and ethics.

Limiting your observations to these populations is not problem-free. A major difficulty is **reversability** (Uttal, 1978). In mathematics, reversability refers to an attempt to determine the problem or equation from a solution. Consider the answer 7. Can we figure out what led to 7? Not without a great deal of additional information. The answer 7 could have come from $4 + 3 = ?$, $377 - 370 = ?$, $\sqrt{49} = ?$, *How many days are in a week?*, and an infinite number of other possibilities. Reversability poses a similar problem in research. Just because a particular behavior is observed both in a rat and in a college sophomore, it does not follow that the underlying processes (the mathematical equation) are the same in both instances. For example, if we damaged a rat brain in order to understand how the human brain works, we have to assume that the brain of a rat works the same way (that it has the same equation) as the human nervous system. Physiological psychologists make the assumption that the solution (the rat's behavior) is unique to a particular equation (the nervous system). In other words, they assume that by reversing the solution we arrive at the problem.

"So what?" some of you might say. "I'm not going to be a physiological psychologist." However, Uttal's point is also relevant to behavioral research that ignores physiological interpretations. Looking for learning in rats or other animals presupposes that there is a mechanism for the process in the same way that damaging a rat brain assumes there is a unique mechanism. Harlow summarized the dilemma this way: "Basically the problems of generalization of behavior between species are simple—one cannot generalize, but one must. If the competent do not wish to generalize, the incompetent will fill the field" (Harlow, Gluck, and Suomi, 1972, p. 716).

Obviously, generalization can be difficult. However, it can also be spectacularly successful. In the nineteenth century, Mendel, a Czechoslovakian monk, determined the basics of genetics by studying garden peas. More recently, the discovery of neurotransmitters in the brain that function like opiate drugs was based on work concerned with neural transmission in the reproductive organs of rats. If we view the results of animal research as a model or analogy, then we recognize that our cross-species generalizations are always tentative. We may have to perform many tests on many species before we can make strong conclusions.

The difficulties we have just examined also pertain to research that uses college students as subjects. How representative are the results obtained from such studies? The answer to this question is vague; it depends on the purposes of the research and the boldness of the investigator. If we are concerned with processes that are likely to be shared by all humans, such as basic sensory processes or simple forms of learning and retention, we can be fairly sure that our data on college students will be representative of human beings in general.

A difficulty arises, however, when we are interested in complex psychological processes. Language, problem solving, and sophisticated memorizing strategies require that the subject possess characteristics that may not be common to everyone. We cannot limit our psychology to normal human adults. Young children, Ibo tribesmen in Africa, and deaf mutes are likely to possess abilities that are different from those of the typical college student. Imagery may enhance memory in college students (Atkinson, 1975; Bower, 1972), but its success for young children (Tversky and Teiffer, 1976) has limits, and cross-cultural differences in the use of imagery exist as well (Cole, Gay, Glick, and Sharp, 1971).

The moral here is that we should be careful in generalizing on the basis of a single sample of subjects from a subset of the population at large. If we are too bold ("Imagery always aids retention, no matter who uses it"), we run the risk of being wrong. Again if we view the college student as a model for psychological processes in the same way that we view the white rat as a model, we will recognize that some of our conclusions must be tentative. This is particularly true when basic research findings are to be used for applied purposes. The generalization should be tried out on the target population before a particular policy or practice is implemented. Time and effort would be wasted if imagery training were instituted in a nursery school for the blind on the basis of Bower's (1972) work with college students.

## Variable Representativeness

Because science is analytic, the scientist usually designs a project that is manageable and direct in its purpose. What this means in practice is that the research project nearly always departs from real life. This is true even in naturalistic observation, in which the observer selects only a subset of the behaviors to record. Scientists also simplify their projects because they do not possess unlimited memory and attention spans. How do we select variables that are reasonable and worthwhile?

In the first place, we may select variables simply because we are interested in them. Scientific nosiness is not only the basis of science; it is also a perfectly respectable attribute. If we are interested in the mating rituals of blue-footed boobies, we go out and observe blue-footed boobies. The role of curiosity in part begs the question, however, because curiosity alone does not provide any clues as to what aspects of the boobies' mating behavior should be observed.

As we discussed in chapter 3, a good researcher must be familiar with the data base of a research problem. We should know what has been done in the past so we do not waste time studying something that has been established as relevant or irrelevant. For example, the boobies' feeding activity may be completely unrelated to their mating behavior. Here, too, theoretical predictions may be crucial. Remember, one of the important criteria of a good theory or a good hypothesis is testability. A theory should tell us what to look for in a particular problem area. From our standpoint, a theory is good as long as it is reasonably explicit in making predictions. Unfortunately, very few psychological theories make straightforward predictions. This ambiguity means that a lot of hypothesis testing depends on the wit and wisdom of the researcher, a state of affairs that makes it difficult to a list a set of rules for hypothesis testing.

Assuming that we have selected variables to observe or manipulate, eventually we will have to consider their representativeness. We can determine variable representativeness in the same way we determined subject representativeness. After we examine the data base and relevant theories, we should repeat our research with minor variations in the variables to begin establishing their representativeness.

## Setting Representativeness

Perhaps the major issue associated with representativeness has to do with the setting. Setting representativeness is often called **ecological validity.** It can be a serious problem in experimentation, where, by definition and through the imposition of control, the experimental setting is an artificial one. Neisser (1976, 1982), for example, questions the ecological validity of laboratory experiments, particularly those involving cognition and memory. He argues that psychologists have avoided studying natural memory in natural settings, which means that "the orthodox psychology of memory has very little to show for a hundred years of effort, perhaps because it has always avoided the interesting issues" (1982, p. 3). Neisser is correct in his concern for ecological validity, but, as we shall see, he is incorrect in his indictment.

When considering the problem of ecological validity, we need to distinguish between **realism** and **generalizability** (Berkowitz and Donnerstein, 1982). Realism refers to whether the experimental setting bears a resemblance to the real world. Do the experiments involving rats learning in Skinner boxes resemble any learning situation in the real world? The answer, of course, is probably not. However, the critical question has to do with the importance of this mundane realism. As was true of the problem of subject representativeness, our concern with ecological validity should be with the psychological processes. If we can demonstrate that the processes exhibited by rats in artificial settings are similar to the processes occurring in the real world, then we can say that realism is not a crucial threat to external validity. Thus, what must be important is the ability of an experimental result to generalize to other situations. Various tests try to determine whether the processes observed in the laboratory are also the processes involved in settings representative of the real world. In the next chapter, we will consider other aspects of generalization, but for now we will examine some direct tests of generalizability.

The strategy used to test the generalizability of experimental results is to repeat the observations in a natural setting—a field study. Obviously, studying memory in a classroom or decision making in a courtroom is less controlled than the corresponding laboratory study. This is why laboratory experiments are conducted—to provide an internally valid causal statement about a psychological process. If we are going to try to generalize our results beyond the laboratory, we may need to conduct a less well controlled field experiment. Before considering such tests of generalization, we should note that field studies do not necessarily permit broad generalization. As pointed out earlier, Dipboye and Flanagan (1979) found that a narrow range of subjects, settings, and variables had been used in field studies done in industrial and organizational psychology. The tests should be varied and not just "natural."

Many applied psychologists have questioned the external validity of laboratory studies on decision making. A substantial amount of laboratory work has examined how people integrate many sources of information to arrive at a decision, and there are many sophisticated mathematical theories describing information integration (Anderson, 1981). Levin, Louviere, and Schepanski (1983) conducted a number of direct tests of the external validity of results from laboratory studies involving decision making, and they found excellent correspondence between the laboratory and the real world. They discovered that the choice of transportation to get to work, as well as choice of shopping location, are almost perfectly predicted by models derived from laboratory studies of decision making. They also report that several other behaviors in the real world coincide with results from strictly controlled experiments. These behaviors include gambling decisions, jury decisions, and occupational choices. Thus, laboratory studies of decision making may be contrived and artificial, but they also predict behavior in the real world.

What about Neisser's criticism of laboratory work in memory? Laboratory procedures do not distort the kinds of relationships that can be found in natural settings. Singer (1982) found that memory for newspaper articles was essentially the same, regardless of whether the setting was a laboratory or a naturalistic, uncontrolled one. Likewise, the pattern of memory loss and memory sparing exhibited by a brain-damaged man was found to be about the same in everyday activities (such as playing golf) and in standard laboratory tasks (Schacter, 1983). Finally, we should note that the kind of everyday memory losses shown by people suffering from minor head injury (so-called closed head wounds, which are usually suffered in automobile accidents) is highly similar to the kind of memory losses they exhibited in some standard laboratory tasks (Sunderland, Harris, and Baddeley, 1983).

All of these results are important because they demonstrate the external validity of procedures that have substantial internal validity. Carefully controlled experiments on decision making or memory allow us to make causal statements, and it appears that the control necessary for adequate causal analysis does not necessarily distort the psychological processes of interest. If Neisser's criticism of memory research has to do with realism, then perhaps he is correct. However, memory research does have much to show for a hundred years of work, because many of its procedures are both internally and externally valid.

Bem and Lord (1979) introduced another promising way of determining the ecological validity of laboratory research. Their procedure is called **template matching,** and it too focuses on whether or not people respond in the laboratory as they do in real life. Instead of trying to determine whether the laboratory setting is analogous to a natural one (that is realistic), Bem and Lord try to see whether similar behaviors occur naturally and in the laboratory (that is, generalizable). First, the behavior in a laboratory task is defined by a *template*. A template in this case is a description of how the person is supposed to behave in that situation. Second, the natural behavior of a person is assessed by means of tests and ratings by friends. Finally, ecological validity is determined by *matching* the natural behavior (determined by friends and tests) with the idealized template (how he or she should respond in the laboratory). Ecological validity is assumed if natural behavior and laboratory behavior match. If they do not match, the assumption is that the experiment is not representative. Let us consider an example. A template for a bargaining task indicates that the ideal cooperative subject will bargain so as to be helpful to other bargainers. Suppose a real subject has been described as being cooperative in everyday affairs. If our subject fails to be cooperative in the laboratory task, then we should question the ecological validity of the study.

Although template matching may be useful, there are some drawbacks. In the first place, realistic templates may be difficult to develop. Knowing how to describe ideal behavior on a task assumes that a great deal is already known about that laboratory setting. Second, getting personality assessments of the real subjects may be time consuming. Finally, we have to be sure that the personality assessments are valid. If the tests or the assessments by the subject's friends are in error, then the template matching will be in error. Our experiment might be valid and our personality assessments invalid (we had an uncooperative subject in our example). Nevertheless, the template-matching technique may be a useful alternative to field research for problems that require ecological validity of the laboratory task.

---

**CONCEPT SUMMARY**

Your choice of

    Subjects

    Variables

    Setting

may all distort the underlying psychological processes.

Generalization can be enhanced by using

    Different subjects

    Different variables

    Different settings

---

## |||| SUMMARY

**1.** Since research is a social endeavor, how your participants react to you and the setting can influence the outcome of your research.

**2.** In descriptive research, motivated forgetting may distort the results.

**3.** The particular response style exhibited by a participant (response acquiescence, response deviation, and social desirability) can contaminate the results of tests, surveys, and interviews. A forced-choice test can minimize the effects of these response styles.

**4.** Volunteer subjects differ in their characteristics from the population in general. Thus, a project may have invalid results if these characteristics are likely to mask the effects of an independent variable or alter performance on a test.

**5.** The demands of an experiment may lead a subject to adopt a particular role: the faithful-subject role, the good-subject role, the negativistic-subject role, or the apprehensive-subject role.

**6.** Evaluation apprehension is likely to be common in experiments, leading subjects to perform in ways that will make them look good to the experimenter.

**7.** Reactivity in experiments may be countered by deception, which means that the participants are blind to certain aspects of the experiment. Simulated experiments also may be useful.

**8.** Deliberate researcher bias, such as faking data, is controlled by replicating the work of others and by the self-correcting nature of science.

**9.** Inadvertent researcher bias is controlled by strict adherence to research procedures for all subjects and by double-blind experiments.

**10.** Operational definitions of concepts, in which the operations needed to produce and measure a concept are clearly specified, are essential for reliable scientific communication.

**11.** Invalid conclusions may be drawn from research if the subjects, variables, or settings distort the underlying psychological processes in question.

**12.** Because experiments are well controlled, and therefore artificial, the ecological validity of experiments is often called into question. The crucial problem is not realism, but whether the experimental results generalize to other settings, which they often do.

**13.** Many field studies (experiments done in natural settings) show that the results of laboratory studies do generalize to the real world.

**14.** Template matching, an alternative to field studies, is a way to check on the ecological validity of an experiment.

## Key Concepts

| | |
|---|---|
| anthropomorphizing | random sample |
| apprehensive-subject role | reactivity |
| blind experiment | realism |
| deception | researcher effects |
| demand characteristics | response acquiescence |
| double-blind design | response deviation |
| ecological validity | response styles or sets |
| evaluation apprehension | retrospective |
| faithful-subject role | reversability |
| field experiments | setting representativeness |
| forced-choice tests | simulated experiment |
| generalizability | social desirability |
| good-subject role | subject representativeness |
| Hawthorne effect | subject roles |
| motivated forgetting | template matching |
| negativistic-subject role | thought experiment |
| operational definition | variable representativeness |
| placebo | volunteer problem |

## Exercises

**1.** [*Special Exercise.*] Design problem. Two men, about to be promoted to assembly-line foremen, were sent by their company to the California Redlands Area School for Supervisors (CRASS) to learn how to be good supervisors. Because the classes at CRASS were oversubscribed, one of the men took a course in Behavioral Administration Development (BAD), and the other took a course in Workers Organizational Reeducation Studies and Training (WORST). On returning to their home office, the men were put in charge of two different shifts of the same assembly line. After two months, the productivity of each shift was determined, and the job satisfaction of the male and female workers was assessed. Productivity under the BAD foreman was about the same as that under the WORST foreman. Furthermore, job satisfaction was only slightly better on the WORST shift than on the BAD shift. The company president decided that the similarity in performance by the BAD and WORST shifts indicated that the CRASS programs were a waste of time and that in the future no new foremen would be sent there. Why might the conclusion of the president be wrong? What pitfalls exist in this training program?

**2.** Which of the following words does not belong with the others? *Hunger, anxiety, learning, response, motivation.* Why?

**3.** You want to do a laboratory experiment on the effects of various mnemonic devices on the learning and retention of textbook material. How would you determine the ecological validity of your task?

**4.** Specify how the volunteer problem could confound the results of an experiment.

**5.** Discuss the issue of subject representativeness. How is subject representativeness a threat to the external validity of an experiment?

## Suggested Readings

Robert Rosenthal has written extensively on subject and experimenter reactivity in research. Although some of his research concerning inadvertent experimenter effects may be overstated (see Barber, 1976), all of his works are valuable.

You will find T. X. Barber's little book, *Pitfalls in human research: ten pivotal points*, (1976), New York: Pergamon, to be an excellent source of information about investigator and experimenter bias. Barber also details many solutions to these problems.

Parsons has suggested that most of the Hawthorne effect can be attributed to operant conditioning (that is, the rewards and feedback provided the assembly-line workers). You might find the article interesting: Parsons, H. M. (1974). What happened at Hawthorne? *Science, 183:* 922–931.

---

## ‖‖ APPLICATION
### Witness Reactivity

Research cited in this chapter indicates that some aspects of hypnotic behavior in the laboratory result from reactivity; that is, people under hypnosis may simply act as if they were hypnotized. When hypnosis is used for practical purposes, the resulting changes in behavior may also occur because of reactivity.

Suppose you are the victim of a mugging. You were roughed up by the perpetrator and were very distraught afterward. You were so upset that you had some difficulty remembering the particulars of the crime, and you were vague about the physical characteristics of the mugger. Police hypnotize you to refresh your memory and you report many details that you did not recall before. Furthermore, you are very confident that one of the members of a lineup is the mugger.

Did the hypnosis enhance your memory? There are several reasons why a positive answer may not be justifiable. First, we do not have a control condition for purposes of comparison. Was the independent variable hypnosis, or was it some other variable such as additional attempts at recall? Second, a review of the laboratory research concerned with hypnotic enhancement of memory indicates that hypnosis does not necessarily lead to better retention (Smith, 1983).

Another research report adds additional cautions to the use of hypnosis as a method of enhancing memory. Sanders and Simmons (1983) had people view a videotape of a person having his pocket picked. Later, the viewers attempted to pick the criminal out of a videotaped lineup and answer some questions about the crime. Half the viewers were tested under ordinary waking conditions, and the other half were hypnotized prior to testing.

Simmons and Sanders found that the hypnotized subjects were less accurate at identifying the pickpocket than were the controls, and the hypnotized subjects were less accurate in answering questions about the crime. The reason the hypnotized people exhibited inaccurate memory was that they were swayed by misleading aspects of the task. For example, in picking a person out of the lineup, they were very likely to choose someone who was wearing clothes similar to those of the criminal, even though the person did not look like the criminal. Furthermore, the hypnotized subjects were just as confident in the correctness of their identifications when they were wrong as when they were correct. Thus, it appears that hypnotized subjects are highly susceptible to misleading information, which could have serious consequences in a real crime.

Current court rulings are in line with the research evidence. In contrast to several years ago, now many states have very stringent guidelines for the use of hypnosis as a possible memory enhancer. Most states do not allow testimony based on hypnotic enhancement. Rather, those states rely on the Frye rule (*Frye* v. *United States,* 1923). This rule of law asserts that scientific procedures will be acceptable in court to the extent that they are generally accepted by the relevant scientific discipline. Attempting to enhance memory by means of hypnosis does not appear to be an acceptable scientific procedure.

*Frye* v. *United States,* 293 F. 1013 (D.C. Cir. 1923).
Sanders, G. S., & Simmons, W. L. (1983). Use of hypnosis to enhance eyewitness accuracy: Does it work? *Journal of Applied Psychology, 68,* 70–77.
Smith, M. C. (1983). Hypnotic memory enhancement: Does it work? *Psychological Bulletin, 94,* 387–407.

## ||||  PSYCHOLOGY IN ACTION
### The Power of Being in an Experiment

As we discussed earlier, people often do things when they are in an experiment that they would not do under other circumstances. You can demonstrate this by performing a simple experiment with your friends. Find ten friends and randomly assign each to either the experimental or the control condition so that there are five people in each group. The independent variable for the two groups is the statement you make at the beginning of the experiment. Say to the experimental subjects: "I would like you to do some things for me as part of a psychology experiment for one of my courses." Say to the control group, "I would like you to do me a favor." Then tell each friend that you have a request; you would like him or her to do five jumping jacks, six sit-ups, four push-ups, and to make a paper airplane as fast as possible. You should have a watch available to time each person. In addition, you should try to elicit comments from the subjects regarding what they thought of the task.

Of course, the small number of subjects in the experiment makes it difficult for you to draw any strong conclusions (you might want to combine your data with that of other classmates). In any event, you will probably make one interesting discovery—the friends you asked to help you with a psychology experiment were probably much more cooperative. They probably did more of the activities, did them faster, and asked fewer questions. People in the control group probably thought you had been studying too hard.

This demonstration shows that psychology experiments do not just provide neutral surveys of behavior; they also can create or alter the behaviors that are studied. When people know they are being observed in an experiment, they may react differently. An even more powerful way of showing this would be to repeat the experiment with strangers, rather than friends, as your subjects. The reactions of the people in the control group are likely to be very interesting. To anticipate the kinds of behaviors you might witness, imagine that a stranger came up to you and said, "Do me a favor—do five jumping jacks, six sit-ups, . . ." What behavior would that experiment produce in you?

| **INTERPRETING THE RESULTS OF RESEARCH** | **Questions to Answer** |
|---|---|
| How to assess whether the research is both reliable and valid | *Is there a scale-attenuation problem?* Are there ceiling or floor effects? |
| | *Is a regresion artifact present?* Do the data provide a "true" measure of the behavior? |
| | *Are the experimental results reliable?* Has the experiment been replicated directly? Have conceptual or systematic replications been undertaken? |
| | *Have the results and concepts been validated by converging operations?* Do the results of several converging observations eliminate alternative explanations of the results? |

# 12 ||| Interpreting the Results of Research

*After you have collected and analyzed your data, you are in a position to interpret them. The purpose of this chapter is to help you understand some of the pitfalls that impede correct interpretation of your data. We will consider problems associated with the interpretation of both specific results and results from a connected series of studies. Your data, even if collected and statistically analyzed correctly, may be difficult to interpret if performance is extremely good or extremely bad (the scale-attenuation problem). Often, your subject's true score or performance differs from the data you have collected, which means that a regression artifact has occurred. Have you obtained reliable results—would you find the same effect if the research were replicated? Are your data valid—do several results converge upon an understanding of a concept? Solutions to these problems are suggested.*

## ||||| INTERPRETING SPECIFIC RESULTS

### The Problem of Scale Attenuation

The first topic we consider here is important but is often overlooked in psychological research. The general problem is how to interpret performance on some dependent variable in an experiment when performance is either nearly perfect (near the *ceiling* of the scale) or nearly lacking altogether (near the *floor*). These effects are called **scale-attenuation effects** (or, more commonly, *ceiling* and *floor effects*).

Suppose two obese men decided to make a bet as to who can lose the greatest amount of weight in a certain amount of time. One man looked much heavier than the other, but neither was sure what he actually weighed, since they both made a point of avoiding scales. The scale they decided to use for the bet was a common bathroom scale that runs from 0 to 300 pounds. On the day they were to begin their weight-loss programs, each man weighed himself while the other watched and, to their great surprise, both men weighed in at exactly the same value, 300 pounds. So despite their different sizes, the men decided that they were beginning their bet at equal weights.

The problem here is one of ceiling effects in the scale of measurement. The weight range of the bathroom scale did not go high enough to record the actual weight of these men. Suppose that one really weighed 300 and the other 350, if their weights had been measured on a scale that had a greater range. After six months on the weight-loss program, let us further suppose, each man actually lost 100 pounds. They reweighed themselves at this point and discovered that one now weighed 200 pounds and the other 250. Since they thought they had both started at the same weight (300), they reached the erroneous conclusion that the person who presently weighed 200 had won the bet (see figure 12–1).

Unfortunately, scale-attenuation effects in research may not be as obvious as the ceiling effect in our contrived example. However, since scale attenuation can lead to highly erroneous conclusions, it is important that you know what to look for in your own research and in the work of others. Not only should you be wary of the scale used to measure behavior, you should also consider the task imposed on the subjects participating in the project. For example, suppose you devised a memory experiment that involved recalling phone numbers. The people in your experiment had to study a typical seven-digit phone number for one minute and then had to dial that number on a telephone. You would probably discover that all of your subjects did fine; in fact, they all remembered the numbers perfectly. What does that tell you? If a task is too easy (or too difficult), differences in behavior will not appear. Whenever you examine research results, you should ask yourself: Are the limits on performance I observe legitimate ones, or are they imposed by the measurement scale or the task used to assess behavior?

**FIGURE 12–1**

The left panel (a) illustrates the situation as the obese men believed it to be—they started at the same weight and one lost twice as much as the other. The right panel (b) reveals the actual case, with the ceiling effect in the scale of measurement removed. In fact, both men lost 100 pounds. Scale attenuation (ceiling and floor effects) can hide actual differences that may exist between conditions in an experiment.

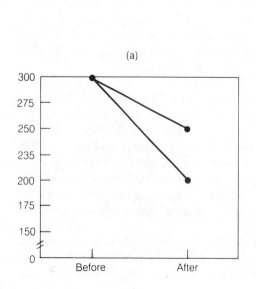

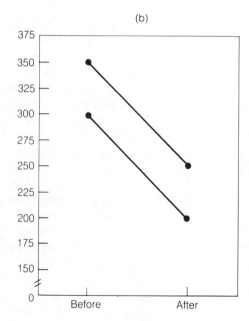

**The eyes have it: Scarborough's experiment.**   Let us consider the results of an experiment that contains a scale-attenuation problem. Scarborough (1972) was interested in the question of modality differences in retention. Do we remember information better if it comes through our eyes or through our ears? Is information better remembered if it is presented to both the ears and the eyes simultaneously than if it is presented to only one or the other? These questions have both theoretical and practical importance. When you look up a phone number and need to remember it while you cross the room to the telephone, is it sufficient to simply read the number silently to yourself as you usually do, or would it be better for you to also read the number aloud so that information enters both your ears and your eyes?

In Scarborough's experiment, all subjects received thirty-six consonant trigrams (for example, *JBT*) presented for .7 second. There were three groups of six subjects; the method by which the trigrams were presented differed for each group. One group saw the trigrams (visual-only condition); another group heard the trigrams (auditory only); and a third group both saw and heard the trigrams (visual plus auditory). Three between-subjects conditions (visual only, auditory only, visual plus auditory) were combined with six within-subjects conditions (retention intervals of 0, 3, 6, 9, 12, or 18 seconds) in the experiment. The retention interval is the delay between trigram presentation and attempted recall.

The results of Scarborough's experiment are reproduced in figure 12–2, where the percentage of times a trigram was correctly reported is plotted as a function of retention interval. It is apparent from this figure (and Scarborough's statistics offer support) that subjects who received only visual presentation of the trigrams generally recalled them a greater percentage of the time than subjects who received only auditory presentation. Furthermore, receiving the information in both modalities simultaneously did not produce any better recall than receiving the information only visually; the percentage correct at each retention interval is roughly the same for visual-only and visual-plus-auditory subjects. So far so good. But what else can we conclude from figure 12–2? Can we conclude anything about the rates of forgetting information that is presented auditorily and visually? Is the rate of forgetting the same or different in the two cases? Did you ask yourself about the source of limitation on performance?

Scarborough was quite careful on this score. Although the auditory-only and visual-only functions appear to diverge increasingly as the retention interval becomes longer, Scarborough did not draw the conclusion that the rate of forgetting is greater for information presented through the ears than through the eyes. However, consider what Massaro (1975) has to say about this experiment:

> The figure shows that the curves intercept the Y ordinate at roughly the same point and diverge significantly. The intercept value at zero sec. provides a measure of the original perception and storage of the stimuli, since it measures how much information the subject has immediately after the presentation of the stimuli, when no forgetting has taken place. The rate of forgetting can be determined from the slopes of the forgetting functions. According to this analysis, Figure

**FIGURE 12–2**
The probability of correctly recalling a stimulus trigram as a function of the three presentation conditions and the duration of the counting task. Notice that (a) visual presentation is generally superior to auditory presentation, and (b) simultaneous auditory and visual presentation is no better than visual-only presentation. (Scarborough, 1972. Copyright 1972 by the American Psychological Association. Reprinted by permission of the author.)

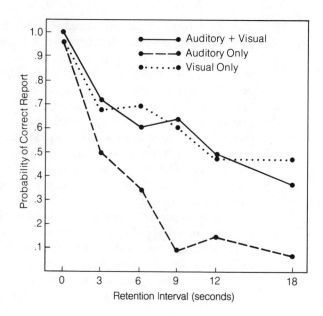

[12–2] shows that the items presented auditorily are forgotten much faster than the items presented visually. (Massaro, 1975, pp. 530–531).

Unfortunately, this conclusion must be called into question. We have the same problem the obese men had: Our scale at the ceiling is not sensitive enough. Performance at the zero-second retention interval is very nearly perfect in all conditions. When performance is perfect, it is impossible to tell whether there are any real differences among conditions because of scale attenuation, in this case a ceiling effect. If the scale of the dependent measure were really long enough, it might show differences between auditory and visual presentation even at the zero-second retention interval. So Massaro's conclusion that the rate of forgetting is greater for auditory than for visual presentation cannot be accepted on the basis of the argument we just quoted, because the assumption of equivalent performance at the zero-second retention interval may not be correct. There is no better way for us to know the rate of forgetting in the two conditions than there is for the obese men to know the rate of weight loss in judging who won their bet. In neither case can we assume equivalent initial scores before the measurement of loss begins.

**Possible solution.**   How can we avoid misinterpretation after the data are collected? (We might have considered using an additional dependent variable, such as time to respond, but the experiment had been completed. Response, or more commonly, reaction time, might have spread out the scale by showing faster times for better-learned trigrams.)

One way to avoid this problem in Scarborough's experiment is to ignore the data points at the zero-second retention interval and ask whether the rate of forgetting is greater between three and eighteen seconds for auditory than for visual presentation. We can do this by computing an interaction between presentation and retention interval over the range of three to eighteen seconds. However, by simply inspecting figure 12–2, we get some idea as to whether the auditory-only and visual-only points are diverging increasingly. We see that they are diverging increasingly between three and nine seconds, but after that the difference between them remains constant. However, this lack of an increasingly larger difference over the last three points may be caused by a floor effect in the auditory-only condition since performance is so poor, especially on the last point (only 7 or 8 percent correct). We must be very careful in interpreting data when ceiling or floor effects exist. A prudent investigator would hesitate to draw any conclusion from the data in figure 12–2 about rates of forgetting, which is just what Scarborough did. But we should also note that over the retention intervals where there are neither ceiling nor floor effects (3, 6, and 9 seconds), forgetting seems to be greater with auditory than with visual presentation.

Unfortunately, there are no hard and fast rules for avoiding scale-attenuation problems. Researchers usually try to design their experiments to avoid extremes in performance, and they often test small groups of pilot subjects (see chapter 3 for a discussion of pilot work). If these subjects perform near the ceiling or floor of the scale, then revision of the experimental task often will be necessary. For example, if performance in a memory experiment is too good (remember the hypothetical telephone-number experiment described at the beginning of the chapter), the amount of material being given can be increased so as to lower performance. Similarly, if the task is so hard that people barely remember anything, the task can be made easier by reducing the amount of material, presenting it more slowly, and so on. The careful investigator will usually take the effort to test pilot subjects before launching into an experiment that may turn out later to have been flawed by ceiling or floor effects. As noted in chapter 3, the testing of pilot subjects also permits the researcher to learn about other problems in the design or procedure of the experiment.

| **CONCEPT SUMMARY** | **Beware of Ceiling and Floor Effects**<br>Conduct pilot work to determine scale sensitivity and task difficulty. |
|---|---|

## Regression Artifacts

A serious problem in many areas of research is known as *statistical regression to the mean,* or the **regression artifact.** The word *artifact* in this context refers to an unwanted effect that occurs during an investigation (thus, it is a synonym for confounding factor), and *regression* means to go back to the mean or true score (this problem was outlined in chapter 10—now we will consider it in detail).

You can best appreciate this unwanted phenomenon by allowing yourself to become a victim of it. Try the following exercise, proceeding through the steps as given:

**1.** Roll six dice on a table in front of you.

**2.** Place the three dice showing the lowest numbers on the left, and the three dice showing the highest numbers on the right. In case of ties, randomly assign the dice to the two groups.

**3.** Compute and record the mean number-per-die for each group of three dice.

**4.** Raise both hands over your head and loudly proclaim, "Improve, in the name of science."

**5.** Roll the three low-scoring dice and compute a new mean number-per-die for the low group.

**6.** Roll the three high-scoring dice and compute a new mean number-per-die for the high group.

**7.** Compare the pre- and post-treatment scores for both groups of dice. Combine your data with that of your classmates, if possible.

On the average, this experiment will produce an increase in the performance of the low group and a decrease in the performance of the high group. You might be tempted to conclude that invoking the name of science has a beneficial effect on underachieving dice, but that overachieving dice require more individual attention to maintain their outstanding performance. Such conclusions, however, fail to consider the effects of regression to the mean. This regression artifact reflects the tendency of many types of measures to yield values close to their mean. You know that the roll of a fair die can yield values from 1 to 6, but that the average value from many rolls will be about 3.5. The likelihood of the average of three dice being close to 3.5 is higher than the likelihood of this average being close to 1 or 6. Thus, when you select three dice that give you a low average and then you roll them again, they will tend to yield a higher average value (a value closer to the mean of 3.5). In the same way, the three dice in the high group should yield a lower value when rolled again.

What does all this have to do with psychological research? By now you are well aware of the fact that accurate measurement lies at the heart of assessing the effects of a variable. Whenever there is a measurement error, such as the regression artifact, there is also the possibility of wrongly concluding that some sort of change has occurred or has failed to occur. Although this statement may appear less than profound to you, a number of psychological studies have been faulted for failing to take adequate account of its truth.

Quasi-experimental designs (see chapter 10), like the dice exercise, are particularly susceptible to bias because of the regression artifact. In such studies, you will remember, subjects are not assigned to treatment and control groups on a random basis, but are matched on some factor or factors (our dice were matched on their value). We noted in chapter 10 that matching on the appropriate dimension may be extremely difficult. In fact, our groups may have been taken from populations that differed on an important dimension prior to the study, or they may have come from the same population and we have matched subjects within groups on an irrelevant variable. Thus, our observations may result from statistical regression to the population mean rather than from our experimental manipulations.

Perhaps another example, closer to home, will help here. Suppose that you are an *A* student and your neighbor is a *C* student, although you both have similar academic backgrounds. On one particular assignment you both receive a *B*. In an effort to improve, your neighbor enrolls in a series of help sessions. Your instructor decides to evaluate the effectiveness of the help sessions by comparing the future grades of help-session students with future grades of non-help-session students who are similar in background and received the same grades on the previous assignment. You are selected as the matched student to be compared with your friend. On your next assignment, you get an *A* − and your friend receives a *C* +. Should the instructor conclude that the help sessions are harmful because your friend went from a *B* to a *C* +, while you went from a *B* to an *A* − ? Probably not, since, just like our low- and high-scoring dice, both of you regressed toward your mean grades. The course of events in this evaluation program is illustrated in table 12–1. The effect on grades is probably not a true treatment effect, but rather a regression artifact caused by the fact that you and your friend were not truly equivalent students. The help sessions may have benefited your friend, since the grade after the sessions *(C* +*)* was higher than the usual grade of *C*. If true *B* students had been randomly assigned to help-session or non-help-session groups, and then compared on grades on the second assignment, accurate assessment of the effect of help sessions on students' grades could have been obtained.

The reason regression to the mean often occurs is that all psychological measures are subject to a certain amount of unreliability. With any measure that is not perfectly reliable, the group of subjects obtaining the highest scores contains not only those who really belong in the highest category, but also others who are placed in this category owing to chance errors of measurement (recall our dice example). On a retest, these chance measurement errors will not necessarily occur in the same direction; they will usually regress toward the true score or population mean. Similarly, a group selected for poor performance on an original test will tend to average higher on a retest, just as was the case with our underachieving dice.

**Regression in compensatory education.**   The importance of regression artifacts in quasi-experimental studies of education has been the subject of much debate. One influential study of the effects of the Head Start pro-

| | | | | |
|---|---|---|---|---|
| **TABLE 12–1**<br>Result of a Hypothetical<br>Evaluation Program | | | | |

| Person | Mean Grade | Matching Grade | Help Session | Criterion Grade |
|---|---|---|---|---|
| You | A | B | No | A − |
| Neighbor | C | B | Yes | C + |

Note: Illustration of regression to the mean confusing the interpretation of the outcome of a quasi-experiment. Although both people were matched as *B* students, their performance, with or without the help session, regressed toward their actual average grade. Did the help session help?

gram of the 1960s (Cicirelli et al., 1969) received particular attention. In this study, called the Westinghouse-Ohio study, children completing their Head Start experience were randomly selected for evaluation. A control population of children from the same area who had been eligible for the program but had not attended was then defined. Control children were selected at random to be matched with experimental children on the basis of sex, racial or ethnic group membership, and kindergarten attendance. After the final selection of experimental and control subjects was made, additional measures of socioeconomic status, demographic status, and attitude were compiled and compared in the two groups. Differences were reported to be slight. Measures of experimental (Head Start) and control (no Head Start) children's academic achievement and potential were then computed and compared. The general conclusion from this large study was that Head Start was not effective in removing the effects of poverty and social disadvantage.

Other psychologists (Campbell and Erlebacher, 1970a) were quick to criticize this study on several grounds. First, they pointed out that the results of the study were undoubtedly caused partially by regression artifacts. Worse, the magnitude of the artifacts could not be estimated, casting doubt over the entire set of findings.

What is the basic problem? Can you see why the matching of subjects may not have been effective? Cicirelli and co-workers laudably tried to match the sample of disadvantaged children who had been in the Head Start program with others from the same area who had not been in the program. Differences that show up later between the two groups should result from the program. Right? Not necessarily. That conclusion is correct only if the two samples came from the same underlying population distributions, which is unlikely.

What is more likely is that the two populations differ, with the disadvantaged "treatment" children coming from a population that is poorer in ability than the "control" children. The treatment children are usually preselected to be from a disadvantaged background (which is why they were included in the program), whereas the controls who are not in the program are likely to be from a different population that is greater in ability (a nonequivalent control group). The basic problem is that subjects are not randomly assigned to conditions, so the researchers must try to match control subjects with experimental subjects. To match samples from these different populations, the experimenters will have to select children *above* the population mean for the disadvantaged treatment group and *below* the population mean for the control group. But when this is done, the dreaded regression artifact will always be introduced. When each group is retested, the subjects' performance will tend to regress to the mean of the group; in other words, the disadvantaged group will tend to perform worse in this example, and the control group will tend to perform better.

Regression to the mean can occur in the absence of any treatment being given and despite matching. The matching effect is the same as that seen in the example concerning grades and help sessions. The grades of the superior student increased to $A-$ from $B$, and the other's decreased from

*B* to *C*+, when the two students were erroneously matched as *B* students. Since in the Head Start study we already expect a difference between groups (favoring the control) because of regression to the mean, how do we evaluate the outcome of the study? Cicirelli and co-workers found no difference between groups. Since we might expect the treatment (Head Start) group to be worse owing to regression to the mean, does this mean the group actually improved because of Head Start?

It is impossible to answer this question, because in the Westinghouse-Ohio evaluation of Head Start the direction or magnitude of regression artifacts could not be assessed. In the preceding paragraph, we made reasonable assumptions concerning regression artifacts in this type of study. Strictly speaking, however, we cannot conclude that Head Start had no effect. In fact, we cannot draw any conclusion on the basis of that study, since we do not know how regression artifacts affected the results.

In general, then, regression artifacts of a difficult-to-estimate magnitude are highly probable in this type of study, a fact acknowledged by most researchers. Why, then, would such studies be conducted, particularly when important political, economic, and social decisions will be based on their results? This question was raised both by Campbell and Erlebacher (1970a, b) and by Cicirelli and his supporters (Cicirelli, 1970; Evans and Schiller, 1970). Their answers were quite different, and they represent the type of issue that frequently confronts scientists but which science can never resolve. Campbell and Erlebacher (1970a) proposed that bad information was worse than no information at all; that if properly controlled experiments could not be performed, then no data should be gathered. On the other side of the issue, Evans and Schiller replied, "This position fails to understand that every program *will* be evaluated by the most arbitrary, anecdotal, partisan, and subjective means" (p. 220). Campbell and Erlebacher concurred but stated that "we judge it fundamentally misleading to lend the prestige of science to any report in a situation where no scientific evaluation is possible" (1970b, p. 224). As a final solution, they proposed that a commission "composed of experts who are not yet partisans in this controversy" be convened to decide the matter.

**Possible solutions.**   We may not be able to decide this issue on strictly rational grounds, but we can all agree that a research study should be conducted according to the best scientific procedures available. After the fact, of course, we are not able to interpret the results of a quasi-experimental study in which there are substantial and unknown regression artifacts. The question becomes: How could the Westinghouse-Ohio study have been properly conducted? The best way would have been to randomly assign participants to either the no-treatment or treatment conditions. There is no substitute for random assignment in eliminating confounding factors (that is, there is no substitute for doing a true experiment). However, it seems unfair to give half the children who seek the help of a remedial program no training whatsoever. Of course, there is no guarantee at the outset that the program will be beneficial to them; that is what the study is designed to discover. The same issue arises in medical research when a control group with a disease is given a placebo rather than a treatment drug. The argument could be made in both cases that in the long run more people will be aided by careful research into the effectiveness of treatments than may be harmed because treatment is withheld. Unfortunately, the issue is not quite that simple. In the case of medical research, for example, preliminary testing of an antiencephalitis drug showed that 72 percent of the patients receiving the drug survived the disease and led normal lives, but only 30 percent of the control group, which received placebos, survived (Katz, 1979). Is such a toll necessary for effective research design in drug development? Again, the issue is difficult to resolve solely on rational or scientific grounds.

There are other solutions to the regression problem (in the Westinghouse-Ohio study) besides random assignment. One is to randomly assign all the children to different groups and put them in different programs to pit the effectiveness of the programs against one another. The difficulty here is that we do not have a no-treatment baseline, and if the programs turn out to be equally effective, we would not know whether any of them were better than no program at all.

---

| CONCEPT SUMMARY | **Regression Artifacts** mask true behavior in quasi-experiments and matching studies. |
| --- | --- |
| | Use random assignment to treatments whenever possible. |

---

## | | | | INTERPRETING PATTERNS OF RESEARCH

The problems of scale attenuation and regression artifacts focus on the results of a particular piece of research. The topics we want to examine now are concerned with interpreting patterns of research. No single observation can stand alone for long. When we are confronted with the results of psychological research, we must always ask whether they are reliable and valid. In chapter 2 we discussed the reliability and validity of data. Here we will expand on some of that discussion so you can grasp the importance of determining whether a particular result displays regularity and whether a particular datum fits with other, related observations.

### Reliability and Replication

Suppose we have been hired to assess presidential preferences in the United States. Our job is to find out who the people seem to prefer for president in the upcoming election. After we develop a survey, we take a random sample of the people in the United States. What sorts of things will make us confident of our results? First, we can be more confident that the results accurately reflect the attitudes of the population if our sample consists of 100,000 people rather than only 100. Second, we should expect a second random sample to yield a similar result (assuming that one of the major candidates has not committed a gross moral or legal transgression during the time between the two surveys). Large numbers of observations and a repeatable result are two key factors to ensure reliability. We should always try to maximize the number of observations and devise our research in a way that allows us to determine whether our results are consistent over time.

**Test reliability.**   In chapter 2, we discussed the ways in which **test reliability** is assessed. Remember that a reliable test is one that yields consistent results. If a test is inconsistent because it is poorly designed (and not because of changes in the person taking the test), we will be unable to determine whether the test is measuring what it is supposed to measure. Thus, an unreliable test is also one that is invalid. The same is true of experiments, which we will discuss next.

**Experimental reliability: Replication.**   The basic issue regarding reliability of experimental results is simply this: If an experiment were repeated, would the results be the same as those found the first time? Obviously, repeatability is a crucial topic in psychological research, for an experimental outcome may be worthless if we cannot have reasonable certainty that the results are reliable. Since we usually are unable to conduct the same study twice using the same subjects (with the possible exception of some small-*n* work), we usually repeat an experiment with a different sample of subjects. If the results of the two experiments are similar, we can be confident that we have demonstrated reliability.

Many psychologists find *experimental reliability* more convincing than statistical reliability, since a statistically reliable finding in a single experiment may be the result of a set of accidental circumstances that favor one condition over another. We emphasize that the results of any particular experiment are to be viewed against the background of others on the same issue. If a phenomenon is not repeatable, we are likely to find out rather quickly. *Replication,* a synonym for *copy* or *reproduction,* is the term usually used to describe experimental reliability. We will now consider an example of replication in the context of a series of famous experiments conducted by Luchins (1942).

**Luchins's Einstellung (set) experiments.**   Abraham S. Luchins (1942) was interested in the following: "Several problems, all solvable by one somewhat complex procedure, are presented in succession. If afterwards a similar task is given which can be solved by a more direct and simpler method, will the individual be blinded to this more direct possibility?" Subjects may construct a set way, or set, to solve experimental tasks. After the problems are changed so that the set way no longer is the most efficient method of solution, will people hang on to the set way or will they recognize the more direct method? The German word for *set* is **Einstellung;** our everyday problem-solving frequently involves an Einstellung: We try our habitual ways of attacking a particular problem even though we may have more efficient procedures readily available to us.

Luchins usually used the water-jar problem in his experiments. People were given two or three jars of varying capacity and were supposed to figure out how to obtain a required amount of water by performing arithmetical operations on the volumes the jars would hold. The basic eleven problems appear in table 12–2. (To become familiar with the Einstellung effect, solve all eleven problems in order before you continue reading.)

In Luchins's first study, the first problem served as an illustration of the task. The appropriate solution is to take the larger jar (29) and subtract the smaller jar (3) three times to get the desired amount (20). Subjects next solved problems 2 through 6, which may be considered set-establishing problems since they all are most easily solved by the same method of solution. In each case, the solution is to take the largest jar (always the middle one), subtract the first jar once, and finally subtract the last jar twice. If we label the jars *A*, *B*, and *C* from left to right, then the set the subjects developed for problems 2 through 6 can be represented as $B - A - 2C$.

Besides the experimental or Einstellung group, there were two others. One group, a control of sorts, began with problems 7 and 8 so that the experimenter could see how the group would solve them with no induced set solution. Another group was treated in the same manner as the Einstellung group, except that before problem 7 each subject wrote "Don't be blind" on the response sheet. Luchins had the subjects write this phrase so that they would be cautious and not be foolish when they solved subsequent problems. Thus, the primary dependent variable was the number of subjects using the Einstellung solution $(B - A - 2C)$ on problems 7 and 8, even though problems 7 and 8 had much more efficient and direct solutions $(A - C$ for 7 and $A + C$ for 8). The results were that none of the control subjects used the inefficient solution in solving problems 7 and 8, 81 percent of the Einstellung subjects used the inefficient solution on 7 and 8, and the "Don't be blind" warning reduced the use of the Einstellung

**TABLE 12–2**

The water-jar problems Luchins used in his Einstellung experiments.

| Problem | Given the following empty jars as measures | | | Obtain the required amount of water |
| | A | B | C | |
|---|---|---|---|---|
| 1 | 29 | 3 | | 20 |
| 2 | 21 | 127 | 3 | 100 |
| 3 | 14 | 163 | 25 | 99 |
| 4 | 18 | 43 | 10 | 5 |
| 5 | 9 | 42 | 6 | 21 |
| 6 | 20 | 59 | 4 | 31 |
| 7 | 23 | 49 | 3 | 20 |
| 8 | 15 | 39 | 3 | 18 |
| 9 | 28 | 76 | 3 | 25 |
| 10 | 18 | 48 | 4 | 22 |
| 11 | 14 | 36 | 8 | 6 |

solution to about 55 percent. Furthermore, after doing problem 9, which cannot be solved via the set-inducing method, 63 percent of the Einstellung subjects continued with the old solution on problems 10 and 11, whereas only 30 percent of the "Don't be blind" subjects reverted to the set solution.

How reliable are the results from this experiment? Luchin's work was published before the use of statistical tests was common in psychological research, so statistical tests to establish reliability were not performed. However, such tests were largely unnecessary in this case, since Luchins provided us with evidence that his results could be replicated in other experiments. Many experiments are included in the original report, and the results are in general agreement with the Einstellung results just outlined. Altogether, Luchins tested more than 9,000 subjects in his original studies. As noted previously, experimental reliability or replication is an exceptionally convincing way to demonstrate the reliability of a phenomenon—the Einstellung effect is a reliable one.

There are three types of replications: direct, systematic, and conceptual. **Direct replication** is simply repeating an experiment as closely as possible with as few changes as possible in the method. Luchins replicated his original experiment several times with only slight changes in the subject population tested; such experiments constitute cases of direct replication.

In a **systematic replication,** all sorts of factors are changed that the investigator considers irrelevant to the phenomenon of interest. If the phenomenon is not illusory, it will survive these changes. So, for example, in a systematic replication of Luchins's experiments, we might vary the nature of the problems so that the set involves a different rule (or several different rules), vary the instructions, vary the type of subjects used, and so on. The Einstellung effect should be robust across all of these manipulations. If it is not, then we have found that variables previously thought to be irrelevant are actually important, and this is crucial knowledge.

In a **conceptual replication,** we attempt to replicate a phenomenon or concept, but in an entirely different way. Luchins examined other tasks besides the water-jar problem to establish the Einstellung phenomenon in diverse situations. He used series of geometry problems, words hidden in letters, and paper mazes. In each case, subjects solved several problems that had a unique solution before they came to the critical problems that could be solved either by the Einstellung solution or by a much more simple and direct solution. Just as in the water-jar experiments, subjects usually used the old, circuitous solution and ignored the more efficient solution. These experiments constitute conceptual replications of the concept of Einstellung.

You should note the following carefully: The problem of reliability of results is interwoven with the problem of generality and validity. As we progress from direct to systematic to conceptual replication, we not only show reliability, we also show increasing validity. Are we studying something that ties in with or is related to our knowledge of other psychological phenomena in a reasonable way? A conceptual replication is closely related to converging operations, which are procedures that validate a hypothetical construct used to explain behavior by eliminating alternative explanations.

<table>
<tr><td>**CONCEPT**<br>**SUMMARY**</td><td>***To ensure experimental reliability, conduct***<br>Direct replications<br>Systematic replications<br>Conceptual replications</td></tr>
</table>

## Converging Operations

Suppose that Luchins had conducted just the one experiment outlined in table 12–2. What sorts of conclusions could he have drawn from his results (assume, too, that he directly replicated the study so that he knew his results were reliable)? Can he legitimately conclude that Einstellung caused the results? Without additional independent evidence, he could have said that the results were owing to a "water-jar effect" or a "$B - A - 2C$ effect" rather than an Einstellung effect. This is because each of these concepts was part of the one experiment, and each is a reasonable cause of the results. By doing systematic and conceptual replications, Luchins ruled out the alternative hypotheses of effects limited to particular variables and made the concept of Einstellung a reasonable explanation of the rigidity seen in many problem-solving situations.

In other words, the results of experiments that had different rules and different problems converged on the Einstellung hypothesis by systematically eliminating alternative hypotheses. *Converging operations*, then, are a set of two or more operations that eliminate alternative concepts that might explain a set of experimental results. The importance of converging operations in psychological research was initially emphasized in a landmark paper by Garner, Hake, and Eriksen (1956). They noted that converging operations are necessary to validate operationally defined constructs (see chapter 11) as well as experimental results. Because converging operations are crucial to an understanding of psychological research and psychological theorizing, we will consider two more examples of converging operations at work.

**Stroop effect: Input or output?**   Before the discussion continues, we want you to try a simple experiment. All you need are some index cards, colored markers, and a watch with a second hand or, even better, a stop watch. Take sixteen index cards and, using your markers, write the name of the color in its color—that is, with green marker write "green," and so on. If you have eight markers, repeat each color twice. If you only have four markers, repeat each color four times. Take another sixteen index cards and write color names that do not correspond to the ink—that is, with a green marker write "red," and so on. Your stimuli are now complete. Pick one of your two decks, and for each card, name the color of the ink. Time how long it takes you to go through all sixteen cards. Do the same for the other deck. Did you go faster using the deck that had compatible color names and inks?

|  | Response | Symbols in Colors | | Color of Patches |
|---|---|---|---|---|
| Neutral Condition | Same | XXXX | XXXX | Both patches red |
|  | Different | XXXX | XXXX | One patch red, one blue |
| Perceptual Inhibition Condition | Same | RED | RED | Both patches red |
|  | Different | RED | RED | One patch red, one blue |
| Response Competition Condition | Same | SAME | SAME | Both patches red |
|  | Different | SAME | SAME | One patch red, one blue |

**FIGURE 12–3**
An outline of some of the conditions in the work by Egeth, Blecker, and Kamlet (1969). In all three conditions, subjects responded SAME when there was agreement among the stimuli and DIFFERENT when there was a mismatch. Subjects saw two colored patches on each trial and responded on the basis of the colors. The Neutral Condition served as a control by having neutral symbols (XXXX) embedded in colored patches. Color names were in the patches in the Perceptual Inhibition Condition—the color names should inhibit the perception of the colors. SAME or DIFFERENT appeared in the patches in the Response Competition Condition—reading the response SAME in different colored patches should inhibit the correct response of DIFFERENT. The Stroop effect occurred in the Response Competition Condition but not in the Perceptual Inhibition Condition.

You probably found that you responded more slowly when ink colors and color names were mismatched than when they were compatible. Furthermore, you probably noticed that you made mistakes, stuttered, and hesitated when the color names and inks were in the incompatible condition. A variation of this frustrating experiment was first done by Stroop (1935); the **Stroop effect** refers to the increase in time required to name the ink color when the ink and color names do not match. This is the same kind of experiment in which you participated in the "Introduction," where the mismatch was between the quantity of the digits and the names of those digits.

The Stroop effect is a highly reliable one; the question is, what causes the Stroop effect? One possibility is that it results from the input or perceptual aspects of the task. Stroop and others found that reading is usually faster than naming; therefore, the perceptual argument is that reading color words inhibits the perception of the ink color. An alternative hypothesis is that output (the subject's responses) is affected, not perception. The output notion goes like this: After the subject has perceived both the ink color and the color word, there is response competition when two different color names are elicited—one by the ink and another by the word. On the basis of Stroop's original work, we have no way of deciding between these two hypotheses. Which is important: the perceptual system or the response system?

A simple but clever experiment was conducted by Egeth, Blecker, and Kamlet (1969) to answer this question by using converging operations. Three important conditions from one of their studies are shown in figure 12–3. The control or baseline condition is shown at the top of the figure (Neutral

Condition). Subjects saw two colored patches with a neutral symbol (XXXX) embedded in them. These patches were either the same color or different colors. An important factor in this study is that instead of responding with color names, the subjects responded SAME when the color of the two patches matched and DIFFERENT when the colors of the two patches were different.

The crucial conditions of the experiment are illustrated in the next rows of figure 12–3. As in the baseline condition, the subject responded SAME or DIFFERENT on the basis of the colors of the two patches. In the Perceptual Inhibition Condition, color names appeared in the colored patches, and on a given trial the same color name appeared in both boxes. Both colored patches could be the same and match the color name (a SAME trial), or the colored patches could be different, with only one patch matching the names (a DIFFERENT trial). Response competition arises when several responses struggle to be executed (Kantowitz, 1974). For example, at a stoplight a red signal calls for a driver to step on the brake with her foot. A green light calls for stepping on the accelerator pedal. If only one signal lamp occurs, there is no response competition. But if the traffic light is defective so that both red and green signals are illuminated, there will be response competition between brake and accelerator pedals because prior learning has strengthened the connections between (1) red traffic lights and brake pedals, and (2) green traffic lights and accelerator pedals.

In the perceptual inhibition condition there is no prior learning to connect color names and the responses SAME or DIFFERENT. Thus, there should be no response competition in this condition. Should responding in this condition be slower than the neutral condition, this result could not be explained by response competition. Therefore, any Stroop effect obtained in the perceptual inhibition condition must result from perceptual inhibition rather than response competition. However, the results obtained by Egeth and his associates were that response times were equal for the perceptual inhibition condition and for the neutral (control) condition. This means that no Stroop effect was obtained. The perceptual similarity between the colors of the patches and the color names failed to produce any Stroop effect. Although this outcome suggests that perceptual factors are not an important cause of Stroop interference, converging operations are needed to bolster this conclusion.

So far so good. We seem to have eliminated one alternative as an explanation of the Stroop effect. Now for a converging operation that will bring back the Stroop effect and identify the processes involved. To accomplish this, Egeth and co-workers used the condition outlined at the bottom of figure 12–3. In the response competition condition, the subjects once again responded SAME and DIFFERENT. However, in this condition the words SAME or DIFFERENT rather than neutral symbols or color names appeared in the colored patches. The experimenters reasoned that if response competition is important, then mismatches between SAME or DIFFERENT and the stimulus information should result in slower responding than in the neutral condition. In other words, if conflict among responses causes the Stroop effect, then responding should be slower in the response competition condition than in the neutral condition. This is exactly what they found. The Stroop effect returned: Now the responses SAME and DIFFERENT took longer when they conflicted with the response in the stimulus. Recall that the identical response words did not produce a Stroop effect in the perceptual inhibition condition. Thus, the converging operations removed the perceptual process as an explanation for the results, leaving us to conclude that a response process accounts for the Stroop effect. Other studies on the Stroop phenomenon also lead to the conclusion that response competition is an important contributing factor to Stroop interference (see Keele, 1973, for an excellent review).

**Personal space.**   The concept of **personal space** implies that people are surrounded by invisible bubbles designed to protect them from a wide variety of social encroachments. How do psychologists know that such a bubble exists? Since it cannot be sensed directly by vision, smell, touch and the other senses, the concept must be evaluated indirectly. The next two experiments demonstrate that there is a personal-space bubble; they use two different kinds of spatial invasion, and yield similar results.

Ironically, the personal-space bubble that helps a person maintain privacy is best studied by invasions that violate the privacy it affords. A simple experiment conducted by Kinzel (1970) shows one operation that defines personal space. Kinzel was interested in the personal-space bubbles surrounding violent and nonviolent prisoners. Thus one independent variable—more precisely, a subject variable (see chapter 10), since it was not manipulated—was classification of prisoners as violent (having inflicted physical injury on another person) or nonviolent. Each prisoner stood in the center of an empty room 20 feet wide and 20 feet long. The experimenter then approached from one of eight directions (the second independent variable) until the prisoner said "Stop" because the experimenter was too close. The dependent variable was the distance between prisoner and experimenter when the prisoner said "Stop." If there is no personal-space bubble, the experimenter should be able to walk right up to the prisoner (distance = 0 feet). Control variables were the room and the experimenter, which were the same throughout the experiment. Results of this experiment are shown in figure 12–4. It is clear that violent prisoners have larger personal-space bubbles than do nonviolent prisoners.

This experiment may not have entirely convinced you that personal-space bubbles exist. A concept based on only one experiment is just a restatement of that particular experimental finding. You may think that in Kinzel's experiment there is something strange about a person walking right up to another person without saying anything. Certainly if this happened to you on the street you would think it unusual, to say the least. The next experiment avoids this potential difficulty.

To avoid actively invading someone's personal-space bubble, Barefoot, Hoople, and McClay (1972) gave subjects the opportunity to invade the experimenter's bubble. The experimenter sat near a water fountain and pretended to read a book. Anyone getting a drink of water had to invade the experimenter's personal space. The independent variable was the dis-

**FIGURE 12–4**

Looking down on the personal-space bubble of violent and nonviolent prisoners. (After Kinzel, *The American Journal of Psychiatry*, vol. 127, pp. 59–64, 1970. Copyright 1970 by the American Psychiatric Association. Reprinted by permission.)

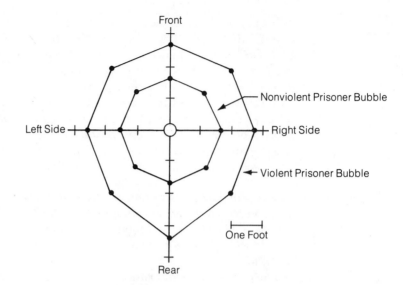

tance between the experimenter and the water fountain. This could be either 1 foot, 5 feet, or 10 feet. This last distance is large enough so that it exceeds the bounds of the experimenter's personal space and thus is a control condition. A confederate kept track of the number of persons passing by the fountain in each of the three experimental conditions. The dependent variable was the percentage of passersby who drank from the fountain. When the experimenter was 1 foot away, only 10 percent drank; 5 feet away, 18 percent drank. Finally, at a distance of 10 feet, 22 percent drank from the fountain.

These results agree with those of the active-invasion paradigm used by Kinzel. The single concept of a personal-space bubble explains findings of both experiments. Hence, the experiments provide converging operations supporting the personal-space concept.

The examples of converging operations we have just detailed are actually rather simple, because only a small number of experiments or conditions were needed to provide validity and generality. In actual practice, many concepts and phenomena require a considerable amount of independent evidence before they can be considered valid.

We also should not be complacent about our understanding of the Stroop effect and the concept of personal space. Additional research is likely to refine our knowledge about these two concepts. For example, there may be tasks involving incompatible stimuli and responses that place exceptional demands on our perceptual system. Thus, some kinds of Stroop phenomena could result from both input and output effects. In a similar fashion, future research may show that the size of the personal-space bubble differs in active and passive situations: your bubble may be smaller when someone invades it than when you enter the personal space of another person.

It seems fitting to end this section and this chapter with a reminder from one of the greatest scientists, Sir Isaac Newton: "Knowledge is gained bit by bit."

| CONCEPT SUMMARY | *Converging operations*<br>Provide **validity** for concepts and hypotheses.<br>Eliminate **alternative explanations** by two or more operations. |
| --- | --- |

## | | | | SUMMARY

**1.** Several pitfalls may make it difficult for experimenters to interpret the results of their research.

**2.** Some of these pitfalls pose problems in particular research projects, and others make it difficult to interpret patterns of research. Scale attenuation and regression artifacts can lead to the misinterpretation of the results of a specific project; replications (reliability) and converging operations (validity) are important for interpreting patterns of research.

**3.** Scale attenuation refers to an inability to observe differences in thought and behavior because performance is either too good (a ceiling effect) or too poor (a floor effect).

**4.** The scale must be spread out or the task modified in order to handle the attenuation problem.

**5.** Regression to the mean is likely to occur whenever subject variables are included in a project. The regression artifact refers to the tendency of the subject's behavior to drift toward his or her mean performance.

**6.** Random assignment is the best way to guard against regression artifacts.

**7.** An experiment that can be replicated is a reliable one, as is a test whose results are consistent.

**8.** The three types of replications are: direct, systematic, and conceptual.

**9.** Converging operations are several independent operations that validate the meaning of constructs.

**10.** The need for converging operations demands that scientific research on a problem be varied and extensive.

### Key Concepts

| | |
| --- | --- |
| ceiling effects | regression artifact |
| conceptual replication | regression to the mean |
| converging operations | replication |
| direct replication | scale-attenuation effects |
| Einstellung | Stroop effect |
| experimental reliability | systematic replication |
| floor effects | test reliability |
| personal space | |

## Exercises

**1.** [*Special Exercises.*] Here is another design problem for you. Reread the description of Luchins's experiment outlined in table 12–2. There seem to be several problems with that study; see whether you can pinpoint two or three of them. As a hint, consider the following questions: Did Luchins use an appropriate control group? If not, what should be the control condition? Are there points in the study that require counterbalancing? What additional dependent variables might have been informative?

**2.** Examine figures and tables in several recent journal articles. See whether you can discover any ceiling or floor effects. If you find any—and it may take a while—read the article to determine whether the investigator was aware of the scale-attenuation problem. Can the problem be rectified?

**3.** Pinpointing regression artifacts may be difficult. However, in an attempt to discover a regression problem, you might find it worthwhile to examine several assessment studies that use subject variables. If you find evidence for a regression artifact, try to determine why the study was published. Remember our discussion of medical research and the difficulty of random assignment. Try these two journals: *Journal of Educational Psychology* and *Journal of Applied Psychology.*

**4.** Try to find an example of each type of replication in recent journals. You may not find any examples of direct replication, and yet Barber (1976) has asserted that direct replications are crucial to the advancement of psychology. Why do direct replications seldom appear in the literature?

**5.** More often than not, good examples of converging operations can be found in a single journal article. Papers by Paivio, Mayer, and Thios and D'Agostino, listed in the suggested readings, offer evidence of converging operations at work. You might take a look at these articles.

## Suggested Readings

The following three articles illustrate both reliability and converging operations. Read them carefully. They are also available in the book *Readings in experimental psychology* by Elmes (Chicago: Rand McNally, 1978): Mayer, R. E. (1977). Problem-solving performance with task overload: Effects of self-pacing and trait anxiety. *Bulletin of the Psychonomic Society, 9,* 283–286; Paivio, A. (1975). Perceptual comparisons through the mind's eye. *Memory and Cognition, 3,* 635–67; Thios, S. J., & D'Agostino, P. R. (1976). Effects of repetition as a function of study-phase retrieval. *Journal of Verbal Learning and Verbal Behavior, 15,* 529–36.

## APPLICATION
### A Failure to Replicate

A variety of behavior-modification techniques (see chapter 7) have been very successful in treating certain kinds of psychological disorders, including phobias and anxiety, among others. However, these techniques have been spectacularly unsuccessful in treating smoking and overeating behaviors. Current estimates indicate that only 10 to 20 percent of the people treated for smoking or obesity maintain the benefits of behavior therapy (Schachter, 1982). In other words, about 80 to 90 percent of the smokers return to smoking after the therapy, and about the same percentage of obese people gain weight after therapy.

Why is there such a dramatic failure to replicate the success seen with other disorders? The standard interpretation is that smoking and overeating are addictions, which means that these habits are more difficult to break than other unfortunate habits, such as snake phobias. Recently, Schachter has argued that this interpretation is misleading. Schachter interviewed a substantial number of people in two areas of New York state. These people, who represented a broad cross-section of the population, were asked a number of health-related questions. What Schachter found was surprising. The success rate for smokers who had tried to quit was nearly 64 percent, and the average length of time they had refrained from smoking was about seven years. The corresponding figures for the obese people who had tried to lose weight were 63 percent and more than eleven years of successful weight reduction. These results are markedly different from the low success rates observed for smokers and overeaters after they had completed formal therapy. Why?

There are at least two reasons Schachter found higher success rates. First, people in the general population are likely to have tried to quit smoking or lose weight several times; in contrast, the therapy results generally refer to one stint in therapy. Thus, the repeated attempts at self-therapy may have increased the number of successful outcomes. Second, those who seek professional help might do so because they have been very unsuccessful in treating themselves. For whatever reason, those who undergo therapy may have a particularly tenacious problem, which would bias against successful results.

Schachter offers his findings as encouragement to those who have tried to lose weight or quit smoking and have failed. "If at first you don't succeed, try, try again."

Schachter, S. (1982). Don't sell habit-breakers short. *Psychology Today, 16*, 27–33.

## PSYCHOLOGY IN ACTION
### Studying Mental Blocks

*Folk* is pronounced *foke*, with the *l* being silent. *Polk* is pronounced *poke*, again with the *l* being silent.
How is the name of the white of an egg pronounced?

If you just pronounced *yolk* in answering the question, this section is for you. *Yolk* is an erroneous answer; the white part of an egg is the *albumen*. The *yolk*, as you probably know, is the yellow part. The sentences prior to the question featured words that rhyme with *yolk* and therefore primed you for the word *yolk*. When you were asked the question about eggs, *yolk* readily came to you as the answer. If you had not been primed with the two sentences, you probably would not have responded *yolk*. The recent experience of reading the sentences blocked you from giving the correct answer.

Here are two more examples, although you may be more wary now:

Pronounce the word produced by the letters *T-O-P-S*. What does a car do at a green light?
Say *tin* out loud ten times. What is an aluminum can made of?

Although you may have answered these questions correctly, if you try them on a friend we think you will find them effective in producing the erroneous answers *stop* and *tin*. You should probably ask the questions aloud, rather than tell your friend to read them.

Such blocks in memory retrieval may play a part in limiting creative thinking (Roediger and Neely, 1982). When people try to solve a problem and fail, they often say that their minds are "in a rut." Usually they mean that when they attempt to solve the problem they are blocked from retrieving a new solution by repeatedly thinking of all the erroneous solutions that previously have been tried. This is the same as the Einstellung effect shown by Luchins's subjects.

You can study the same effect by having some friends read through the priming sentences before the target ones. Compare their behavior with others who do not read the priming sentences. You should consider having the latter group read (or hear) some nonpriming sentences in order to control for the amount of mental work you have your subjects do.

If you are interested in additional ways of studying mental blocks, the following references may be of interest.

Fingerman, P., & Levine, M. (1974). Nonlearning: The completeness of the blindness. *Journal of Experimental Psychology, 102,* 720–721.
Roediger, H. L., & Neely, J. H. (1982). Retrieval blocks in episodic and semantic memory. *Canadian Journal of Psychology, 36,* 213–242.

## RESEARCH REPORTS
### How to read and write them

| | | |
|---|---|---|
| **What to Look for in the . . .** | *Abstract:* | What was done to whom, and what was found |
| | *Introduction:* | What the author proposes; the hypotheses tested |
| | *Method:* | Dependent, independent, subject, and control variables; does the method test the hypothesis? |
| | *Results:* | Do the results support or reject the hypothesis? |
| | *Discussion:* | What conclusions are stated? |
| | *References:* | Other reports you might read: Are citations complete? |
| **What to Include in the . . .** | *Abstract:* | What you did to whom and what you found |
| | *Introduction:* | Why are you doing this research; the hypothesis you are testing |
| | *Method:* | A description of all variables; enough detail so that someone else can repeat your project. |
| | *Results:* | Tables and/or figures that summarize your results, point the reader to the most pertinent data |
| | *Discussion:* | State how your results relate to the hypotheses tested; include relevant inferences and conclusions |
| | *References:* | All references cited in your paper belong here |

# 13 ||| How to Read and Write a Research Report

Unless you read articles in journals of psychology, you may have difficulty understanding psychological research. The data base associated with a particular problem area resides in journals. Thus, to understand those data, you will need to be able to comprehend the research reports. The first section of this chapter explains the format and style of articles and gives you some hints to help you become a critical reader. Because you will probably have to report the results of your own research, the second part of this chapter deals with writing a research report.

## |||| HOW TO READ A JOURNAL ARTICLE

Trying to comprehend a psychology article can be difficult for the novice. In this section, we prepare you for your first encounter with a journal article by explaining the format and style of journal reports. In addition, you will be given some clues about how to be a critical reader of research reports.

### The Parts of an Article

The format of journal articles in psychology is governed by the *Publication Manual of the American Psychological Association*, which was revised in 1983. This manual is well worth reading, especially when you start to write your own research reports. The typical psychology article consists of seven parts: title and author(s), abstract, introduction, method, results, discussion, and references. The main purpose and content of each section are summarized below.

**Title, author(s), and abstract.** From these sections, you can decide whether you want to read the entire article. The title and abstract let you know what variables were manipulated or selected, and you should be able to determine what was measured. The abstract tells you something about the results that were obtained. If the title is mysterious or not particularly informative, the abstract should clear up ambiguities. The name of the researcher is important for two reasons: You can make sure you have found the article you are looking for (referencing is done by author's surname); and if you are familiar with an author's research, you may be able to anticipate some of the content of the article.

**Introduction.**   The introduction specifies the problem to be studied and tells why it is important. A good introduction also specifies the hypotheses to be tested and gives the rationale behind any predictions. You will find short references to other research reports, such as: *Brown (1979) found ...* or *It has been argued that (Brown, 1979). ...* These statements refer to the author of another research report and the date when the report was published. The complete reference to the research is found in the reference section at the end of the report. Statements are referenced to indicate the source of hypotheses or research findings. You may find it necessary to read some of these other reports to fully understand the one you are currently reading.

**Method.**   The method section describes in detail the operations performed by the experimenter. It is usually printed in smaller type to conserve space, but this should not mislead you into believing that it is an unimportant section to be quickly skimmed over. It should contain enough information to allow another experimenter to replicate the study.

It is customary to divide the method section into subsections that cover subjects, apparatus, and procedure. The "Subjects" subsection tells how many subjects there were, how they were selected, and who they were (college students or rats). The "Apparatus" subsection indicates any special equipment that was used. If the equipment is commercially available, then the brand name and model number are usually specified. If custom-built equipment was used, then construction details and measurements are presented. The "Procedure" subsection explains what happened to the subjects, including instructions (for human subjects), special handling (for animals), statistical design features, and so forth. If uncommon materials such as special nonsense syllables, an original survey, or a new personality test were used, there may be a "Materials" subsection. The materials subsection will provide details about the test or other novel materials and may contain a sample of the materials or even a listing of all materials used. Often you will find a "Design" subsection that includes a description of the experimental plan and additional features of the statistical techniques.

**Results.**   This section tells what data were obtained. Descriptive statistics summarize the results (it is unusual to find raw data or individual scores reported). Inferential statistics are presented so that the reader can decide whether or not to believe the data. Since you may be reading articles soon, you need to know that a statement like "$F(4, 60) = 2.93, p < .05$" means that if the experiment were repeated, the odds of obtaining an $F$-statistic at least as large as 2.93 by chance would be less than 5 percent.

Tables or graphs may be used to summarize data. Tables present a summary of the dependent variable. Graphs are called figures, and the way they are drawn can be misleading. If an article contains several figures, check to see whether the scales are comparable so that the effects can be easily compared across different figures. In most figures, the dependent variable (what is measured) is plotted on the ordinate—the vertical axis. The independent variable (what is manipulated in an experiment) or a subject variable (such as personality type or age in a quasi-experimental study) is usually plotted on the abscissa—the horizontal axis. The results of several conditions can be shown in one figure by using different types of lines and symbols for each condition (see the articles later in this chapter).

**Discussion.**    The discussion section is the most creative part of an article. Here the author presents conclusions about the results and often offers a theoretical analysis of them. In the words of the *Publication Manual:* "In the discussion section, you are free to examine, interpret, and qualify your results, as well as draw inferences from them." Authors are given enough rope to hang themselves in the discussion. Hence, although all parts of an article should be approached with caution, an extra degree of skepticism is required for discussion sections.

**References.**    These are found at the end of the article. For the student, the references are primarily valuable as a guide to related information. The references cited will indicate the research that the author thinks is most relevant. When you have become familiar with a research area, you may know of additional, pertinent work that the author overlooked (or at least failed to cite). In this instance, you might be able to make an important criticism of the work and develop some ideas for additional research.

### Exceptions to the Format

Some exceptions to the standard format are common. The exception you are most likely to encounter involves a combination of the results and discussion sections. Fortunately, such combinations are labeled "Results and Discussion." These combined sections often are found in short articles (such as those published in the *Bulletin of the Psychonomic Society*). Combined results and discussion sections are also found in articles that report more than one experiment; each study has its own results and discussion section. When more than one study is reported in an article, there is usually a final section devoted to interpretation of all the results. This last section is generally called "General Discussion" or "Conclusions."

### Order of Reading Sections

Most readers start at the beginning of an article and dutifully plod their way through to the references, except perhaps those who enjoy mystery novels and thus reverse the process. As you become more and more familiar with a research area, it becomes less necessary to follow the order of sections presented in journals. For example, if you are truly an expert in some area, merely reading the results section may be enough for you to infer the rest of the article. After you have read a few articles, do not be afraid to depart from the usual order.

### | | | | CHECKLIST FOR THE CRITICAL READER

In this section, we offer some hints to help you become a better consumer of the information presented in psychological journals. Our most important suggestion is that you avoid rushing through the article. Instead, you should stop after each section and write down the answers to the questions we list here. This will be difficult at first, but with practice the process becomes automatic and requires little extra time. We suggest that you write down the answers for several articles. Once you get into the habit of being an active, critical reader, you may omit written answers to all the questions. However, you should keep a written summary of the articles you read (on index cards or in a notebook). The purpose of these notes is to give you ready access to the data base relevant to a particular problem. The questions listed here indicate some of the information that should be in your summaries. We have also included some suggestions from an article by M. Anisfeld (1987), which you might want to consult further for additional hints about how to read an empirical research paper critically.

## Introduction

**1.** *What is the author proposing?* Skeptics regard the introduction as a sales pitch for the article. Try to determine the author's bias. Sometimes it is helpful to play devil's advocate and adopt an alternative bias to help you identify possible distortions in the author's exposition (Anisfeld, 1987). Experienced readers can probably figure out why the author is arguing for some point of view, but beginners need a straightforward answer to the question.

**2.** *What hypotheses will be tested?* The answer to this question should be obvious and stated directly.

**3.** *How would I test this hypothesis?* This is the key question for the introduction. You should answer this question *before* you go on to the method section. If the author has any skill as a wordsmith, once you have finished the next section you are likely to agree with the method advocated in the article. In fact, a really clever author will, in the introduction itself, hint at the method, which makes it harder for the reader to answer this question without being biased by the author's persuasiveness. Write down the major ideas for your method of testing the hypothesis.

## Method

Compare your answer to question 3 with the author's. They probably will differ, if you have not peeked. Now answer question 4a.

**4a.** *Is my proposed method better than the author's?* Regardless of who had the better method, you or the author, this forced comparison will make you think about the method section critically, instead of passively accepting it.

**4b.** *Does the method actually test the hypothesis?* The hypothesis is sometimes the first casuality, disappearing between the introduction and method sections. Always check that the method used is adequate and relevant to the hypothesis.

**4c.** *What are the independent, dependent, subject, and control variables?* This is an obvious question and can be answered quickly. Listing the variables help you avoid passive reading of the method section. After you have resolved differences between your proposed method and the author's, answer the next question.

**5.** *Using the subjects, apparatus, and procedures described by the author, what results would I predict for this experiment?* It is essential that you answer this before reading the results section. You may find it impossible to predict a single outcome. This is not really a problem, since the author probably had more than one prediction also, and then went back and "polished" the introduction once results were in. Draw a rough sketch illustrating the most likely outcomes.

## Results

Compare the author's results with your predictions. If they are the same, go on to question 7. If not, answer question 6.

**6.** *Did the author get unexpected results?* After some thought, you will reach one of two conclusions. Either your prediction was wrong or the results are hard to believe. Perhaps the method was inappropriate or perhaps these results would not be obtained again if the experiment were repeated. If you are bothered by the results, you might even try your own experiment.

**7.** *How would I interpret these results?* You should answer this before reading the discussion. Look at the data in different ways to determine whether the results are internally consistent and substantiate the author's interpretation. Carefully scrutinize the data presented in the text, tables, and graphs, and reorganize them in other ways that are meaningful to you. For example, you can retabulate data, or you can graph data that are presented in the tables and text. This can help you generate alternative interpretations of the data, identify interesting results that the author overlooked, or find contradictory trends that the author would rather ignore. Look for biases in both the analysis and the interpretation of the results (Anisfeld, 1987).

## Discussion

Compare your interpretation with the author's. Answer question 8a or 8b, whichever is appropriate.

**8a.** *Why didn't I think of that?* (Author wins.)

**8b.** *Why didn't the author think of that?* (You win.) The discussion section is the most difficult to evaluate. Often only future research can determine whether the interpretation is correct. Frequently, authors have already done some of this future research but have not yet gotten around to reporting it. In such cases, the discussion often sets up this "new" research.

## Checklist Summary

If you read your first article carefully and wrote down the answers to all eight questions, by now you should be pleasantly exhausted. To help you recover, we will present a typical psychology article and analyze it according to the checklist summarized in table 13–1.

|||| **SAMPLE JOURNAL ARTICLE**

In this section, we have reprinted a short article from the *Bulletin of the Psychonomic Society*. The answers to the checklist questions were distilled from answers given in one of the author's classes. Most of those students were college sophomores who had taken two courses in psychology. The article is about experiments that have been interpreted as showing that a particular type of brain wave (alpha waves) can be conditioned in human subjects.

Most articles are written for experts in a particular area, so the authors of a report assume that their readers have some knowledge of the topic under investigation. In addition, most journals set page limitations on articles, which means that some information may be missing or presented very tersely. The assumptions made by the authors and the brevity of many articles pose a problem for the novice reader. The novice may have to read other articles or textbooks in order to understand a particular report. To help you understand the following report, we present some background information.

The article by Lindholm and Lowry (1978) is about learning to control a particular brain wave—the alpha wave. Alpha waves are prominent during meditation and relaxed wakefulness, and these waves are often associated with a pleasant emotional state that is called the alpha experience.

In a typical study about learning to control brain waves, the subject is connected to an electroencephalograph (EEG), a device that measures brain waves. The EEG is constructed so that it can provide a feedback signal to

---

**TABLE 13–1**
Questions for Critical Readers

*Introduction*
  1. What is the author proposing?
  2. What hypotheses will be tested?
  3. How would I test this hypothesis?

*Method*
  4a. Is my proposed method better than the author's?
  4b. Does the method actually test the hypothesis?
  4c. What are the independent, dependent, subject, and important control variables?
  5. Using this method, what results would I predict?

*Results*
  6. Did the author get unexpected results?
  7. How would I interpret these results?

*Discussion*
  8. Is my interpretation better than the author's?

the subject when a particular brain wave, such as the alpha wave, is present. The feedback, usually a tone, is supposed to work as a reinforcer does in operant conditioning; that is, the feedback tells the subject when alpha is occurring. So, when the feedback is contingent upon the appearance of alpha waves (feedback occurs only when alpha occurs), the alpha waves should occur more often than when feedback is noncontingent (the occurrence of feedback is unrelated to the occurrence of alpha). The logic here is precisely the same as that of reinforcing a hungry rat with food when the rat makes a particular response. If food is contingent upon a particular response, then that response will increase in likelihood. If food is presented noncontingently with respect to that response, then it will not increase in likelihood.

Some earlier alpha-wave studies seemed to show that alpha would increase even when the feedback was noncontingent. Thus, Lindholm and Lowry wanted to examine the effects of false (noncontingent) feedback on alpha-wave production. If alpha waves increase when feedback is noncontingent, then we can conclude that something other than operant conditioning increases the frequency of alpha production.

Lindholm and Lowry also studied the effects of relaxation on the production of alpha. They do not detail the method of inducing relaxation, but we will. The procedure used was Jacobson's (1978) method of progressive relaxation. This technique involves training people to alternately tense and relax small groups of muscles until the entire body is in a state of relaxation. This progressive relaxation usually starts with the toes, works up through the legs, the torso, arms, neck, and finally the face.

The following report is brief. One question you might try to answer is: "Could I replicate this study on the basis of the information presented?"

---

## Alpha production in humans under conditions of false feedback

Ernest Lindholm and Steven Lowry
Arizona State University, Tempe, Arizona 85281

Subjects were pretrained in either Jacobson's relaxation or a control relaxation technique, then served in four daily sessions of biofeedback training. On some days, the feedback was veridical with respect to alpha production, while on other days, the feedback falsely indicated either success or failure at the control task. The results showed that alpha increased over trials, but this increase was independent of feedback contingency. Subjective reports of mood were not influenced by feedback falsely indicating success or failure at the control task, and there were no reliable relationships between mood and amount of alpha actually produced. Prior training on Jacobson's relaxation did not enhance alpha production. It is concluded that alpha production and positive mood states are not systematically related and that neither of these variables is operantly conditioned through biofeedback.

Brown (1970, 1971, 1974), Kamiya (1968, 1969) and others have reported that humans can learn to control their alpha production and that successful learning is accompanied by a variety of positive mood states (e.g., euphoria, well-being) collectively referred to as the "alpha experience." Others (e.g., Lynch, Paskewitz, & Orne, 1974) have argued that alpha production is not learned, that rather, subjects habituate to the strangeness of the experimental environment and over time, engage in fewer activities that tend to block alpha, such as visual fixation on objects in the room. Regarding mood states, Plotkin, Mazer, and Lowey (1976) found no relationship between mood and the amount of alpha produced, although they suggested the possibility that the subjects' perceived success or failure might influence subjective reports of mood; that is, subjects who thought they were successful might report more positive mood states than subjects who thought they were not successful at the control task.

The Lynch et al. (1974) position that alpha enhancement is not learned is questioned by the results of Brolund and Schallow (1976), who showed that combining feedback and reward led to greater alpha enhancement than feedback alone, suggesting that experimental contingencies were controlling the behavior (alpha production) to some reliable degree. Further, Lynch et al. (1974) employed a noncontingent feedback control in which the noncontingent feedback of one subject is a replay of the contingent feedback received by another. This may well be inappropriate for alpha learning experiments, since subjects do (by whatever means) increase alpha over trials, thus the replay of increasing density of feedback over trials might serve to fortuitously reinforce almost anything the control subject does which works in the direction of increasing alpha. This could introduce a bias in the direction of reducing group differences between contingent and noncontingent groups and obscure real differences between groups.

The other type of control group used in alpha experiments is the no-feedback control, which simply requires subjects to sit in a comfortable chair in a quiet room for the duration of the experiment (Browland & Schallow, 1976). The problem here is that these subjects receive less stimulation than subjects receiving feedback (contingent or otherwise) and thus might display enhanced alpha due to a movement toward a sleep or semisleep state. It appears, therefore, that while some argue that alpha enhancement is not a learned phenomenon, the lack of appropriate control groups detracts from the force of these arguments.

There appear to be four important questions that require evaluation before the worth of alpha conditioning experiments can be adequately evaluated: (1) Are alpha increases learned as a result of experimental contingencies? (2) Is the "alpha experience" closely related to the amount of alpha actually produced? (3) Is the intensity of the "alpha experience" influenced by the subject's perceived success or failure? (4) Is the amount of alpha produced and the intensity of the "alpha experience" influenced by the subject's ability to relax? There is an implicit assumption that alpha density and relaxation are closely related, yet this assumption has never been directly tested by manipulating relaxation as an independent variable.

**Question 1.** What is the author proposing? The authors propose that the results of research concerned with learning to control alpha waves are equivocal. They seem to favor the idea that you cannot learn to control alpha.

**Question 2.** What hypotheses will be tested? The hypotheses are listed as questions to be answered before one can accept alpha conditioning:

(1) Does alpha increase because of the feedback provided? (2) What is the relation between the amount of alpha produced and the alpha experience? (3) What is the relation between the alpha experience and the subject's perceived failure or success? (4) What is the relation between the subject's ability to relax and the production of alpha (and the alpha experience)?

**Question 3.** How would I test these hypotheses? With respect to the first one, you could try to fool the subject in some way so that the feedback provided on the production of alpha is not correct. You could, for example, randomly present feedback to the subject—sometimes when alpha is being produced, and sometimes when it is not being produced. If alpha increases under random feedback, then it is not learned. With regard to the second hypothesis, you could correlate some measure of the subject's mood (the alpha experience) and the amount of alpha that is produced. For the third hypothesis, you could tell some subjects that they are doing well and compare their alpha production to that of subjects who are told that they are not doing well. One way to examine the final hypothesis would be to provide a relaxing atmosphere for some subjects and compare their alpha to the alpha of subjects who are trained in a more tense environment.

---

## Method

### Subjects
Ten male and 10 female subjects were solicited by advertisement to participate in an experiment in which they could learn self-relaxation techniques and control of brainwaves. All were members of psychology classes regularly offered at Arizona State University.

### Apparatus
Brain activity was recorded from occipital-occipital placements referenced to left mastoid using Grass silver disk electrodes and Grass electrode paste. Signals were amplified by a Beckman Type 411 dynograph, the high-level output of which was fed to the input of a DEC-LAB-8 computer that was programmed to detect alpha activity according to the following criteria: (1) There must be 1½ cycles of activity falling within the 8-to 12-Hz frequency band, and (2) the amplitude of the activity must exceed the Schmitt trigger threshold set for each subject during the baseline sessions. When both criteria were met, the computer software turned on the biofeedback display which consisted of a 61 × 61 cm sheet of milk-white Plexiglas located 61 cm from the subject's face and back-lighted by a 15-W ac bulb. The Plexiglas formed the face of a plywood box, thus providing a diffuse low-intensity glow that covered a large portion of the visual field and minimized focusing.

### Procedure
Relaxation training. The 20 subjects were divided into two groups of 5 males and 5 females each. The subjects in the Jacobson's group received 3 h of relaxation training, as did the subjects in the control relaxation group; the latter were told only to listen to white noise played at a low intensity and to relax as best they could.

Biofeedback training. Four 54-min sessions of biofeedback training were employed. Subjects were told that each session investigated a different brainwave, and that recent research indicated that relaxation enhanced control of all brain-waves, *thus they should use their prior relaxation training to keep the feedback light on as much as possible. This was deception. In fact, the four sessions operated as follows: Contingent Day 1 (CD1) was the first day of feedback for all subjects. Feedback was contingent on alpha production and this was true also for the fourth day (Contingent Day 4, abbreviated (CD4). Days 2 and 3 were either false increasing (FI) or false decreasing (FD) feedback, counterbalanced across subjects. Under FI, the feedback density started at low level and increased over trials while the reverse was true for the FD condition. To make the illusion of "real" feedback convincing, the amounts delivered on Days 2 and 3 were based on individual subject's Day 1 performance, and were programmed for delivery according to an unpredictable computerized schedule, the only constraint being that feedback increased and decreased over trials for the FI and FD groups, respectively. Thus, the amount of feedback presented to each individual subject was both a familiar and credible amount, referenced to his or her Day 1 performance. The rationale for this particular design was as follows: The first day must be contingent to establish baseline performance, and the last day should also be contingent to assess time-dependent changes in alpha production. The middle 2 days were FI and FD to assess perceived success on mood and also to determine whether feedback contingency was systematically related to alpha production.*

---

**Question 4a.**   Is my method better than the authors'? Their methods are at least as good as ours, if not better.

**Question 4b.**   Does the method actually test the hypotheses? Yes, the methods should test the four hypotheses. One problem that does exist is that all subjects receive contingent feedback on the first day. Although that procedure seems necessary to provide a baseline of alpha production, its effects could carry over throughout the next three days and mask the other manipulations. However, the effects of false feedback on the second two days probably will not carry over because the order of presenting the two conditions was counterbalanced across subjects. Counterbalancing means that some subjects received false increasing feedback about their brain waves on the second day and decreasing feedback on the third day. The rest of the subjects received those conditions in the reverse order.

**Question 4c.**   What are the variables (independent, dependent, subject, control)? Independent variables: type of feedback, type of relaxation training, trials, and days. Dependent variables: amount of alpha, mood. It is not clear how or when mood will be assessed. Subject variables: sex. Control variables: amount of feedback on the false feedback days determined by the subject's alpha level on the first day. Session length was controlled, as were the number of training days.

**Question 5.**   What do I predict? Since previous studies have reported reliable alpha conditioning, we predict that increases in alpha will be observed only on the first and last days (that is, only when the feedback is contingent on alpha production). Furthermore, we expect that alpha will increase with increases in the alpha experience and with perceived success. We expect that the ability to relax will enhance alpha.

### Results and Discussion

The .95 confidence level was adopted throughout as indicating the presence of a reliable difference.

The percent alpha produced during all phases of the experiment are displayed in Figure 1. All functions superficially resemble "learning curves," since performance during Trial 4 was generally superior to performance during Trial 1. An ANOVA revealed main effects for trials and rest vs. feedback. The main effect for sessions approached the .05 level and was therefore further analyzed by comparing CD1 alone with CD2, as a test for extreme differences. This analysis also failed to detect reliable sessions differences. No other main effect or interaction approached significance in either ANOVA.

The interpretation of these results is straightforward: The Jacobson's relaxation and control relaxation groups behaved similarly throughout the experiment. Both displayed more alpha as a function of trials and both displayed more alpha during feedback than during rest periods. However, the amount of alpha produced was not affected by whether the feedback was veridical or false, demonstrating that alpha production was not under the control of the experimental contingencies. We also analyzed the data from the viewpoint of net alpha change, for example, alpha produced during each feedback period minus alpha produced during the preceding rest period. This "change score" produced functions (not shown) that varied in a nonsystematic manner and remained close to 0% change. An ANOVA in this case produced no main effects or interactions that approached reliability.

The mood scores (responses on the Mood Adjective Check List, MACL, Nowlis, 1965) were analyzed by ANOVA, Mann-Whitney U, and parametric and nonparametric correlational methods. None of these analyses even hinted at a reliable relationship among the variables of amount of alpha actually produced, subjective report of mood, prior exposure to relaxation training, or perceived success or failure

**FIGURE 1**

Percent alpha produced by the Jacobson's relaxation group (solid circles) and the control relaxation group (open circles) as a function of sessions and trials. Abbreviations: CD1 and CD2, Contingent Days 1 and 2, respectively; FI and FD, false increasing and false decreasing biofeedback, respectively. R and F, rest and feedback, respectively. The first R period in each session is the mean of the baseline recording period.

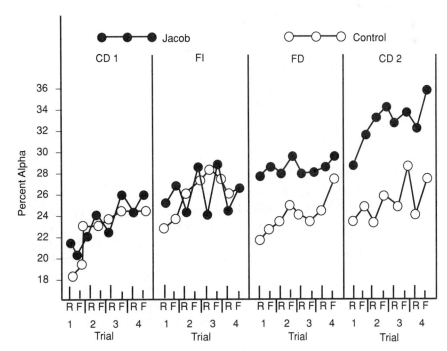

on the control task. Differences attributable to sex of subject were sought in all of the above analyses, but none were found.

We purposely used visual feedback since the early positive reports of alpha conditioning used visual feedback while more recent, negative findings employed non-visual feedback designs. Also, we designed control groups that we feel eliminated or circumvented the problems inherent in the control groups used by others. Additionally, we used a computerized system for detecting alpha activity that circumvented the "roll off" problems inherent in the "active filter" systems used by others. Finally, we gathered data on our subjects over a 4-day period (plus relaxation pretraining) which is longer than other published experiments. Nonetheless, there was no evidence that changes in alpha production were learned through operant conditioning, since the response (alpha production) was not under the control of reinforcement contingencies (biofeedback being verdical or false). We did replicate Brown's (1971) finding that alpha production is greater during feedback than during rest periods. While Brown interpreted this finding as evidence for alpha learning, we point out that feedback need not be contingent to produce this effect, and if alpha is considered to be change scores, no evidence for learning is apparent. Finally, the "alpha experience" appears to be nothing more than suggestibility; empirically, mood was not related to the amount of alpha produced nor to perceived success or failure.

## References

Brolund, J. W., & Schallow, J. R. (1976). The effects of reward on occipital alpha facilitation by biofeedback. *Psychophysiology,* **13** 236–241.

Brown, B. B. (1970). Recognition of aspects of consciousness through association with EEG activity represented by a light signal. *Psychophysiology,* **6,** 442–452.

Brown, B. B. (1971). Awareness of EEG subjective activity relationships within a closed feedback system. *Psychophysiology,* **7,** 451–464.

Brown, B. B. (1974). *New mind, new body.* New York: Harper & Row.

Kamiya, J. (1968). Conscious control of brainwaves. *Psychology Today,* **1,** 57–60.

Kamiya, J. (1969). Operant control of the EEG alpha rhythm and some of its reported effects on consciousness. In C. Tart (Ed.), *Altered states of consciousness: A book of readings.* New York: Wiley.

Lynch, J. J., Paskewitz, D. A., & Orne, M. T. (1974). Some factors in the feedback control of human alpha rhythm. *Psychosomatic Medicine,* **36,** 399–410.

Nowlis, V. (1965). Research with the mood adjective check list. In S. S. Tomkins & C. E. Izard (Eds.), *Affect, cognition, and personality.* New York: Springer.

Plotkin, W. B., Mazer, C., & Lowey, D. (1976). Alpha enhancement and the likelihood of an alpha experience. *Psychophysiology,* **13,** 466–471.

(Received for publication November 9, 1977.)

---

**Question 6.**   Did the author get unexpected results? The only prediction of ours that was correct concerned the positive effect of false increasing feedback on the amount of alpha. However, this is a small victory, since alpha also increased under false decreasing feedback. It looks as if the subjects who received real relaxation training did better on the last day or two than did the control subjects. However, the authors report that there were no interactions between relaxation and sessions. This means that the effects of relaxation training did not differ reliably across sessions. "ANOVA" refers to "analysis of variance," a type of statistical test discussed in appendix B.

**Question 7.**   How would I interpret the results? Subjects might have increased alpha because they wanted to. In other words, the important variable in an alpha conditioning study is not the relation between feedback and alpha production. Rather, subjects may perceive alpha waves as being desirable, and thus may try to have an alpha experience. Since most college students have heard about meditation and brain waves, these subjects may well have tried to relax in order to increase alpha. Furthermore, since these subjects were introductory psychology students, it is likely that they knew quite a bit about alpha waves and the alpha experience.

**Question 8.**   Is my interpretation better than the authors's? The authors simply point out that the results are not owing to conditioning (alternative explanations are mentioned in the introduction). They do argue that the alpha experience is caused by suggestibility, which is somewhat similar to our interpretation of the conditioning results.

If you are interested in alpha experiences and alpha conditioning, you will find a review by Plotkin (1979) to be thought provoking. Plotkin suggests that there are no unequivocal demonstrations of alpha conditioning, and he offers eight hypotheses for the development of the alpha experience during laboratory studies of alpha.

Table 3–1 in chapter 3 lists many important journals that contain psychological research. You might examine these journals and start being a critical consumer of psychological research. Practice might not make you a perfect reader of journal reports, but it will help, especially if you follow the checklist for critical readers.

## | | | | WRITING A RESEARCH REPORT

You have gotten an idea, reviewed the pertinent literature, designed a procedure, collected your data, and analyzed the results. Your course may require a written record of your research. Even if it does not, you are obligated to publicize the results of a carefully done project. We believe that to maintain the self-correcting nature of science, it is important to publish good data. However, this does not mean that journals should be cluttered with information derived from every undergraduate project. If your research is promising, you will receive encouragement from your instructor.

In this section, we will review the format of a typical report and discuss some of the stylistic considerations that make up a comprehensible paper. If you follow our suggestions for reading articles, you will have a pretty good idea about the format of a research report, and you will probably have a good feel for technical writing style. Some aspects of technical writing are not too obvious, so we will discuss them here. What we present are general guidelines. If you need additional information, examine R. J. Sternberg's book, *The Psychologist's Companion* and D. J. Bem's (1987) chapter, "Writing the Empirical Journal Article." The 1983 revision of the *Publication Manual of the American Psychological Association* (third edition) will also help, because it is the official arbiter of style for almost all of the journals listed in table 3–1 (chapter 3), as well as for many other journals in psychology and education.

## Format

The outline of a typical report in figure 13–1 emphasizes the sequence of pages you will have to put together in your APA-style manuscript. This version of the article is known as the *copy* manuscript, and is assembled in a particular manner to facilitate the editorial and publication processes. A run through that sequence will give you an idea of what you are supposed to include. Your cover page contains the title of your project, your name, and your affiliation (your institution or place of business). The short title that appears at the top of each page of the copy manuscript consists of the first few words of the title and is used to identify the manuscript during the editorial process only. The heading that will appear at the top of each page of the *published* article is called the running head, and this is typed in capital letters near the bottom of the cover page of the copy manuscript. The short title and running head should not be confused. The next page, page 2, contains the heading "Abstract" and the abstract itself. On this page and on all subsequent ones (except the figures), you should have an ab-

**FIGURE 13–1**

Page sequence for a report in APA format.

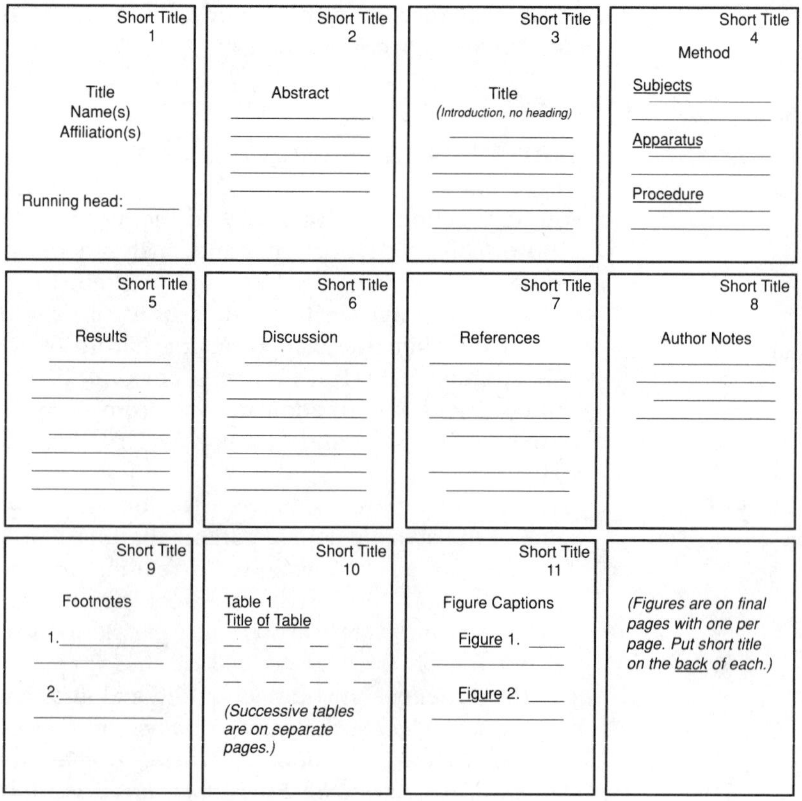

breviated title and the page number in the top right-hand corner of the page. Page 3 repeats the whole title and includes your introductory material. Ordinarily, you do not have a heading for the introduction. After your introduction is finished, the method section begins. Note the format shown for the headings on page 4 in figure 13–1. The side headings, like "Subjects" and "Apparatus," help guide the reader to pertinent information. The results section immediately follows the method. Do not include figures and tables in the body of this section (they come at the end of the report). Instead, indicate their approximate location as shown in page 5 of figure 13–1. Next comes the discussion, which ends the major textual portion of your report.

The references begin on a separate page. The format for presenting references is complex, and you should use care in preparing them. The article reprinted in this chapter contains most of the different styles of references that you will have to document. Look them over carefully, and, if you have any questions, ask you instructor. You might also study the APA manual and recent journal articles. Any author notes and footnotes appear on separate pages after the references. For most college laboratory reports, footnotes are not necessary. When you prepare something for publication, you may acknowledge financial and intellectual support, which should appear on the author-note page. General acknowledgments are not numbered. Other, perhaps peripheral, information should appear as numbered footnotes on a separate footnote page, but such footnotes are generally discouraged.

Following the footnotes are your data tables mentioned in the results section. Each table should be on a separate page and numbered consecutively, according to its appearance in the results section. Make the titles of your tables short but communicative. Captions for your figures are numbered consecutively and appear on a separate page following the data tables. Finally, you have your figures, each on a separate piece of paper. Put your name (or the short title) and the number of the figure on the back.

As mentioned before, copy manuscripts are organized in this fashion to accommodate the publisher. However, you should note that there is a special section in the *APA Publication Manual* about the accepted format for student papers submitted for a course requirement but not for publication. For example, in student papers, tables and figures may be interspersed in the text. You should check with your professor or department regarding the preferred format for class projects. However, we recommend learning the APA publication format because it provides good practice for preparing your future publications.

A sample manuscript appears on the following pages. You should note the sequence of pages, where typing begins on a new page, and what information is provided in each section. The only aspect missing from this manuscript that may appear in one of yours is a separate footnote page. Note carefully how the references are cited in the reference section.

The following paper is copyright 1987 by the American Psychological Association. Reprinted by permission of the author. Comish, S. E. (1987). Recognition of facial stimuli following an intervening task involving the Identi-kit. *Journal of Applied Psychology, 72,* 488–491.

Recognition of Facial Stimuli

1

Recognition of Facial Stimuli Following an Intervening

Task Involving the Identi-kit

Sara Elizabeth Comish

University of Alberta

Running head:   RECOGNITION OF FACIAL STIMULI

Recognition of Facial Stimuli

2

## Abstract

The Identi-kit is a tool for constructing a facial composite.  The types of errors made on a recognition task, following an intervening task involving the Identi-kit, were examined in this study.  One hundred and eight introductory psychology students viewed a target composite-face and made an Identi-kit reconstruction.  Subsequently, they were required to identify the original composite-face from a lineup of six composite-faces. Subjects who made an Identi-kit reconstruction were prone to make more errors on the recognition task than participants in a control condition, $p < .01$.  False alarms were promoted when the subjects saw a lineup containing foils modified to resemble the subjects' own reconstruction errors, $p < .05$.  This finding suggests that memory for facial stimuli can be influenced by viewing misleading information.

Recognition of Facial Stimuli Following an Intervening

Task Involving the Identi-kit

There is a commonly held belief that memory for faces is
immune to interference; this belief is expressed by the oft heard
statement, "I never forget a face."  Support for the role of
interference in facial memory, however, can be found in
experimental studies.  Deffenbacher, Carr, and Leu (1981) found
that individual's memory for photographs of faces was highly
susceptible to retroactive interference, unlike their memory for
nouns and objects, which was relatively immune to the
interference.  Loftus and Greene (1980) examined the extent to
which facial memory was influenced by reading misleading
descriptions of a previously shown target face.  In a later
recognition task with the target face absent, the majority of
subjects who had read the misleading information picked a face
with the misleading information.  This finding raises the issue of
whether facial memory can be altered by viewing misleading
information.

A useful tool for studying this issue is the Identi-kit, a
technique that consists of transparencies of line drawings of
different facial features that can be superimposed on each other
to make a composite-face.  A similar system is the Photofit, which
consists of actual photographs of features instead of line
drawings.  Studies that have used composite techniques to examine

Recognition of Facial Stimuli

4

interference in memory for faces have yielded conflicting results. Mauldin and Laughery (1981) found that use of the Identi-kit to construct a target face improved recognition of the same target face in a later recognition task. On the other hand, Davies, Ellis, and Shepherd (1978) found different results. They found a trend in the opposite direction, which indicated that making a Photofit reconstruction could interfere with later recognition of a target face (although this difference failed to attain statistical significance). In both of these studies, subjects viewed a target face and then made a composite reconstruction. The recognition tasks that were used to assess memory involved photograph lineups that were not altered to resemble subjects' composite reconstructions.

It is reasonable to assume, however, that the source of any interference from Identi-kit reconstruction may result from viewing one's own errors in Identi-kit reconstruction as a holistic face and that maximum interference can be expected when the distractors used during the recognition task are similar to the individual's errors in Identi-kit reconstruction. The purpose of this study was to determine the effect of an intervening task involving misleading information on later recognition. In order to test this, subjects in two conditions made Identi-kit reconstructions of a target composite-face. The third condition was a control condition in which subjects did not make an Identi-kit reconstruction.  For the subsequent recognition task, subjects saw a lineup consisting of the original target composite-face and five foils.  The subjects were yoked on the recognition task to allow for the determination of whether interference was a result of making Identi-kit reconstructions per se or if it occurred only when the distractor foils resembled the participants' own Identi-kit reconstruction errors.

Method

Subjects

One hundred and eight introductory psychology students participated in partial fulfillment of a course requirement. Thirty-six subjects were randomly assigned to each of the three conditions.

Materials

The Identi-kit, available from Smith and Wesson, Inc., is a box containing transparencies of facial features.  It is accompanied by the Identi-kit Handbook, which is a pictorial index of the features available in the kit.

Design and Procedure

A three-group design was employed.  In the Identi-kit/own-errors condition, subjects made an Identi-kit reconstruction of a target composite-face and, in a later recognition task, encountered foils modified to resemble the subjects' own Identi-

Recognition of Facial Stimuli

6

kit reconstruction errors.  Subjects in the Identi-kit/other-errors conditions also made an Identi-kit reconstruction but were yoked to a subject in the Identi-kit/own-errors condition so that the foils in the recognition task were those of a subject in the Identi-kit/own-errors condition.  In the control/other-errors condition, subjects saw the target composite-face but did not make an Identi-kit reconstruction.  They were also yoked so that the foils in the recognition task were those of a subject in the Identi-kit/own-errors condition.

Initially, all subjects viewed one of two target composite-faces -- photocopies of an Identi-kit reconstruction of either a man or a woman -- for 10 s until it was removed.  Subjects in the Identi-kit/own-errors condition and the Identi-kit/other-errors condition then made an Identi-kit reconstruction that involved an initial choice of facial features from the Identi-kit Handbook.  A composite face was made using these features and shown to the subjects, who were allowed to change any of the features.  On average, the reconstruction process took 13 min.  Following this, subjects performed a filler task in which they were given 7 min to rate two photograph faces on trait dimensions.  In order to ensure that the time that elapsed between the initial exposure to the target composition-face and the recognition task was the same for subjects in all conditions, the subjects in the control/other-errors condition spent 20 min rating the two photograph faces.

Finally, the subjects performed the recognition task, in which they were asked to select the original composite-face from a lineup consisting of the original target composite-face and five distractors. This task was not a forced choice and subjects were allowed to indicate that the target composite-face was not present in the lineup. In the Identi-kit/own-errors condition, each distractor foil was the same as the original target composite-face except that one error from the individual's Identi-kit reconstruction was substituted for one feature of each distractor. Thus, the first distractor was the same as the target except for the hair, the second distractor was the same as the target except for the nose, the third differed on the lips, the fourth differed on the eyes, and the fifth differed on the eyebrows (see Figure 1 for an example of a typical lineup). These distractor foils were photocopied and placed in a lineup, counterbalanced to vary the order of the target and the foils. Using this technique the target appeared in each position six times in each condition, with the positions of the foils randomly determined. Subjects in the Identi-kit/other-errors condition and control/other-errors condition saw the same lineup in the recognition task as the subject in the Identi-kit/own errors condition to whom they were yoked.

Recognition of Facial Stimuli

8

---------------------------

Insert Figure 1 about here

---------------------------

The data from an additional four participants in the Identi-kit/own-errors condition and from an additional three subjects in the Identi-kit yoked condition were not included in the analyses because one or more features in the Identi-kit reconstruction was identical to the original target composite-face. When the correct feature was selected for the Identi-kit reconstruction, it was not possible to modify the lineup distractor foils in the manner described previously. These subjects were replaced.

The dependent variable was scored as a hit, a miss, or a false alarm. A hit was a correct recognition of the original target composite-face; a miss was an incorrect "not present" decision; and a false alarm was an incorrect selection of a distractor foil. In addition, subjects' satisfaction with their reconstruction and the subjects' certainty with regard to their recognition were obtained on scales from not at all satisfied (1) to totally satisfied (7) and from not at all certain (1) to totally certain (7), respectively.

Results

All data were collapsed over the two target composite-faces and converted to percentages, which are presented by condition in Table 1. A one-way analysis of variance (ANOVA) across the three conditions was performed on the number of overall errors.  A significant difference was found for the overall number of recognition errors, $\underline{F}$(2, 105) = 4.86, $\underline{p}$ < .01.  A Newman-Keuls comparison revealed that the control/other-errors condition produced significantly fewer errors than either of the Identi-kit reconstruction conditions.  The estimated $\omega^2$ was .065.

--------------------------

Insert Table 1 about here

--------------------------

A further one-way ANOVA was performed on the number of false alarms.  A significant difference was found among the conditions, $\underline{F}$(2, 105) = 4.46, $\underline{p}$ < .05.  A Newman-Keuls comparison revealed that the Identi-kit/own-errors condition differed significantly from the other two conditions, demonstrating that when the foils resembled subjects' Identi-kit errors, subjects were more prone to incorrectly identify the modified foils.  In this case, the estimated $\omega^2$ was .059.

Although an ANOVA on the number of overall errors and on both of the types of errors is redundant -- because the two types of errors sum to give the number of overall errors -- the effect of Identi-kit use on the different types of errors is of particular interest in this study.  Therefore, an additional ANOVA was performed on the number of "not present" responses (misses).  There was a significant different among the conditions, $\underline{F}$(2, 105)

Recognition of Facial Stimuli

10

= 3.75, $\underline{p}$ < .05, and the Newman-Keuls comparison revealed that the subjects in the Identi-kit/other errors condition made significantly more "not present" responses than subjects in either the Identi-kit/own-errors condition or the control/other-errors condition.  The estimated $\omega^2$ was .047.

An ANOVA was performed on subjects' confidence ratings, and there were no significant differences among the conditions, $\underline{F}$(2, 105) = 1.46, ns.  Wells and Lindsay (1985) have suggested that confidence ratings of "choosers only" (i.e., those subjects that make a recognition choice rather than those that indicate that the target composite-face was not present) should be analyzed separately to determine whether confidence ratings have predictive use.  No significant differences were found among the conditions when a one-way ANOVA was performed on the confidence ratings of "choosers only," $\underline{F}$(2, 89) = 0.422, ns.  The low accuracy-confidence correlation, however, is consistent with previous eyewitness studies (see Wells & Murray, 1984).

A point-biserial correlation between confidence and accuracy was performed for "choosers only" by condition and was not significant, highest $\underline{r}$ = -.221.  Further, it was not significant when performed on the data of all subjects, highest $\underline{r}$ = -.24.  A point-biserial correlation between subjects' satisfaction with their Identi-kit reconstruction and accuracy of recognition was also not significant for all subjects ratings nor was it

Recognition of Facial Stimuli

11

significant when the analysis was performed on "choosers only,"
highest $r$ = -.27.

## Discussion

The use of the Identi-kit itself promotes overall errors on
the recognition task. The lineup foils in this study were
modified by only one feature to resemble the Identi-kit
reconstructions. This was sufficient, however, to bias people in
favor of foils that resembled their own Identi-kit
reconstructions. When the lineup foils resemble people's own
Identi-kit reconstructions, the errors that are promoted are false
alarms to composite-faces that resemble their Identi-kit
reconstructions. Errors are promoted even when the composite-
faces in the lineup are not similar to the subject's original
Identi-kit reconstruction. In these cases, the predominant errors
are misses, that is, failures to correctly identify the original
target composite-face by saying that it is not present.
Therefore, it appears that people who make an Identi-kit
reconstruction are biased away from the original target composite-
face.

The findings in this study appear to conflict with the
results obtained by Davies et al. (1978) and Mauldin and Laughery
(1981). The differences between the present study and the
experiments of Davies et al. and Mauldin and Laughery are,

however, numerous.  Their null results, for example, may be due to a failure to allow the subject to make a "not present" response. Alternatively, the high similarity between distractors and target achieved in the present study, compared with the others, might account for the different results.  Most important, no study prior to this has used Identi-kit reconstruction errors to build distractor composite-faces in which the target is embedded.  This contingency between Identi-kit reconstructions and the recognition task in the Identi-kit/own-errors condition allowed for an optimal test of the potential interference effects of the Identi-kit task on subsequent recognition.

What is the source of the recognition errors?  It is possible that the Identi-kit task creates interference because it involves viewing the misleading errors incorporated into a complete face. A person making a recognition decision may be easily confused between the original memory and the memory of the Identi-kit reconstruction.  This is particularly likely to occur when a composite-face similar to a person's own Identi-kit reconstruction is present in the lineup.

The distribution of facial features in the foils that subjects had falsely identified was also examined.  In general, people seem to make more recognition errors when features of less importance, such as eyebrows and lips, were altered.  This is consistent with previous studies (see Ellis, 1984, for a review).

Recognition errors involving the more important features, hair and eyes, were primarily made only when the altered features resembled the Identi-kit reconstruction.  This suggests that more confusions occur for less important features and for important features that resemble Identi-kit reconstructions.

Although the Identi-kit task was shown to interfere with recognition in this study, there are a number of caveats to consider in generalizing these findings to police lineups.  First, it is not known how representative Identi-kit composite-faces are of photographs of real individuals, let alone the extent to which Identi-kit encoding operations compare with the encoding of live faces.  Thus, performance on an Identi-kit lineup task may not be indicative of performance on a real lineup task.  Second, the lineups used in this experiment consisted of highly similar composite-faces, faces much more similar than a typical police lineup.  In the first condition, the foils were altered so that one feature was precisely the same as the subjects' Identi-kit reconstruction--an occurrence that is highly unlikely in a typical police lineup.  Third, the target stimuli in this study were limited to only two Identi-kit composites that may not be representative of other faces.  Fourth, the reconstructions from which the lineups were created shared no features with the target composite.  Finally, the subjects in this study may have had poorer memories for the target than aroused witnesses to a crime

Recognition of Facial Stimuli

14

and thus made poorer reconstructions.  For these reasons, it is necessary to be cautious in extrapolating from these results to police lineups.

Recognition of Facial Stimuli

15

## References

Davies, G. M., Ellis, H. D., & Shepherd, J. W. (1978). Face identification:  The influence of delay upon accuracy of Photofit construction.  Journal of Police Science and Administration, 6, 35-42.

Deffenbacher, K. A., Carr, T. H., & Leu, J. R. (1981).  Memory for words, pictures and faces:  Retroactive interference, forgetting and reminiscence.  Journal of Experimental Psychology:  Human Learning and Memory, 7, 299-305.

Ellis, H. D. (1984).  Practical aspects of face memory.  In G. L. Wells & E. F. Loftus (Eds.), Eyewitness testimony: Psychological perspectives (pp. 12-37).  New York:  Cambridge University Press.

Loftus, E., & Greene, E. (1980).  Warning:  Even memory for faces may be contagious.  Law and Human Behavior, 4, 323-334.

Mauldin, M., & Laughery, K. (1981).  Composite production effects on subsequent facial identification.  Journal of Applied Psychology, 66, 351-357.

Wells, G. L., & Lindsay, R. C. L. (1985).  Methodological notes on the accuracy-confidence relation in eyewitness identifications. Journal of Applied Psychology, 70, 413-419.

Recognition of Facial Stimuli

16

Wells, G. L., & Murray, D. M. (1984).  Eyewitness confidence.  In

G. L. Wells & E. F. Loftus (Eds.), Eyewitness testimony:

Psychological perspectives (pp. 155-170).  New York:  Cambridge

University Press.

Recognition of Facial Stimuli

17

## Author Notes

Portions of this article were presented at the meeting of the Canadian Psychological Association held in Toronto, Canada, June 1986.

I am indebted to Gary Wells for the thoughtful help and guidance he provided during the course of this research. In addition, I am grateful to John Pullyblank, John Turtle, and Brendan Rule for their comments on an earlier version of this article; to Constable Bates of the Royal Canadian Mounted Police for his time and comments; and to two anonymous reviewers for their extremely helpful and meticulous comments.

Correspondence concerning this article should be addressed to Sara Elizabeth Comish, who is now at the Department of Psychology, University of Victoria, P. O. Box 1700, Victoria, British Columbia, Canada, V8W 2Y2.

Recognition of Facial Stimuli

18

Table 1

Performance on the Recognition Task:  Data Converted Into

Percentages by Condition

|  | Condition | | |
|---|---|---|---|
| Performance | Identi-kit (own errors) | Identi-kit (yoked) | Control (yoked) |
| Total errors | $86.11_a$ | $77.78_a$ | $56.56_b$ |
| Misses | $8.33_a$ | $27.78_b$ | $8.33_a$ |
| False alarms | $77.78_a$ | $50.00_b$ | $47.22_b$ |
| Correct (hits) | 13.89 | 22.22 | 44.44 |

Note.  Percentages that do not share a common subscript differ at $p < .05$.

Recognition of Facial Stimuli

19

Figure Caption

<u>Figure</u> 1. The original target face, a typical Identi-kit

reconstruction, and the subsequent lineup. (Foils are identical

to the original target face, except for the indicated facial

feature obtained from the reconstruction.)

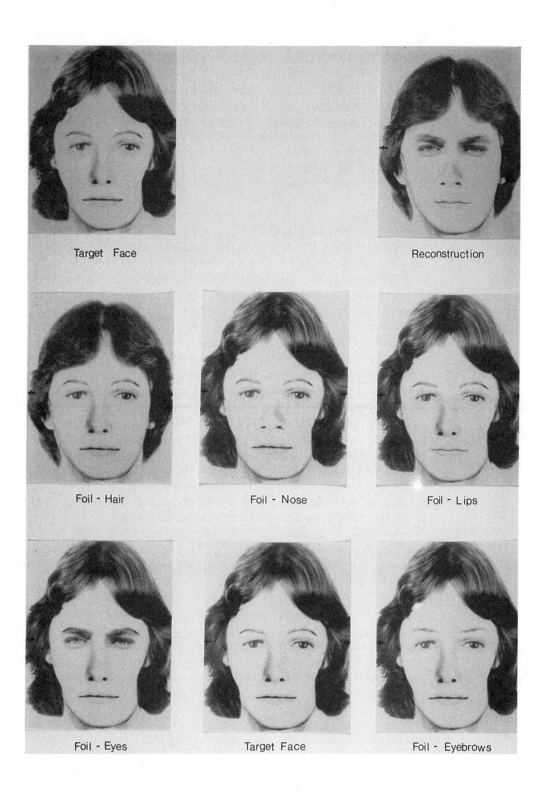

Target Face

Reconstruction

Foil - Hair

Foil - Nose

Foil - Lips

Foil - Eyes

Target Face

Foil - Eyebrows

## Style

Now that you have some idea of format, let us consider style. After you have suffered through some obscurely written article, you will no doubt recognize the advantage of clear, unambiguous writing. The APA format helps standardize the order and general content. However, making sure that the reader understands what you are saying is up to you. We have read many research reports prepared for our classes—some good, some awful, most of them in between—and we have found that the biggest problem is transition, or flow, from one section to the next. Deliberately or not, many students write as if they were composing a surprise-ending short story, even though their report should be as straightforward as possible.

Your abstract should include your variables (independent, dependent, and important control variables), number and type of subjects, major results, and important conclusions. The body of your report should expand upon the abstract. (This is why most abstracts are written last, even though the report might be clearer if it were written first, as an outline for the main part of the work.) You should remember the following: In the introduction, state why you are interested in particular variables and what other investigators have found; in the method section, state how you examined those variables; in the results section, state what happened when you examined the variables; and in your discussion, state what the effects of the variables mean. Thus, the body of your report should represent a tight package, not a disjointed essay containing sections that seem independent of each other. You have to tell your readers what you were trying to do, over and over again. Do not be afraid to be somewhat redundant by having each section build on the previous one. If you repeat the purpose of your research often enough, even the dullest reader will have gotten something from your report by the time he or she gets to the reference list. Table 13–2 summarizes the information that should be included in each section of your report.

The APA publication manual outlines style considerations as follows: Use the precise word, avoid ambiguity, order presentation of ideas, and consider the reader. These guidelines warrant some discussion.

Scientific writing demands clarity, so each word has to be chosen carefully. Consider these sentences that regularly appear in undergraduate research reports: "I ran the subjects individually." "The white albino rat was introduced to the Skinner box." Actually, none of the subjects in the study from which the first sentence was pulled did any running during the course of the project. What the author meant to say was, "I tested the subjects individually," or "The subjects were tested individually." From reading about rats introduced to Skinner boxes, you might conclude that the researcher had very clever rats. The rat did not shake hands with a box; all that happened was that the rat was put into the operant-conditioning chambers. Furthermore, "white albino" is redundant. All albino rats are white. The lesson here is that in scientific writing you must be careful to choose the correct word or phrase and avoid ambiguity. Also, be cautious when using pronouns such as *which, this, that, these,* and *those.* Many students find it irresistible to begin a paragraph with one of these pronouns, and more often than not the referent for the pronoun is not very easy to

**TABLE 13-2**

A summary of the information in each section of a research report.

| Section | Content |
|---------|---------|
| Title | Experiments: State independent and dependent variables—<br>    "The effects of X on Y."<br>Other studies: State the relationships examined—<br>    "The relation between X and Y." |
| Abstract | In less than 150 words, state what was done to whom and summarize the most important results. |
| Introduction | State what you plan to do and why (you may have to review results from related research). Predicted results may be appropriate. |
| Method | Present enough information to allow someone else to repeat your study exactly the way you did it. For clarity use subheadings (*Subjects, Apparatus,* etc.), and make sure that dependent, independent, subject, and control variables are specified. |
| Results | Summarize important results in tables or figures. Direct the reader to data that seem most relevant to the purpose of the research. |
| Discussion | State how the results relate to the hypotheses or predictions stated in the introduction. Inferences and theoretical statements are appropriate. |
| References | In APA format, list only those references that were cited in your report. |

determine. You can usually avoid any ambiguity by including the referent of the pronoun each time it is used.

After you have decided on your words and phrases, put them together carefully. A common problem among some writers is to shift verb tenses abruptly. In general, use the past tense in the review of other studies in your introduction (Smith *found*) and in your method (The subjects *were*). When you are describing and discussing your data, the present tense is usually appropriate (The data *show* that . . ., which *means* that).

Make sure that collective and plural nouns agree with their verbs and pronouns. Plural words that end in *a* are troublesome, such as *data, criteria,* and *phenomena.* Each of these nouns is plural, so they each require plural verbs and pronouns. "These data *are*" is correct, but "this phenomena *is*" is not correct. The singular forms for these nouns are: *datum, criterion,* and *phenomenon* (This phenomenon *is*).

Many scientific writers overuse the passive voice in their reports. Consider this statement: "It is thought that forgetting is caused by interference." Although this sentence is fairly concise (and it is precise), it is also stuffy and less direct than "We think that interference causes forgetting," which is really what was meant. Be careful about using either the active or passive voice too much. If you overuse the passive voice, your report sounds stuffy. If you overuse the active voice, you may take interest away from what you did and place too much emphasis on yourself (I think, I did, and so on) If you want to emphasize what was done and not who did it and why, use the passive construction. On the other hand, if you think that the agent of the activity is also important, or if the reason for the action is important, use the active voice.

The careful writer tries to avoid language that is sexist. The APA recommends that the use of *he* (and *his* and *him*) as a generic pronoun be avoided by changing to a plural construction or by using something like *he* and *she*. Generally, the writer should strive for accurate, unbiased communication.

Writing a cogent, well-organized research article is a skill that requires considerable effort and practice. More is involved than simply allocating information to the correct sections. There are many fine points of style, usage, and exposition that distinguish lucid, well-written articles from obscure and tortuous ones. While writing your report, you should make frequent use of standard references for points of style and grammar. In addition, consult the *APA Publication Manual* regarding aspects of technical writing that are particularly relevant to psychology journal articles, including the organization and content of each section, economy and precision in the expression of ideas, the presentation of data and statistics, and so forth. Finally, we highly recommend the aforementioned book by Sternberg (1987) and the chapter by Bem (1987) for excellent advice and specific examples of good and poor style, phrasing, and organization in psychology articles.

## Publishing an Article

Assume that your article has been written, proofread, corrected, and the last page has just emerged from a steaming typewriter. Now what? Although it is unlikely that your first student effort will produce an article of professional quality, you may nevertheless find it interesting to discover what happens when an article is submitted to a journal by a professional psychologist.

The first step is to send copies of the manuscript (the technical term for an unpublished work) to a small number of trusted associates who can check it over to make sure that it has no obvious or elementary flaws and that it is written clearly. Once the comments come back, the indicated corrections are made and, with some trepidation, the author commits the manuscript to the mail, addressed to the editor of the most appropriate journal. After this, it is necessary to forget about it entirely for the next few months or otherwise exhibit great patience. The review process is slow. (The editor who receives the manuscript is a harried, overworked, tired individual who often regrets accepting the editorship. Editors of journals, like elected politicians, serve a fixed term of office, usually four to six years.) About two or three weeks after submitting the article, the author receives a form letter that thanks him or her for interest in the journal and acknowledges receipt of the manuscript. The manuscript gets a number (like 86–867) and if an associate editor has been assigned to handle it, the author is instructed to direct all future correspondence to that editor.

The editor then sends copies of the manuscript to two or three reviewers. It is unlikely that both of them will be good friends of the author. Some journals allow the author to have blind reviewing, where the author conceals his or her identity. Blind reviewing is for those who do not believe in the impartiality of reviewers. The reviewer, who may also review for several other journals, puts the manuscript in the pile on his or her desk. A conscientious reviewer may take up to a day or two to carefully read and evaluate a manuscript. When each reviewer gets around to it, a summary statement is sent to the editor. When the reviewers are in agreement, the editor's decision is easy. Should the reviewers disagree, the editor must carefully read the manuscript and sometimes may request a third opinion. Finally, an editorial decision is reached and the author receives a letter stating either (1) why the manuscript cannot be published, (2) what kind of revisions are needed to make the manuscript acceptable, or (3) that the journal will publish the article. Since rejection rates for manuscripts are quite high in most journals (above 80 percent), editors spend a great deal of time devising tactful letters of rejection.

Whether or not the article was accepted, the comments of the reviewers are most valuable. The best psychologists in the area have provided, free of charge, their careful opinions about the research. Of course, reviewers can also make mistakes. Any author who disagrees with a review has the privilege, even the responsibility, of writing to the editor. Although this action will usually not result in the article being accepted, it is important that rejected authors have the right to appeal or protest. Anyway, there are always other journals.

If the article was accepted for publication, the author is still not yet finished. Some revision of the manuscript may be required. The copyright for the article is signed over to the publisher. Some months later, the author receives galley or page proofs from the publisher. These must be carefully checked to ensure that the words and tables set in type by the printer match those in the original manuscript. After making corrections (and the author is charged for excessive changes that do not result from the printer's errors), the author returns the article to the publisher. Several months later, the article finally appears in the journal. The entire process, from submission of the manuscript until final publication, takes a year or more. Authors do not get paid for articles in journals, but on the other hand, neither do they get charged for the privilege of appearing in print.

As you might expect, it is a great thrill to see your name in print, especially the first time. An even greater thrill, however, is the knowledge that you may have added some small amount to our understanding of why people and animals think and act as they do.

# ||||Statistical Appendixes

## DESCRIPTIVE STATISTICS
### Organizing and summarizing

| Useful Computational Formulae | Measures of Central Tendency | Measures of Dispersion |
|---|---|---|
| | *Mode* <br> The most frequent score <br> *Median* <br> The middle score <br> *Mean* <br> $\overline{X} = \Sigma X/n$ | *Variance* <br> $s^2 = \dfrac{\Sigma X^2}{n} - \overline{X}^2$ <br><br> *Standard Deviation* <br> $s = \sqrt{\dfrac{\Sigma X^2}{n} - \overline{X}^2}$ |

| Facts about the Normal Distribution | |
|---|---|
| | 1. Of all scores, 68 percent are within $\pm$ 1 standard deviation of the mean. |
| | 2. Of all scores, nearly 96 percent are within $\pm$ 2 standard deviations of the mean. |
| | 3. Of all scores, 99.74 percent are within $\pm$ 3 standard deviations of the mean. |
| | 4. Standard scores (z scores) are differences between individual scores and the mean expressed in units of standard deviations. |

| Explanation of Symbols | | | |
|---|---|---|---|
| | 1. $X$ and $Y$ are individual scores (data). | 2. $n$ is the number of observations or subjects. | 3. $\Sigma$ refers to the act of adding (or summing). |
| | 4. $X^2$ is each score squared. | 5. $\Sigma X^2$ refers to adding up the scores after each has been squared. | 6. $(\Sigma X)^2$ means the square of the sum of the raw scores. |

# A ||| Descriptive Statistics

We have conducted research in order to collect data about a psychological topic. What are we going to do with the numbers? First, we need to systematize and organize them. We do not have to look at the whole array of numbers produced by subjects in the different conditions of an experiment. Instead, we can look at a briefer version. Descriptive statistics provide the summarizing and systematizing function. The two main types of descriptive statistics are *measures of central tendency* and *measures of dispersion* (variability).

Let us consider a hypothetical experiment. A drug company has sponsored a test of the effects of LSD on the behavior of rats, so we decide to see how the drug affects the rats' running speed. Forty food-deprived rats have been trained to run a straight-alley maze for a food reward. We randomly assign them to two groups. To one group we administer LSD by injection and observe the effect on the speed with which the rats run the alley for food thirty minutes after the injection. The other group is tested in a similar manner thirty minutes after receiving an injection of an inert substance. The following are the running times (in seconds) for the twenty control subjects: 13, 11, 14, 18, 12, 14, 10, 13, 13, 16, 15, 9, 12, 20, 11, 13, 12, 17, 15, and 14. The running times for the subjects receiving the LSD injections are 17, 15, 16, 20, 14, 19, 14, 13, 18, 18, 26, 17, 19, 13, 16, 22, 18, 16, 18, and 9. Now that we have the running times, what do we do with them? We might want some sort of graphical representation of the numbers. One type of graph is the **histogram** shown in the two panels of figure A–1, where the running speeds in seconds appear along the abscissa (*x*-axis), and the frequency with which each occurred in the two conditions is displayed along the ordinate (*y*-axis). Running times for the control subjects are given in the top histogram, and those for the experimental subjects are shown in the bottom one. Another way to represent the same information is a **frequency polygon.** Its construction is equivalent to that of the histogram; you can visualize this type of graph by connecting the midpoints of the bars in the histogram. (Examples of *frequency polygons* appear in figure A–2.) Notice that in both conditions in figure A–1, the greatest number of scores occurs in the middle and the scores tend to decrease in frequency

**Figure A–1.**

Histograms representing scores for twenty subjects in the control and experimental conditions of the hypothetical LSD experiment.

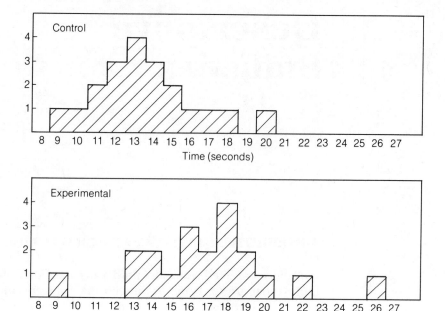

as running times become smaller or larger. Both the histogram and frequency polygon are types of **frequency distributions.** They help systematize the data, but there are more efficient summary descriptions.

## Central Tendency

The most common summary description of data is a measure of central tendency, which indicates the center of the distribution of scores. By far the most common measure of central tendency in psychological research is the **mean.** The mean $(\bar{X})$ is the sum of all the scores $(\Sigma X)$ divided by the number of scores $(n)$, or $\bar{X} = \Sigma X/n$. It is what most people think of as the average of a set of numbers, although the term *average* technically applies to any measure of central tendency. The sums of the running times for the experimental and control conditions in our hypothetical experiment were 338 and 272 seconds, respectively. Since there were twenty observations in each condition, the means are 16.9 seconds for the experimental condition and 13.6 for the control group.

The mean is by far the most useful measure of central tendency and almost all inferential statistics, which we come to later, are based on it. Therefore, this statistic is used whenever possible. However, two other measures of central tendency are sometimes employed. The second most common measure is the **median.** It is the score above which half of the distribution lies and below which the other half lies. The median, then, is the midpoint of the distribution. When there is an odd number of scores in the distribution, such as 27, the median is the 14th score from the bottom or top, since that score divides the distribution into two groups of thirteen scores. When the number of scores $(n)$ is an even number, the median is the arithmetic mean of the two middle scores, if the scores are not tied. So the median of the scores 66, 70, 72, 76, 80, and 96 is (72 + 76)/2, or 74. When the two middle scores are tied, as in the distribution of scores from the hypothetical LSD experiment, the convention is to designate the median as the appropriate proportion of the distance between the limits of the particular score, where the limits are a half score above and below the tied score. Consider the distributions of scores from our experiment. If we arrange the twenty control running times from lowest to highest, we discover that the eighth, nineth, tenth, and eleventh scores are all 13. Under such conditions, the tenth score is considered the median and it lies three quarters of the distance between the limits of 12.5 and 13.5. So the median would be 12.5 + .75, or 13.25, for the control subjects. By the same reasoning (and you should try it yourself), we find that the median for the experimental subjects is 17.

Why is the median used? The primary reason is that it has the desirable property of being insensitive to extreme scores. In the distribution of scores of 66, 70, 72, 76, 80, and 96, the median of the distribution would remain exactly the same if the lowest score were 1 rather than 66 or the highest score were 1,223 rather than 96. The mean, on the other hand, would differ widely with these other scores. Often this benefit can be extremely useful in summarizing data. In our LSD experiment, suppose that one of the rats given LSD had stopped halfway down the alley to examine a particularly interesting feature of the runway before continuing on its way to the goal box, and its time to complete the runway was 45 minutes or 2,700 seconds. If this score replaced the 26-second score in the original distribution, the mean would go from 16.9 seconds to 150.6, or from 3.30 seconds greater than the control mean to 137.0 seconds greater, because of only one very deviant score. In such cases, researchers frequently use the median score rather than the mean to represent the central tendency. Using the mean seems to give an unrepresentative estimate of central tendency because of the great influence of the one deviant score. However, using the median often severely limits any statistical tests that can be applied to the data.

The final measure of central tendency, almost never reported in psychological research, is the **mode,** or the most frequent score in the distribution. In the distribution of control scores in our experiment, it is 13, and in the distribution of experimental scores, it is 18.

### Measures of Dispersion: Variability in Data

Measures of central tendency indicate the center of the scores, whereas measures of dispersion indicate how the scores are spread out about the center. The simplest measure of dispersion is the **range,** which is the difference between the highest and lowest scores in the distribution. For the control rats in the LSD experiment the range is 11 (20 − 9), and for the experimental rats it is 17 (26 − 9). Since the range indicates only the extreme scores, it is rarely used.

The most useful measures of dispersion are the **standard deviation** and the **variance** of a distribution. The standard deviation is most useful as a descriptive statistic, whereas the variance of a distribution is employed in inferential statistics. As we shall see, the two are closely related.

One number that reflects the amount of spread that the scores exhibit around some central-tendency measure, usually the mean, is the *mean deviation*. This is calculated by taking the difference between the mean and every score in a distribution, summing these differences, and then dividing by the number of scores. However, we need to take the mean *absolute* difference (that is, to ignore the sign of the difference or whether the score was greater or less than the mean). The reason is that the sum of the deviations of scores about the mean is always zero, a defining characteristic of the mean (see table A–1). Thus, the mean deviation must be the *absolute* mean deviation. The mean deviations for our hypothetical experimental conditions in the LSD experiment are calculated in table A–1. The symbol ∥ indicates the absolute value of a number, so $|-6| = 6$.

The absolute mean deviation of a set of scores is an adequate measure of dispersion and is based on the same logic involved in finding the mean of a distribution. However, the standard deviation and variance are preferred to the mean deviation because they have mathematical properties that make them much more useful in advanced statistical computations. The logic behind their calculation is quite similar to that of the mean deviation, which is why we have considered the mean deviation here. In calculating the mean deviation, we had to determine the absolute value of the difference of each score from the mean so that these differences would not sum to zero. Instead of taking the absolute difference, we could have gotten rid of the troublesome negative numbers by squaring the differences. This is

**TABLE A–1**

Calculation of the mean deviations and absolute mean deviations from two sets of scores. Notice that the sum of the deviations (differences) in calculating the mean deviation is zero, which is why it is necessary to use the absolute mean deviation.

| | Control group | | | Experimental group | |
|---|---|---|---|---|---|
| $X$ | $(X - \bar{X})$ | $|X - \bar{X}|$ | $X$ | $(X - \bar{X})$ | $|X - \bar{X}|$ |
| 9 | −4.60 | 4.60 | 9 | −7.90 | 7.90 |
| 10 | −3.60 | 3.60 | 13 | −3.90 | 3.90 |
| 11 | −2.60 | 2.60 | 13 | −3.90 | 3.90 |
| 11 | −2.60 | 2.60 | 14 | −2.90 | 2.90 |
| 12 | −1.60 | 1.60 | 14 | −2.90 | 2.90 |
| 12 | −1.60 | 1.60 | 15 | −1.90 | 1.90 |
| 12 | −1.60 | 1.60 | 16 | − .90 | .90 |
| 13 | − .60 | .60 | 16 | − .90 | .90 |
| 13 | − .60 | .60 | 16 | − .90 | .90 |
| 13 | − .60 | .60 | 17 | + .10 | .10 |
| 13 | − .60 | .60 | 17 | + .10 | .10 |
| 14 | + .40 | .40 | 18 | +1.10 | .10 |
| 14 | + .40 | .40 | 18 | +1.10 | 1.10 |
| 14 | + .40 | .40 | 18 | +1.10 | 1.10 |
| 15 | +1.40 | 1.40 | 18 | +1.10 | 1.10 |
| 15 | +1.40 | 1.40 | 19 | +2.10 | 2.10 |
| 16 | +2.40 | 2.40 | 19 | +2.10 | 2.10 |
| 17 | +3.40 | 3.40 | 20 | +3.10 | 3.10 |
| 18 | +4.40 | 4.40 | 22 | +5.10 | 5.10 |
| 20 | +6.40 | 6.40 | 26 | +9.10 | 9.10 |
| $\Sigma X = 272$ | Total = 0.00 | Total = 41.20 | $\Sigma X = 338$ | Total = 0.00 | Total = 52.20 |
| $\bar{X} = 13.60$ | | | $\bar{X} = 16.90$ | | |

Absolute mean deviation $= \dfrac{41.20}{20} = 2.06$  Absolute mean deviation $= \dfrac{52.20}{20} = 2.61$

**TABLE A–2**

Calculation of the standard deviation, s, for the control and experimental conditions by the mean-deviation method.

| Control group | | | Experimental group | | |
|---|---|---|---|---|---|
| $X$ | $(X-\bar{X})$ | $(X-\bar{X})^2$ | $X$ | $(X-\bar{X})$ | $(X-\bar{X})^2$ |
| 9 | −4.60 | 21.16 | 9 | −7.90 | 62.41 |
| 10 | −3.60 | 12.96 | 13 | −3.90 | 15.21 |
| 11 | −2.60 | 6.76 | 13 | −3.90 | 15.21 |
| 11 | −2.60 | 6.76 | 14 | −2.90 | 8.41 |
| 12 | −1.60 | 2.56 | 14 | −2.90 | 8.41 |
| 12 | −1.60 | 2.56 | 15 | −1.90 | 3.61 |
| 12 | −1.60 | 2.56 | 16 | − .90 | .81 |
| 13 | − .60 | .36 | 16 | − .90 | .81 |
| 13 | − .60 | .36 | 16 | − .90 | .81 |
| 13 | − .60 | .36 | 17 | + .10 | .01 |
| 13 | − .60 | .36 | 17 | + .10 | .01 |
| 14 | + .40 | .16 | 18 | +1.10 | 1.21 |
| 14 | + .40 | .16 | 18 | +1.10 | 1.21 |
| 14 | + .40 | .16 | 18 | +1.10 | 1.21 |
| 15 | +1.40 | 1.96 | 18 | +1.10 | 1.21 |
| 15 | +1.40 | 1.96 | 19 | +2.10 | 4.41 |
| 16 | +2.40 | 5.76 | 19 | +2.10 | 4.41 |
| 17 | +3.40 | 11.56 | 20 | +3.10 | 9.61 |
| 18 | +4.40 | 19.36 | 22 | +5.10 | 26.01 |
| 20 | +6.40 | 40.96 | 26 | +9.10 | 82.81 |

$\Sigma X=272$  Total $=0.00$  $\Sigma(X-\bar{X})^2=138.80$      $\Sigma X=338$  Total $=0.00$  $\Sigma(X-\bar{X})^2=247.80$
$\bar{X}=13.60$                                                        $\bar{X}=16.90$

$$s = \sqrt{\frac{\Sigma(X-\bar{X})^2}{n}}$$

$$s = \sqrt{\frac{138.80}{20}}$$

$$s = 2.63$$

$$s = \sqrt{\frac{\Sigma(X-\bar{X})^2}{n}}$$

$$s = \sqrt{\frac{247.80}{20}}$$

$$s = 3.52$$

exactly what is done in calculating the variance and standard deviation of a distribution.

The *variance* of a distribution is defined as *the sum of the squared deviations from the mean, divided by the number of scores*. In other words, each score is subtracted from the mean and squared; then all these values are summed and divided by the number of scores. The formula for the variance is

$$s^2 = \frac{\Sigma(X - \bar{X})^2}{n} \tag{A–1}$$

where $s^2$ represents the variance, $X$ the individual scores, $\bar{X}$ the mean, and $n$ the number of scores or observations. The *standard deviation* is simply *the square root of the variance*, and is therefore represented by $s$. So

$$s = \sqrt{\frac{\Sigma(X - \bar{X})^2}{n}} \tag{A–2}$$

Calculation of the standard deviations for the control and experimental conditions in the LSD experiment by the mean-deviation method is illustrated in table A–2.

The formulas for the variance and standard deviation of a distribution shown in equations A–1 and A–2 are rather cumbersome, and in practice, the equivalent computational formulas are used. The standard-deviation formula is

$$s = \sqrt{\frac{\Sigma X^2}{n} - \overline{X}^2} \tag{A-3}$$

where $\Sigma X^2$ is the sum of the squares of all the scores, $\overline{X}$ is the mean of the distribution, and $n$ is the number of scores. Similarly, the formula for variance is

$$s^2 = \frac{\Sigma X^2}{n} - \overline{X}^2 \tag{A-4}$$

The standard deviations for the experimental and control scores are calculated by the computational formula shown in table A–3. Notice that the value in each case is the same as when the definitional formula is used.

To describe an array of data, psychologists usually present two descriptive statistics, the mean and the standard deviation. Although there are other measures of central tendency and dispersion, these are most useful for descriptive purposes. Variance is used extensively in inferential statistics (see appendix B).

**Table A–3**

Calculation of the standard deviation, s, for the control and experimental conditions by using the computational formula (also called the raw-score method). Notice that the same values are obtained as when the definitional formula is used (see table A–2), but that the calculations are much easier to perform.

| $X$ | $X^2$ | $X$ | $X^2$ |
|---|---|---|---|
| 9 | 81 | 9 | 81 |
| 10 | 100 | 13 | 169 |
| 11 | 121 | 13 | 169 |
| 11 | 121 | 14 | 196 |
| 12 | 144 | 14 | 196 |
| 12 | 144 | 15 | 225 |
| 12 | 144 | 16 | 256 |
| 13 | 169 | 16 | 256 |
| 13 | 169 | 16 | 256 |
| 13 | 169 | 17 | 289 |
| 13 | 169 | 17 | 289 |
| 14 | 196 | 18 | 324 |
| 14 | 196 | 18 | 324 |
| 14 | 196 | 18 | 324 |
| 15 | 225 | 18 | 324 |
| 15 | 225 | 19 | 361 |
| 16 | 256 | 19 | 361 |
| 17 | 289 | 20 | 400 |
| 18 | 324 | 22 | 484 |
| 20 | 400 | 26 | 676 |
| $\Sigma X = 272$ | $\Sigma X^2 = 3838$ | $\Sigma X = 338$ | $\Sigma X^2 = 5960$ |

$$\overline{X} = 13.60 \qquad\qquad \overline{X} = 16.90$$

$$\overline{X}^2 = 184.96 \qquad\qquad \overline{X}^2 = 285.61$$

$$s = \sqrt{\frac{\Sigma X^2}{n} - \overline{X}^2} \qquad\qquad s = \sqrt{\frac{\Sigma X^2}{n} - \overline{X}^2}$$

$$s = \sqrt{\frac{3838}{20} - 184.96} \qquad\qquad s = \sqrt{\frac{5960}{20} - 285.61}$$

$$s = 2.63 \qquad\qquad s = 3.52$$

## |||| THE NORMAL DISTRIBUTION

In the histograms in figure A–1 representing the running times of the rats in the two conditions of our hypothetical experiment, most of the scores pile up in the center and tail off toward the ends (or tails) of the distribution, especially for control subjects. Most psychological data tend to look like this when represented graphically; they often approximate the **normal curve** or **standard normal distribution,** where scores are most numerous in the middle, decline in frequency with distance from the middle, and do so in a fairly symmetrical way. A score ten points above the middle is about as common as a score ten points below it. Several examples of normal curves are shown in figure A–2. First note that in all three distributions, the mean, median, and mode are the same. The main difference in the distributions is in their variability. The tall, thin curve A has a smaller variance (and, of course, standard deviation) than the other two, whereas the flat, broad curve C has a larger variance than the others. All three curves, though, are normal curves.

Notice that on each side of the normal curve there is a point where the curve slightly reverses its direction; it starts bending outward more. This is called the *inflection point* and is labeled in the normal curve shown in figure A–3. The inflection point in the curve is always one standard deviation from the mean, and the normal curve has the useful property that specific proportions of the distribution of scores it represents are contained within specific areas of the curve itself. About 68 percent of all scores are contained within one standard deviation of the mean (34 percent on each side). Similarly, almost 96 percent of the scores are contained within two standard deviations of the mean, and 99.74 percent of the scores are within three standard deviations. The percentage in each area is shown in figure A–3. This is true of all normal curves, no matter how sharp or flat they are.

**Figure A–2**

Three examples of the normal curve that differ in variability. C has the greatest variability and A the least. The normal curve is a symmetrical distribution in which the mean, median, and mode all have the same value.

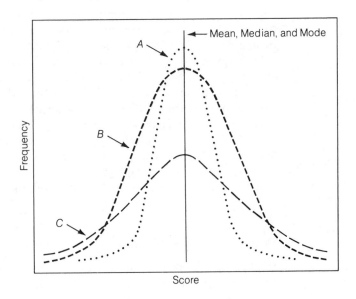

**Figure A–3**

*Proportions of scores in specific areas under the normal curve. The inflection points are one standard deviation from the mean.*

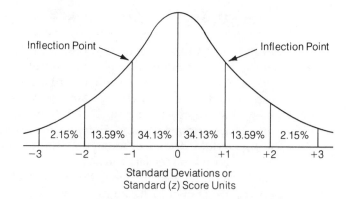

This property of normal curves is extremely useful because if we know an individual's score and the mean and standard deviation in the distribution of scores, we also know the person's relative rank. For example, most IQ tests are devised so that the population mean is 100 and the standard deviation is 15. If a person has an IQ of 115, we know that he or she scored higher than 84 percent of all people on the test (50 percent of the people below the mean and 34 percent above). Similarly, a person with an IQ of 130 scored higher than almost 98 percent of all people, and a person with an IQ of 145 scored higher than 99.87 percent of the population. See whether you can arrive at these percentages by adding up the appropriate areas in figure A–3.

Most distributions of scores in psychological data are, or at least are assumed to be, normal. (Often with small samples, as in our hypothetical data in figure A–1, it is difficult to tell whether the distribution is normal.) Scores are compared across normal distributions with different means and variances in terms of **standard scores** or *z-scores*. This score is simply the difference between an individual score and the mean expressed in units of standard deviations. So an IQ of 115 translates to a z-score of 1.00, that is, $[115 - 100]/15$; and an IQ of 78 translates to a z score of $-1.47$, that is, $[78 - 100]/15$. Standard scores are useful since they allow comparison of the relative ranks of scores for a person across distributions in which the means and standard deviations vary greatly. Grades in courses should be calculated in terms of z-scores if the means and standard deviations of the scores vary widely from one test to the next. Thus, a person's eventual rank in the class is calculated more faithfully by finding the mean of the z-scores than by finding the mean of the raw scores of the tests.

When data in an experiment are said to be *normally distributed* it means that, if they were graphed, they would form a normal distribution, as in figure A–3. Thus *normal,* as it is used in psychological research, usually refers to a type of distribution (there are many other types of distributions) and is not a value judgment as to the goodness or badness of the scores.

## Correlation Coefficient

In chapter 9, correlational research is described. The purpose of correlational research is to see how two or more attributes of an organism vary

**319**

together. The strength and direction of a correlation are determined by the calculation of a correlation coefficient. We will consider just one: *Pearson product-moment correlation coefficient* or *r*. Shown in box A–1 is the calculation formula for *r*, using the hypothetical data relating head size to memory performance discussed in chapter 9. Box A–2 repeats this analysis, using the computerized statistical package called MINITAB.

Regardless of how you calculate *r*, you should read the appropriate sections of chapter 9 that discuss the use and interpretation of a correlation coefficient.

---

**BOX A–1**
Computing Pearson *r*

Let us call one set of numbers in table A–4 *X* scores and the other set *Y* scores. For example, head sizes might be *X* scores and words recalled *Y* scores. The formula for computing Pearson *r* from the raw scores in panels (a), (b), or (c) of table 9–1 is as follows:

$$r = \frac{n \Sigma XY - (\Sigma X)(\Sigma Y)}{\sqrt{[n \Sigma X^2 - (\Sigma X)^2][n \Sigma Y^2 - (\Sigma Y)^2]}} \tag{A–5}$$

The *n* refers to the number of subjects on which observations are taken (here, 10); the terms $\Sigma X$ and $\Sigma Y$ are the totals of the *X* and *Y* scores, respectively; $\Sigma X^2$ and $\Sigma Y^2$ are the sum of all the *X* (or *Y*) values after each is squared; and the $(\Sigma X)^2$ and $(\Sigma Y)^2$ are the total of all the *X* or *Y* values with the entire total or sum squared. This leaves the value $\Sigma XY$, or the sum of the cross-products. This is obtained very simply by multiplying each *X*-value by its corresponding *Y* and then summing these products. You may see other formulas for calculation of Pearson *r* besides the raw-score formula in equation A–5, but these will be equivalent (in general) to the one presented here. An illustration of how Pearson *r* is calculated using this raw-score formula is presented in table A–4 using the data from the (a) column of table 9–1 (chapter 9). You should try to work out the values for Pearson *r* for the (b) and (c) panels yourself, to make certain you understand how to calculate the values and to gain an intuitive feel for the concept of correlation. The values of *r* are given below the appropriate columns in table 9–1.

TABLE A–4. CALCULATION OF PEARSON *R* FOR THE DATA IN THE FIRST (A) COLUMN OF TABLE 9–1, BY THE RAW-SCORE FORMULA (EQUATION A–5).

| Subject number | X Head size (cm.) | X² | Y Words recalled | Y² | X · Y |
|---|---|---|---|---|---|
| 1 | 50.8 | 2580.64 | 17 | 289 | 863.60 |
| 2 | 63.5 | 4032.25 | 21 | 441 | 1330.50 |
| 3 | 45.7 | 2088.49 | 16 | 256 | 731.20 |
| 4 | 25.4 | 645.16 | 11 | 121 | 279.40 |
| 5 | 29.2 | 852.64 | 9 | 81 | 262.80 |
| 6 | 49.5 | 2450.25 | 15 | 225 | 742.50 |
| 7 | 38.1 | 1451.61 | 13 | 169 | 495.30 |
| 8 | 30.5 | 930.25 | 12 | 144 | 366.00 |
| 9 | 35.6 | 1267.36 | 14 | 196 | 498.40 |
| 10 | 58.4 | 3410.56 | 23 | 529 | 1343.20 |
| $n =$ 10 | $\Sigma X =$ 426.70 | $\Sigma X^2 =$ 19,709.21 | $\Sigma Y =$ 151 | $\Sigma Y^2 =$ 2451 | $\Sigma XY =$ 6915.90 |

$$r = \frac{n\Sigma XY - (\Sigma X)(\Sigma Y)}{\sqrt{[n\Sigma X^2 - (\Sigma X)^2][n\Sigma Y^2 - (\Sigma Y)^2]}}$$

$$r = \frac{10(6915.90) - (426.70)(151)}{\sqrt{[(10)(19,709.21) - (426.70)^2][(10)(2451) - (151)^2]}}$$

$$r = \frac{69,159.00 - 64,431.70}{\sqrt{[197,092.10 - 182,072.89][24,510 - 22,801]}}$$

$$r = \frac{4727.30}{\sqrt{[15,019.21][1709]}} = \frac{4727.30}{\sqrt{25,667,829.89}}$$

$$r = \frac{4727.30}{5066.34}$$

$$r = +.93$$

**BOX A–2**

Calculation of r by a Computer

One popular statistical package on many large computers is called MINITAB. The MINITAB program will compute r, as well as many other statistics. We have outlined a typical session on a computer in which MINITAB is used to calculate r for the data in Box A–1. The entries shaded are what you type into the computer, and the other information is what the computer presents to you. After you have signed on to the computer, you need to gain access to MINITAB, which in this case is done by typing MINITAB. (However, different computer systems may have other ways of accessing MINITAB; check with your computer center before trying to run MINITAB.) Then, you are likely to see some information about the MINITAB program, followed by "MTB." MTB means that you should enter the appropriate MINITAB command, and it is here that you need to tell MINITAB that you are entering data to be "read" for analysis. So, the appropriate command is: "READ INTO C1, C2." This tells MINITAB that you are entering two columns of data (C1 and C2). Then MINITAB asks for the two columns by printing "DATA," next to which you enter the two scores for a particular subject. You continue to enter pairs of scores until the data for all subjects have been entered (ten pairs in this case), after which you type "END." You then enter the command "CORRELATION BETWEEN C1 AND C2," which tells MINITAB to compute the r between the ten pairs of scores. MINITAB tells you that ten rows of data were read (a handy check that you have entered the correct number of pairs of scores), and then prints out the correlation. The correlation computed by MINITAB is identical to the one in table A–4. Next, MINITAB asks for additional commands. When you enter "STOP," you leave the MINITAB program. You are now ready to sign off the computer. (You could have entered another MINITAB command besides "STOP" if you had additional statistical computations to perform.)

```
MINITAB RELEASE 82.1 *** COPYRIGHT - PENN STATE UNIV. 1982
APRIL 25, 1984 *** CONVERTED AT U. OF WISC. WAISMAN CENTER
STORAGE AVAILABLE   41099

MTB > READ INTO C1, C2
DATA> 50.8 17
DATA> 63.5 21
DATA> 45.7 16
DATA> 25.4 11
DATA> 29.2 9
DATA> 49.5 15
DATA> 38.1 13
DATA> 30.5 12
DATA> 35.6 14
DATA> 58.4 23
DATA> END
    10 ROWS READ
MTB > CORRELATION BETWEEN C1 AND C2

    CORRELATION OF       C1 AND C2      = 0.933

MTB > STOP

*** MINITAB *** STATISTICS DEPT * PENN STATE UNIV. * RELEASE 82.1 *
STORAGE AVAILABLE    41099
```

**The results of a computer session with MINITAB. MINITAB has
calculated the *r* for the data presented in Box A–1. Shaded entries
are typed in by the user, and the other information is printed by the
computer program.**

There are several other statistical packages for computers (for example, SPSS and
BMD) that may be available to you; whichever one is available, we recommend
you become familiar with it. Computer analysis is faster and more accurate than
doing statistical work by hand or step by step on a calculator.

# INFERENTIAL STATISTICS
## What statistical test should I use when ...

***I have one independent variable that has two levels?***

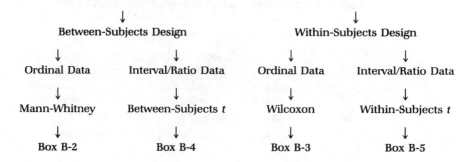

| ↓ | | | ↓ |
|---|---|---|---|
| Between-Subjects Design | | Within-Subjects Design | |
| ↓ | ↓ | ↓ | ↓ |
| Ordinal Data | Interval/Ratio Data | Ordinal Data | Interval/Ratio Data |
| ↓ | ↓ | ↓ | ↓ |
| Mann-Whitney | Between-Subjects *t* | Wilcoxon | Within-Subjects *t* |
| ↓ | ↓ | ↓ | ↓ |
| Box B-2 | Box B-4 | Box B-3 | Box B-5 |

***I have one independent variable that has more than two levels?***

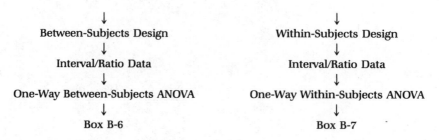

| ↓ | ↓ |
|---|---|
| Between-Subjects Design | Within-Subjects Design |
| ↓ | ↓ |
| Interval/Ratio Data | Interval/Ratio Data |
| ↓ | ↓ |
| One-Way Between-Subjects ANOVA | One-Way Within-Subjects ANOVA |
| ↓ | ↓ |
| Box B-6 | Box B-7 |

***I have two independent variables, each with at least two levels?***

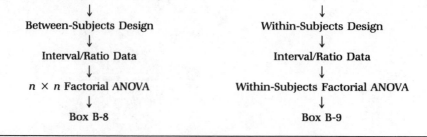

| ↓ | ↓ |
|---|---|
| Between-Subjects Design | Within-Subjects Design |
| ↓ | ↓ |
| Interval/Ratio Data | Interval/Ratio Data |
| ↓ | ↓ |
| *n* × *n* Factorial ANOVA | Within-Subjects Factorial ANOVA |
| ↓ | ↓ |
| Box B-8 | Box B-9 |

# B ||| Inferential Statistics

**STATISTICAL REASONING**

Descriptive statistics are concerned with describing or summarizing data. The results from our LSD experiment (in appendix A) can be summarized by saying that the control group had a mean running time of 13.60 seconds and a standard deviation of 2.63, whereas the experimental rats injected with LSD had a mean of 16.90 seconds and a standard deviation of 3.52 seconds. On average, the experimental rats ran 3.30 seconds slower than the controls, but should we take this difference seriously? Perhaps it resulted from chance factors such as measurement error or a few rats in the control group having a particularly good day and thus feeling like running a bit faster. How can we judge whether the difference between the two conditions is real (reliable) or a fluke? Inferential statistics are used to answer this question.

It is not too complicated to answer this question in actual practice. We choose an appropriate statistical test for the experimental situation, perform a few straightforward computations on a calculator (or computer), and then consult a special table. The table informs us of the probability that the difference we found between our conditions is a result of chance factors. If it is sufficiently unlikely to have occurred by chance, we conclude that the difference is statistically significant, or reliable. The computational procedures are often quite simple, but the logic behind them needs to be explained so you will understand how statistical inferences are made.

## Sampling

A **population** is a complete set of measurements (or individuals or objects) having some common observable characteristic (see box B–1). Examples of populations are all U.S. citizens of voting age, all albino rats that have had injections of LSD, and all people asked to remember a list of fifty words. Of course, it is impossible to study the entire population in any of these cases. If we could measure the entire population of rats for running speed after either an injection of LSD or an injection of a chemically inert substance, we would have a better idea of the effects of LSD. (Any difference, of course, might still be attributable to measurement error.) But since it is almost always impractical to measure an entire population, we must sample from it. A **sample** is a subset of a population, and it is what we are usually examining when we compare experimental conditions. Thus, we make statistical inferences when we draw a conclusion about an entire population on the basis of only a sample of observations. We really want to know about the effects of LSD and the inert substance on rats in general, but we hope to draw this conclusion from a sample of, say, twenty rats in each condition.

Technically, we can only *generalize* about the population from which we have sampled, but if we took this statement literally, experimental research would hardly be worth doing. If we received fifty rats from a supply house, and we selected a sample of forty and randomly assigned them to the two conditions of our experiment, would our conclusions be true only of the population of fifty rats? Well, perhaps technically, but no one would care about the result if this were so, and we would not have wasted our time doing the experiment. We at least want to assume that the results are characteristic of that strain of rats, and, perhaps, that these results also generalize to other species, including human beings. The problem is the same in research with human beings. Suppose you are a researcher at the University of Toronto interested in some aspect of social behavior. You ready your experiment, which has three conditions, and you plan to use students from introductory psychology courses as subjects, a common practice. You display a sign-up sheet, randomly assign the volunteers to the three experimental conditions when they show up, and collect your data. To whom do your conclusions generalize? To introductory psychology students at

---

**BOX B–1**
Statistical Notation

Characteristics of a population of scores are called *parameters,* and characteristics of a sample of scores drawn from a larger population are *statistics.* The mean of an entire population of scores is a parameter, and the mean of a sample is a statistic. Different symbols are used for population parameters and sample statistics. Some of the most frequent are listed here. Several of the concepts have already been explained, and the others will be discussed in the next few pages.

$N$ = number of scores in a population

$n$ = number of scores in a sample

$\mu$ = population mean ($\mu$ is pronounced mu)

$\bar{X}$ = sample mean

$\sigma^2$ = population variance ($\sigma$ is pronounced sigma)

$s^2$ = sample variance $\dfrac{\Sigma(X - \bar{X})^2}{n}$

$\hat{s}^2$ = unbiased estimate of population variance $\dfrac{\Sigma(X - \bar{X})^2}{n - 1}$

$\sigma$ = population standard deviation

$s$ = sample standard deviation

$\hat{s}$ = sample standard deviation based on the unbiased variance estimate

$\sigma_{\bar{x}}$ = standard error of the mean, $\dfrac{\sigma}{\sqrt{N}}$

$s_{\bar{x}}$ = estimated standard error of the mean, $\dfrac{s}{\sqrt{n}}$ or $\dfrac{s}{\sqrt{n - 1}}$

the University of Toronto who volunteered for your experiment? If so, who cares about what you found? In practice, psychologists assume that their results generalize more widely than to the limited population from which they sampled for their experiment.

**The distribution of sample means.**   One way we could check on the reliability of our hypothetical LSD experiment would be to perform the experiment repeatedly using new groups of rats. Of course, obtaining exactly the same mean running times for the experimental and control conditions in these replications would be unlikely. The means in seconds for the experimental and control conditions in four replications might be 17.9 and 12.5, 16.0 and 13.4, 16.6 and 14.5, and 15.4 and 15.1. Since the experimental rats that receive the LSD always run slower than the control rats, we would have more confidence in our original finding, although the difference is rather small in the last replication. If we repeated the experiment like this and plotted the distribution of the sample means obtained in the two conditions, the distributions would tend to be normal, and they would have all the characteristics of a normal distribution, such as a certain proportion of the scores falling under a certain part of the curve. A plot of the difference between the sample means in each experiment would also be normally distributed.

To give you a better idea of the **distribution** of sample means concept, let us borrow an example from a class demonstration by Horowitz (1974, pp. 179–182). Horowitz manufactured a population of 1,000 normally distributed scores so that the mean and standard deviation of the entire population would be known, which is almost never the case in actual research situations. His 1,000 scores ranged from 0 to 100 and had a mean of 50 and a standard deviation of 15.8. The scores were listed on 1,000 slips of paper and placed in a container. Horowitz had ninety-six students take samples of ten slips from the container and calculate the mean. On each draw from the container, the student took out a slip, noted its number, and then replaced the slip. The slips were then somewhat mixed up in the container, another slip was drawn, and so on. After each student calculated the mean of the ten scores in his or her sample, Horowitz collected all ninety-six sample means and plotted their distribution, which is represented in table B–1. The intervals between which means might fall are on the left and the number of means falling within each interval is on the right. Notice that the distribution is almost perfectly symmetrical, with almost as many scores in any interval a certain distance below the true mean of the population (50) as above it. Also, the mean of the ninety-six sample means (49.99) is quite close to the actual mean of the population (50). The main thing you should notice in table B–1 is the great variability among the sample means. Although each sample of ten was presumably random, not biased in any way, and came from the same population, one sample had a mean of 37.8, while another had a mean of 62.3. If you did an experiment and found two very different sample means, and you tried to decide whether they came from the same underlying distribution or two different distributions, you might think that such a large difference indicated that they came from different distributions. In other words, you would think that the experi-

| Interval | Frequency | |
|----------|-----------|---|
| 62.0–63.9 | 1 | |
| 60.0–61.9 | 1 | |
| 58.0–59.9 | 3 | |
| 56.0–57.9 | 7 | |
| 54.0–55.9 | 9 | |
| 52.0–53.9 | 12 | |
| 50.0–51.9 | 15 | Mean of sample means = 49.99 |
| 48.0–49.9 | 15 | Standard deviation (s) of |
| 46.0–47.9 | 13 | sample means = 5.01 |
| 44.0–45.9 | 9 | |
| 42.0–43.9 | 6 | |
| 40.0–41.9 | 3 | |
| 38.0–39.9 | 1 | |
| 36.0–37.9 | 1 | |
| | 96 samples | |

mental treatment produced scores reliably different (from a different distribution) than the control scores. Usually this is a good rule—the larger the difference between means in the conditions, the more likely the means are to be reliably different—but as we have seen, even random sampling from a known distribution can produce sample means that differ greatly from each other and from the true population mean, which is known in this case. While pondering small differences between means, keep this lesson in mind. Is the 3.30-second difference between experimental and control means in our hypothetical LSD experiment really reliable?

**The standard error of the mean.** The **standard error of the mean** is the standard deviation of a distribution of sample means. In the data in table B–1, it is 5.01. The standard error of the mean gives us some idea as to the amount of variability in the distribution of sample means, or how likely it is that the value of any particular sample mean is in error. Large standard errors indicate great variability, whereas small ones tell us that a particular sample mean is likely to be quite close to the actual population mean. Thus, the standard error of the mean is a very useful number.

You might be wondering why we bother to tell you about the standard error of the mean if in order to calculate it you must repeat an experiment numerous times to get the distribution of sample means and then calculate its standard deviation. Fortunately, you do not. The formula for finding the standard error of the mean (represented by $\sigma_{\bar{x}}$) is simply the standard deviation of the population ($\sigma$) divided by the square root of the number of observations ($\sqrt{n}$). Or

$$\sigma_{\bar{x}} = \frac{\sigma}{\sqrt{n}} \tag{B–1}$$

Now, if you are still with us you might well be thinking, "Terrific. What good does this do me since the standard deviation of the population, the numerator in equation B–1, is never known?" That question has occurred to statisticians, too, so they have devised a method for estimating the standard deviation of the population from the standard deviation of a sample. If you look back at equation A–2, in appendix A, where the formula for the

**TABLE B-2**

The distribution of sample means for the 96 samples taken by students when sample size (n) = 50. The distribution is again normal, as in table B–1, but when each sample is based on a larger sample size, as it is here, the variability of the distribution (represented by the standard error of the mean) is much smaller. (After Horowitz, 1974, *Elements of Statistics for Psychology and Education*, table 8.2. Copyright 1974 by McGraw-Hill. Reprinted with permission.)

| Interval | Frequency | |
|----------|-----------|---|
| 55.0–55.9 | 1 | |
| 54.0–54.9 | 3 | |
| 53.0–53.9 | 5 | |
| 52.0–52.9 | 9 | |
| 51.0–51.9 | 13 | |
| 50.0–50.9 | 17 | |
| 49.0–49.9 | 16 | Mean of sample means = 49.95 |
| 48.0–48.9 | 14 | Standard deviation (s) of sample means = 2.23 |
| 47.0–47.9 | 9 | |
| 46.0–46.9 | 6 | |
| 45.0–45.9 | 2 | |
| 44.0–44.9 | 1 | |
| | 96 samples | |

standard deviation of a sample *(s)* appears, and simply replace the *n* in the denominator by *n* − 1, you have the formula for getting an unbiased estimate of σ, the standard deviation of the population. The equation for finding the standard error of distribution of sample means (called the standard error of the mean, or $s_{\bar{x}}$ is

$$\text{Estimated } \sigma_{\bar{x}} = s_{\bar{x}} = \frac{s}{\sqrt{n-1}} \qquad (\text{B–2})$$

Since the standard error of the mean indicates our error in assuming that our sample mean represents the population mean, we want it to be as small as possible. Equations B–1 and B–2 tell us how to do this: Increase the size of the sample, *n*, which increases the denominator in the equation. The greater is *n*, the sample size, the smaller will be the standard error of the mean, $s_{\bar{x}}$. In a population involving 1,000 scores, the sample mean should be closer to the population mean if there are 500 observations in the sample rather than only 10.

Horowitz drove this point home to the ninety-six students in his class by having them repeat the exercise of drawing slips from the population of 1,000 scores and calculating the mean again, but this time he had them sample fifty slips rather than only ten. The resulting distribution of sample means is shown in table B–2. This time, with larger samples, there is much less variability in the sample means. They are much closer to the actual population mean of 50. The standard deviation of the distribution of sample means, or the standard error of the mean, is 2.23, as opposed to 5.01 when the sample size was only 10. If *n* = 100 in a sample from the 1,000 scores, the standard error of the mean would be 1.59; with a sample of 500 it would be .71, and with 1,000 scores in a sample it would be only .50. (These were calculated from equation B–1 since the standard deviation, σ, is known for the entire population.) The reason we might not get the population mean even with a sample of 1,000 is that the sampling was done with *replacement;* that is, after a slip was drawn it was returned to the container and it might have been drawn again and again, but some slips were never drawn.

The lesson to be learned is that we should always try to maximize the number of observations—the sample size—in experimental conditions so that the statistics obtained will be as close as possible to the population parameters.

## Testing Hypotheses

Scientists set up experiments to test hypotheses. The conventional statistical logic for testing hypotheses goes something like this. An experimenter arranges conditions, such as the experimental (LSD) and control (placebo) in our experiment with rats in order to test an *experimental hypothesis*. The experimental hypothesis in this case is that LSD will have some effect on running speed. This is tested against the *null hypothesis*, which maintains that the two conditions do not differ in their effects on running speed. In other words, the experimental hypothesis holds that the samples of running speeds come from two different underlying populations (that is, populations with different distributions), and the null hypothesis maintains that the two samples come from the same distribution. Statistical tests allow us to find the likelihood with which the null hypothesis can be rejected. How unlikely must a null hypothesis be to be rejected? If an experimental result differs from that to be expected by the null hypothesis (so much so that a difference that great would be expected on the basis of chance only 5 times in 100), we conclude that the null hypothesis can be rejected. This .05 *level of significance* is just a convention; many psychologists prefer a more conservative .01 level for rejection, so that a null hypothesis is rejected only if the experimental result is likely to occur by chance in one case in 100. At any rate, the experimental hypothesis is tested, in a sense, indirectly. It is not affirmed, but the null hypothesis is rejected.

The logic of pitting an experimental hypothesis against the null hypothesis has come under attack in recent years for several reasons. Some argue that it gives a misleading idea about how scientists operate. For one thing, not many researchers wander about the world losing any sleep over or investing any thought into the null hypothesis. In general, experiments are set up to test our theories, and what is of primary concern is how the results can be interpreted or accounted for by our theories. Of special interest is the case in which important experimental results seem irreconcilable with the major theories of a phenomenon. Experiments are important because of what they tell us about our theories and ideas—this is why we designed them in the first place—and not about rejection of the null hypothesis. But the logic of testing hypotheses against the null hypothesis is widely used as an introduction, however oversimplified to the way scientific inference proceeds. Thus we present it here.

**Testing hypotheses: Parameters known.**   The logic of testing hypotheses against the null hypothesis can be aptly illustrated in cases in which the parameters of a population are known and we wish to determine whether a particular sample comes from the population. Such cases are quite unusual in actual research, of course, since population parameters are rarely known. Suppose you were interested in whether the members of your experimental-psychology class were reliably above the national mean in intelligence as measured by IQ tests (or reliably below, as the case may be). We know the population parameters in this case; the mean is 100 and the standard deviation is 15. You could test your class easily enough by giving them the short form of some intelligence test, such as the Otis, developed for group testing. Suppose you randomly sampled 25 people from your class of 100 and found the mean IQ of the sample to be 108 with a standard deviation of 5.

How do we go about testing the experimental hypothesis that the class is reliably brighter than the population as a whole? First let us consider the hypotheses. The experimental hypothesis is that the students are brighter than people in the nation as a whole, or that the IQ scores of the students sampled come from a different population than randomly selected people. The null hypothesis is that there is no reliable difference between our sample and the national mean, or that the students in the class are a sample from the same national population. If the null hypothesis were actually the case, the difference between the sample mean of 108 and the population parameter mean ($\mu$) of 100 would result from random factors. Certainly this is not implausible, because we have seen from our discussion of the distribution of sample means how much a sample mean can differ from a population parameter, even when the sample is selected in an unbiased manner. Remember Horowitz's classroom demonstration, the results of which are portrayed in tables B–1 and B–2.

The normal curve, the distribution of sample means, and z scores can help us determine how likely it is that the null hypothesis is false. When unbiased samples are taken from a larger population, the means of these samples are normally distributed. With normal distributions we can specify what proportion of the distribution falls under each part of the curve (as shown in figure A–3 in appendix A). Remember also that z-scores are the calculation of any score in a normal distribution in standard deviation units from the mean.

All this is by way of review. Now how does this help us? What we do in testing the hypothesis that the sample is actually from a population with a mean IQ greater than the population at large is to treat the sample mean as an individual score (in terms of our earlier discussion) and calculate a z-score on the basis of the deviation of the sample mean from the population mean. In our case, we know the population mean is 100 and the class mean of the randomly selected students is 108. To calculate the z-score, we also need to know the standard error of the mean, the standard deviation of the distribution of sample means. The equation for the z-score here is

$$z = \frac{\bar{X} - \mu}{\sigma_{\bar{x}}} \tag{B–3}$$

The standard error of the mean ($\sigma_{\bar{x}}$) is found by dividing the standard deviation of the population ($\sigma$) by $\sqrt{n}$ (see Equation B–1), so $\sigma_{\bar{x}}$ is $15/\sqrt{25}$, or 3. Thus z is $(108 - 100)/3$, or 2.67. This result, 2.67, allows us to reject the null hypothesis with reasonable confidence and conclude in favor of the alternative hypothesis, that the class is actually superior in IQ to the population at large. We establish this by asking the question: How likely is a z-score of 2.67 when a sample mean is drawn from a larger population whose mean is actually 100? The answer is that it will occur only .0038 of the time, or 38 times in 10,000. (In the next paragraph we will discuss how this was calculated.) The custom in rejecting the null hypothesis is that if it could only occur 1 time in 20 by chance, we would reject it, so the difference in the class sample mean is *reliably different* or *significantly different* from the mean of the population.

To explain how this rather remarkable conclusion is reached, we need to refer again to the special property of the normal curve, which is that a certain proportion of cases fall under each part of the curve. Looking back to figure A–3, we see that having a z-score of $\pm 2.00$ is highly improbable. Greater scores in either direction occur only 2.15 percent of the time. In other words, the probability of such an occurrence is .0215. This is also below the 5 percent or .05 level of significance, so any mean score two or more standard deviations from the population mean is considered, using the logic we have outlined here, significantly different from the population mean. In fact, the critical z-value for rejecting the null hypothesis at the .05 level of significance, is $\pm 1.96$. Table C–1 (in appendix C) presents (1) z-scores from zero to four, with (2) the amount of area between the mean and z, and (3) most important, the amount of area beyond z. The amount of area beyond z is the probability of finding a score that distant from the mean on the basis of chance alone. Once again, when this probability falls below .05, as it does with z scores of $\pm 1.96$ (or more), we reject the null hypothesis. Notice that with a z of 2.67, as in our IQ example, the probability of such a rare occurrence is only .0038. See figure B–1.

The statistical problem we have just considered—comparing a sample mean to a population parameter to see whether the sample came from that population—is rather artificial, since population parameters are rarely known. But this example does exhibit characteristics of most common statistical tests. In all tests, some computations are performed on the data or raw scores, a value is found as in the z-score just calculated, and then this value is compared with a distribution of values so that we can determine the likelihood that such a value could be obtained if the null hypothesis were in fact true. This distribution tells us, then, with what probability our result could be attributed to random variation. If the probability is less than 5 cases in 100 ($p < .05$), then we say the null hypothesis can be rejected.

**Figure B–1**
Standard Normal
Distribution

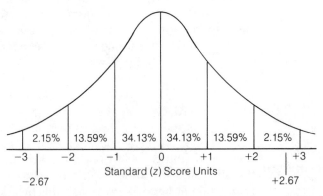

This is the standard normal distribution shown in figure A–3 (in appendix A). There are two sides or tails to the distribution, positive and negative. If an experimenter simply asserts that there should be a difference between an experimental and control condition but does not specify the direction of the difference, this is called a nondirectional hypothesis. If a $z = 2.67$ is found, it is necessary to look up the probability that this will occur in both the positive and negative tails of the distribution and add the two, since the experimenter did not specify whether the difference should be positive or negative. When the experimenter has specified the direction of difference, we need only look up the probability in one tail. Since the distribution is symmetrical, the probability that the null hypothesis can be rejected is half as great with a one-tailed as with a two-tailed test. The less certain we are about the outcome of an experiment, the greater the difference between conditions must be for us to decide that it is not a result of chance.

This probability is sometimes called the **alpha ($\alpha$) level** and, as already mentioned, some psychologists prefer values of .01 or even smaller so that they can be more certain that the null hypothesis should be rejected.

Our z-score test can also serve to introduce you very briefly to other important statistical concepts. First, let us consider two types of errors that can be made by applying statistical tests to experimental data. A *type 1 error* is rejection of the null hypothesis when it is actually true, and the probability that this error will occur is indexed by the alpha level, which the experimenter selects. If the alpha level is $p = .05$, then we shall mistakenly reject the null hypothesis in 5 cases in 100. This illustrates the probabilistic nature of inferential statistics; we are not absolutely certain that a null hypothesis can be rejected, only reasonably certain. Thus the lower $\alpha$ level or $p$ level we use in determining statistical significance, the less chance we have of making a type 1 error. However, this increases the probability of a *type 2 error*, which occurs when we *fail* to reject the null hypothesis when it is actually *false*. Thus by setting $\alpha$ levels at different points we systematically decrease and increase the two types of errors.

Scientists are generally conservative in such matters, so the $\alpha$ level is usually kept fairly small, such as .05 or .01 (rather than, say, .10 or .15). Thus we minimize the error of rejecting the null hypothesis when it is true, or claiming a difference in our results when a difference is not there. As a consequence, though, we increase the probability of type 2 errors. A *conservative* statistical test minimizes type 1 errors, whereas more *liberal* statistical tests increase the probability of a type 1 error but decrease that of a type 2 error.

Unfortunately, we can never know positively in our experimental situations whether we are committing type 1 or type 2 errors. We find this out primarily by doing experimental replications of our results, but also by calculating the power of a statistical test. The *power* of a test is the probability of rejecting the null hypothesis when it is actually false; thus we always want to maximize the power of our statistical tests. This is not the place to describe how the power of tests is calculated, but we will note the two main factors that influence power. Look back to the z-score formula in equation B–3. Whatever would make the z score larger would increase the power of the statistical test, or the likelihood of rejecting the null hypothesis. The value $\mu$, the population mean, is fixed. Thus only two changes in the values of equation B–3 can affect z. One is the difference between the sample mean and the population mean $(\overline{X} - \mu)$ and the other is $n$, the size of the sample. If the discrepancy between $\mu$ and $\overline{X}$ is increased (or in other cases, if the difference between sample means in an experimental comparison is increased), the probability of rejecting the null hypothesis is also increased.

However, there is nothing we can do about the size of the difference between means; it is fixed. We can increase the power of our statistical tests by increasing the sample size. The reason is that with larger samples we can be more confident that our sample means represent the mean of the populations from which they are drawn, and thus we can be more confident that any difference between a sample mean and a population mean (or between two sample means) is reliable. Sample size can have a great effect on the power of a test, as shown in table B–3. Presented there are the

**TABLE B–3**

How varying sample size (*n*) affects the power of a statistical test, or how likely it is that the null hypothesis can be rejected when the test is used. The example is from the *z* score (calculated in the text) on a mean sample IQ of 108, where

$$z = \frac{\bar{X} - \mu}{\sigma_{\bar{x}}}$$

If the mean difference remains the same but *n* increases, *z* increases because

$$\sigma_{\bar{x}} = \frac{\sigma}{\sqrt{n}}$$

| n | $\bar{X} - \mu$ | $\sigma_{\bar{x}}$ | z | p† |
|---|---|---|---|---|
| 2 | 8 | 13.14 | .61 | .2709 |
| 5 | 8 | 6.70 | 1.19 | .1170 |
| 7 | 8 | 5.67 | 1.41 | .0793 |
| 10 | 8 | 4.74 | 1.69 | .0455* |
| 12 | 8 | 4.33 | 1.85 | .0322* |
| 15 | 8 | 3.88 | 2.06 | .0197* |
| 17 | 8 | 3.64 | 2.20 | .0139* |
| 20 | 8 | 3.35 | 2.38 | .0087* |
| 25 | 8 | 3.00 | 2.67 | .0038* |
| 50 | 8 | 2.12 | 3.77 | .0001* |
| 75 | 8 | 1.73 | 4.62 | <.00003* |
| 100 | 8 | 1.50 | 5.33 | <.00003* |

\* All these values meet the conventional level of statistical significance, $p < .05$ (one-tailed).

† $p$ values are one-tailed.

z-scores and *p* values for our difference between a sample mean of 108 IQ points and the population mean of 100 as the sample size varies. As the sample size varies, so will our conclusion as to whether the sample came from a national population or a more restricted, high-IQ population. If we assume that the null hypothesis is actually false here, then by increasing sample size we decrease the probability of a type 2 error, or increase the power of the test we are using.

One final issue to consider is the *directionality* of statistical tests. According to conventional logic involved in testing an alternative hypothesis against the null hypothesis, the alternative hypothesis may be **directional** or **nondirectional.** If an experimental and a control group are in an experiment, a nondirectional alternative hypothesis would be that the two groups differ in performance on the dependent variable. A directional hypothesis would, in addition, state the predicted direction of the difference; for example, the experimental group might be predicted to do better than the control.

This distinction is important, because if the alternative hypothesis is directional, a **one-tailed** (or *one-sided*) **statistical test** is used, but if the alternative hypothesis is nondirectional, a **two-tailed** *(two-sided)* **test** is used. One versus two "tails" refers to whether we consider one or both tails of the distribution when we look up a *p* level associated with the result of a statistical test (say, z = 1.69).

Examine figure B–1 once again. We took a sample (*n* = 25) of students, determined that the mean IQ of the sample was 108, and calculated a z = + 2.67 in testing to see whether this was different from the mean population IQ of 100. If we had no prior expectation of how the sample IQ should deviate from the normal population—if we thought it could be either higher or lower—this would have been a nondirectional hypothesis. In fact, we did expect the sample IQ to be greater than 100, so we tested a directional hypothesis and thus used a one-tailed test. This means we looked up the resulting z-score in only one tail of the normal distribution, that greater than zero. A z = + 2.67 leads to a one-tailed *p* value of .0038. If the hypothesis were nondirectional, then we have no a priori right to expect the resultant z score to be greater instead of less than zero. The z score could be in the positive or negative tail. Since the difference could have occurred in either direction, we use a two-tailed test. In practice, since the two tails of the distribution are symmetrical, we simply double the $p$ level for the one-tailed test. In our example, if the hypothesis had been nondirectional, $p$ would equal $2 \times .0038$, or $.0076$, still well below $.05$.

Two-tailed tests are more conservative and less powerful than one-tailed tests: it is harder to reject the null hypothesis. If we are uncertain about the outcome of an experiment, we need a greater value of the statistic to allow us to declare a difference. In practice, most investigators prefer to use the more conservative two-tailed test with sufficient power ensured by fairly large sample sizes.

In the remainder of this appendix, we show you how to calculate several statistical tests. We believe it is important for you to do some of these calculations by hand or with a calculator. When you carefully work through the calculations, you become familiar with the logic and components of the statistical test. However, as we noted in Appendix A (see Box A–2), many statistical tests can be done automatically by sophisticated calculators and computers. All you need to do is access a particular statistical program and then enter your data. Most of the statistical tests outlined in this appendix can be done by the computer package, MINITAB. We suggest you become familiar with the statistical capabilities of the computing equipment available to you. Computers can conduct statistical tests faster and more accurately than you can, and they relieve some of the tedium associated with the more complex statistical tests that require numerous complicated calculations.

## Tests for Differences Between Two Groups

A variety of statistical tests exist for almost every purpose. At present, we are interested in discussing tests that assess the reliability of a difference between two groups or conditions. How do we pick an appropriate test from all those available? There is no hard-and-fast rule. Tests vary in the assumptions they make, their power, and the types of situation for which they are appropriate. Perhaps the most popular test for the difference between two means in psychological research is the *t*-test. Since the *t*-test provides the same estimate of reliability as does the simple analysis of variance (discussed next), we will first concentrate on two other tests, the Mann-Whitney $U$-test and the Wilcoxon signed-ranks test. These tests also are useful in introducing yet another type of statistical test.

The Mann-Whitney and Wilcoxon tests are **nonparametric statistics** as opposed to **parametric statistics.** Parametric statistical tests, such as analysis of variance and $t$, are those which make assumptions about the underlying population parameters of the samples on which the tests are performed. Common assumptions of parametric tests are that the variances of the underlying populations being compared are equivalent, that the underlying distributions are normal, and that the level of measurement is at least an interval scale. If these assumptions are not met, the test may be inappropriate. But how can we ever know whether the assumptions underlying the test are met since we do not know the population parameters? Usually we cannot, except by estimating population parameters from sample statistics. However, if we turn to nonparametric statistical tests, the problem does not arise, because these tests make no assumptions about the underlying population parameters. This is why these tests are often called distribution-free statistics. Since the parameters cannot be known anyway, this provides an important reason for using nonparametric tests. Another reason is that these tests are generally very easy to calculate and can often even be done by hand. However, nonparametric tests are usually less powerful than parametric tests used in the same situation; that is, they are less likely to allow the null hypothesis to be rejected.

The *Mann-Whitney* U *test* is used when we want to compare two samples and decide whether they come from the same or different underlying populations. It is used when the two samples are composed of different subjects—between-subjects designs. The underlying rationale for the Mann-Whitney test will not be discussed here. The logic is the same as in other statistical tests in which a value is computed from the test and compared with a distribution of values in order to determine whether the null hy-

---

**BOX B–2**
Calculation of a Mann-Whitney *U* Test

These data are from our hypothetical experiment involving the effects of LSD on the running speeds of rats. Using the Mann-Whitney *U test* to test the reliability of the difference between our two samples, we follow these steps:

*Step 1.* Rank all the numbers for *both groups* together, beginning with the smallest number. Assign it the lowest rank.

| CONTROL (PLACEBO) | | EXPERIMENTAL (LSD) | |
|---|---|---|---|
| Latency (sec.) | Rank | Latency (sec.) | Rank |
| 9 | 1.5 | 9 | 1.5 |
| 10 | 3 | 13 | 11.5 |
| 11 | 4.5 | 13 | 11.5 |
| 11 | 4.5 | 14 | 17 |
| 12 | 7 | 14 | 17 |
| 12 | 7 | 15 | 21 |
| 12 | 7 | 16 | 24.5 |
| 13 | 11.5 | 16 | 24.5 |
| 13 | 11.5 | 16 | 24.5 |
| 13 | 11.5 | 17 | 28 |
| 13 | 11.5 | 17 | 28 |
| 14 | 17 | 18 | 32 |
| 14 | 17 | 18 | 32 |
| 14 | 17 | 18 | 32 |
| 15 | 21 | 18 | 32 |
| 15 | 21 | 19 | 35.5 |
| 16 | 24.5 | 19 | 35.5 |
| 17 | 28 | 20 | 37.5 |
| 18 | 32 | 22 | 39 |
| 20 | 37.5 | 26 | 40 |
| | $\Sigma$ rank$_1$ 295.5 | | $\Sigma$ rank$_2$ 524.5 |

Note: When scores are tied, assign the mean value of the tied ranks to each. Thus, for both 9-second times in this example, the rank 1.5 is assigned (the mean of 1 and 2).

*Step 2.* The equations for finding $U$ and $U'$ are as follows, where $n_1$ is the size of the smaller sample, $n_2$ is the size of the larger sample, $\Sigma R_1$ is the sum of the ranks of the smaller sample, and $\Sigma R_2$ is the sum of the ranks of the larger sample. The subscripts are important only if the sample sizes are unequal, which is not the case here.

$$U = n_1 n_2 + \frac{n_1(n_1 + 1)}{2} - \Sigma R_1$$

$$U = (20)(20) + \frac{(20)(21)}{2} - 295.5$$

$$U = 400 + 210 - 295.5$$

$$U = 314.5$$

$$U' = n_1 n_2 + \frac{n_2(n_2 + 1)}{2} - \Sigma R_2$$

$$U' = (20)(20) + \frac{(20)(21)}{2} - 524.5$$

$$U' = 85.5$$

Actually, it is only necessary to compute $U$ or $U'$, because the other can be found according to the equation:

$$U = n_1 n_2 - U'$$

or

$$U' = n_1 n_2 - U.$$

*Step 3.* Take $U$ or $U'$, whichever value is *smaller*, and look at table C–2 (in appendix C) to see whether the difference between the two groups is reliable. The values in the table are recorded by different sample sizes. In this case, both sample sizes are 20, so the critical value from the table is 88. In order for the difference between the two groups to be judged reliable, the $U$ or $U'$ from the experiment must be *less than* the appropriate value shown in Table C–2. Since 85.5 is less than 88, we can conclude that the difference between the two groups is reliable at the .001 level of significance.

Note: Table C–2 is only appropriate when the sizes of the two samples are between 8 and 21. For other cases, consult an advanced text.

pothesis should be rejected. The way in which the Mann-Whitney test is applied to data is outlined in box B–2, where the reliability of the difference between the two samples in our hypothetical LSD experiment is tested.

The *Wilcoxon signed-ranks test* is also used in testing for the difference between two samples, but in this case the design must be a *related-measures design*. In other words, either the same subjects must serve in both the experimental and control groups (a within-subjects design), or the subjects must be matched in some way. Of course, precautions must be taken in within-subjects designs to ensure that a variable such as practice or fatigue is not confounded with the variable of interest.

Before considering the signed-ranks test, let us examine its simpler cousin, the sign test, which is appropriate in the same situations. The sign test is the essence of simplicity. Suppose we have twenty-six subjects serving in both conditions of an experiment, and we predict that when subjects are in the experimental condition they will do better than when they are in the control condition. Now suppose that nineteen subjects actually do better in the experimental condition than in the control, and the reverse is true for the other seven. Is this difference reliable? The sign test yields an answer to this question without our needing to know what the actual scores were. Under the null hypothesis, we might expect thirteen subjects to perform better in the experimental condition and thirteen to perform better in the control. The sign test allows us to compute the exact probability that the null hypothesis is false when there are nineteen cases in the predicted direction but also seven reversals or exceptions. The null hypothesis can be rejected in this case with a .014 significance level (one-tailed); with a nondirectional prediction, $p$ equals .028 (two-tailed). In table C-3 (in appendix C) are the $\alpha$ levels (one-tailed) for situations with sample sizes from three to forty-two when there are $x$ number of exceptions to the predicted hypothesis. So, for example, when there are sixteen subjects in the experiment (remember, in both conditions) and thirteen show the predicted pattern of results whereas three exhibit reversals, we can reject the null hypothesis at the .011 level of significance (one-tailed).

The sign test uses very little of the data from an experiment, just whether the subjects performed better or worse in one condition than in another. For the sign test, the direction of the difference and not its magnitude is what matters. The sign test therefore wastes much of the information gathered in an experiment and is not a very powerful statistical test. The Wilcoxon signed-ranks test is used as the sign test in situations where the same (or matched) subjects are in two conditions and the direction of the difference is taken into account. However, in the Wilcoxon test the size of the difference is taken into account, too. For this reason it is also called the *sized sign test*. The Wilcoxon test is more powerful than the sign test. Box B-3 shows how the Wilcoxon signed-ranks test is used.

---

**BOX B-3**
Calculation of the Wilcoxon Signed-Ranks Test

Imagine an experiment designed to test whether Professor von Widget's memory course really works. A group of thirty subjects is presented with fifty words to remember. Then the subjects are randomly separated into two groups, and a check indicates that the groups do not differ reliably in terms of the mean number of words recalled. The experimental group is given Professor von Widget's three-week course, and the control group is not. Then all thirty subjects are tested again on another fifty-word list. The controls show no improvement from one list to another. The question is whether the experimental subjects' memories were reliably improved. (Note: We could—and should—also compare the experimental subjects' performance on the second test with that of the controls. The Mann-Whitney test is appropriate for this comparison. Do you know why?) We use the Wilcoxon signed-ranks test to assess whether the experimental subjects improved reliably from the first test to the second.

*Step 1.* Place the data in a table (such as the one that follows) where both scores for each subject (before and after the memory course) are paired together. Find and record the difference between the pairs.

| | MEAN NUMBER OF WORDS RECALLED | | | |
|---|---|---|---|---|
| Subject | Before | After | Difference | Rank |
| 1 | 11 | 17 | + 6 | 14 |
| 2 | 18 | 16 | − 2 | 5.5 |
| 3 | 9 | 21 | +12 | 15 |
| 4 | 15 | 16 | + 1 | 2.5 |
| 5 | 14 | 17 | + 3 | 8.5 |
| 6 | 12 | 15 | + 3 | 8.5 |
| 7 | 17 | 16 | − 1 | 2.5 |
| 8 | 16 | 17 | + 1 | 2.5 |
| 9 | 15 | 20 | + 5 | 13 |
| 10 | 19 | 16 | − 3 | 8.5 |
| 11 | 12 | 13 | + 1 | 2.5 |
| 12 | 16 | 14 | − 2 | 5.5 |
| 13 | 10 | 14 | + 4 | 11.5 |
| 14 | 17 | 20 | + 3 | 8.5 |
| 15 | 6 | 10 | + 4 | 11.5 |
| | $\bar{X} = 13.80$ | $\bar{X} = 16.07$ | | |

Step 2.   Rank the values of the differences according to size, beginning with the smallest. *Ignore the sign.* Use the absolute values of the numbers. For tied ranks, assign each the mean value of the ranks. (See the right-hand column of the table here.)

Step 3.   Add the ranks for all the difference values that are negative (5.5 + 2.5 + 8.5 + 5.5 = 22.0) and positive (14 + 15 + 2.5 + 8.5 + 8.5 + 2.5 + 13 + 2.5 + 11.5 + 8.5 + 11.5 = 98.0). These are the signed-rank values.

Step 4.   Take the signed-rank value that is smallest (22) and go to table C−4 in appendix C. Look up the number of pairs of observations (listed as *n* on the left). There are 15 in this case. Then look at the number under the desired level of significance. Since the direction of the outcome was predicted (we expected the memory course to help rather than hurt recall of words), let us choose the value under the .025 level of significance for a one-tailed test. This value is 25. If the smaller of the two values from the experiment is *below* the appropriate value in the table, then the result is reliable. Since 22 is below 25, we can conclude that Professor von Widget's course really did help subjects recall words.

Note: Remember that the controls showed no improvement in performance from one test to the other. This is a crucial bit of information, for otherwise we could not rule out two plausible competing hypotheses— one is that the improvement on the second list was simply owing to practice on the first, and the other is that the second list was easier than the first.

In boxes B−4 and B−5 we present the corresponding *t*-tests for the analyses presented in the previous two boxes. The *t*-test is a parametric test, which means that we assume that the underlying distributions are roughly normal in shape. Furthermore, the *t*-test and other parametric tests were designed to be used on data that are at least interval in nature. The *U*-test and the sign test require only ordinal data. The *t*-tests are essentially based on z-scores having to do with the standard error of the difference between means. Thus, even if the computational formulas appear unusual at first, the underlying logic is the same as that discussed earlier in this chapter.

**BOX B–4**
Calculation of a
Between-Subjects
*t* Test

These are hypothetical experimental data previously discussed (see Box B–2). The calculation formula is:

$$t = \frac{\bar{X}_1 - \bar{X}_2}{\sqrt{\left[\dfrac{\Sigma X_1^2 - \dfrac{(\Sigma X_1)^2}{N_1} + \Sigma X_2^2 - \dfrac{(\Sigma X_2)^2}{N_2}}{N_1 + N_2 - 2}\right]\left[\dfrac{1}{N_1} + \dfrac{1}{N_2}\right]}}$$

$\bar{X}_1$ = mean of group 1
$\bar{X}_2$ = mean of group 2
$N_1$ = number of scores in group 1
$N_2$ = number of scores in group 2

$\Sigma X_1^2$ = sum of squared scores in
$\Sigma X_2^2$ = group 1
$(\Sigma X_1)^2$ = sum of squared scores in
$(\Sigma X_2)^2$ = group 2
     square of group-1 sum
     square of group-2 sum

| CONTROL (PLACEBO) | | | | EXPERIMENTAL (LSD) | | | |
| --- | --- | --- | --- | --- | --- | --- | --- |
| *X* | *X²* | *X* | *X²* | *X* | *X²* | *X* | *X²* |
| 9 | 81 | 13 | 169 | 9 | 81 | 17 | 289 |
| 10 | 100 | 14 | 196 | 13 | 169 | 18 | 324 |
| 11 | 121 | 14 | 196 | 13 | 169 | 18 | 324 |
| 11 | 121 | 14 | 196 | 14 | 196 | 18 | 324 |
| 12 | 144 | 15 | 225 | 14 | 196 | 18 | 324 |
| 12 | 144 | 15 | 225 | 15 | 225 | 19 | 361 |
| 12 | 144 | 16 | 256 | 16 | 256 | 19 | 361 |
| 13 | 169 | 17 | 289 | 16 | 356 | 20 | 400 |
| 13 | 169 | 18 | 324 | 16 | 356 | 22 | 484 |
| 13 | 169 | 20 | 400 | 17 | 289 | 26 | 676 |

$\Sigma X = 272$         $\Sigma X^2 = 3838$         $\Sigma X = 338$         $\Sigma X^2 = 5960$
$\bar{X} = 13.60$                                           $\bar{X} = 16.90$

*Step 1.* After calculating $\Sigma X$, $\Sigma X^2$, and $\bar{X}$ for each group (by the way, there is no need to rank order our data), we need to calculate $(\Sigma X)^2/N$ for each group: $(272)^2/20 = 3699.20$ and $(338)^2/20 = 5712.20$. Then we need to determine $\Sigma X^2 - (\Sigma X)^2/N$ for each group: $3838 - 3699.2 = 138.8$ and $5960 - 5712.2 = 247.8$.

*Step 2.* Now we add the two group figures we obtained in the last step: $247.8 + 138.8$, and divide this sum by $N_1 + N_2 - 2$: $386.6/38 = 10.17$.

*Step 3.* The quotient obtained in Step 2 (10.17) is multiplied by

$$\left[\frac{1}{N_1} + \frac{1}{N_2}\right]: (10.17)(2/20) = 1.02.$$

*Step 4.* We now take the square root of the product obtained in Step·3: $\sqrt{1.02} = 1.01$.

*Step 5.* We find the absolute difference between the mean scores of the two groups (by subtracting one from the other, and ignoring the sign): $16.90 - 13.60 = 3.30$.

*Step 6.* $t$ = the difference between means (Step 5) divided by the results of Step 4: $3.30/1.01 = 3.27$. So, our $t = 3.27$. To evaluate this, we look in the tabled values of $t$ in table C–5 in appendix C. We enter this table with the number of degrees of freedom (*df*) in our experiment, which means the number of scores that are free to vary. For a between-subjects $t$, the degrees of freedom are $N_1 + N_2 - 2$, in this case $df = 38$. For $p = .05$ and $df = 38$, the critical value of $t$ is 2.04 in our table (always take the next lowest $df$ to calculate the critical value). Since our obtained $t$ exceeds the critical value, we can reject the hypothesis that our two groups have the same running scores; that is, LSD had an effect on the behavior of our subjects.

**BOX B–5**
Calculation of a
Within-Subjects $t$ Test

The hypothetical data are from Professor Widget's experiment (see Box B–3). The computational formula for the within-subjects $t$ test is as follows:

$$t = \sqrt{\frac{N - 1}{[N \Sigma D^2 / (\Sigma D)^2] - 1}}$$

where $N$ = number of subjects; and $D$ = difference in the scores of a given subject (or matched subject pair) in the two conditions.

| MEAN NUMBER OF WORDS RECALLED | | | | |
|---|---|---|---|---|
| Subject | Before | After | Difference | $D^2$ |
| 1 | 11 | 17 | + 6 | 36 |
| 2 | 18 | 16 | − 2 | 4 |
| 3 | 9 | 21 | + 12 | 144 |
| 4 | 15 | 16 | + 1 | 1 |
| 5 | 14 | 17 | + 3 | 9 |
| 6 | 12 | 15 | + 3 | 9 |
| 7 | 17 | 16 | − 1 | 1 |
| 8 | 16 | 17 | + 1 | 1 |
| 9 | 15 | 20 | + 5 | 25 |
| 10 | 19 | 16 | − 3 | 9 |
| 11 | 12 | 13 | + 1 | 1 |
| 12 | 16 | 14 | − 2 | 4 |
| 13 | 10 | 14 | + 4 | 16 |
| 14 | 17 | 20 | + 3 | 9 |
| 15 | 6 | 10 | + 4 | 16 |
| | $\bar{X} = 13.80$ | $\bar{X} = 16.07$ | $\Sigma D = 35$<br>$(\Sigma D)^2 = 1{,}225$ | $\Sigma D^2 = 285$ |

*Step 1.* After you arrange the scores for each subject in pairs as shown in this table, record the difference between each pair and then square each of these difference scores.

*Step 2.* Add the difference scores across subjects, which yields $\Sigma D$, then square this sum to get $(\Sigma D)^2$: $\Sigma D = 35$; and $(\Sigma D)^2 = 1{,}225$.

*Step 3.* Calculate the sum of the squared difference scores to get $\Sigma D^2 = 285$.

*Step 4.* Multiply $\Sigma D^2$ (Step 3) by the number of subjects: $285 \times 15 = 4{,}275$.

*Step 5.* Divide the product found in Step 5 by $(\Sigma D)^2$: $4{,}275/1{,}225 = 3.49$, and then subtract 1 from the result: $3.49 - 1 = 2.49$.

*Step 6.* Divide the number of subjects less 1 $(N - 1)$ by the result of Step 5: $14/2.49 = 5.62$.

*Step 7.* $t = \sqrt{5.62} = 2.37.$

*Step 8.* To evaluate *t,* compare it to the critical values shown in Table C–5 in Appendix C. Enter the table with $N - 1$ *df,* and for this study *df* = 14. With *df* = 14, the critical value of *t* is 2.145 for $p$ = .05. Since the obtained *t* exceeds the critical value, we can conclude that von Widget's course really did affect word recall.

## The Analysis of Variance

Most psychological research has progressed beyond the stage where there are only two conditions, an experimental and a control that are compared with each other. Investigators typically have more than two conditions in psychological research. In our example of the effects of LSD on running speed of rats, it may be quite useful to vary the amount of LSD administered to the rats. Perhaps low dosages and high dosages produce different effects. We could not determine this from the two-group design where one group received LSD in some amount and the other did not. In order to evaluate the results of such an experiment with multiple groups, we must use the analysis of variance. A simple analysis of variance is used in situations where one factor or independent variable (such as amount of LSD) is varied systematically, and thus is usually called a *one-factor analysis of variance.*

Often researchers are interested in varying more than one factor. They may want to vary two or more factors simultaneously. In such complex or multifactor experimental designs, the analysis of variance is also appropriate, but it is more complex. In this section, we introduce you to the logic of both simple and multifactor analyses of variance (abbreviated *ANOVA*).

**Simple analysis of variance.**   The heart of the analysis-of-variance procedure is a comparison of variance estimates. We have already discussed the concept of variance and how it is estimated from one particular sample of observations. You should refer back to the section on measures of dispersion if the concept of variance is unclear. Recall that the equation for the unbiased estimate of the population variance is

$$\hat{s}^2 = \frac{\Sigma(X - \overline{X})^2}{n - 1} \tag{B–4}$$

and that when the deviation of scores from the mean is large, the variance will be great. Similarly, when the deviations from the mean are small, the variance will be small.

In the analysis of variance, two independent estimates of variance are obtained. One is based on the variability between the different experimental groups—how much the means of the different groups differ from one another. Actually, the variance is computed as to how much the individual group means differ from the overall mean of all scores in the experiment. The greater the difference among the means of the groups, the greater will be the **between-groups variance**.

The other estimate of variance is the **within-groups variance.** This is the concept we discussed in considering estimates of variance from individual samples. Now we are concerned with finding an estimate of within-groups variance that is representative of all the individual groups, so we take the mean of the variances of these groups. The within-groups variance gives us an estimate of how much the subjects in the groups differ from one another (or the mean of the group). Two variance estimates are obtained, one for the variance within groups and one for the variance between groups. Now what good does this do?

The basic logic of testing to see whether the scores of the different groups or conditions are reliably different is as follows. The null hypothesis is that all the subjects in the various conditions are drawn from the same underlying population; the experimental variable has no effect. If the null hypothesis were true and all the scores in the different groups came from the same population, then the between-groups variance should be the same as the within-groups variance. The means of the different groups should differ from one another no more nor less than do the scores within the groups. For us to reject the null hypothesis, then, the means of the different groups must vary from one another more than the scores vary within the groups. The greater the variance (differences) between the groups of the experiment, the more likely the independent variable is to have had an effect, especially if the within-groups variance is low.

The person who originated this logic was the eminent British statistician R. A. Fisher, and the test is referred to as an *F-test* in his honor. The *F*-test is simply a ratio of the between-groups variance estimate to the within-groups variance estimate, so

$$F = \frac{\text{between-groups variance}}{\text{within-groups variance}} \qquad \text{(B--5)}$$

According to the logic just outlined, the *F*-ratio under the null hypothesis should be 1.00, because the between-groups variance should be the same as the within-groups variance. The greater the between-groups variance is than the within-groups variance and, consequently, the greater the *F*-ratio is than 1.00, the more confident we can be in rejecting the null hypothesis. Exactly how much greater the *F*-ratio must be than 1.00 depends on the **degrees of freedom** in the experiment, or how free the measures are to vary. This depends both on the number of groups or conditions in the experiment and on the number of observations in each group. The greater the number of degrees of freedom, the smaller need be the value of the *F*-ratio to be judged a reliable effect, as you can see from examining table C--6 in appendix C. Follow the computational example in box B--6 carefully to get a feel for the analysis of variance.

---

**BOX B--6**
Computing Simple
Analysis of Variance:
One Variable—
Between Subjects

This ANOVA is often called a *one-way ANOVA* because there is only *one* independent variable. Imagine you have just performed an experiment testing the effects of LSD on the running speeds of rats, but that there were three levels of LSD administered, rather than two as in our earlier example. Ten rats received no LSD, ten others received a small amount, and a third group received a great amount. Thus the experiment uses a between-subjects design where amount of LSD (none, small, large) is the independent variable and running time is the dependent variable. First calculate the sum of the scores ($\Sigma X$) and the sum of the squared values of the scores ($\Sigma X^2$).

| | | AMOUNT OF LSD | |
|---|---|---|---|
| | **None** | **Small** | **Large** |
| | 13 | 17 | 26 |
| | 11 | 15 | 20 |
| | 14 | 16 | 29 |
| | 18 | 20 | 31 |
| | 12 | 13 | 17 |
| | 14 | 19 | 25 |
| | 10 | 18 | 26 |
| | 13 | 17 | 23 |
| | 16 | 19 | 25 |
| | 12 | 21 | 27 |
| $\Sigma X$ = | 133 | 175 | 249 |
| $\overline{X}$ = | 13.30 | 17.50 | 24.90 |
| $\Sigma X^2$ = | 1819 | 3115 | 6351 |
| $\Sigma\Sigma X$ = | 557 | $\Sigma\Sigma X^2 = 11285$ | |

A basic quantity in calculating analysis of variance is the *sum of squares*, which is an abbreviation for the *sum of squared deviations from the mean*. If you look back to equation A–1 (in appendix A), which defines the variance of a sample, you will see that the sum of squares is the numerator. Three sum of squares are of interest. First, there is the total sum of squares (*SS* Total), which is the sum of the squared deviations of the individual scores from the grand mean or the mean of all scores in all groups in the experiment. Second, there is the sum of squares between groups (*SS* Between), which is the sum of the squared deviations of the group means from the grand mean. Third, the sum of squares within groups (*SS* Within) is the mean of the sum of the squared deviations of the individual scores within groups or conditions from the group means. It turns out that *SS* Total = *SS* Between + *SS* Within, so that in practice only two sums of squares need be calculated; the third can be found by subtraction.

These sums of squares could be calculated by taking the deviations from the appropriate means, squaring them, and then finding the sum, but such a method would take much time and labor. Fortunately, there are computational formulas that allow the calculations to be done more easily, especially if the values of $\Sigma X$ and $\Sigma X^2$ have been found for each group, as in the present data. The formula for finding the total sum of squares is

$$SS \text{ Total} = \Sigma\Sigma X^2 - \frac{T^2}{N} \tag{B–6}$$

where $\Sigma\Sigma X^2$ means that each score within each group is squared ($X^2$) and all these squared values are added together, so $\Sigma X^2$. There are two summation signs, one for summing the squared values within groups and one for then summing these $\Sigma X^2$ across the different groups. The $T$ is the total of all scores, and $N$ is the total number of scores in the experiment. So *SS* Total in our example is calculated in the following way:

$$SS \text{ Total} = \Sigma\Sigma X^2 - \frac{T^2}{N}$$

$$SS \text{ Total} = 1819 + 3115 + 6351 - \frac{(133 + 175 + 249)^2}{30}$$

$$SS \text{ Total} = 11{,}285 - \frac{310{,}249}{30}$$

$$SS \text{ Total} = 11{,}285 - 10{,}341.63$$

$$SS \text{ Total} = 943.37$$

The between-groups sum of squares is calculated with the following formula:

$$SS \text{ Between} = \Sigma \frac{(\Sigma X)^2}{n} - \frac{T^2}{N} \qquad (B-7)$$

The first part of the formula means that the sum of the values for each group is squared and then divided by the number of observations on which it is based, or $(\Sigma X)^2/n$; then these values are summed across groups, so $\Sigma(\Sigma X)^2/n$. The second part of the formula is the same as for the $SS$ Total:

$$SS \text{ Between} = \Sigma \frac{(\Sigma X)^2}{n} - \frac{T^2}{N}$$

$$SS \text{ Between} = \frac{17{,}689}{10} + \frac{30{,}625}{10} + \frac{62{,}001}{10} - 10{,}341.63$$

$$SS \text{ Between} = 11{,}031.50 - 10{,}341.63$$

$$SS \text{ Between} = 689.87$$

The sum of squares within groups can be found by subtracting $SS$ Between from $SS$ Total, so $SS$ Within $= 943.37 - 689.87 = 253.50$. As a check, we should also calculate it directly. This is done by computing an $SS$ Total (as in equation B–6) for each group and summing all these sums of squares for the individual groups. Unless we have made an error, this quantity should equal $SS$ Within obtained by subtraction. Note that

$$\frac{(\Sigma\Sigma X)^2}{N} \text{ or } \frac{T^2}{N}$$

is called the *correction term* because it is taken out of most $SS$.

After we have obtained the various sums of squares, it is convenient to construct an analysis-of-variance table such as the one that follows. In the far left column appears the source of variance, or source. Keep in mind that there are two primary sources of variance we are interested in comparing—between groups and within groups.

In the next column are the number of degrees of freedom $(df)$. These can be thought of as the number of scores that are free to vary, given that the total is fixed. For the degrees of freedom between-groups, if the overall total is fixed, all groups are free to vary except one. Thus, the between-groups $df$ is the number of groups minus one. In our example, then, it is $3 - 1 = 2$. The within-groups $df$ is equal to the total number of scores minus the number of groups, because there is one score in each group that cannot vary if the group total is fixed. So within-groups $df$ is $30 - 3 = 27$. The total $df$ = between-groups $df$ + within-groups $df$.

The third column includes the **sum of squares** $(SS)$, which have already been calculated. The fourth column represents the *mean squares*, $(MS)$, which are found by dividing the $SS$ by the $df$ for each row. Each mean square is an estimate of the population variance if the null hypothesis is true. But if the independent variable had an effect, the between-groups mean square should be larger than the within-groups mean square.

As discussed in the text, these two values are compared by computing an $F$-ratio, which is found by dividing the $MS$ Between by the $MS$ Within. Once the $F$ value is calculated, it is necessary to determine whether the value reaches an acceptable level of statistical significance. By looking at table C–6 in appendix C, we can see that for 2 and 26 degrees of freedom (the closest we can get to 2 and 27), an F value of 9.12 is needed for the .001 level of significance. Our F value surpasses 9.12, so we can conclude that the groups varied reliably in running speed because of variation in the independent variable—amount of LSD injected.

| Source | df | SS | MS | F | p |
|---|---|---|---|---|---|
| Between-groups | 2 | 689.87 | 344.94 | 36.73 | <.001 |
| Within-groups | 27 | 253.50 | 9.39 | | |
| Total | 29 | 943.37 | | | |

Note: If you compute analyses of variance with the aid of a calculator, watch out for errors. If you come up with a negative sum of squares within-groups (by subtracting SS Between from SS Total), you will know you made an error. You cannot have a negative sum of squares. You should compute SS Within both by subtraction and directly, anyway, as a check. One common error is to confuse $\Sigma X^2$ (square each number and then sum the squares) with $(\Sigma X)^2$, which is the square of the total of the scores.

If the simple analysis of variance yields a significant F–ratio, there is still more we would like to know, in particular, which of the individual conditions vary among themselves. This is especially important in cases where manipulation of the independent variable is qualitative in nature. *Quantitative* variation of an independent variable is when the quantity of an independent variable is manipulated (for example, amount of LSD), whereas *qualitative* variation is when conditions vary but not in some easily specified quantitative manner. An example of qualitative variation is an instructional manipulation in which the different conditions vary in terms of the instructions given at the beginning of the experiment. In such situations, it is not enough simply to say that the conditions vary reliably from one another. It is of interest to know which particular conditions differ. To answer this question, we need to perform tests after the simple analysis of variance. In these follow-up tests (generally called post hoc tests), the conditions of the experiment are taken two at a time and compared so that we can see which pairs are reliably different. There are several statistical tests for this purpose. We could perform analyses of variance on groups taken as pairs, which is equivalent to performing t-tests, but usually other tests are done. These include the Newman-Keuls test, the Scheffé test, Duncan's multiple-range test, Tukey's HSD (Honestly Significant Differences) test, and Dunnett's test. These tests vary in their assumptions and their power. You should consult statistical texts when you need to use a follow-up test. Follow-up tests are also used when manipulation of the independent variable is quantitative in nature. These are called *trend tests* (we will not discuss them here).

**BOX B–7**
Within-Subjects (Treatments × Subjects) ANOVA—One Variable (One-way ANOVA)

We could have conducted the previous three-level LSD study with a within-subjects rather than a between-subjects design. Of course, we would have counterbalanced the order of administering dosages across subjects. Let us assume that we used nine subjects in our within-subjects LSD study: Three subjects received the dose order None-Large-Small; three received the doses in the Small-None-Large order; and three were dosed in the order Large-Small-None. After each dose of LSD, the rats' running time in the straight alley was recorded. We could analyze the effects of order by a two-factor, within-subjects ANOVA (see Box B–9), but for the purposes of this illustration, we will ignore the effects of treatment order.

In a within-subjects ANOVA, we need to calculate the following kinds of variability:

**SS Total**—This is the variation about the mean of all the scores. SS Total is the sum of the remaining sums of squares.

**SS Treatment**—This is the difference among the treatment conditions and is calculated like SS Between in the previous ANOVA.

**SS Subjects**—This estimates the differences among individuals in our experiment and is used to calculate the next SS.

**SS Error** or **SS Treatment × Subject**—This represents the random variability that would occur in the scores of the same individuals in the same conditions. This interaction gives the ANOVA the name **Treatments × Subjects.** Usually, this SS is called *error variance,* and it is the denominator of the F-ratio of the treatment effect.

We will use the hypothetical data from the first nine subjects of the LSD study shown in box B–6. We will assume the ordering of treatments as mentioned earlier. You should set up your data table as follows, so that the scores for each subject are in a row. Leave room so that a given subject's total score summed across treatments can appear in the table. You might also want to leave room for the squares of the scores and the squares of the subjects' totals.

| | | RUNNING TIMES | | | |
|---|---|---|---|---|---|
| | | **Amount of LSD** | | **Subject** | **Subject** |
| **Subject** | **None** | **Small** | **Large** | **Total** | **Total Squared** |
| 1 | 13 | 17 | 26 | 56 | 3136 |
| 2 | 11 | 15 | 20 | 46 | 2116 |
| 3 | 14 | 16 | 29 | 59 | 3481 |
| 4 | 18 | 20 | 31 | 69 | 4761 |
| 5 | 12 | 13 | 17 | 42 | 1764 |
| 6 | 14 | 19 | 25 | 58 | 3364 |
| 7 | 10 | 18 | 26 | 54 | 2916 |
| 8 | 13 | 17 | 23 | 53 | 2809 |
| 9 | 16 | 19 | 25 | 60 | 3600 |
| $\Sigma X =$ | 121 | 154 | 222 | 497 | |
| $\Sigma X^2 =$ | 1675 | 2674 | 5622 | | 27497 |

$$\Sigma\Sigma X = 497 \quad \Sigma\Sigma X^2 = 9971 \ (1675 + 2674 + 5622)$$

*Step 1.* When you calculate $\Sigma\Sigma X$ by adding the three treatment totals (121 + 154 + 222), you can check your accuracy by adding up the subject totals, the sum of which should equal $\Sigma\Sigma X$. Calculate $\Sigma X^2$ for each treatment, $\Sigma\Sigma X^2$, and the sum of the squares of the subject totals (last column).

*Step 2.* Calculation of the correction term, C.

$C = (\Sigma\Sigma X)^2/N$, where $N$ = the number of scores in the table (9 subjects × 3 scores for each subject)

$= 497^2/27$

$= 247009/27$

$= 9148.48$

*Step 3.* SS Total $= \Sigma\Sigma X^2 -$ Step 2
$\phantom{Step 3. SS Total }= 9971 - 9148.48$
$\phantom{Step 3. SS Total }= 822.52$

*Step 4.* SS Treatments $=$ SS Dose. SS Dose is calculated by summing the squares of the treatment totals, dividing that sum by the number of scores in each treatment, and then subtracting C (Step 2).

$$SS \text{ Dose} = \frac{121^2 + 154^2 + 222^2}{9} - \text{Step 2}$$

$\phantom{SS Dose }= 87419/9 - \text{Step 2}$
$\phantom{SS Dose }= 9737.89 - 9148.48$
$\phantom{SS Dose }= 589.41$

*Step 5.* SS Subject $=$ Sum of the squared subject totals (final column in the table) divided by the number of scores per subject (3) minus C.
$\phantom{SS Subject }= 27947/3 - \text{Step 2}$
$\phantom{SS Subject }= 9315.67 - 9148.48$
$\phantom{SS Subject }= 167.19$

*Step 6.* SS Error $=$ SS Total $-$ SS Dose $-$ SS Subject
$\phantom{SS Error }= \text{Step 3} - \text{Step 4} - \text{Step 5}$
$\phantom{SS Error }= 822.52 - 589.41 - 167.19$
$\phantom{SS Error }= 65.92$

*Step 7.* Determination of *df.*

$df$ Total $= \#$ scores $- 1 = 26$
$df$ Dose $= \#$ treatments $- 1 = 2$
$df$ Subject $= \#$ subjects $- 1 = 8$
$df$ Error $= (df \text{ Dose})(df \text{ Subject}) = 16$

*Step 8.* Determination of MS.

MS Dose $=$ SS Dose/$df$ Dose $= 589.41/2 = 294.71$
MS Error $=$ SS Error/$df$ Error $= 65.92/16 = 4.12$

*Step 9.* $F =$ MS Dose/MS Error $= 294.71/4.12 = 71.53$.

*Step 10.* Summary Table.

| Source | SS | df | MS | F |
|--------|-----|----|------|------|
| Subjects | 167.19 | 8 | | |
| Dose | 589.41 | 2 | 294.71 | 71.53 |
| Error | 65.92 | 16 | 4.12 | |
| Total | 822.52 | 26 | | |

We determine the significance of the *F*-ratio by entering table C–6 (in appendix C) with 2 and 16 degrees of freedom. Since our obtained *F* greatly exceeds those needed for significance with 2 and 16 *df*, we can conclude that dose level of LSD influenced the running times of our rats.

**Multifactor analysis of variance.** To discover the multiple determinants of behavior and how they interact, we must perform experiments in which more than one factor is varied simultaneously. The appropriate procedure for analyzing results of such experiments is *multifactor analysis of variance.* There may be any number of factors in the experiment, but it is rare to find more than four variables of interest manipulated simultaneously. When there are two factors, the analysis is referred to as a two-way ANOVA; when there are three factors, it is a three-way ANOVA; and so on.

The importance of such complex designs involving more than one factor is that they allow the experimenter to assess how different factors may *interact* to produce a result. Recall that an interaction occurs when the effect of one experimental variable is influenced by the level of the other experimental variable. When performing a complex analysis of variance, we find out the separate effects of each factor in the experiment (called **main effects**), and also how the variables affect one another (called **interaction effects,** or simply *interactions*).

In the following two boxes, we present some recipes for complex ANOVAs. Because of space limitations, we have refrained from presenting much of the logic behind these tests. However, you should find the examples useful in analyzing your own results even if you have not had a formal course in statistics.

---

**BOX B–8**
Calculation of a
2 × 2 ANOVA

This is a between-subjects design. The data are from a memory experiment in which subjects had to remember words of either high imagery (cigar) or low imagery (democracy). Some subjects simply said the words to themselves as they were presented (rote rehearsal), and the other subjects tried to get a mental image of the words (elaborative rehearsal).

| | HIGH-IMAGERY WORDS | | LOW-IMAGERY WORDS | |
|---|---|---|---|---|
| | **Rote Rehearsal** | **Elaborative Rehearsal** | **Rote Rehearsal** | **Elaborative Rehearsal** |
| | 5 | 8 | 4 | 7 |
| | 7 | 8 | 1 | 6 |
| | 6 | 9 | 5 | 3 |
| | 4 | 7 | 6 | 3 |
| | 4 | 10 | 4 | 5 |
| | 9 | 10 | 3 | 6 |
| | 7 | 8 | 4 | 2 |
| | 5 | 9 | 4 | 4 |
| | 5 | 8 | 5 | 5 |
| | 6 | 9 | 3 | 4 |
| $\Sigma X =$ | 58 | 86 | 39 | 45 |
| $\Sigma X^2 =$ | 358 | 748 | 169 | 225 |

$\Sigma\Sigma X^2 = (358 + \ldots + 225) = 1500 \qquad \Sigma\Sigma X = 228$

*Step 1.* Square the grand sum $(\Sigma\Sigma X = 228)$ and divide by the total number of scores (40). $(\Sigma\Sigma X)^2/N = (228)^2/40 = 1299.6$. This is the correction term.

*Step 2. SS* Total $= \Sigma\Sigma X^2 - (\Sigma\Sigma X)^2/N$. Subtract the results of Step 1 from 1500. *SS* Total $= 200.4$.

*Step 3. SS* Imagery. Get the sum of all scores in each imagery condition, square each sum, then divide each sum by the number of scores yielding each sum, add the two quotients, and then subtract the results of Step 1 from the last sum.

$$SS \text{ Imagery} = (58 + 86)^2/20 + (39 + 45)^2/20 - \text{Step 1}$$

$$= \frac{144^2 + 84^2}{20} - 1299.6$$

$$= 1389.6 - 1299.6$$

$$= 90$$

*Step 4. SS* Rehearsal. This is calculated in the same manner as Step 3, except that you base your calculations on the grand sum of each type of rehearsal.

$$SS \text{ Rehearsal} = \frac{(86 + 45)^2 + (58 + 39)^2}{20} - \text{Step 1}$$

$$= 1328.5 - 1299.6$$

$$= 28.9$$

*Step 5. SS* Imagery $\times$ Rehearsal. Square each group sum and add the squares. Then divide each sum by the number of scores in each sum. From the last result, subtract the *SS* Imagery (Step 3), *SS* Rehearsal (Step 4), and Step 1.

$$SS I \times R = \frac{58^2 + 86^2 + 39^2 + 45^2}{10} - \text{Step 1} - \text{Step 3} - \text{Step 4}$$

$$= 14306/10 - 1299.6 - 90 - 28.9$$

$$= 12.1$$

*Step 6. SS* Error. Subtract each of your treatments *SS* from *SS* Total.

$$SS \text{ Error} = 200.4 - 90 - 28.9 - 12.1$$

$$= 69.4$$

*Step 7.* Determining degrees of freedom.

$df$ Total $=$ the number of measures less one $(40 - 1) = 39$
$df$ Imagery $=$ number of levels of Imagery less one $(2 - 1) = 1$
$df$ Rehearsal $=$ number of levels of Rehearsal less one $(2 - 1) = 1$
$df$ I $\times$ R $= df$ Imagery X $df$ Rehearsal $(1 \times 1) = 1$
$df$ Error $= df$ Total $- df$ Imagery $- df$ Rehearsal $- df$ I $\times$ R
$(39 - 1 - 1 - 1) = 36$

*Step 8.* Summary table. Calculate mean squares (*MS*) by dividing *SS* by the number of *df*. Then calculate the *F* ratios by dividing the treatment *MS* by the *MS* Error.

| SUMMARY TABLE OF A 2 × 2 ANOVA | | | | | |
|---|---|---|---|---|---|
| **Source** | **SS** | **df** | **MS** | **F** | **p** |
| Imagery | 90. | 1 | 90. | 46.6 | <.05 |
| Rehearsal | 28.9 | 1 | 28.9 | 15.0 | <.05 |
| Imagery X Rehearsal | 12.1 | 1 | 12.1 | 6.3 | <.05 |
| Error | 69.4 | 36 | 1.9 | | |

*Step 9.* To determine the significance of the *F* ratio, enter Statistical Table C–6 with the *df* for the numerator (in this case it is always 1), and with the *df* for the denominator (*df* Error), which is 36, for any effect you are interested in.

We can conclude that the type of words and type of rehearsal both influenced recall. But we should note that the effects of word type were dependent on the type of rehearsal (that is, we obtained an interaction).

---

**BOX B–9**

Factorial ANOVA with Repeated Measures (Within-Subjects)

In a within-subjects ANOVA, we need to calculate both column (treatment) and row (subject) totals, because subjects are serving as their own control condition. In fact, our error variance is estimated by the interaction of subjects within treatments (see Box B–7). Arrange your data table so that the scores of a single subject are in a row. It is usually a good idea to leave room so that treatment totals for a single subject may be placed in the table. We will analyze the data from Experiment 1 by Elmes and Bjork (1975). In their study, subjects either rote or elaboratively rehearsed words, and then they performed a distracting math task for 2 or 12 seconds before attempting to recall the words. Thus, this is a 2 × 2 within-subjects design. The individual subjects' total recall scores are shown in the following table.

| Subject | ROTE REHEARSAL Retention Interval | | ELABORATE REHEARSAL Retention Interval | | SUBJECT TOTAL | REHEARSAL TOTAL | | RETENTION TOTAL | |
|---|---|---|---|---|---|---|---|---|---|
| | 2 sec | 12 sec | 2 sec | 12 sec | | Rote | Elab. | 2 sec | 12 sec |
| 1 | 15 | 3 | 11 | 11 | 40 | 18 | 22 | 26 | 14 |
| 2 | 20 | 15 | 19 | 18 | 72 | 35 | 37 | 39 | 33 |
| 3 | 18 | 2 | 18 | 19 | 57 | 20 | 37 | 36 | 21 |
| 4 | 15 | 13 | 16 | 15 | 59 | 28 | 31 | 31 | 28 |
| 5 | 10 | 1 | 17 | 12 | 40 | 11 | 29 | 27 | 13 |
| 6 | 14 | 5 | 16 | 13 | 48 | 19 | 29 | 30 | 18 |
| 7 | 17 | 6 | 19 | 18 | 60 | 23 | 37 | 36 | 24 |
| 8 | 19 | 12 | 16 | 19 | 66 | 31 | 35 | 35 | 31 |
| 9 | 11 | 4 | 9 | 12 | 36 | 15 | 21 | 20 | 16 |
| 10 | 17 | 10 | 14 | 7 | 48 | 27 | 21 | 31 | 17 |
| 11 | 18 | 11 | 18 | 10 | 57 | 29 | 28 | 36 | 21 |
| 12 | 18 | 4 | 20 | 19 | 61 | 22 | 39 | 38 | 23 |
| 13 | 16 | 9 | 19 | 18 | 62 | 25 | 37 | 35 | 27 |
| 14 | 18 | 6 | 19 | 17 | 60 | 24 | 36 | 37 | 23 |
| 15 | 10 | 5 | 10 | 7 | 32 | 15 | 17 | 20 | 12 |
| 16 | 16 | 5 | 19 | 18 | 58 | 21 | 37 | 35 | 23 |
| $\Sigma X =$ | 252 | 111 | 260 | 233 | 856 | 363 | 493 | 512 | 344 |
| $\Sigma X^2 =$ | 4114 | 1033 | 4408 | 3669 | 47776 | 24820 | | 24910 | |
| $\Sigma\Sigma X =$ | 856 | $\Sigma\Sigma X^2 =$ | 13224 | | | | | | |

*Step 1.* Determine the total score/subject (row) and total score/treatment combination (column). Find each subject's total score for every independent variable. The subject totals for a particular independent variable (for example, subject #1 has rehearsal totals of 18 and 22) should add up to that subject's total score (in this case, 40). Determine each treatment total by adding the appropriate column sums; check your answer by also adding the subject totals for that level of the independent variable. For example, the Rote Rehearsal total = 252 + 111 = 363 (sum of columns 1 and 2, which is equal to the sum of column 6).

*Step 2.* Determine the correction term ($C$). $C = (\Sigma\Sigma X)^2/N$, where $N$ = the number of measures in the table. $N = 16$ subjects $\times$ 4 scores $= 64$.

$C = 856^2/64$
$\quad = 732736/64$
$\quad = 11449$

*Step 3.* SS Total $= \Sigma\Sigma X^2 -$ Step 2
$\qquad\qquad\quad = 13224 - 11449$
$\qquad\qquad\quad = 1775$

*Step 4.* SS Subjects. Square each subject's total score (column 5), add the squares, and divide that total by the number of scores for each subject (4), then subtract the results of Step 2.

SS Subject $= 47776/4 -$ Step 2
$\qquad\qquad = 11944 - 11449$
$\qquad\qquad = 495$

*Step 5.* SS Rehearsal $= (363^2 + 493^2)/32 -$ Step 2
$\qquad\qquad\qquad\; = 374818/32 -$ Step 2
$\qquad\qquad\qquad\; = 11713.06 - 11449$
$\qquad\qquad\qquad\; = 264.06$

*Step 6.* MS Rehearsal. Divide the SS Rehearsal by the *df* for Rehearsal. The *df* Rehearsal = the number of levels of Rehearsal $- 1$.

*df* Rehearsal $= 2 - 1$.
MS Rehearsal $= 264.06/1$
$\qquad\qquad\quad = 264.06$

*Step 7.* SS Error Rehearsal. The error term for Rehearsal is the interaction of subjects with rehearsal. Square the subject totals for each level of Rehearsal (columns 6 and 7), add the squares, divide by the number of scores needed to get each sum (2 in this case), then subtract $C$ (Step 2), SS Subject (Step 4), and SS Rehearsal (Step 5).

$$SS\ Error\ Rehearsal = \frac{18^2 + 22^2 + ... + 21^2 + 37^2}{2} - \text{Steps 2, 4, and 5}$$
$\qquad\qquad\qquad\quad = 24820/2 -$ Steps 2, 4, and 5
$\qquad\qquad\qquad\quad = 12410 - 11449 - 495 - 264.06$
$\qquad\qquad\qquad\quad = 201.94$

*Step 8.* MS Error Rehearsal. Divide SS Error Rehearsal by *df* Error Rehearsal.

$df = (\#\text{Subject} - 1)(df\ \text{Rehearsal}) = (15)(1)$
MS Error Rehearsal $= 201.94/15$
$\qquad\qquad\qquad\quad = 13.46$

*Step 9.* F Rehearsal $=$ MS Rehearsal/MS Error Rehearsal
$\qquad\qquad\qquad = $ Step 6/Step 8
$\qquad\qquad\qquad = 264.06/13.46$
$\qquad\qquad\qquad = 19.62$

*Step 10.* Repeat Steps 5–9 to find the *F* for Retention Interval (RI)

SS RI $= (512^2 + 344^2)/32 -$ Step 2
$\qquad = 441.00$
MS RI $= 441.00/(2 - 1)$
$\qquad = 441.00$

$$SS \text{ Error RI} = \frac{26^2 + 14^2 + \ldots + 35^2 + 23^2}{2} - \text{Step 2, Step 4, and } SS \text{ RI}$$

$$= 24910/2 - C - SS \text{ Subject} - SS \text{ RI}$$
$$= 12455 - 11449 - 495 - 441$$
$$= 70$$

$$MS \text{ Error RI} = SS \text{ Error RI}/(16 - 1)(2 - 1)$$
$$= 70/15$$
$$= 4.67$$

$$F \text{ RI} = 441.00/4.67$$
$$= 94.43$$

*Step 11.* $SS$ Rehearsal $\times$ RI $= \dfrac{252^2 + 111^2 + 260^2 + 233^2}{16} - C$

$$- SS \text{ Reh} - SS \text{ RI}$$
$$= 12357.13 - 11449 - 264.06 - 441.00$$
$$= 203.07$$

*Step 12.* $MS$ Rehearsal $\times$ RI $= 203.07/(df \text{ Rehearsal})(df \text{ RI})$
$$= 203.07/1$$
$$= 203.07$$

*Step 13.* $SS$ Error Rehearsal $\times$ RI. Calculate this triple interaction by subtracting all the $SS$ you have calculated from $SS$ Total.

$SS$ Error Rehearsal $\times$ RI $= SS$ Total $- SS$ Subject $- SS$ Rehearsal $- SS$ RI
$$- SS \text{ Rehearsal} \times \text{RI} - SS \text{ Error Rehearsal}$$
$$- SS \text{ Error RI}$$
$$= 1775 - 495 - 264.06 - 441 - 203.07 - 204.94 - 70$$
$$= 99.93$$

*Step 14.* $MS$ Error Rehearsal $\times$ RI $= 99.93/(\#\text{Subject} - 1)(df \text{ Rehearsal})(df \text{ RI})$
$$= 99.93/15$$
$$= 6.66$$

*Step 15.* $F$ Rehearsal $\times$ RI $= MS$ Rehearsal $\times$ RI/$MS$ Error Rehearsal $\times$ RI
$$= 203.07/6.66$$
$$= 30.49$$

*Step 16.* Summary table of 2 $\times$ 2 within-subjects ANOVA

| Source | SS | df | MS | F |
|---|---|---|---|---|
| Subjects | 495.00 | 15 | | |
| Rehearsal | 264.06 | 1 | 264.06 | 19.62 |
| Error Reh | 201.94 | 15 | 13.46 | |
| Retention Interval | 441.00 | 1 | 441.00 | 94.43 |
| Error RI | 70.00 | 15 | 4.67 | |
| Reh $\times$ RI | 203.07 | 1 | 203.07 | 30.49 |
| Error Reh $\times$ RI | 99.93 | 15 | 6.66 | |
| Total | 1775.00 | 63 | | |

To determine significance, enter table C–6 with the appropriate degrees of freedom for each $F$-ratio. (In this case, the $df = 1$ and 15). Note that both rehearsal and retention interval had significant effects on recall, and that the effects of type of rehearsal are dependent on the length of the retention interval.

# C ||| Statistical Tables

---

**TABLE C–1**
**Proportions of Area under the Normal Curve**

*Column A* gives the positive z-score.

*Column B* gives the area between the mean and z. Since the curve is symmetrical, areas for negative z-scores are the same as for positive ones.

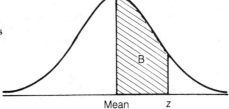

*Column C* gives the area that is beyond z.

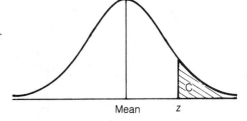

*How to Use Table A:* The values in this table represent the proportion of areas in the standard normal curve, which has a mean of 0, a standard deviation of 1.00, and a total area equal to 1.00. The raw scores must first be transformed into a z-score. Column A represents this z score, Column B represents the distance between the mean of the standard normal distribution (0) and the z-score, and Column C represents the proportion of the area beyond a given z.

---

**TABLE C–1
(Continued)**

| (A) z | (B) area between mean and z | (C) area beyond z | (A) z | (B) area between mean and z | (C) area beyond z | (A) z | (B) area between mean and z | (C) area beyond z |
|---|---|---|---|---|---|---|---|---|
| 0.00 | .0000 | .5000 | 0.50 | .1915 | .3085 | 1.00 | .3413 | .1587 |
| 0.01 | .0040 | .4960 | 0.51 | .1950 | .3050 | 1.01 | .3438 | .1562 |
| 0.02 | .0080 | .4920 | 0.52 | .1985 | .3015 | 1.02 | .3461 | .1539 |
| 0.03 | .0120 | .4880 | 0.53 | .2019 | .2981 | 1.03 | .3485 | .1515 |
| 0.04 | .0160 | .4840 | 0.54 | .2054 | .2946 | 1.04 | .3508 | .1492 |
| 0.05 | .0199 | .4801 | 0.55 | .2088 | .2912 | 1.05 | .3531 | .1469 |
| 0.06 | .0239 | .4761 | 0.56 | .2123 | .2877 | 1.06 | .3554 | .1446 |
| 0.07 | .0279 | .4721 | 0.57 | .2157 | .2843 | 1.07 | .3577 | .1423 |
| 0.08 | .0319 | .4681 | 0.58 | .2190 | .2810 | 1.08 | .3599 | .1401 |
| 0.09 | .0359 | .4641 | 0.59 | .2224 | .2776 | 1.09 | .3621 | .1379 |
| 0.10 | .0398 | .4602 | 0.60 | .2257 | .2743 | 1.10 | .3643 | .1357 |
| 0.11 | .0438 | .4562 | 0.61 | .2291 | .2709 | 1.11 | .3665 | .1335 |
| 0.12 | .0478 | .4522 | 0.62 | .2324 | .2676 | 1.12 | .3686 | .1314 |
| 0.13 | .0517 | .4483 | 0.63 | .2357 | .2643 | 1.13 | .3708 | .1292 |
| 0.14 | .0557 | .4443 | 0.64 | .2389 | .2611 | 1.14 | .3729 | .1271 |
| 0.15 | .0596 | .4404 | 0.65 | .2422 | .2578 | 1.15 | .3749 | .1251 |
| 0.16 | .0636 | .4364 | 0.66 | .2454 | .2546 | 1.16 | .3770 | .1230 |
| 0.17 | .0675 | .4325 | 0.67 | .2486 | .2514 | 1.17 | .3790 | .1210 |
| 0.18 | .0714 | .4286 | 0.68 | .2517 | .2483 | 1.18 | .3810 | .1190 |
| 0.19 | .0753 | .4247 | 0.69 | .2549 | .2451 | 1.19 | .3830 | .1170 |
| 0.20 | .0793 | .4207 | 0.70 | .2580 | .2420 | 1.20 | .3849 | .1151 |
| 0.21 | .0832 | .4168 | 0.71 | .2611 | .2389 | 1.21 | .3869 | .1131 |
| 0.22 | .0871 | .4129 | 0.72 | .2642 | .2358 | 1.22 | .3888 | .1112 |
| 0.23 | .0910 | .4090 | 0.73 | .2673 | .2327 | 1.23 | .3907 | .1093 |
| 0.24 | .0948 | .4052 | 0.74 | .2704 | .2296 | 1.24 | .3925 | .1075 |
| 0.25 | .0987 | .4013 | 0.75 | .2734 | .2266 | 1.25 | .3944 | .1056 |
| 0.26 | .1026 | .3974 | 0.76 | .2764 | .2236 | 1.26 | .3962 | .1038 |
| 0.27 | .1064 | .3936 | 0.77 | .2794 | .2206 | 1.27 | .3980 | .1020 |
| 0.28 | .1103 | .3897 | 0.78 | .2823 | .2177 | 1.28 | .3997 | .1003 |
| 0.29 | .1141 | .3859 | 0.79 | .2852 | .2148 | 1.29 | .4015 | .0985 |
| 0.30 | .1179 | .3821 | 0.80 | .2881 | .2119 | 1.30 | .4032 | .0968 |
| 0.31 | .1217 | .3783 | 0.81 | .2910 | .2090 | 1.31 | .4049 | .0951 |
| 0.32 | .1255 | .3745 | 0.82 | .2939 | .2061 | 1.32 | .4066 | .0934 |
| 0.33 | .1293 | .3707 | 0.83 | .2967 | .2033 | 1.33 | .4082 | .0918 |
| 0.34 | .1331 | .3669 | 0.84 | .2995 | .2005 | 1.34 | .4099 | .0901 |
| 0.35 | .1368 | .3632 | 0.85 | .3023 | .1977 | 1.35 | .4115 | .0885 |
| 0.36 | .1406 | .3594 | 0.86 | .3051 | .1949 | 1.36 | .4131 | .0869 |
| 0.37 | .1443 | .3557 | 0.87 | .3078 | .1922 | 1.37 | .4147 | .0853 |
| 0.38 | .1480 | .3520 | 0.88 | .3106 | .1894 | 1.38 | .4162 | .0838 |
| 0.39 | .1517 | .3483 | 0.89 | .3133 | .1867 | 1.39 | .4177 | .0823 |
| 0.40 | .1554 | .3446 | 0.90 | .3159 | .1841 | 1.40 | .4192 | .0808 |
| 0.41 | .1591 | .3409 | 0.91 | .3186 | .1814 | 1.41 | .4207 | .0793 |
| 0.42 | .1628 | .3372 | 0.92 | .3212 | .1788 | 1.42 | .4222 | .0778 |
| 0.43 | .1664 | .3336 | 0.93 | .3238 | .1762 | 1.43 | .4236 | .0764 |
| 0.44 | .1700 | .3300 | 0.94 | .3264 | .1736 | 1.44 | .4251 | .0749 |
| 0.45 | .1736 | .3264 | 0.95 | .3289 | .1711 | 1.45 | .4265 | .0735 |
| 0.46 | .1772 | .3228 | 0.96 | .3315 | .1685 | 1.46 | .4279 | .0721 |
| 0.47 | .1808 | .3192 | 0.97 | .3340 | .1660 | 1.47 | .4292 | .0708 |
| 0.48 | .1844 | .3156 | 0.98 | .3365 | .1635 | 1.48 | .4306 | .0694 |
| 0.49 | .1879 | .3121 | 0.99 | .3389 | .1611 | 1.49 | .4319 | .0681 |

**TABLE C-1 (Continued)**

| (A) z | (B) area between mean and z | (C) area beyond z | (A) z | (B) area between mean and z | (C) area beyond z | (A) z | (B) area between mean and z | (C) area beyond z |
|---|---|---|---|---|---|---|---|---|
| 1.50 | .4332 | .0668 | 2.00 | .4772 | .0228 | 2.50 | .4938 | .0062 |
| 1.51 | .4345 | .0655 | 2.01 | .4778 | .0222 | 2.51 | .4940 | .0060 |
| 1.52 | .4357 | .0643 | 2.02 | .4783 | .0217 | 2.52 | .4941 | .0059 |
| 1.53 | .4370 | .0630 | 2.03 | .4788 | .0212 | 2.53 | .4943 | .0057 |
| 1.54 | .4382 | .0618 | 2.04 | .4793 | .0207 | 2.54 | .4945 | .0055 |
| 1.55 | .4394 | .0606 | 2.05 | .4798 | .0202 | 2.55 | .4946 | .0054 |
| 1.56 | .4406 | .0594 | 2.06 | .4803 | .0197 | 2.56 | .4948 | .0052 |
| 1.57 | .4418 | .0582 | 2.07 | .4808 | .0192 | 2.57 | .4949 | .0051 |
| 1.58 | .4429 | .0571 | 2.08 | .4812 | .0188 | 2.58 | .4951 | .0049 |
| 1.59 | .4441 | .0559 | 2.09 | .4817 | .0183 | 2.59 | .4952 | .0048 |
| 1.60 | .4452 | .0548 | 2.10 | .4821 | .0179 | 2.60 | .4953 | .0047 |
| 1.61 | .4463 | .0537 | 2.11 | .4826 | .0174 | 2.61 | .4955 | .0045 |
| 1.62 | .4474 | .0526 | 2.12 | .4830 | .0170 | 2.62 | .4956 | .0044 |
| 1.63 | .4484 | .0516 | 2.13 | .4834 | .0166 | 2.63 | .4957 | .0043 |
| 1.64 | .4495 | .0505 | 2.14 | .4838 | .0162 | 2.64 | .4959 | .0041 |
| 1.65 | .4505 | .0495 | 2.15 | .4842 | .0158 | 2.65 | .4960 | .0040 |
| 1.66 | .4515 | .0485 | 2.16 | .4846 | .0154 | 2.66 | .4961 | .0039 |
| 1.67 | .4525 | .0475 | 2.17 | .4850 | .0150 | 2.67 | .4962 | .0038 |
| 1.68 | .4535 | .0465 | 2.18 | .4854 | .0146 | 2.68 | .4963 | .0037 |
| 1.69 | .4545 | .0455 | 2.19 | .4857 | .0143 | 2.69 | .4964 | .0036 |
| 1.70 | .4554 | .0446 | 2.20 | .4861 | .0139 | 2.70 | .4965 | .0035 |
| 1.71 | .4564 | .0436 | 2.21 | .4864 | .0136 | 2.71 | .4966 | .0034 |
| 1.72 | .4573 | .0427 | 2.22 | .4868 | .0132 | 2.72 | .4967 | .0033 |
| 1.73 | .4582 | .0418 | 2.23 | .4871 | .0129 | 2.73 | .4968 | .0032 |
| 1.74 | .4591 | .0409 | 2.24 | .4875 | .0125 | 2.74 | .4969 | .0031 |
| 1.75 | .4599 | .0401 | 2.25 | .4878 | .0122 | 2.75 | .4970 | .0030 |
| 1.76 | .4608 | .0392 | 2.26 | .4881 | .0119 | 2.76 | .4971 | .0029 |
| 1.77 | .4616 | .0384 | 2.27 | .4884 | .0116 | 2.77 | .4972 | .0028 |
| 1.78 | .4625 | .0375 | 2.28 | .4887 | .0113 | 2.78 | .4973 | .0027 |
| 1.79 | .4633 | .0367 | 2.29 | .4890 | .0110 | 2.79 | .4974 | .0026 |
| 1.80 | .4641 | .0359 | 2.30 | .4893 | .0107 | 2.80 | .4974 | .0026 |
| 1.81 | .4649 | .0351 | 2.31 | .4896 | .0104 | 2.81 | .4975 | .0025 |
| 1.82 | .4656 | .0344 | 2.32 | .4898 | .0102 | 2.82 | .4976 | .0024 |
| 1.83 | .4664 | .0336 | 2.33 | .4901 | .0099 | 2.83 | .4977 | .0023 |
| 1.84 | .4671 | .0329 | 2.34 | .4904 | .0096 | 2.84 | .4977 | .0023 |
| 1.85 | .4678 | .0322 | 2.35 | .4906 | .0094 | 2.85 | .4978 | .0022 |
| 1.86 | .4686 | .0314 | 2.36 | .4909 | .0091 | 2.86 | .4979 | .0021 |
| 1.87 | .4693 | .0307 | 2.37 | .4911 | .0089 | 2.87 | .4979 | .0021 |
| 1.88 | .4699 | .0301 | 2.38 | .4913 | .0087 | 2.88 | .4980 | .0020 |
| 1.89 | .4706 | .0294 | 2.39 | .4916 | .0084 | 2.89 | .4981 | .0019 |
| 1.90 | .4713 | .0287 | 2.40 | .4918 | .0082 | 2.90 | .4981 | .0019 |
| 1.91 | .4719 | .0281 | 2.41 | .4920 | .0080 | 2.91 | .4982 | .0018 |
| 1.92 | .4726 | .0274 | 2.42 | .4922 | .0078 | 2.92 | .4982 | .0018 |
| 1.93 | .4732 | .0268 | 2.43 | .4925 | .0075 | 2.93 | .4983 | .0017 |
| 1.94 | .4738 | .0262 | 2.44 | .4927 | .0073 | 2.94 | .4984 | .0016 |
| 1.95 | .4744 | .0256 | 2.45 | .4929 | .0071 | 2.95 | .4984 | .0016 |
| 1.96 | .4750 | .0250 | 2.46 | .4931 | .0069 | 2.96 | .4985 | .0015 |
| 1.97 | .4756 | .0244 | 2.47 | .4932 | .0068 | 2.97 | .4985 | .0015 |
| 1.98 | .4761 | .0239 | 2.48 | .4934 | .0066 | 2.98 | .4986 | .0014 |
| 1.99 | .4767 | .0233 | 2.49 | .4936 | .0064 | 2.99 | .4986 | .0014 |

**TABLE C–1
(Continued)**

| (A) z | (B) area between mean and z | (C) area beyond z | (A) z | (B) area between mean and z | (C) area beyond z | (A) z | (B) area between mean and z | (C) area beyond z |
|---|---|---|---|---|---|---|---|---|
| 3.00 | .4987 | .0013 | 3.15 | .4992 | .0008 | 3.50 | .4998 | .0002 |
| 3.01 | .4987 | .0013 | 3.16 | .4992 | .0008 | 3.60 | .4998 | .0002 |
| 3.02 | .4987 | .0013 | 3.17 | .4992 | .0008 | 3.70 | .4999 | .0001 |
| 3.03 | .4988 | .0012 | 3.18 | .4993 | .0007 | 3.80 | .4999 | .0001 |
| 3.04 | .4988 | .0012 | 3.19 | .4993 | .0007 | 3.90 | .49995 | .00005 |
| 3.05 | .4989 | .0011 | 3.20 | .4993 | .0007 | 4.00 | .49997 | .00003 |
| 3.06 | .4989 | .0011 | 3.21 | .4993 | .0007 | | | |
| 3.07 | .4989 | .0011 | 3.22 | .4994 | .0006 | | | |
| 3.08 | .4990 | .0010 | 3.23 | .4994 | .0006 | | | |
| 3.09 | .4990 | .0010 | 3.24 | .4994 | .0006 | | | |
| 3.10 | .4990 | .0010 | 3.25 | .4994 | .0006 | | | |
| 3.11 | .4991 | .0009 | 3.30 | .4995 | .0005 | | | |
| 3.12 | .4991 | .0009 | 3.35 | .4996 | .0004 | | | |
| 3.13 | .4991 | .0009 | 3.40 | .4997 | .0003 | | | |
| 3.14 | .4992 | .0008 | 3.45 | .4997 | .0003 | | | |

**TABLE C–2
Critical Values of the $U$ Statistic of the Mann-Whitney $U$ Test**

To use these four subtables, first decide what level of significance you want with either a one- or a two-tailed test. For example, if you want $p = .05$, two-tailed, use subtable c. Then locate the number of cases or measures ($n$) in both groups in the particular subtable you have chosen. The $U$ value you have calculated must be *less* than that at the appropriate place in the table. For example, if you had 18 subjects in each group of an experiment, and calculated $U = 90$, you could conclude that the null hypothesis can be rejected because the critical $U$ value with groups of these sizes is 99 (see subtable c).

*(a)* Critical Values of $U$ for a One-Tailed Test at .001 or for a Two-Tailed Test at .002

| $n_1$ \ $n_2$ | 9 | 10 | 11 | 12 | 13 | 14 | 15 | 16 | 17 | 18 | 19 | 20 |
|---|---|---|---|---|---|---|---|---|---|---|---|---|
| 1 | | | | | | | | | | | | |
| 2 | | | | | | | | | | | | |
| 3 | | | | | | | | | 0 | 0 | 0 | 0 |
| 4 | | 0 | 0 | 0 | 1 | 1 | 1 | 2 | 2 | 3 | 3 | 3 |
| 5 | 1 | 1 | 2 | 2 | 3 | 3 | 4 | 5 | 5 | 6 | 7 | 7 |
| 6 | 2 | 3 | 4 | 4 | 5 | 6 | 7 | 8 | 9 | 10 | 11 | 12 |
| 7 | 3 | 5 | 6 | 7 | 8 | 9 | 10 | 11 | 13 | 14 | 15 | 16 |
| 8 | 5 | 6 | 8 | 9 | 11 | 12 | 14 | 15 | 17 | 18 | 20 | 21 |
| 9 | 7 | 8 | 10 | 12 | 14 | 15 | 17 | 19 | 21 | 23 | 25 | 26 |
| 10 | 8 | 10 | 12 | 14 | 17 | 19 | 21 | 23 | 25 | 27 | 29 | 32 |
| 11 | 10 | 12 | 15 | 17 | 20 | 22 | 24 | 27 | 29 | 32 | 34 | 37 |
| 12 | 12 | 14 | 17 | 20 | 23 | 25 | 28 | 31 | 34 | 37 | 40 | 42 |
| 13 | 14 | 17 | 20 | 23 | 26 | 29 | 32 | 35 | 38 | 42 | 45 | 48 |
| 14 | 15 | 19 | 22 | 25 | 29 | 32 | 36 | 39 | 43 | 46 | 50 | 54 |
| 15 | 17 | 21 | 24 | 28 | 32 | 36 | 40 | 43 | 47 | 51 | 55 | 59 |
| 16 | 19 | 23 | 27 | 31 | 35 | 39 | 43 | 48 | 52 | 56 | 60 | 65 |
| 17 | 21 | 25 | 29 | 34 | 38 | 43 | 47 | 52 | 57 | 61 | 66 | 70 |
| 18 | 23 | 27 | 32 | 37 | 42 | 46 | 51 | 56 | 61 | 66 | 71 | 76 |
| 19 | 25 | 29 | 34 | 40 | 45 | 50 | 55 | 60 | 66 | 71 | 77 | 82 |
| 20 | 26 | 32 | 37 | 42 | 48 | 54 | 59 | 65 | 70 | 76 | 82 | 88 |

**TABLE C–2 (Continued)**

*(b)* Critical Values of *U* for a One-Tailed Test at .01 or for a Two-Tailed Test at .02

| $n_1$ \ $n_2$ | 9 | 10 | 11 | 12 | 13 | 14 | 15 | 16 | 17 | 18 | 19 | 20 |
|---|---|---|---|---|---|---|---|---|---|---|---|---|
| 1 | | | | | | | | | | | | |
| 2 | | | | | 0 | 0 | 0 | 0 | 0 | 0 | 1 | 1 |
| 3 | 1 | 1 | 1 | 2 | 2 | 2 | 3 | 3 | 4 | 4 | 4 | 5 |
| 4 | 3 | 3 | 4 | 5 | 5 | 6 | 7 | 7 | 8 | 9 | 9 | 10 |
| 5 | 5 | 6 | 7 | 8 | 9 | 10 | 11 | 12 | 13 | 14 | 15 | 16 |
| 6 | 7 | 8 | 9 | 11 | 12 | 13 | 15 | 16 | 18 | 19 | 20 | 22 |
| 7 | 9 | 11 | 12 | 14 | 16 | 17 | 19 | 21 | 23 | 24 | 26 | 28 |
| 8 | 11 | 13 | 15 | 17 | 20 | 22 | 24 | 26 | 28 | 30 | 32 | 34 |
| 9 | 14 | 16 | 18 | 21 | 23 | 26 | 28 | 31 | 33 | 36 | 38 | 40 |
| 10 | 16 | 19 | 22 | 24 | 27 | 30 | 33 | 36 | 38 | 41 | 44 | 47 |
| 11 | 18 | 22 | 25 | 28 | 31 | 34 | 37 | 41 | 44 | 47 | 50 | 53 |
| 12 | 21 | 24 | 28 | 31 | 35 | 38 | 42 | 46 | 49 | 53 | 56 | 60 |
| 13 | 23 | 27 | 31 | 35 | 39 | 43 | 47 | 51 | 55 | 59 | 63 | 67 |
| 14 | 26 | 30 | 34 | 38 | 43 | 47 | 51 | 56 | 60 | 65 | 69 | 73 |
| 15 | 28 | 33 | 37 | 42 | 47 | 51 | 56 | 61 | 66 | 70 | 75 | 80 |
| 16 | 31 | 36 | 41 | 46 | 51 | 56 | 61 | 66 | 71 | 76 | 82 | 87 |
| 17 | 33 | 38 | 44 | 49 | 55 | 60 | 66 | 71 | 77 | 82 | 88 | 93 |
| 18 | 36 | 41 | 47 | 53 | 59 | 65 | 70 | 76 | 82 | 88 | 94 | 100 |
| 19 | 38 | 44 | 50 | 56 | 63 | 69 | 75 | 82 | 88 | 94 | 101 | 107 |
| 20 | 40 | 47 | 53 | 60 | 67 | 73 | 80 | 87 | 93 | 100 | 107 | 114 |

**TABLE C–2 (Continued)**

*(c)* Critical Values of *U* for a One-Tailed Test at .025 or for a Two-Tailed Test at .05

| $n_1$ \ $n_2$ | 9 | 10 | 11 | 12 | 13 | 14 | 15 | 16 | 17 | 18 | 19 | 20 |
|---|---|---|---|---|---|---|---|---|---|---|---|---|
| 1 | | | | | | | | | | | | |
| 2 | 0 | 0 | 1 | 1 | 1 | 1 | 1 | 1 | 2 | 2 | 2 | 2 |
| 3 | 2 | 3 | 3 | 4 | 4 | 5 | 5 | 6 | 6 | 7 | 7 | 8 |
| 4 | 4 | 5 | 6 | 7 | 8 | 9 | 10 | 11 | 11 | 12 | 13 | 13 |
| 5 | 7 | 8 | 9 | 11 | 12 | 13 | 14 | 15 | 17 | 18 | 19 | 20 |
| 6 | 10 | 11 | 13 | 14 | 16 | 17 | 19 | 21 | 22 | 24 | 25 | 27 |
| 7 | 12 | 14 | 16 | 18 | 20 | 22 | 24 | 26 | 28 | 30 | 32 | 34 |
| 8 | 15 | 17 | 19 | 22 | 24 | 26 | 29 | 31 | 34 | 36 | 38 | 41 |
| 9 | 17 | 20 | 23 | 26 | 28 | 31 | 34 | 37 | 39 | 42 | 45 | 48 |
| 10 | 20 | 23 | 26 | 29 | 33 | 36 | 39 | 42 | 45 | 48 | 52 | 55 |
| 11 | 23 | 26 | 30 | 33 | 37 | 40 | 44 | 47 | 51 | 55 | 58 | 62 |
| 12 | 26 | 29 | 33 | 37 | 41 | 45 | 49 | 53 | 57 | 61 | 65 | 69 |
| 13 | 28 | 33 | 37 | 41 | 45 | 50 | 54 | 59 | 63 | 67 | 72 | 76 |
| 14 | 31 | 36 | 40 | 45 | 50 | 55 | 59 | 64 | 67 | 74 | 78 | 83 |
| 15 | 34 | 39 | 44 | 49 | 54 | 59 | 64 | 70 | 75 | 80 | 85 | 90 |
| 16 | 37 | 42 | 47 | 53 | 59 | 64 | 70 | 75 | 81 | 86 | 92 | 98 |
| 17 | 39 | 45 | 51 | 57 | 63 | 67 | 75 | 81 | 87 | 93 | 99 | 105 |
| 18 | 42 | 48 | 55 | 61 | 67 | 74 | 80 | 86 | 93 | 99 | 106 | 112 |
| 19 | 45 | 52 | 58 | 65 | 72 | 78 | 85 | 92 | 99 | 106 | 113 | 119 |
| 20 | 48 | 55 | 62 | 69 | 76 | 83 | 90 | 98 | 105 | 112 | 119 | 127 |

**TABLE C–2 (Continued)**

(d) Critical Values of $U$ for a One-Tailed Test at .05 or for a Two-Tailed Test at .10

| $n_1$ \ $n_2$ | 9 | 10 | 11 | 12 | 13 | 14 | 15 | 16 | 17 | 18 | 19 | 20 |
|---|---|---|---|---|---|---|---|---|---|---|---|---|
| 1 | | | | | | | | | | | 0 | 0 |
| 2 | 1 | 1 | 1 | 2 | 2 | 2 | 3 | 3 | 3 | 4 | 4 | 4 |
| 3 | 3 | 4 | 5 | 5 | 6 | 7 | 7 | 8 | 9 | 9 | 10 | 11 |
| 4 | 6 | 7 | 8 | 9 | 10 | 11 | 12 | 14 | 15 | 16 | 17 | 18 |
| 5 | 9 | 11 | 12 | 13 | 15 | 16 | 18 | 19 | 20 | 22 | 23 | 25 |
| 6 | 12 | 14 | 16 | 17 | 19 | 21 | 23 | 25 | 26 | 28 | 30 | 32 |
| 7 | 15 | 17 | 19 | 21 | 24 | 26 | 28 | 30 | 33 | 35 | 37 | 39 |
| 8 | 18 | 20 | 23 | 26 | 28 | 31 | 33 | 36 | 39 | 41 | 44 | 47 |
| 9 | 21 | 24 | 27 | 30 | 33 | 36 | 39 | 42 | 45 | 48 | 51 | 54 |
| 10 | 24 | 27 | 31 | 34 | 37 | 41 | 44 | 48 | 51 | 55 | 58 | 62 |
| 11 | 27 | 31 | 34 | 38 | 42 | 46 | 50 | 54 | 57 | 61 | 65 | 69 |
| 12 | 30 | 34 | 38 | 42 | 47 | 51 | 55 | 60 | 64 | 68 | 72 | 77 |
| 13 | 33 | 37 | 42 | 47 | 51 | 56 | 61 | 65 | 70 | 75 | 80 | 84 |
| 14 | 36 | 41 | 46 | 51 | 56 | 61 | 66 | 71 | 77 | 82 | 87 | 92 |
| 15 | 39 | 44 | 50 | 55 | 61 | 66 | 72 | 77 | 83 | 88 | 94 | 100 |
| 16 | 42 | 48 | 54 | 60 | 65 | 71 | 77 | 83 | 89 | 95 | 101 | 107 |
| 17 | 45 | 51 | 57 | 64 | 70 | 77 | 83 | 89 | 96 | 102 | 109 | 115 |
| 18 | 48 | 55 | 61 | 68 | 75 | 82 | 88 | 95 | 102 | 109 | 116 | 123 |
| 19 | 51 | 58 | 65 | 72 | 80 | 87 | 94 | 101 | 109 | 116 | 123 | 130 |
| 20 | 54 | 62 | 69 | 77 | 84 | 92 | 100 | 107 | 115 | 123 | 130 | 138 |

**TABLE C–3**
**Distribution for**
**the Sign Test**

This table shows alpha levels of the sign test for pairs of observations ranging from 3 to 42. The symbol $x$ denotes the number of exceptions (the number of times the difference between conditions is in the unexpected direction), and the $p$ level indicates the probability that that number of exceptions could occur by chance. If, out of 28 paired observations, 20 are ordered in the expected direction and only 8 are exceptions, the probability that this could occur by chance is .018.

| x | p | x | p | x | p | x | p | x | p | x | p |
|---|---|---|---|---|---|---|---|---|---|---|---|
| $n = 3$ | | $n = 12$ | | $n = 19$ | | $n = 25$ | | $n = 31$ | | $n = 37$ | |
| 0 | .125 | 1 | .003 | 3 | .002 | 5 | .002 | 7 | .002 | 10 | .004 |
| $n = 4$ | | 2 | .019 | 4 | .010 | 6 | .007 | 8 | .005 | 11 | .010 |
| 0 | .062 | 3 | .073 | 5 | .032 | 7 | .022 | 9 | .015 | 12 | .024 |
| 1 | .312 | 4 | .194 | 6 | .084 | 8 | .051 | 10 | .035 | 13 | .049 |
| $n = 5$ | | $n = 13$ | | 7 | .180 | 9 | .115 | 11 | .075 | 14 | .094 |
| 0 | .031 | 1 | .002 | $n = 20$ | | 10 | .212 | 12 | .141 | 15 | .162 |
| 1 | .188 | 2 | .011 | 3 | .001 | $n = 26$ | | $n = 32$ | | $n = 38$ | |
| $n = 6$ | | 3 | .016 | 4 | .006 | 6 | .005 | 8 | .004 | 10 | .003 |
| 0 | .016 | 4 | .133 | 5 | .021 | 7 | .014 | 9 | .010 | 11 | .007 |
| 1 | .109 | $n = 14$ | | 6 | .058 | 8 | .038 | 10 | .025 | 12 | .017 |
| 2 | .344 | 1 | .001 | 7 | .132 | 9 | .084 | 11 | .055 | 13 | .036 |
| $n = 7$ | | 2 | .006 | $n = 21$ | | 10 | .163 | 12 | .108 | 14 | .072 |
| 0 | .008 | 3 | .029 | 4 | .004 | $n = 27$ | | 13 | .189 | 15 | .128 |
| 1 | .062 | 4 | .090 | 5 | .013 | 6 | .003 | $n = 33$ | | $n = 39$ | |
| 2 | .227 | 5 | .212 | 6 | .039 | 7 | .010 | 8 | .002 | 11 | .005 |
| $n = 8$ | | $n = 15$ | | 7 | .095 | 8 | .026 | 9 | .007 | 12 | .012 |
| 0 | .004 | 1 | .000 | 8 | .192 | 9 | .061 | 10 | .018 | 13 | .027 |
| 1 | .035 | 2 | .004 | $n = 22$ | | 10 | .124 | 11 | .040 | 14 | .054 |
| 2 | .145 | 3 | .018 | 4 | .002 | 11 | .221 | 12 | .081 | 15 | .100 |
| $n = 9$ | | 4 | .059 | 5 | .008 | $n = 28$ | | 13 | .148 | 16 | .168 |
| 0 | .002 | 5 | .151 | 6 | .026 | 6 | .002 | $n = 34$ | | $n = 40$ | |
| 1 | .020 | $n = 16$ | | 7 | .067 | 7 | .006 | 9 | .005 | 11 | .003 |
| 2 | .090 | 2 | .002 | 8 | .143 | 8 | .018 | 10 | .012 | 12 | .008 |
| 3 | .254 | 3 | .011 | $n = 23$ | | 9 | .044 | 11 | .029 | 13 | .019 |
| $n = 10$ | | 4 | .038 | 4 | .001 | 10 | .092 | 12 | .061 | 14 | .040 |
| 0 | .001 | 5 | .105 | 5 | .005 | 11 | .172 | 13 | .115 | 15 | .077 |
| 1 | .011 | 6 | .227 | 6 | .017 | $n = 29$ | | 14 | .196 | 16 | .134 |
| 2 | .055 | $n = 17$ | | 7 | .047 | 7 | .004 | $n = 35$ | | $n = 41$ | |
| 3 | .172 | 2 | .001 | 8 | .105 | 8 | .012 | 9 | .003 | 11 | .002 |
| $n = 11$ | | 3 | .006 | 9 | .202 | 9 | .031 | 10 | .008 | 12 | .006 |
| 0 | .000 | 4 | .025 | $n = 24$ | | 10 | .068 | 11 | .020 | 13 | .014 |
| 1 | .006 | 5 | .072 | 5 | .008 | 11 | .132 | 12 | .045 | 14 | .030 |
| 2 | .033 | 6 | .166 | 6 | .011 | $n = 30$ | | 13 | .088 | 15 | .059 |
| 3 | .113 | $n = 18$ | | 7 | .032 | 7 | .003 | 14 | .155 | 16 | .106 |
| 4 | .274 | 3 | .004 | 8 | .076 | 8 | .008 | $n = 36$ | | 17 | .174 |
| | | 4 | .015 | 9 | .154 | 9 | .021 | 9 | .002 | $n = 42$ | |
| | | 5 | .048 | | | 10 | .049 | 10 | .006 | 12 | .004 |
| | | 6 | .119 | | | 11 | .100 | 11 | .014 | 13 | .010 |
| | | 7 | .240 | | | 12 | .181 | 12 | .033 | 14 | .022 |
| | | | | | | | | 13 | .066 | 15 | .044 |
| | | | | | | | | 14 | .121 | 16 | .082 |
| | | | | | | | | 15 | .203 | 17 | .140 |

## TABLE C-4
## Critical Values of
## Wilcoxon's T
## Statistic for the
## Matched-Pairs
## Signed-Ranks
## Test

In using this table, first locate the number of *pairs* of scores in the $n$ column. The critical values for several levels of significance are listed in the columns to the right. For example, if $n$ were 15 and the computed value 19, we could conclude that since 19 is less than 25, the difference between conditions is significant beyond the .02 level of significance for a two-tailed test.

| | Level of significance for one-tailed test | | |
| | .025 | .01 | .005 |
| | Level of significance for two-tailed test | | |
| $n$ | .05 | .02 | .01 |
|---|---|---|---|
| 6 | 1 | — | — |
| 7 | 2 | 0 | — |
| 8 | 4 | 2 | 0 |
| 9 | 6 | 3 | 2 |
| 10 | 8 | 5 | 3 |
| 11 | 11 | 7 | 5 |
| 12 | 14 | 10 | 7 |
| 13 | 17 | 13 | 10 |
| 14 | 21 | 16 | 13 |
| 15 | 25 | 20 | 16 |
| 16 | 30 | 24 | 19 |
| 17 | 35 | 28 | 23 |
| 18 | 40 | 33 | 28 |
| 19 | 46 | 38 | 32 |
| 20 | 52 | 43 | 37 |
| 21 | 59 | 49 | 43 |
| 22 | 66 | 56 | 49 |
| 23 | 73 | 62 | 55 |
| 24 | 81 | 69 | 61 |
| 25 | 90 | 77 | 68 |

**TABLE C–5
Critical Values
of $t$**

To find the appropriate value of $t$, read across the row that contains the number of degrees of freedom in your experiment. The columns are determined by the level of significance you have chosen. The value of $t$ you obtain must be *greater* than that in the table in order to be significant. For example, with $df = 15$ and $p = .05$ (two-tailed test), your $t$ value must be greater than 2.131.

| | Level of significance for one-tailed test | | | | | |
| | .10 | .05 | .025 | .01 | .005 | .0005 |
| --- | --- | --- | --- | --- | --- | --- |
| | Level of significance for two-tailed test | | | | | |
| df | .20 | .10 | .05 | .02 | .01 | .001 |
| 1 | 3.078 | 6.314 | 12.706 | 31.821 | 63.657 | 636.619 |
| 2 | 1.886 | 2.920 | 4.303 | 6.965 | 9.925 | 31.598 |
| 3 | 1.638 | 2.353 | 3.182 | 4.541 | 5.841 | 12.941 |
| 4 | 1.533 | 2.132 | 2.776 | 3.747 | 4.604 | 8.610 |
| 5 | 1.476 | 2.015 | 2.571 | 3.365 | 4.032 | 6.859 |
| 6 | 1.440 | 1.943 | 2.447 | 3.143 | 3.707 | 5.959 |
| 7 | 1.415 | 1.895 | 2.365 | 2.998 | 3.449 | 5.405 |
| 8 | 1.397 | 1.860 | 2.306 | 2.896 | 3.355 | 5.041 |
| 9 | 1.383 | 1.833 | 2.262 | 2.821 | 3.250 | 4.781 |
| 10 | 1.372 | 1.812 | 2.228 | 2.764 | 3.169 | 4.587 |
| 11 | 1.363 | 1.796 | 2.201 | 2.718 | 3.106 | 4.437 |
| 12 | 1.356 | 1.782 | 2.179 | 2.681 | 3.055 | 4.318 |
| 13 | 1.350 | 1.771 | 2.160 | 2.650 | 3.012 | 4.221 |
| 14 | 1.345 | 1.761 | 2.145 | 2.624 | 2.977 | 4.140 |
| 15 | 1.341 | 1.753 | 2.131 | 2.602 | 2.947 | 4.073 |
| 16 | 1.337 | 1.746 | 2.120 | 2.583 | 2.921 | 4.015 |
| 17 | 1.333 | 1.740 | 2.110 | 2.567 | 2.898 | 3.965 |
| 18 | 1.330 | 1.734 | 2.101 | 2.552 | 2.878 | 3.922 |
| 19 | 1.328 | 1.729 | 2.093 | 2.539 | 2.861 | 3.883 |
| 20 | 1.325 | 1.725 | 2.086 | 2.528 | 2.845 | 3.850 |
| 21 | 1.323 | 1.721 | 2.080 | 2.518 | 2.831 | 3.819 |
| 22 | 1.321 | 1.717 | 2.074 | 2.508 | 2.819 | 3.792 |
| 23 | 1.319 | 1.714 | 2.069 | 2.500 | 2.807 | 3.767 |
| 24 | 1.318 | 1.711 | 2.064 | 2.492 | 2.797 | 3.745 |
| 25 | 1.316 | 1.708 | 2.060 | 2.485 | 2.787 | 3.725 |
| 26 | 1.315 | 1.706 | 2.056 | 2.479 | 2.779 | 3.707 |
| 27 | 1.314 | 1.703 | 2.052 | 2.473 | 2.771 | 3.690 |
| 28 | 1.313 | 1.701 | 2.048 | 2.467 | 2.763 | 3.674 |
| 29 | 1.311 | 1.699 | 2.045 | 2.462 | 2.756 | 3.659 |
| 30 | 1.310 | 1.697 | 2.042 | 2.457 | 2.750 | 3.646 |
| 40 | 1.303 | 1.684 | 2.021 | 2.423 | 2.704 | 3.551 |
| 60 | 1.296 | 1.671 | 2.000 | 2.390 | 2.660 | 3.460 |
| 120 | 1.289 | 1.658 | 1.980 | 2.358 | 2.617 | 3.373 |
| ∞ | 1.282 | 1.645 | 1.960 | 2.326 | 2.576 | 3.291 |

Table C–5 is taken from Table III of Fisher & Yates': *Statistical Tables for Biological, Agricultural and Medical Research.* Published by Longman Group UK Ltd. London (previously published by Oliver and Boyd Ltd. Edinburgh) and by permission of the authors and publishers.

**TABLE C–6**
**Critical Values of**
**the F Distribution**

Find the appropriate values in the table by looking up the degrees of freedom in the numerator and denominator of the $F$-ratio. After you have decided on the level of significance desired, the obtained $F$-ratio must be *greater* than that in the table. For example, with $p = .05$ and 9 $df$ in the numerator and 28 in the denominator, your $F$ value must be greater than 2.24 to be reliable.

| df for denom. | α | \multicolumn{9}{c}{df for numerator} |
| | | 1 | 2 | 3 | 4 | 5 | 6 | 7 | 8 | 9 |
|---|---|---|---|---|---|---|---|---|---|---|
| 3 | .25 | 2.02 | 2.28 | 2.36 | 2.39 | 2.41 | 2.42 | 2.43 | 2.44 | 2.44 |
| | .10 | 5.54 | 5.46 | 5.39 | 5.34 | 5.31 | 5.28 | 5.27 | 5.25 | 5.24 |
| | .05 | 10.1 | 9.55 | 9.28 | 9.12 | 9.01 | 8.94 | 8.89 | 8.85 | 8.81 |
| | .025 | 17.4 | 16.0 | 15.4 | 15.1 | 14.9 | 14.7 | 14.6 | 14.5 | 14.5 |
| | .01 | 34.1 | 30.8 | 29.5 | 28.7 | 28.2 | 27.9 | 27.7 | 27.5 | 27.4 |
| | .001 | 167 | 148 | 141 | 137 | 135 | 133 | 132 | 131 | 130 |
| 4 | .25 | 1.81 | 2.00 | 2.05 | 2.06 | 2.07 | 2.08 | 2.08 | 2.08 | 2.08 |
| | .10 | 4.54 | 4.32 | 4.19 | 4.11 | 4.05 | 4.01 | 3.98 | 3.95 | 3.94 |
| | .05 | 7.71 | 6.94 | 6.59 | 6.39 | 6.26 | 6.16 | 6.09 | 6.04 | 6.00 |
| | .025 | 12.2 | 10.6 | 9.98 | 9.60 | 9.36 | 9.20 | 9.07 | 8.98 | 8.90 |
| | .01 | 21.2 | 18.0 | 16.7 | 16.0 | 15.5 | 15.2 | 15.0 | 14.8 | 14.7 |
| | .001 | 74.1 | 61.2 | 56.2 | 53.4 | 51.7 | 50.5 | 49.7 | 49.0 | 48.5 |
| 5 | .25 | 1.69 | 1.85 | 1.88 | 1.89 | 1.89 | 1.89 | 1.89 | 1.89 | 1.89 |
| | .10 | 4.06 | 3.78 | 3.62 | 3.52 | 3.45 | 3.40 | 3.37 | 3.34 | 3.32 |
| | .05 | 6.61 | 5.79 | 5.41 | 5.19 | 5.05 | 4.95 | 4.88 | 4.82 | 4.77 |
| | .025 | 10.0 | 8.43 | 7.76 | 7.39 | 7.15 | 6.98 | 6.85 | 6.76 | 6.68 |
| | .01 | 16.3 | 13.3 | 12.1 | 11.4 | 11.0 | 10.7 | 10.5 | 10.3 | 10.2 |
| | .001 | 47.2 | 37.1 | 33.2 | 31.1 | 29.8 | 28.8 | 28.2 | 27.6 | 27.2 |
| 6 | .25 | 1.62 | 1.76 | 1.78 | 1.79 | 1.79 | 1.78 | 1.78 | 1.78 | 1.77 |
| | .10 | 3.78 | 3.46 | 3.29 | 3.18 | 3.11 | 3.05 | 3.01 | 2.98 | 2.96 |
| | .05 | 5.99 | 5.14 | 4.76 | 4.53 | 4.39 | 4.28 | 4.21 | 4.15 | 4.10 |
| | .025 | 8.81 | 7.26 | 6.60 | 6.23 | 5.99 | 5.82 | 5.70 | 5.60 | 5.52 |
| | .01 | 13.8 | 10.9 | 9.78 | 9.15 | 8.75 | 8.47 | 8.26 | 8.10 | 7.98 |
| | .001 | 35.5 | 27.0 | 23.7 | 21.9 | 20.8 | 20.0 | 19.5 | 19.0 | 18.7 |
| 7 | .25 | 1.57 | 1.70 | 1.72 | 1.72 | 1.71 | 1.71 | 1.70 | 1.70 | 1.69 |
| | .10 | 3.59 | 3.26 | 3.07 | 2.96 | 2.88 | 2.83 | 2.78 | 2.75 | 2.72 |
| | .05 | 5.59 | 4.74 | 4.35 | 4.12 | 3.97 | 3.87 | 3.79 | 3.73 | 3.68 |
| | .025 | 8.07 | 6.54 | 5.89 | 5.52 | 5.29 | 5.12 | 4.99 | 4.90 | 4.82 |
| | .01 | 12.2 | 9.55 | 8.45 | 7.85 | 7.46 | 7.19 | 6.99 | 6.84 | 6.72 |
| | .001 | 29.2 | 21.7 | 18.8 | 17.2 | 16.2 | 15.5 | 15.0 | 14.6 | 14.3 |
| 8 | .25 | 1.54 | 1.66 | 1.67 | 1.66 | 1.66 | 1.65 | 1.64 | 1.64 | 1.63 |
| | .10 | 3.46 | 3.11 | 2.92 | 2.81 | 2.73 | 2.67 | 2.62 | 2.59 | 2.56 |
| | .05 | 5.32 | 4.46 | 4.07 | 3.84 | 3.69 | 3.58 | 3.50 | 3.44 | 3.39 |
| | .025 | 7.57 | 6.06 | 5.42 | 5.05 | 4.82 | 4.65 | 4.53 | 4.43 | 4.36 |
| | .01 | 11.3 | 8.65 | 7.59 | 7.01 | 6.63 | 6.37 | 6.18 | 6.03 | 5.91 |
| | .001 | 25.4 | 18.5 | 15.8 | 14.4 | 13.5 | 12.9 | 12.4 | 12.0 | 11.8 |
| 9 | .25 | 1.51 | 1.62 | 1.63 | 1.63 | 1.62 | 1.61 | 1.60 | 1.60 | 1.59 |
| | .10 | 3.36 | 3.01 | 2.81 | 2.69 | 2.61 | 2.55 | 2.51 | 2.47 | 2.44 |
| | .05 | 5.12 | 4.26 | 3.86 | 3.63 | 3.48 | 3.37 | 3.29 | 3.23 | 3.18 |
| | .025 | 7.21 | 5.71 | 5.08 | 4.72 | 4.48 | 4.32 | 4.20 | 4.10 | 4.03 |
| | .01 | 10.6 | 8.02 | 6.99 | 6.42 | 6.06 | 5.80 | 5.61 | 5.47 | 5.35 |
| | .001 | 22.9 | 16.4 | 13.9 | 12.6 | 11.7 | 11.1 | 10.7 | 10.4 | 10.1 |

**TABLE C–6**
**(Continued)**

| df for denom. | α | 1 | 2 | 3 | 4 | 5 | 6 | 7 | 8 | 9 |
|---|---|---|---|---|---|---|---|---|---|---|
| | | | | | df for numerator | | | | | |
| 10 | .25 | 1.49 | 1.60 | 1.60 | 1.59 | 1.59 | 1.58 | 1.57 | 1.56 | 1.56 |
| | .10 | 3.29 | 2.92 | 2.73 | 2.61 | 2.52 | 2.46 | 2.41 | 2.38 | 2.35 |
| | .05 | 4.96 | 4.10 | 3.71 | 3.48 | 3.33 | 3.22 | 3.14 | 3.07 | 3.02 |
| | .025 | 6.94 | 5.46 | 4.83 | 4.47 | 4.24 | 4.07 | 3.95 | 3.85 | 3.78 |
| | .01 | 10.0 | 7.56 | 6.55 | 5.99 | 5.64 | 5.39 | 5.20 | 5.06 | 4.94 |
| | .001 | 21.0 | 14.9 | 12.6 | 11.3 | 10.5 | 9.92 | 9.52 | 9.20 | 8.96 |
| 11 | .25 | 1.47 | 1.58 | 1.58 | 1.57 | 1.56 | 1.55 | 1.54 | 1.53 | 1.53 |
| | .10 | 3.23 | 2.86 | 2.66 | 2.54 | 2.45 | 2.39 | 2.34 | 2.30 | 2.27 |
| | .05 | 4.84 | 3.98 | 3.59 | 3.36 | 3.20 | 3.09 | 3.01 | 2.95 | 2.90 |
| | .025 | 6.72 | 5.26 | 4.63 | 4.28 | 4.04 | 3.88 | 3.76 | 3.66 | 3.59 |
| | .01 | 9.65 | 7.21 | 6.22 | 5.67 | 5.32 | 5.07 | 4.89 | 4.74 | 4.63 |
| | .001 | 19.7 | 13.8 | 11.6 | 10.4 | 9.58 | 9.05 | 8.66 | 8.35 | 8.12 |
| 12 | .25 | 1.46 | 1.56 | 1.56 | 1.55 | 1.54 | 1.53 | 1.52 | 1.51 | 1.51 |
| | .10 | 3.18 | 2.81 | 2.61 | 2.48 | 2.39 | 2.33 | 2.28 | 2.24 | 2.21 |
| | .05 | 4.75 | 3.89 | 3.49 | 3.26 | 3.11 | 3.00 | 2.91 | 2.85 | 2.80 |
| | .025 | 6.55 | 5.10 | 4.47 | 4.12 | 3.89 | 3.73 | 3.61 | 3.51 | 3.44 |
| | .01 | 9.33 | 6.93 | 5.95 | 5.41 | 5.06 | 4.82 | 4.64 | 4.50 | 4.39 |
| | .001 | 18.6 | 13.0 | 10.8 | 9.63 | 8.89 | 8.38 | 8.00 | 7.71 | 7.48 |
| 13 | .25 | 1.45 | 1.55 | 1.55 | 1.53 | 1.52 | 1.51 | 1.50 | 1.49 | 1.49 |
| | .10 | 3.14 | 2.76 | 2.56 | 2.43 | 2.35 | 2.28 | 2.23 | 2.20 | 2.16 |
| | .05 | 4.67 | 3.81 | 3.41 | 3.18 | 3.03 | 2.92 | 2.83 | 2.77 | 2.71 |
| | .025 | 6.41 | 4.97 | 4.35 | 4.00 | 3.77 | 3.60 | 3.48 | 3.39 | 3.31 |
| | .01 | 9.07 | 6.70 | 5.74 | 5.21 | 4.86 | 4.62 | 4.44 | 4.30 | 4.19 |
| | .001 | 17.8 | 12.3 | 10.2 | 9.07 | 8.35 | 7.86 | 7.49 | 7.21 | 6.98 |
| 14 | .25 | 1.44 | 1.53 | 1.53 | 1.52 | 1.51 | 1.50 | 1.49 | 1.48 | 1.47 |
| | .10 | 3.10 | 2.73 | 2.52 | 2.39 | 2.31 | 2.24 | 2.19 | 2.15 | 2.12 |
| | .05 | 4.60 | 3.74 | 3.34 | 3.11 | 2.96 | 2.85 | 2.76 | 2.70 | 2.65 |
| | .025 | 6.30 | 4.86 | 4.24 | 3.89 | 3.66 | 3.50 | 3.38 | 3.29 | 3.21 |
| | .01 | 8.86 | 6.51 | 5.56 | 5.04 | 4.69 | 4.46 | 4.28 | 4.14 | 4.03 |
| | .001 | 17.1 | 11.8 | 9.73 | 8.62 | 7.92 | 7.43 | 7.08 | 6.80 | 6.58 |
| 15 | .25 | 1.43 | 1.52 | 1.52 | 1.51 | 1.49 | 1.48 | 1.47 | 1.46 | 1.46 |
| | .10 | 3.07 | 2.70 | 2.49 | 2.36 | 2.27 | 2.21 | 2.16 | 2.12 | 2.09 |
| | .05 | 4.54 | 3.68 | 3.29 | 3.06 | 2.90 | 2.79 | 2.71 | 2.64 | 2.59 |
| | .025 | 6.20 | 4.77 | 4.15 | 3.80 | 3.58 | 3.41 | 3.29 | 3.20 | 3.12 |
| | .01 | 8.68 | 6.36 | 5.42 | 4.89 | 4.56 | 4.32 | 4.14 | 4.00 | 3.89 |
| | .001 | 16.6 | 11.3 | 9.34 | 8.25 | 7.57 | 7.09 | 6.74 | 6.47 | 6.26 |
| 16 | .25 | 1.42 | 1.51 | 1.51 | 1.50 | 1.48 | 1.47 | 1.46 | 1.45 | 1.44 |
| | .10 | 3.05 | 2.67 | 2.46 | 2.33 | 2.24 | 2.18 | 2.13 | 2.09 | 2.06 |
| | .05 | 4.49 | 3.63 | 3.24 | 3.01 | 2.85 | 2.74 | 2.66 | 2.59 | 2.54 |
| | .025 | 6.12 | 4.69 | 4.08 | 3.73 | 3.50 | 3.34 | 3.22 | 3.12 | 3.05 |
| | .01 | 8.53 | 6.23 | 5.29 | 4.77 | 4.44 | 4.20 | 4.03 | 3.89 | 3.78 |
| | .001 | 16.1 | 11.0 | 9.00 | 7.94 | 7.27 | 6.81 | 6.46 | 6.19 | 5.98 |
| 17 | .25 | 1.42 | 1.51 | 1.50 | 1.49 | 1.47 | 1.46 | 1.45 | 1.44 | 1.43 |
| | .10 | 3.03 | 2.64 | 2.44 | 2.31 | 2.22 | 2.15 | 2.10 | 2.06 | 2.03 |
| | .05 | 4.45 | 3.59 | 3.20 | 2.96 | 2.81 | 2.70 | 2.61 | 2.55 | 2.49 |
| | .025 | 6.04 | 4.62 | 4.01 | 3.66 | 3.44 | 3.28 | 3.16 | 3.06 | 2.98 |
| | .01 | 8.40 | 6.11 | 5.18 | 4.67 | 4.34 | 4.10 | 3.93 | 3.79 | 3.68 |
| | .001 | 15.7 | 10.7 | 8.73 | 7.68 | 7.02 | 6.56 | 6.22 | 5.96 | 5.75 |

**TABLE C–6
(Continued)**

| df for denom. | α | df for numerator 1 | 2 | 3 | 4 | 5 | 6 | 7 | 8 | 9 |
|---|---|---|---|---|---|---|---|---|---|---|
| 18 | .25 | 1.41 | 1.50 | 1.49 | 1.48 | 1.46 | 1.45 | 1.44 | 1.43 | 1.42 |
| | .10 | 3.01 | 2.62 | 2.42 | 2.29 | 2.20 | 2.13 | 2.08 | 2.04 | 2.00 |
| | .05 | 4.41 | 3.55 | 3.16 | 2.93 | 2.77 | 2.66 | 2.58 | 2.51 | 2.46 |
| | .025 | 5.98 | 4.56 | 3.95 | 3.61 | 3.38 | 3.22 | 3.10 | 3.01 | 2.93 |
| | .01 | 8.29 | 6.01 | 5.09 | 4.58 | 4.25 | 4.01 | 3.84 | 3.71 | 3.60 |
| | .001 | 15.4 | 10.4 | 8.49 | 7.46 | 6.81 | 6.35 | 6.02 | 5.76 | 5.56 |
| 19 | .25 | 1.41 | 1.49 | 1.49 | 1.47 | 1.46 | 1.44 | 1.43 | 1.42 | 1.41 |
| | .10 | 2.99 | 2.61 | 2.40 | 2.27 | 2.18 | 2.11 | 2.06 | 2.02 | 1.98 |
| | .05 | 4.38 | 3.52 | 3.13 | 2.90 | 2.74 | 2.63 | 2.54 | 2.48 | 2.42 |
| | .025 | 5.92 | 4.51 | 3.90 | 3.56 | 3.33 | 3.17 | 3.05 | 2.96 | 2.88 |
| | .01 | 8.18 | 5.93 | 5.01 | 4.50 | 4.17 | 3.94 | 3.77 | 3.63 | 3.52 |
| | .001 | 15.1 | 10.2 | 8.28 | 7.26 | 6.62 | 6.18 | 5.85 | 5.59 | 5.39 |
| 20 | .25 | 1.40 | 1.49 | 1.48 | 1.47 | 1.45 | 1.44 | 1.43 | 1.42 | 1.41 |
| | .10 | 2.97 | 2.59 | 2.38 | 2.25 | 2.16 | 2.09 | 2.04 | 2.00 | 1.96 |
| | .05 | 4.35 | 3.49 | 3.10 | 2.87 | 2.71 | 2.60 | 2.51 | 2.45 | 2.39 |
| | .025 | 5.87 | 4.46 | 3.86 | 3.51 | 3.29 | 3.13 | 3.01 | 2.91 | 2.84 |
| | .01 | 8.10 | 5.85 | 4.94 | 4.43 | 4.10 | 3.87 | 3.70 | 3.56 | 3.46 |
| | .001 | 14.8 | 9.95 | 8.10 | 7.10 | 6.46 | 6.02 | 5.69 | 5.44 | 5.24 |
| 22 | .25 | 1.40 | 1.48 | 1.47 | 1.45 | 1.44 | 1.42 | 1.41 | 1.40 | 1.39 |
| | .10 | 2.95 | 2.56 | 2.35 | 2.22 | 2.13 | 2.06 | 2.01 | 1.97 | 1.93 |
| | .05 | 4.30 | 3.44 | 3.05 | 2.82 | 2.66 | 2.55 | 2.46 | 2.40 | 2.34 |
| | .025 | 5.79 | 4.38 | 3.78 | 3.44 | 3.22 | 3.05 | 2.93 | 2.84 | 2.76 |
| | .01 | 7.95 | 5.72 | 4.82 | 4.31 | 3.99 | 3.76 | 3.59 | 3.45 | 3.35 |
| | .001 | 14.4 | 9.61 | 7.80 | 6.81 | 6.19 | 5.76 | 5.44 | 5.19 | 4.99 |
| 24 | .25 | 1.39 | 1.47 | 1.46 | 1.44 | 1.43 | 1.41 | 1.40 | 1.39 | 1.38 |
| | .10 | 2.93 | 2.54 | 2.33 | 2.19 | 2.10 | 2.04 | 1.98 | 1.94 | 1.91 |
| | .05 | 4.26 | 3.40 | 3.01 | 2.78 | 2.62 | 2.51 | 2.42 | 2.36 | 2.30 |
| | .025 | 5.72 | 4.32 | 3.72 | 3.38 | 3.15 | 2.99 | 2.87 | 2.78 | 2.70 |
| | .01 | 7.82 | 5.61 | 4.72 | 4.22 | 3.90 | 3.67 | 3.50 | 3.36 | 3.26 |
| | .001 | 14.0 | 9.34 | 7.55 | 6.59 | 5.98 | 5.55 | 5.23 | 4.99 | 4.80 |
| 26 | .25 | 1.38 | 1.46 | 1.45 | 1.44 | 1.42 | 1.41 | 1.39 | 1.38 | 1.37 |
| | .10 | 2.91 | 2.52 | 2.31 | 2.17 | 2.08 | 2.01 | 1.96 | 1.92 | 1.88 |
| | .05 | 4.23 | 3.37 | 2.98 | 2.74 | 2.59 | 2.47 | 2.39 | 2.32 | 2.27 |
| | .025 | 5.66 | 4.27 | 3.67 | 3.33 | 3.10 | 2.94 | 2.82 | 2.73 | 2.65 |
| | .01 | 7.72 | 5.53 | 4.64 | 4.14 | 3.82 | 3.59 | 3.42 | 3.29 | 3.18 |
| | .001 | 13.7 | 9.12 | 7.36 | 6.41 | 5.80 | 5.38 | 5.07 | 4.83 | 4.64 |
| 28 | .25 | 1.38 | 1.46 | 1.45 | 1.43 | 1.41 | 1.40 | 1.39 | 1.38 | 1.37 |
| | .10 | 2.89 | 2.50 | 2.29 | 2.16 | 2.06 | 2.00 | 1.94 | 1.90 | 1.87 |
| | .05 | 4.20 | 3.34 | 2.95 | 2.71 | 2.56 | 2.45 | 2.36 | 2.29 | 2.24 |
| | .025 | 5.61 | 4.22 | 3.63 | 3.29 | 3.06 | 2.90 | 2.78 | 2.69 | 2.61 |
| | .01 | 7.64 | 5.45 | 4.57 | 4.07 | 3.75 | 3.53 | 3.36 | 3.23 | 3.12 |
| | .001 | 13.5 | 8.93 | 7.19 | 6.25 | 5.66 | 5.24 | 4.93 | 4.69 | 4.50 |
| 30 | .25 | 1.38 | 1.45 | 1.44 | 1.42 | 1.41 | 1.39 | 1.38 | 1.37 | 1.36 |
| | .10 | 2.88 | 2.49 | 2.28 | 2.14 | 2.05 | 1.98 | 1.93 | 1.88 | 1.85 |
| | .05 | 4.17 | 3.32 | 2.92 | 2.69 | 2.53 | 2.42 | 2.33 | 2.27 | 2.21 |
| | .025 | 5.57 | 4.18 | 3.59 | 3.25 | 3.03 | 2.87 | 2.75 | 2.65 | 2.57 |
| | .01 | 7.56 | 5.39 | 4.51 | 4.02 | 3.70 | 3.47 | 3.30 | 3.17 | 3.07 |
| | .001 | 13.3 | 8.77 | 7.05 | 6.12 | 5.53 | 5.12 | 4.82 | 4.58 | 4.39 |

**TABLE C−6**
**(Continued)**

| df for denom. | α | df for numerator | | | | | | | | |
|---|---|---|---|---|---|---|---|---|---|---|
| | | 1 | 2 | 3 | 4 | 5 | 6 | 7 | 8 | 9 |
| 40 | .25 | 1.36 | 1.44 | 1.42 | 1.40 | 1.39 | 1.37 | 1.36 | 1.35 | 1.34 |
| | .10 | 2.84 | 2.44 | 2.23 | 2.09 | 2.00 | 1.93 | 1.87 | 1.83 | 1.79 |
| | .05 | 4.08 | 3.23 | 2.84 | 2.61 | 2.45 | 2.34 | 2.25 | 2.18 | 2.12 |
| | .025 | 5.42 | 4.05 | 3.46 | 3.13 | 2.90 | 2.74 | 2.62 | 2.53 | 2.45 |
| | .01 | 7.31 | 5.18 | 4.31 | 3.83 | 3.51 | 3.29 | 3.12 | 2.99 | 2.89 |
| | .001 | 12.6 | 8.25 | 6.60 | 5.70 | 5.13 | 4.73 | 4.44 | 4.21 | 4.02 |
| 60 | .25 | 1.35 | 1.42 | 1.41 | 1.38 | 1.37 | 1.35 | 1.33 | 1.32 | 1.31 |
| | .10 | 2.79 | 2.39 | 2.18 | 2.04 | 1.95 | 1.87 | 1.82 | 1.77 | 1.74 |
| | .05 | 4.00 | 3.15 | 2.76 | 2.53 | 2.37 | 2.25 | 2.17 | 2.10 | 2.04 |
| | .025 | 5.29 | 3.93 | 3.34 | 3.01 | 2.79 | 2.63 | 2.51 | 2.41 | 2.33 |
| | .01 | 7.08 | 4.98 | 4.13 | 3.65 | 3.34 | 3.12 | 2.95 | 2.82 | 2.72 |
| | .001 | 12.0 | 7.76 | 6.17 | 5.31 | 4.76 | 4.37 | 4.09 | 3.87 | 3.69 |
| 120 | .25 | 1.34 | 1.40 | 1.39 | 1.37 | 1.35 | 1.33 | 1.31 | 1.30 | 1.29 |
| | .10 | 2.75 | 2.35 | 2.13 | 1.99 | 1.90 | 1.82 | 1.77 | 1.72 | 1.68 |
| | .05 | 3.92 | 3.07 | 2.68 | 2.45 | 2.29 | 2.17 | 2.09 | 2.02 | 1.96 |
| | .025 | 5.15 | 3.80 | 3.23 | 2.89 | 2.67 | 2.52 | 2.39 | 2.30 | 2.22 |
| | .01 | 6.85 | 4.79 | 3.95 | 3.48 | 3.17 | 2.96 | 2.79 | 2.66 | 2.56 |
| | .001 | 11.4 | 7.32 | 5.79 | 4.95 | 4.42 | 4.04 | 3.77 | 3.55 | 3.38 |
| ∞ | .25 | 1.32 | 1.39 | 1.37 | 1.35 | 1.33 | 1.31 | 1.29 | 1.28 | 1.27 |
| | .10 | 2.71 | 2.30 | 2.08 | 1.94 | 1.85 | 1.77 | 1.72 | 1.67 | 1.63 |
| | .05 | 3.84 | 3.00 | 2.60 | 2.37 | 2.21 | 2.10 | 2.01 | 1.94 | 1.88 |
| | .025 | 5.02 | 3.69 | 3.12 | 2.79 | 2.57 | 2.41 | 2.29 | 2.19 | 2.11 |
| | .01 | 6.63 | 4.61 | 3.78 | 3.32 | 3.02 | 2.80 | 2.64 | 2.51 | 2.41 |
| | .001 | 10.8 | .91 | 5.42 | 4.62 | 4.10 | 3.74 | 3.47 | 3.27 | 3.10 |

**TABLE C–7**
**Random Numbers**

| | 1 | 2 | 3 | 4 | 5 | 6 | 7 | 8 | 9 |
|---|---|---|---|---|---|---|---|---|---|
| 1 | 32942 | 95416 | 42339 | 59045 | 26693 | 49057 | 87496 | 20624 | 14819 |
| 2 | 07410 | 99859 | 83828 | 21409 | 29094 | 65114 | 36701 | 25762 | 12827 |
| 3 | 59981 | 68155 | 45673 | 76210 | 58219 | 45738 | 29550 | 24736 | 09574 |
| 4 | 46251 | 25437 | 69654 | 99716 | 11563 | 08803 | 86027 | 51867 | 12116 |
| 5 | 65558 | 51904 | 93123 | 27887 | 53138 | 21488 | 09095 | 78777 | 71240 |
| 6 | 99187 | 19258 | 86421 | 16401 | 19397 | 83297 | 40111 | 49326 | 81686 |
| 7 | 35641 | 00301 | 16096 | 34775 | 21562 | 97983 | 45040 | 19200 | 16383 |
| 8 | 14031 | 00936 | 81518 | 48440 | 02218 | 04756 | 19506 | 60695 | 88494 |
| 9 | 60677 | 15076 | 92554 | 26042 | 23472 | 69869 | 62877 | 19584 | 39576 |
| 10 | 66314 | 05212 | 67859 | 89356 | 20056 | 30648 | 87349 | 20389 | 53805 |
| 11 | 20416 | 87410 | 75646 | 64176 | 82752 | 63606 | 37011 | 57346 | 69512 |
| 12 | 28701 | 56992 | 70423 | 62415 | 40807 | 98086 | 58850 | 28968 | 45297 |
| 13 | 74579 | 33844 | 33426 | 07570 | 00728 | 07079 | 19322 | 56325 | 84819 |
| 14 | 62615 | 52342 | 82968 | 75540 | 80045 | 53069 | 20665 | 21282 | 07768 |
| 15 | 93945 | 06293 | 22879 | 08161 | 01442 | 75071 | 21427 | 94842 | 26210 |
| 16 | 75689 | 76131 | 96837 | 67450 | 44511 | 50424 | 82848 | 41975 | 71663 |
| 17 | 02921 | 16919 | 35424 | 93209 | 52133 | 87327 | 95897 | 65171 | 20376 |
| 18 | 14295 | 34969 | 14216 | 03191 | 61647 | 30296 | 66667 | 10101 | 63203 |
| 19 | 05303 | 91109 | 82403 | 40312 | 62191 | 67023 | 90073 | 83205 | 71344 |
| 20 | 57071 | 90357 | 12901 | 08899 | 91039 | 67251 | 28701 | 03846 | 94589 |
| 21 | 78471 | 57741 | 13599 | 84390 | 32146 | 00871 | 09354 | 22745 | 65806 |
| 22 | 89242 | 79337 | 59293 | 47481 | 07740 | 43345 | 25716 | 70020 | 54005 |
| 23 | 14955 | 59592 | 97035 | 80430 | 87220 | 06392 | 79028 | 57123 | 52872 |
| 24 | 42446 | 41880 | 37415 | 47472 | 04513 | 49494 | 08860 | 08038 | 43624 |
| 25 | 18534 | 22346 | 54556 | 17558 | 73689 | 14894 | 05030 | 19561 | 56517 |
| 26 | 39284 | 33737 | 42512 | 86411 | 23753 | 29690 | 26096 | 81361 | 93099 |
| 27 | 33922 | 37329 | 89911 | 55876 | 28379 | 81031 | 22058 | 21487 | 54613 |
| 28 | 78355 | 54013 | 50774 | 30666 | 61205 | 42574 | 47773 | 36027 | 27174 |
| 29 | 08845 | 99145 | 94316 | 88974 | 29828 | 97069 | 90327 | 61842 | 29604 |
| 30 | 01769 | 71825 | 55957 | 98271 | 02784 | 66731 | 40311 | 88495 | 18821 |
| 31 | 17639 | 38284 | 59478 | 90409 | 21997 | 56199 | 30068 | 82800 | 69692 |
| 32 | 05851 | 58653 | 99949 | 63505 | 40409 | 85551 | 90729 | 64938 | 52403 |
| 33 | 42396 | 40112 | 11469 | 03476 | 03328 | 84238 | 26570 | 51790 | 42122 |
| 34 | 13318 | 14192 | 98167 | 75631 | 74141 | 22369 | 36757 | 89117 | 54998 |
| 35 | 60571 | 54786 | 26281 | 01855 | 30706 | 66578 | 32019 | 65884 | 58485 |
| 36 | 09531 | 81853 | 59334 | 70929 | 03544 | 18510 | 89541 | 13555 | 21168 |
| 37 | 72865 | 16829 | 86542 | 00396 | 20363 | 13010 | 69645 | 49608 | 54738 |
| 38 | 56324 | 31093 | 77924 | 28622 | 83543 | 28912 | 15059 | 80192 | 83964 |
| 39 | 78192 | 21626 | 91399 | 07235 | 07104 | 73652 | 64425 | 85149 | 75409 |
| 40 | 64666 | 34767 | 97298 | 92708 | 01994 | 53188 | 78476 | 07804 | 62404 |
| 41 | 82201 | 75694 | 02808 | 65983 | 74373 | 66693 | 13094 | 74183 | 73020 |
| 42 | 15360 | 73776 | 40914 | 85190 | 54278 | 99054 | 62944 | 47351 | 89098 |
| 43 | 68142 | 67957 | 70896 | 37983 | 20487 | 95350 | 16371 | 03426 | 13895 |
| 44 | 19138 | 31200 | 30616 | 14639 | 44406 | 44236 | 57360 | 81644 | 94761 |
| 45 | 28155 | 03521 | 36415 | 78452 | 92359 | 81091 | 56513 | 88321 | 97910 |
| 46 | 87971 | 29031 | 51780 | 27376 | 81056 | 86155 | 55488 | 50590 | 74514 |
| 47 | 58147 | 68841 | 53625 | 02059 | 75223 | 16783 | 19272 | 61994 | 71090 |
| 48 | 18875 | 52809 | 70594 | 41649 | 32935 | 26430 | 82096 | 01605 | 65846 |
| 49 | 75109 | 56474 | 74111 | 31966 | 29969 | 70093 | 98901 | 84550 | 25769 |
| 50 | 35983 | 03742 | 76822 | 12073 | 59463 | 84420 | 15868 | 99505 | 11426 |

# |||| References

Adams, J.A. (1972). Research and the future of engineering psychology. *American Psychologist, 27,* 615–622.

Alsip, J.E., & Chezik, D.D. (1974). *Research guide in psychology.* Morristown, NJ: General Learning Press.

American Psychological Association. (1972). Guidelines for psychologists for the use of drugs in research. *American Psychologist, 27,* 336.

American Psychological Association. (1981a). Ethical principles of psychologists. *American Psychologist, 36,* 633–638.

American Psychological Association. (1981b). Guidelines for the use of animals in school-science behavior projects. *American Psychologist, 36,* 686.

American Psychological Association (1982). *Ethical principles in the conduct of research with human behavior.* Washington, DC: Author.

American Psychological Association. (1983). *Publication manual of the American Psychological Association* (3d ed.). Washington, DC: Author.

American Psychological Association. (1987). *Casebook on ethical issues.* Washington, DC: Author.

Anderson, N.H. (1981). *Foundations of information integration theory.* New York: Academic Press.

Anisfield, M. (1987). A course to develop competence in critical reading of empirical research in psychology. *Teaching of Psychology, 14,* 224–227.

Atkinson, R.C. (1975). Mnemotechnics and second-language learning. *American Psychologist, 30,* 821–828.

Bachman, J.D., & Johnston, L.D. (1979). The freshman. *Psychology Today, 13,* 78–87.

Barber, T.X. (1976). *Pitfalls in human research: Ten pivotal points.* New York: Pergamon.

Barefoot, J.C., Hoople, H., & McClay, D. (1972). Avoidance of an act which would violate personal space. *Psychonomic Science, 28,* 205–206.

Bem, D.J. (1987). Writing the empirical journal article. In M.P. Zanna & J.M. Darley (Eds.), *The compleat academic: A practical guide for the beginning social scientist.* New York: Random House.

Bem, D.J., & Lord, C.G. (1979). Template matching: A proposal for probing the ecological validity of experimental settings in social psychology. *Journal of Personality and Social Psychology, 37,* 833–846.

Berkowitz, L., & Donnerstein, E. (1982). External validity is more than skin deep. *American Psychologist, 37,* 245–257.

Blaney, R.H. (1986). Affect and memory: A review. *Psychological Bulletin, 99,* 229–246.

Boe, R., & Winokur, S. (1978). A procedure for studying echoic control in verbal behavior. *Journal of the Experimental Analysis of Behavior, 30,* 213–217.

Boice, R. (1983). Observational skills. *Psychological Bulletin, 93,* 3–29.

Boring, E. G. (1950). *A history of experimental psychology*. New York: Appleton-Century-Crofts.

Boring, E. G. (1954). The nature and history of experimental control. *American Journal of Psychology, 67*, 573–589.

Bouffard, J.-P., & Jarrard, L. E. (1988). Acquisition of a complex place task in rats with selective ibotenate lesions of hippocampal formation: Combined lesions of subiculum and enthorhinal cortex vs. hippocampus. *Behavioral Neuroscience, 102*.

Bowd, A. D. (1980). Ethical reservations about psychological research with animals. *Psychological Record, 30*, 201–210.

Bower, G. H. (1972). Mental imagery and associative learning. In L. Gregg (Ed.), *Cognition in learning and memory*. New York: Wiley.

Brady, J. V. (1958). Ulcers in "executive" monkeys. *Scientific American, 199*, 92–100.

Brady, J. V., Porter, R. W., Conrad, D. G., & Mason, J. W. (1958). Avoidance behavior and the development of gastroduodenal ulcers. *Journal of the Experimental Analysis of Behavior, 1*, 69–72.

Broadbent, D. E. (1971). *Decision and stress*. London: Academic Press.

Broadbent, D. E. (1973). *In defence of empirical psychology*. London: Methuen.

Brownell, K. D., & Stunkard, A. J. (1982). The double-blind in danger: Untoward consequences of informed consent. *American Journal of Psychiatry, 139*, 1487–1489.

Cairns, R. B., & Ornstein, P. A. (1979). Developmental psychology. In E. Hearst (Ed.), *The first century of experimental psychology*. Hillsdale, NJ: Erlbaum.

Calfee, R. C. (1975). *Human experimental psychology*. New York: Holt, Rinehart & Winston.

Campbell, D. T., & Erlebacher, A. (1970a). How regression artifacts can mistakenly make compensatory education look harmful. In J. Helmuth (Ed.), *Compensatory education: A national debate: Vol. 3. Disadvantaged child*. New York: Brunner/Mazel.

Campbell, D. T., & Erlebacher, A. (1970b). Reply to the replies. In J. Helmuth (Ed.), *Compensatory education: A national debate: Vol. 3. Disadvantaged child*. New York: Brunner/Mazel.

Campbell, D. T., & Stanley, J. C. (1963). *Experimental and quasi-experimental designs for research*. Chicago: Rand McNally.

Carver, C. S., Coleman, A. E., & Glass, D. C. (1976). The coronary-prone behavior pattern and the suppression of fatigue on a treadmill test. *Journal of Personality and Social Psychology, 33*, 460–466.

Cicirelli, V. (1970). The relevance of the regression artifact problem to the Westinghouse-Ohio evaluation of Head Start: A reply to Campbell and Erlebacher. In J. Helmuth (Ed.), *Compensatory education: A national debate: Vol. 3. Disadvantaged child*. New York: Brunner/Mazel.

Cicirelli, V. et al. (1969, June). *The impact of Head Start on children's cognitive and affective development*. A report presented to the Office of Economic Opportunity pursuant to Contract B89–4536. Westinghouse Learning Corporation, Ohio University. (Distributed by Clearinghouse for Federal Scientific and Technical Information, U.S. Department of Commerce, National Bureau of Standards, Institute for Applied Technology, PB 184 328.)

Clark, W. C., & Yang, J. C. (1974). Acupunctural analgesia: Evaluation by signal detection theory. *Science, 184*, 1096–1098.

Cole, M., Gay, J., Glick, J. A., & Sharp, D. W. (1971). *The cultural context of learning and thinking*. New York: Basic Books.

Comish, S. E. (1987). Recognition of facial stimuli following an intervening task involving the Identi-kit. *Journal of Applied Psychology, 72*, 488–491.

Cook, T. D., & Campbell, D. T. (1979). *Quasi-experimentation: Design and analysis for field settings*. Chicago: Rand McNally.

Cornsweet, T. N. (1962). The staircase method in psychophysics. *American Journal of Psychology, 75,* 485–491.

Craik, F. I. M. (1977). Age differences in human memory. In J. E. Birren & W. Schaie (Eds.), *Handbook of the psychology of aging.* New York: Van Nostrand Reinhold.

DeGreene, K. B. (Ed.). (1970). *Systems psychology.* New York: McGraw-Hill.

Dewing, K., & Hetherington, P. (1974). Anagram solving as a function of word imagery. *Journal of Experimental Psychology, 102,* 764–767.

Dipboye, R. L., & Flanagan, M. F. (1979). Research settings in industrial and organizational psychology. *American Psychologist, 34,* 141–150.

Edwards, A. L. (1953). The relationship between the judged desirability of a trait and the probability that the trait will be endorsed. *Journal of Applied Psychology, 37,* 90–93.

Edwards, A. L. (1957). *The social desirability variable in personality research.* New York: Dryden.

Egeth, H., Blecker, D. L., & Kamlet, A. S. (1969). Verbal interference in a perceptual comparison task. *Perception & Psychophysics, 6,* 355–356.

Eibl-Eibesfeldt, I. (1970). *Ethology: The biology of behavior.* New York: Holt, Rinehart & Winston.

Eibl-Eibesfeldt, I. (1972). Similarities and differences between cultures in expressive movements. In R. A. Hinde (Ed.), *Non-verbal communication.* Cambridge, England: Cambridge University Press.

Elmes, D. G. (1978). *Readings in experimental psychology.* Chicago: Rand McNally.

Elmes, D. G., & Bjork, R. A. (1975). The interaction of encoding and rehearsal processes in the recall of repeated and nonrepeated items. *Journal of Verbal Learning and Verbal Behavior, 14,* 30–42.

Elmes, D. G., Chapman, P. F., & Selig, C. W. (1984). Role of mood and connotation in the spacing effect. *Bulletin of the Psychonomic Society, 22,* 186–188.

Eron, L. D. (1982). Parent-child interaction, television violence, and aggression of children. *American Psychologist, 37,* 197–211.

Eron, L. D., Huesman, L. R., Lefkowitz, M. M., & Walder, L. O. (1972). Does television violence cause aggression? *American Psychologist, 27,* 253–263.

Etaugh, C., & Michaels, D. (1975). Effect on reading comprehension of preferred music and frequency of studying to music. *Perceptual and Motor Skills, 41,* 533–554.

Evans, J. W., & Schiller, J. (1970). How preoccupation with possible regression artifacts can lead to a faulty strategy for the evaluation of social action programs: A reply to Campbell and Erlebacher. In J. Helmuth (Ed.), *Compensatory education: A national debate: Vol. 3. Disadvantaged child.* New York: Brunner/Mazel.

Feingold, B. F. (1975). Hyperkinesis and learning disabilities linked to artificial food flavors and colors. *American Journal of Nursing, 75,* 797–803.

Festinger, L., Riecken, H. W., & Schachter, S. (1956). *When prophecy fails.* Minneapolis: University of Minnesota Press.

Fingerman, P., & Levine, M. (1974). Nonlearning: The completeness of the blindness. *Journal of Experimental Psychology, 102,* 720–721.

Fossey, D. (1972). Living with mountain gorillas. In T. B. Allen (Ed.), *The marvels of animal behavior.* Washington, DC: National Geographic Society.

Frye v. United States, 293F.1013 (D.C. Cir. 1923).

Gabrenya, W. K., Latané, B., & Wang, Y. (1983). Social loafing in cross-cultural perspective: Chinese on Taiwan. *Journal of Cross-Cultural Psychology, 14,* 368–384.

Gallup, G. G., & Suarez, S. D. (1985). Alternatives to the use of animals in psychological research. *American Psychologist, 40,* 1104–1111.

Garner, W. R., Hake, H., & Eriksen, C. W. (1956). Operationism and the concept of perception. *Psychological Review, 63,* 149–159.

Gescheider, G. A. (1976). *Psychophysics: Method and theory.* Hillsdale, NJ: Erlbaum.

Glass, D. C., & Singer, J. E. (1972a). Behavioral after effects of unpredictable and uncontrollable aversive events. *American Scientist, 60,* 457–465.

Glass, D. C., & Singer, J. E. (1972b). *Urban stress: Experiments on noise and social stressors.* New York: Academic Press.

Glenberg, A. M. (1988). *Learning from data.* San Diego: Harcourt Brace Jovanovich.

Graessle, O. A., Ahbel, K., & Porges, S. W. (1978). Effects of mild prenatal decompressions on growth and behavior in the rat. *Bulletin of the Psychonomic Society, 12,* 329–331.

Guilford, J. P. (1967). *The nature of human intelligence.* New York: McGraw-Hill.

Hanson, N. R. (1958). *Patterns of discovery.* Cambridge: Cambridge University Press.

Harkins, S. G., Latané, B., & Williams, K. (1980). Social loafing: Allocating effort or taking it easy? *Journal of Experimental Social Psychology, 16,* 457–465.

Harlow, H. F. (1958). The nature of love. *American Psychologist, 13,* 673–685.

Harlow, H. F. (1959, June). Love in infant monkeys. *Scientific American, 200(6),* 68–74.

Harlow, H. F., Gluck, J. P., & Suomi, S. J. (1972). Generalization of behavioral data between nonhuman and human animals. *American Psychologist, 27,* 709–716.

Harlow, H. F., & Harlow, M. K. (1966). Learning to love. *American Scientist, 54,* 244–272.

Harré, R. (1983). *Great scientific experiments.* Oxford: Oxford University Press.

Hart, B. M., Allen, K. E., Buell, J. S., Harris, F. R., & Wolf, M. M. (1964). Effects of social reinforcement on operant crying. *Journal of Experimental Child Psychology, 1,* 145–153.

Helson, H. (1964). *Adaptation-level theory: An experimental and systematic approach to behavior.* New York: Harper & Row.

Hicks, E. A., & Kilcourse, J. (1983). Habitual sleep duration and the incidence of headaches in college students. *Bulletin of the Psychonomic Society, 21,* 119.

Hintzman, D. L., Carre, F. A., Eskridge, V. L., Owens, A. M., Shaff, S. S., & Sparks, M. E. (1972). "Stroop" effect: Input or output phenomenon? *Journal of Experimental Psychology, 95,* 458–459.

Hoff, C. (1980). Immoral and moral uses of animals. *New England Journal of Medicine, 302,* 115–118.

Homa, D. (1983). An assessment of two extraordinary speed-readers. *Bulletin of the Psychonomic Society, 21,* 123–126.

Homans, G. C. (1965). Group factors in worker productivity. In H. Proshansky and L. Seidenberg (Eds.), *Basic studies in social psychology.* New York: Holt.

Horowitz, L. M. (1974). *Elements of statistics for psychology and education.* New York: McGraw Hill.

Huff, D. (1954). *How to lie with statistics.* New York: Norton.

Hyman, R. (1964). *The nature of psychological inquiry.* Englewood Cliffs, N.J.: Prentice-Hall.

Imber, S. D., Glanz, L. M., Elkin, I., Sotsky, S. M., Boyer, J. L., & Leber, W. R. (1986). Ethical issues in psychotherapy research: Problems in a collaborative clinical study. *American Psychologist, 41,* 137–146.

Jacobson, E. (1978). *You must relax* (5th ed.). New York: McGraw-Hill.

Jarrard, L. E. (1963). Effects of d-lysergic acid diethylamide on operant behavior in the rat. *Psychopharmacologia, 5,* 39–46.

Jensen, A. R. (1969). How much can we boost I.Q. and scholastic achievement? *Harvard Educational Review, 39,* –123.

Jones, R. F. (1982). *Ancients and moderns.* New York: Dover.

Kantowitz, B. H. (1974). Double stimulation. In B. H. Kantowitz (Ed.), *Human information processing—Tutorials in performance and cognition.* Hillsdale, NJ: Erlbaum.

Kantowitz, B. H., Roediger, H. L., & Elmes, D. G. (1988). *Experimental psychology:*

*Understanding behavioral research* (3d ed.). St. Paul, MN: West.

Kaplan, R. M., & Saccuzzo, D. P. (1982). *Psychological testing: Principles, applications, and issues.* Monterey, CA: Brooks/Cole.

Katz, D. (1979, February 7). Paying the price for drug development. *Roanoke Times & World News.*

Keele, S. W. (1973). *Attention and human performance.* Pacific Palisades, CA: Goodyear.

Kendler, H. H. (1981). *Psychology: A science in conflict.* New York: Oxford.

Kerlinger, F. (1986). *Foundations of behavioral research.* New York: Holt, Rinehart & Winston.

Kinsey, A. C., Pomeroy, W. B., & Martin, C. E. (1953). *Sexual behavior in the human female.* Philadelphia: Saunders.

Kinzel, A. F. (1970). Body-buffer zone in violent prisoners. *The American Journal of Psychiatry, 127,* 59–64.

Kuhn, T. S. (1962). *The structure of scientific revolutions.* Chicago: University of Chicago Press.

Latané, B. (1981). The psychology of social impact. *American Psychologist, 36,* 343–356.

Latané, B., & Darley, J. M. (1970). *The unresponsive bystander—Why doesn't he help?* New York: Appleton-Century-Crofts.

Latané, B., Williams, K., & Harkins, S. (1979). Many hands make light the work: Causes and consequences of social loafing. *Journal of Personality and Social Psychology, 37,* 822–832.

Lester, B. M., & Brazelton, T. B. (1982). Cross-cultural assessment of neonatal behavior. In D. A. Wagner & H. W. Stevenson (Eds.), *Cultural perspectives on child development.* San Francisco: Freeman.

Levin, I. P., Louviere, J. J., & Schepanski, A. A. (1983). External validity tests of laboratory studies of information integration. *Organizational Behavior and Human Performance, 31,* 173–193.

Lindholm, E., & Lowry, S. (1978). Alpha production in humans under conditions of false feedback. *Bulletin of the Psychonomic Society, 11,* 106–108.

Luchins, A. S. (1942). Mechanization in problem solving: The effect of Einstellung. *Psychological Monographs, 54* (6, Whole No. 181).

Marriot, P. (1949). Size of working groups and output. *Occupational Psychology, 23,* 47–57.

Masling, J. (1966). Role-related behavior of the subject and psychologist and its effects upon psychological data. *Nebraska symposium on motivation* (Vol. 14). Lincoln: University of Nebraska Press.

Massaro, D. W. (1975). *Experimental psychology and information processing.* Chicago: Rand McNally.

Mayer, R. E. (1977). Problem-solving performance with task overload: Effects of self-pacing and trait anxiety. *Bulletin of the Psychonomic Society, 9,* 283–286.

Mayr, E. (1982). *The growth of biological thought.* Cambridge, MA: Belknap Press.

Mayzner, M. S., & Tresselt, M. E. (1966). Anagram solution times: A function of multiple solution anagrams. *Journal of Experimental Psychology, 71,* 66–73.

McClelland, I. L., & Ward, J. S. (1982). The ergonomics of toilet seats. *Human Factors, 24,* 713–725.

McSweeny, A. J. (1978). The effects of response cost on the behavior of a million persons: Charging for directory assistance in Cincinnati. *Journal of Applied Behavior Analysis, 11,* 47–51.

Melton, G., & Gray, J. (1988). Ethical dilemmas in AIDS research: Individual privacy and public health. *American Psychologist, 43,* 60–64.

Milgram, S. (1963). Behavioral study of obedience. *Journal of Abnormal and Social Psychology, 67,* 371–378.

Milgram, S. (1977). Ethical issues in the study of obedience. In B. Milgram (Ed.), *The individual in a social world* (pp. 188–199). Reading, MA: Addison-Wesley.

Mill, J. S. (1930). *A system of logic.* London: Longmans Green. (Original work published 1843).

Miller, D. B. (1977). Roles of naturalistic observation in comparative psychology. *American Psychologist, 32,* 211–219.

Moede, W. (1927). Die richtlinien der leistungs—Psychologie. *Industrielle Psychotechnik, 4,* 193–207.

Mook, D. G. (1983). In defense of external invalidity. *American Psychologist, 38,* 379–387.

Moran, S. L. V., & Loeb, M. (1977). Annoyance and behavioral aftereffects following interfering and noninterfering aircraft noise. *Journal of Applied Psychology, 62,* 719–726.

Morin, R. E., & Grant, D. A. (1954). Learning and performance of a keypressing task as a function of the degree of spatial stimulus-response correspondence. *Journal of Experimental Psychology, 49,* 39–47.

Natsoulas, T. (1967). What are perceptual reports about? *Psychological Bulletin, 67,* 249–272.

Neisser, U. (1976). *Cognition and reality: Principles and implications of cognitive psychology.* San Francisco: Freeman.

Neisser, U. (1982). *Memory observed: Remembering in natural contexts.* San Francisco: Freeman.

Notterman, J. M., & Mintz, D. E. (1965). *Dynamics of response.* New York: Wiley.

Orne, M. T. (1962). On the social psychology of the psychological experiment: With particular reference to demand characteristics and their implications. *American Psychologist, 17,* 776–783.

Orne, M. T. (1969). Demand characteristics and the concept of quasi-controls. In R. Rosenthal & R. L. Rosnow (Eds.), *Artifact in behavioral research.* New York: Academic Press.

Orne, M. T., & Evans, T. J. (1965). Social control in the psychological experiment: Antisocial behavior and hypnosis. *Journal of Personality and Social Psychology, 1,* 189–200.

Paivio, A. (1975). Perceptual comparisons through the mind's eye. *Memory & Cognition, 3,* 635–647.

Parducci, A. (1968). The relativism of absolute judgments. *Scientific American, 219,* 84–90.

Parsons, H. M. (1974). What happened at Hawthorne? *Science, 183,* 922–931.

Pavlov, I. P. (1963). *Lectures on conditioned reflexes.* New York: International Publishers.

Peirce, C. S. (1877). The fixation of belief. *Popular Science Monthly, 12,* 1–15. Reprinted in E. C. Moore (Ed.). (1972). *Charles S. Peirce: The essential writings.* New York: Harper & Row.

Phillips, D. P. (1972). Deathday and birthday: An unexpected connection. In J. Tanur, F. Mosteller, W. H. Kruskal, R. F. Link, R. S. Peters, & G. R. Rising (Eds.), *Statistics: A guide to the unknown.* San Francisco: Holden Day.

Phillips, D. P. (1977). Motor vehicle fatalities increase just after publicized suicide stories. *Science, 196,* 1464–1465.

Phillips, D. P. (1978). Airplane accident fatalities increase just after stories about murder and suicide. *Science, 201,* 148–150.

Phillips, D. P. (1983). The impact of mass media violence on U.S. homicides. *American Sociological Review, 48,* 560–568.

Piaget, J., & Inhelder, B. (1969). *The Psychology of the child.* London: Routledge & Kegan Paul.

Piliavin, I. M., Piliavin, J. A., & Rodin, J. (1975). Costs, diffusion, and the stigmatized victim. *Journal of Personality and Social Psychology, 32,* 429–438.

Platt, J. R. (1964). Strong inference. *Science, 146*, 347–353.

Plotkin, W. B. (1979). The alpha experience revisited: Biofeedback in the transformation of psychological state. *Psychological Bulletin, 86*, 1132–1148.

Popper, K. R. (1961). *The logic of scientific discovery.* New York: Basic Books.

Poulton, E. C. (1982). Influential companions: Effects of one strategy on another in the within-subjects designs of cognitive psychology. *Psychological Bulletin, 9*, 673–690.

Pratkanis, A. R., Greenwald, A. G., Leippe, M. R., & Baumgardner, M. H. (1988). In search of reliable persuasion effects: The sleeper effect is dead. Long live the sleeper effect. *Journal of Personality and Social Psychology, 54*, 203–218.

Read, J. D. (1983). Detection of Fs in a single statement: The role of phonetic recoding. *Memory & Cognition, 11*, 390–399.

Richman, C. L., Mitchell, D. B., & Reznick, J. S. (1979). Mental travel: Some reservations. *Journal of Experimental Psychology: Human Perception and Performance, 5*, 13–18.

Robbins, L. C. (1963). The accuracy of parental recall of aspects of child development and of child-rearing practices. *Journal of Abnormal and Social Psychology, 66*, 261–270.

Roberts, C. (1971). Debate I. Animal experimentation and evolution. *American Scholar, 40*, 497–503.

Roediger, H. L., & Neely, J. H. (1982). Retrieval blocks in episodic and semantic memory. *Canadian Journal of Psychology, 36*, 213–242.

Rogosa, D. (1980). A critique of the cross-lagged correlation. *Psychological Bulletin, 88*, 245–248.

Rollin, B. E. (1985). The moral status of research animals in psychology. *American Psychologist, 40*, 920–926.

Rose, T. L. (1978). The functional relationship between artificial food colors and hyperactivity. *Journal of Applied Behavior Analysis, 11*, 439–446.

Rosenberg, M. J. (1969). The conditions and consequences of evaluation apprehension. In R. Rosenthal & R. L. Rosnow (Eds.), *Artifact in behavioral research.* New York: Academic Press.

Rosnow, R. L., & Aiken, L. S. (1973). Mediation of artifacts in behavorial research. *Journal of Experimental Social Psychology, 9*, 181–201.

Rosnow, R. L., & Rosenthal, R. (1970). Volunteer effects in behavioral research. In *New directions in psychology 4.* New York: Holt, Rinehart & Winston.

Rowland, L. W. (1939). Will hypnotized persons try to harm themselves or others? *Journal of Abnormal and Social Psychology, 34*, 114–117.

Saari, L. M., & Latham, G. P. (1982). Employee reactions to continuous and variable ratio reinforcement schedules involving a monetary incentive. *Journal of Applied Psychology, 67*, 506–508.

Sanders, G. S., & Simmons, W. L. (1983). Use of hypnotism to enhance eyewitness accuracy: Does it work? *Journal of Applied Psychology, 68*, 70–77.

Scarborough, D. L. (1972). Stimulus modality effects on forgetting in short-term memory. *Journal of Experimental Psychology, 95*, 285–289.

Scarr, S. (1988). Race and gender as psychological variables: Social and ethical issues. *American Psychologist, 43*, 56–59.

Schachter, S. (1982). Don't sell habit-breakers short. *Psychology Today, 16*, 27–33.

Schacter, D. L. (1983). Amnesia observed: Remembering and forgetting in a natural environment. *Journal of Abnormal Psychology, 92*, 236–242.

Schaie, K. W. (1977). Quasi-experimental designs in the psychology of aging. In J. E. Birren & K. W. Schaie (Eds.), *Handbook of the psychology of aging.* New York: Van Nostrand.

Schreibman, L., O'Neill, R. E., & Koegel, R. L. (1983). Behavioral training for siblings of autistic children. *Journal of Applied Behavior Analysis, 16*, 129–138.

Sidman, M. (1960). *Tactics of scientific research*. New York: Basic Books.

Sieber, J. E., & Stanley, B. (1988). Ethical and professional dimensions of socially sensitive research. *American Psychologist, 43*, 49–55.

Singer, M. (1982). Comparing memory for natural and laboratory reading. *Journal of Experimental Psychology: General, 111*, 331–347.

Singer, P. (1978). Animal experimentation: Philosophical perspectives. In W. T. Reich (Ed.), *Encyclopedia of bioethics*. New York: Free Press.

Skinner, B. F. (1938). *The behavior of organisms: An experimental analysis*. New York: Appleton-Century-Crofts.

Skinner, B. F. (1956). A case history in scientific method. *American Psychologist, 11*, 221–233.

Smith, C. P. (1983). Ethical issues: Research on deception, informed consent, and debriefing. In L. Wheeler & P. Shaver (Eds.), *Review of personality and social psychology* (Vol. 4, pp. 297–328). Beverly Hills, CA: Sage.

Smith, M. C. (1983). Hypnotic memory enhancement: Does it work? *Psychological Bulletin, 94*, 387–407.

Spreen, O., & Schulz, R. W. (1966). Parameters of abstraction, meaningfulness, and pronunciability [sic] for 329 nouns. *Journal of Verbal Learning and Verbal Behavior, 5*, 459–468.

Sternberg, R. J. (1987). *The psychologist's companion: A guide to scientific writing for students and researchers*. Cambridge: Cambridge University Press.

Stroop, J. R. (1935). Studies of interference in serial verbal reactions. *Journal of Experimental Psychology, 18*, 643–662.

Sunderland, A., Harris, J. E., & Baddeley, A. D. (1983). Do laboratory tests predict everyday memory? A neuropsychological study. *Journal of Verbal Learning and Verbal Behavior, 22*, 341–357.

Suppes, P., & Zinnes, J. L. (1963). Basic measurement theory. In R. Luce, R. Brush, & E. Galanter (Eds.), *Handbook of mathematical psychology* (Vol. 1). New York: Wiley.

Thios, S. J., & D'Agostino, P. R. (1976). Effects of repetition as a function of study-phase retrieval. *Journal of Verbal Learning and Verbal Behavior, 15*, 529–536.

Thompson, J. B., & Buchanan, W. (1979). *Analyzing psychological data*. New York: Scribner's.

Tolman, E. C., & Honzik, C. H. (1930). Introduction and removal of reward and maze performance in rats. *University of California Publications in Psychology, 4*, 257–275.

Tulving, E., & Pearlstone, Z. (1966). Availability versus accessibility of information in memory for words. *Journal of Verbal Learning and Verbal Behavior, 5*, 381–391.

Tversky, B., & Teiffer, E. (1976). Development of strategies for recall and recognition. *Developmental Psychology, 12*, 406–410.

Underwood, B. (1957). *Psychological research*. New York: Appleton.

Underwood, B. J. (1975). Individual differences as a crucible in theory construction. *American Psychologist, 30*, 128–134.

Uttal, W. R. (1978). *The psychobiology of mind*. Hillsdale, NJ: Erlbaum.

Velten, E. A. (1968). A laboratory task for the induction of mood states. *Behavior Research and Therapy, 6*, 473–478.

Walters, C., Shurley, J. T., & Parsons, O. A. (1962). Differences in male and female responses to underwater sensory deprivation: An exploratory study. *Journal of Nervous and Mental Disease, 135*, 302–310.

Warren, R. M. (1963). Are loudness judgments based on distance estimates? *Journal of the Acoustical Society of America, 35*, 613–614.

Webb, E. J., Campbell, D. T., Schwartz, R. D., & Sechrist, L. (1981). *Unobtrusive measures: Nonreactive research in the social sciences*. Chicago: Rand McNally.

Weber, S. J., & Cook, T. D. (1972). Subject effects in laboratory research: An examination of subject roles, demand characteristics, and valid inference. *Psychological Bulletin, 77,* 273–295.

Weinstein, N. D. (1978). Individual differences in reactions to noise: A longitudinal study in a college dormitory. *Journal of Applied Psychology, 63,* 458–466.

Weinstock, S. (1958). Acquisition and extinction of a partially reinforced running response at a 24-hour intertrial interval. *Journal of Experimental Psychology, 56,* 151–158.

Weiss, J. M. (1968). Effects of coping responses on stress. *Journal of Comparative and Physiological Psychology, 65,* 251–260.

Weiss, J. M. (1971). Effects of coping behavior in different warning signal conditions on stress pathology in rats. *Journal of Comparative and Physiological Psychology, 77,* 1–13.

White, R. J. (1971). Debate II. Antivivisection: The reluctant hydra. *American Scholar, 40,* 503–512.

Wildman, B. G., & Erickson, M. T. (1977). Methodological problems in behaviorial observation. In J. D. Cone and R. P. Hawkins (Eds.), *Behaviorial assessment.* New York: Brunner/Mazel.

Williams, K., Harkins, S., & Latané, B. (1981). Identifiability as a deterrent to social loafing: Two cheering experiments. *Journal of Personality and Social Psychology, 40,* 303–311.

Williams, R. D., & Long, J. D. (1979). *Toward a self-managed life style* (2d ed.). Boston: Houghton-Mifflin.

Windes, J. D. (1968). Reaction time for numerical coding and naming of numerals. *Journal of Experimental Psychology, 78,* 318–322.

Wohwill, J. F. (1970). Methodology and research strategy in the study of developmental change. In L. R. Goulet & P. B. Baltes (Eds.), *Life-span developmental psychology: Research and theory.* New York: Academic Press.

Wolf, M. M., & Risley, T. R. (1971). Reinforcement: Applied research. In R. Glaser (Ed.), *The nature of reinforcement.* New York: Academic Press.

Wolf, R. H., & Weiner, F. (1972). Effect of four noise conditions on arithmetic performance. *Perceptual and Motor Skills, 35,* 938–940.

Woods, P. J. (1976). *Career opportunities for psychologists.* Washington, DC: American Psychological Association.

Woolfolk, M. E. (1981). The eye of the beholder: Methodological considerations when observers assess nonverbal communication, *Journal of Nonverbal Behavior, 5,* 199–204.

Woolfolk, M. E., Castellan, W., & Brooks, C. I. (1983). Pepsi versus Coke: Labels, not tastes, prevail. *Psychological Reports, 52,* 185–186.

Wright, L. (1988). The Type A behavior pattern and coronary artery disease. *American Psychologist, 43,* 2–14.

Young, P. C. (1952). Antisocial uses of hypnosis. In L. M. LeCron (Ed.), *Experimental hypnosis.* New York: Macmillan.

Zajonc, R. B., & Marcus, N. (1975). Birth order and intellectual development. *Psychological Review, 82,* 74–88.

# |||| Glossary

**ABA and ABAB designs** see *reversal design*

**ABBA counterbalancing** intrasubject counterbalancing in which treatments or conditions A and B are administered in the ABBA or BAAB order

**Abscissa** the horizontal axis (or $x$-axis) in a graph

**Absolute threshold** the average point on a sensory continuum (such as light intensity) at which an observer detects a stimulus

**Adaptation level** a source of difficulty in psychophysical studies resulting from the context or reference level surrounding a given psychophysical judgment

**Aftercare** the need for experimenters to guard the welfare of their subjects subsequent to the research manipulation; especially important in drug research

**Alpha level** see *significance level*

**Analysis of variance** a statistical test appropriate for analyzing reliability from experiments with any number of levels on one or more independent variables

**Anthropomorphizing** attributing human characteristics or emotions, such as happiness, to animals

**APA format** the journal article format specified by the American Psychological Association (APA)

**A priori method** according to Peirce, a way of fixing belief due to the reasonableness of the event (see *method of tenacity, method of authority,* and *empirical*)

**Apprehensive-subject role** a presumed role taken by a research subject who dislikes being evaluated; *see evaluation apprehension* and *reactive*

**Balanced Latin square** counterbalancing scheme in which each condition is preceded and followed equally often by every other condition

**Baseline** the "normal" or typical behavior used as a standard of comparison in an experiment

**Beta** the criterion of the decision process in signal detection measured by the slope of the receiver-operating-characteristic (ROC) function at the point of interest

**Between-groups variance** a measure of the dispersion among groups in an experiment

**Between-subjects design** an experimental design in which each subject is tested under only one level of each independent variable

**Blind experiment** experiment in which subjects do not know whether or not they are in the treatment condition (see *double blind*)

**Block randomization** a counterbalancing technique in which the treatment orders are randomized in successive blocks (groups) of presenting those conditions

**377**

**Carryover effect** relatively permanent effect that testing subjects in one condition has on their later behavior in another condition

**Case study** intensive investigation of a particular instance, or cases, of some behavior; does not allow inferences of cause and effect but is merely descriptive

**Ceiling effect** see *scale-attenuation effects*

**Central tendency** descriptive statistics indicating the center of a distribution of scores; see *mean, median,* and *mode*

**Cohorts** the people (and society in general) living at the time a given individual is developing; a potential confound when age is a subject variable that may be likened to the "generation gap"

**Computerized literature search** a method of searching the data base in a library that uses a computer

**Conceptual replication** attempt to demonstrate an experimental phenomenon with an entirely new paradigm or set of experimental conditions (see *converging operations*)

**Confidence level** see *significance level*

**Confidentiality** information obtained about subjects should remain confidential unless otherwise agreed

**Confounding** simultaneous variation of a second variable with an independent variable of interest so that any effect on the dependent variable cannot be attributed with certainty to the independent variable; inherent in correlational research

**Construct validity** when several measures fit sensibly with other results, we are measuring an underlying psychological concept

**Continuous reinforcement** schedule of reinforcement in which a reward follows every time the appropriate behavior is emitted

**Control** the technique of producing comparisons and holding other variables constant

**Control group** the group in an experiment that receives a comparison level of the independent variable

**Control variable** a potential independent variable that is held constant in an experiment

**Convergent validity** when two or more test results are highly correlated with each other but not with the results of other tests (see *discriminant validity*)

**Converging operations** a set of related lines of investigation that all bolster a common conclusion

**Correlation** a measure of the extent to which two variables are related, not necessarily causally

**Correlation coefficient** a number that can vary from $-1.00$ to $+1.00$ and indicates the degree of relation between two variables

**Counterbalancing** refers to any technique used to vary systemically the order of conditions in an experiment to distribute the effects of time of testing (e.g., practice and fatigue) so they are not confounded with conditions

**Counting** a measurement procedure leading to a ratio scale in which measurable attributes are enumerated

**Criterion** an independent means of determining the validity of an observation, experiment, or judgment; and the decision point in a signal detection experiment at which an observer decides to say yes or no

**Critical experiments** experiments designed to test the predictions of two or more theories

**Cross-lagged panel correlation** calculating several correlation coefficients across time on the same participants in order to increase the internal validity of correlational research

**Cross-sectional studies** taking a large sample of the population of various ages at one time and testing them (contrast with *longitudinal studies*)

**Cross-sequential design** a quasi-experimental design used when age is a subject variable to try to control for cohort and time of testing effects; involves testing several different age groups at several different time periods (see *longitudinal studies* and *cross-sectional studies*)

**$d'$** the sensitivity of an observer in a signal detection experiment; the distance between signal and noise distributions

**Data** the scores obtained on a dependent variable

**Debriefing** when subjects are told all details of an experiment after they have participated; an ethical obligation of the researcher

**Deception** a research technique in which the participant is mislead about some aspect of the project; may be unethical (see *double blind*)

**Decision process** evaluation of the sensory impression of a stimulus

**Deduction** reasoning from the general to the particular

**Degrees of freedom** the number of values free to vary if the total number of values and their sum are fixed

**Demand characteristics** those cues available to subjects in an experiment that may enable them to determine the purpose of the experiment, or what is expected by the experimenter

**Dependent variable** the variable measured and recorded by the experimenter

**Description** a determination of the quantity (frequency, magnitude) of behavior resulting from observation, case study, survey, and testing methods

**Descriptive statistics** methods of organizing and summarizing data

**Deviant case analysis** investigation of similar cases that differ in outcome in an attempt to specify the reasons for the different outcomes

**Difference threshold** the average point at which two stimuli are judged to be different (half of the interval of uncertainty)

**Directional/nondirectional statistical tests** see *one-* and *two-tailed tests*

**Direct measurement** the observer applies his or her scale in assigning numbers (see *indirect measurement*)

**Direct replication** repeating an experiment as closely as possible to determine whether or not the same results will be obtained

**Discounting cue** a message, signal, or pertinent fact that makes you doubt the accuracy or credibility of a persuasive message

**Discriminant validity** when two or more test results supposedly measuring different traits are not correlated with each other (see *convergent validity*)

**Dispersion** the amount of spread in a distribution of scores

**Distribution** a set of values of a variable

**Double blind** experimental technique in which neither the subject nor the experimenter knows which subjects are in which treatment conditions

**Ecological validity** the extent to which a research setting matches the environment of the problem under investigation; a threat to the external validity of experiments

**Einstellung** see *set*

**Empirical** relying upon or derived from observation or experiment

**Ethogram** a data sheet providing categories for making naturalistic observations

**Ethology** the systematic study of behavior; usually animal behavior in natural settings

**Evaluation apprehension** a source of reactivity in which subjects are uneasy about being evaluated in an experiment (see reactivity)

**Experiment** the systematic manipulation of some environment in order to observe the effect of this manipulation upon behavior; a particular comparison is produced

**Experimental control** holding constant extraneous variables in an experiment so that any effect on the dependent variable can be attributed to manipulation of the independent variable

**Experimental group** the group in an experiment that receives the level of interest of the independent variable

**Experimental reliability** see *replication*

**Explanation** a causal statement about why or when a particular event occurs resulting from experimental methods (see *joint method of agreement and difference*)

**Ex post facto** literally, "after the fact"; refers to conditions in an experiment that are not determined prior to the experiment, but only after some manipulation has occurred naturally

**External validity** refers to the generality of research; externally valid research is representative of real life and does not distort the question under investigation

**Face validity** when a measuring instrument intuitively seems to measure what it is supposed to measure

**Factorial design** an experimental design in which each level of every independent variable occurs with all levels of the other independent variable

**Faithful-subject role** when subjects do their utmost to follow the demands of the experimenter (see *reactive*)

**False alarm** saying yes when a signal is not present (in contrast to a hit)

**Falsifiability view** the assertion by Popper that negative results are more informative than positive results

**Field research** research conducted in natural settings in which subjects typically do not know that they are in an experiment

**Floor effect** see *scale-attenuation effects*

**Forced-choice tests** tests in which the participant must select between two or more statements; often used to control response styles

***F*-ratio** a ratio of between-groups variance to within-groups variance; forms the basis of the analysis of variance

**Freedom to withdraw** experimenter is ethically obligated to allow their subjects to discontinue participation in the research

**Frequency distribution** a set of scores arranged in order along a distribution indicating the number of times each score occurs

**Frequency polygon** a frequency distribution in which the height of the curve indicates the frequency of scores (see *histogram*)

**Fundamental question** why do organisms think and act as they do?

**Generality of results** the issue of whether or not a particular experimental result will be obtained under different circumstances, such as with a different subject population or in a different experimental setting

**Generalizability** see *generality of results*

**Good-subject role** when a subject attempts to determine the purposes of an experiment and reacts accordingly; see *demand characteristics* and *reactive*

**Hawthorne effect** refers to conditions under which performance in an experiment is affected by the knowledge of participants that they are in an experiment; see *demand characteristics*

**Heterogeneous** dissimilar

**Histogram** a frequency distribution in which the height of bars in the graph indicates the frequency of a class of scores; also called a bar graph

**History** a possible confound in research that inadvertently takes place between measurements because of historical changes in the participant

**Hit** saying yes when a signal is presented (see *false alarm*)

**Homogeneous** similar

**Hypothesis** a testable statement that offers a predicted relationship between dependent and independent variables

**Independent variable** the variable manipulated by the experimenter

**Indirect measurement** the observer limits judgments to a small set of categories in order to scale the attribute in question (contrast with *direct measurement*)

**Individual differences** a problem that may confound the results of a between-subjects experiment

**Induction** reasoning from the particular to the general

**Inferential statistics** procedures for determining the reliability and generality of a particular experimental finding

**Inferential validity** the idea that sound scientific inferences depend upon situations having a combination of internal, external, and construct validity

**Informed consent** potential subjects must be in a position to decide whether to participate in an experiment

**Interactions** experimental results that occur when the levels of one independent variable are differentially affected by the levels of other independent variables

**Internal distribution** the presumed sensory impressions in signal-detection theory

**Internal validity** allows straightforward statements about causality; experiments are usually internally valid because the joint method of agreement and difference is employed

**Interrupted-time-series design** a quasi-experiment that involves examination of a naturally occurring treatment on the behavior of a large number of participants

**Interval of uncertainty** the difference between the upper and lower thresholds in the determination of a difference threshold

**Interval scale** a scale with equal intervals but without a true zero point (for example, temperature)

**Intrasubject counterbalancing (ABBA)** see *ABBA counterbalancing*

**Introspection** literally, "looking within"; a way of obtaining subjective reports from observers

**Itch of research** the need or desire to solve a particular practical problem

**Joint method of agreement and difference** in Mill's system a situation, such as an experiment, in which $X$ always follows $A$ and never occurs when $A$ is not present

**Longitudinal studies** testing one group of people repeatedly as they age (contrast with cross-sectional studies)

**Magnitude estimation** observers assign numbers to attributes usually without restriction except that the numbers be assigned proportionately to the judged magnitude (a ratio scale)

**Main effect** when the effect of one independent variable is the same at all levels of another independent variable

**Mann-Whitney $U$ test** see U-*test*

**Matched groups design** experimental design in which subjects are matched on some variable assumed to be correlated with the dependent variable and then randomly assigned to conditions

**Matching** see *subject variables* and *matched groups design*

**Maturation** changes in people over time because of growth and other historical factors; may be a source of confounding in quasi-experiments

**Mean** measure of central tendency; the sum of all the scores divided by the number of scores

**Measurement** the systematic assignment of numbers to objects or attributes of objects

**Measurement scales** in order of increasing power: nominal, ordinal, interval, and ratio

**Median** measure of central tendency; the middle score of a distribution, or the one that divides a distribution in half

**Method of adjustment** a psychophysical procedure in which the observer adjusts a comparison stimulus to equate it with a standard

**Method of agreement** asserts that if event $A$ is always followed by result $X$, then $A$ is the likely cause of $X$ (see *method of difference*)

**Method of authority** a method of fixing belief in which an authority's word is taken on faith (contrast with *empirical*)

**Method of difference** according to J. S. Mill if $A$ is not present, then $X$ will not occur

**Method of limits** a psychophysical procedure for determining thresholds in which ascending and descending sequences of stimuli are presented

**Method of magnitude estimation** a direct psychophysical procedure in which observers assign values to their judgments according to the perceived magnitude of the perception usually resulting in a ratio scale

**Method of tenacity** a way of fixing belief involving a steadfast adherence to a particular belief, regardless of contrary arguments (see *empirical*)

**Mixed design** an experimental design that contains both between-subjects and within-subjects manipulations of the independent variables

**Mode** a measure of central tendency; the most frequent score

**Modulus** an anchor point sometimes used in the method of magnitude estimation to indicate an average value of the dimension

**Monotonic relationship** relationship between two variables in which an increase on one variable is accompanied by a consistent increase or decrease on the other variable

**Mortality** a possible source of confounding in research resulting from subjects dropping out either because they will not participate or because they cannot participate

**Motivated forgetting** distortions of past events reported retrospectively because of the emotional nature of those events

**Multiple-baseline design** a small-$n$ design in which different behaviors (or different people) receive baseline periods of varying lengths prior to the introduction of the independent variable

**Naturalistic observation** description of naturally occurring events without intervention on the part of the investigator

**Negativistic-subject role** when a subject deliberately attempts to sabotage an experiment

**Noise** a random disturbance that can be confused with signals in a signal-detection experiment

**Nominal scale** a scale in which objects are named or categorized—the weakest measurement scale

**Nonequivalent control group** in quasi-experiments a control group that is not determined by random assignment but is usually selected after the fact and is supposed to be equivalent to the naturally treated group

**Nonreactive** term to describe observations that are not influenced by the presence of the investigator; nonreactive methods are also referred to as unobtrusive

**Normal curve** a distribution of events that, when plotted, results in a bell-shaped curve. In a normal curve the mean, the median, and the mode are all equal

**Normal distribution** one producing a symmetric bell-shaped curve

**Nonparametric statistics** statistical tests that do not make any assumptions about the underlying distribution of scores; ordinarily require just ordinal-level data (see *parametric statistics*)

**Null hypothesis** states that the independent variable will have no effect on the dependent variable

**Null result** an experimental outcome where the dependent variable was not influenced by the independent variable

**Observation-treatment-observation** a quasi-experimental design; usually includes a nonequivalent control group

**Observational methods** research techniques based on simply observing behavior without trying to manipulate it experimentally

**One-shot case study** (see *case study*) a quasi-experiment in which the behavior of a single individual is studied and "explained" in terms of life events (see also *deviant case analysis*)

**One-tailed test** test that places the rejection area at one end of a distribution

**Operational definition** a definition of a concept in terms of the operations that must be performed to demonstrate the concept

**Ordinal scale** a measurement scale in which objects or attributes are ordered but in which the intervals between points are not equal

**Ordinate** the vertical axis (or *y*-axis) in a graph

**Organization** one function of a theory is to collect or organize what is known into a coherent statement

**Parallel forms** two alternative forms of a test

**Parametric statistics** statistical tests that make assumptions about the distribution of scores (e.g., normally distributed); require interval or ratio data

**Parsimony** a good, powerful theory should explain many events with few statements or explanatory concepts; thus, refers to simplicity

**Participant observation** an observation procedure in which the observer participates with those being observed; e.g., living with gorillas in the wild

**Pearson *r*** one form of correlation coefficient

**Personal space** the "invisible bubble" surrounding a person

**Pilot research** preliminary research undertaken to discover problems of method and design for a subsequent full-scale project

**Placebo** see *placebo effect*

**Placebo effect** improvement often shown in drug effectiveness studies in which patients believe they have received a drug when they actually received an inert substance

**Point of subjective equality** the mean of the upper and lower thresholds in a difference-threshold experiment

**Population** the total set of potential observations from which a sample is drawn

**Power (of a statistical test)** the probability of rejecting the null hypothesis in a statistical test when it is in fact false

**Precision** a good theory should be precise in its predictions

**Prediction** a specification of relationships resulting from correlational methods (see method of agreement); also one aim of a theory

**Predictive validity** when a test can predict a particular outcome

**Protection from harm** ethical researchers protect their subjects from any harm

**Protocol** a recipe to be followed exactly in conducting a research project

**Psychometrics** the judged specification of psychological attributes that do not have a known physical dimension; e.g., friendliness

**Psychophysics** judgment of stimuli along a known physical dimension; e.g., the perceived brightness of lights of different intensities

**Quasi-experiment** an experiment in which the independent variable occurs naturally and is not under direct control of the experimenter (see *ex post facto*)

**Random assignment** a crucial tool in experimentation whereby subjects are assigned to conditions in an unbiased fashion

**Random groups design** when subjects are randomly assigned to conditions in a between-subjects design

**Random sample** a sample from a population that has been selected in an unbiased way

**Random sampling** (see *random sample*)

**Range** descriptive measure of dispersion; the difference between the largest and smallest score in a distribution

**Rating technique** a measurement procedure in which observers arrange the attributes in question into groups or categories along some continuum (see *indirect measurement*)

**Ratio scale** the highest form of scale in which there is a true zero and in which it is meaningful to consider multiplicative differences among attributes

**Reactive** term to describe observations that are influenced by (or may be, in part, a reaction to) the detected presence of the investigator

**Realism** the extent to which a research procedure matches the characteristics of the real world; contrast with *generality of results*

**Receiver-operating-characteristic (ROC)** a plot of hits against false alarms in signal-detection experiments

**Regression artifacts** an artifact in the measurement of change on a variable when groups of subjects who scored at the extremes on the variable are tested again (see *regression to the mean*)

**Regression to the mean** tendency for extreme measures on some variable to be closer to the group mean when remeasured, due to unreliability of measurement

**Reliability** refers to the repeatability of an experimental result; inferential statistics provide an estimation of how likely it is that a finding is repeatable; also refers to the consistency of a test or measuring instrument determined by computing a correlation between scores obtained by subjects taking the test twice (test-retest reliability), or taking two different parallel forms of the test, or scores obtained on each half of the test (split-half reliability)

**Removing harmful consequences** ethical researchers remove any harmful consequences that their subjects may have incurred

**Repeated measures design** several measures are taken on the same subject, such as several learning trials or numerous psychophysical judgments; a type of within-subject experiment

**Replication** the repetition of an earlier experiment to duplicate (and perhaps extend) its findings (see also *systematic replication*)

**Reproduceability** see *reliability*

**Researcher bias** deliberate or inadvertent bias in which data are misanalyzed or participants are differentially treated over and above any planned differences in treatment

**Response acquiescence** a habitual way of responding on tests that involves frequently responding "yes" (see *response styles*)

**Response deviation** a habitual way of responding on tests that involves frequently responding "no" (see *response styles*)

**Response styles** habitual ways of responding on a test that are independent of the particular test item; see *response deviation, response acquiescence,* and *social desirability*

**Retroactive interference** forgetting of material produced by learning of subsequent material

**Retrospective report** in case studies when the person has to report on events that occurred in the distant past; subject to ordinary and motivated forgetting

**Reversability** an assumption made in research that the characteristics of different populations and species of subjects have the same underlying process; the behavioral "equation" can be determined from the behavior that is observed

**Reversal (ABA) design** small-*n* design in which a subject's behavior is measured under a baseline (A) condition, then an experimental treatment is applied during the B phase and any changes in behavior are observed; finally, the original baseline (A) conditions are reinstituted to ensure that the experimental treatment was responsible for any observed change during the B phase

**Sample** observations selected from a population

**Scale-attenuation effects** difficulties in interpreting results when performance on the dependent variable is either nearly perfect (a ceiling effect) or nearly lacking altogether (a floor effect)

**Scatter diagrams** a graphical relationship indicating degree of correlation between two variables made by plotting the scores of individuals on two variables

**Selection bias** occurs when subjects are not selected randomly; see *subject attrition* and *matching*

**Self-correction** science is self-correcting because it relies on public, empirical observation; old beliefs are discarded if they do not fit the empirical data

**Sensory impresssion** a hypothetical process that depends on the intensity of the stimulus in a signal-detection experiment

**Set** the effect of expectancy on cognition; for example, if the people solve problems in one particular way, they will often approach new problems in the same set way even when the original strategy is no longer effective

**Setting representativeness** see *ecological validity*

**Shadowing task** a form of dichotic listening in which the listener is required to repeat aloud (shadow) the message presented in one ear as it occurs

**Significance level** probability that an experimental finding is due to chance, or random fluctuation, operating in the data

**Simulated experiment** a fake experiment in which subjects are told to simulate the behavior of real subjects in a particular experiment; also called a *thought experiment*

**Skewed distribution** a nonsymmetrical distribution

**Sleeper effect** an improvement in the effect of a persuasive message with the passage of time

**Small-*n* design** research design utilizing a small number of subjects

**Social desirability** a habitual way of responding on tests that involves making socially desirable responses (see *response styles*)

**Social loafing** the decrease in individual effort that sometimes occurs when other people are present and when group performance is measured

**Speciesism** a term used to describe the view that animal life is qualitatively different from human life and, therefore, a form of bigotry

**Split-half reliability** determining reliability of a test by dividing the test items into two arbitrary groups and correlating the scores obtained on the two halves of the test

**Staircase method** an abbreviated version of the method of limits in which only stimuli around the threshold value are presented

**Standard deviation** descriptive measure of dispersion; square root of the sum of squared deviations of each score from the mean divided by the number of scores

**Standard error of the mean** the standard deviation of the distribution of sample means

**Standard normal distribution** a distribution of events that, when plotted, results in a bell-shaped curve. In a standard normal distribution the mean, the median, and the mode are all equal

**Standard scores** also called z-scores; differences between individual scores and the mean score expressed in units of standard deviations

**Statistical reliability** rejecting the null hypothesis on the basis of a statistical test that yields an alpha level of less than .05

**Strong inference** Platt's view that scientific progress comes about through a series of tests of alternative theoretical outcomes

**Stroop effect** difficulty in naming the color of an object when the color conflicts with the name of the object (when the word *blue* is printed in red ink)

**Subject attrition** when a subject fails to complete an experiment, which may destroy the basis of matching subjects across groups

**Subject representativeness** determination of generality of results across different subject populations

**Subject roles** how a subject reacts in an experiment; see *apprehensive-subject role, faithful-subject role, good-subject role*, and *negativistic-subject role*

**Subject variable** some characteristics of people that can be measured or described but cannot be varied experimentally (e.g., height, weight, sex, IQ, etc.)

**Sum of squares (SS)** sum of the squared scores used to calculate effects via analysis of variance

**Survey research** technique of obtaining a limited amount of information from a large number of people, usually through random sampling

**Synergism** a term used in medical research to describe an interaction; see interaction

**Systematic replication** repeating an experiment while varying numerous factors considered to be irrelevant to the phenomenon to see if it will survive these changes

**Template matching** a procedure involving a match between the behavior in a research setting and the behavior in real life; a way to determine the ecological validity of research

**Test reliability** see *test-retest reliability* and *split-half reliability*

**Testability** a good theory needs to be capable of disproof

**Test-retest reliability** giving the same test twice in succession over a short interval to see if the scores are stable, or reliable; generally expressed as a correlation between scores on the tests

**Theory** a collection of ideas whose purpose is to describe and predict

**Theory of signal detection** states that sensory impressions and decision processes control our detection of signals

**Thought experiment** see *simulated experiment*

**Threshold** in psychophysics the hypothetical barrier a stimulus must cross to be detected

**Time-lag design** a quasi-experimental design used when age is a subject variable in order to control time of testing effects; subjects of a particular age (e.g., 19-year-olds) are tested at different time periods

**Treatment × treatment × subjects design** a within-subjects factorial design with two independent variables

**Truncated range** a problem in interpreting low correlations; the amount of dispersion (or range) of scores on one variable may be small, thus leading to the low correlation found

**$t$-tests** parametric tests for testing differences between two groups

**Two by two factorial design** ($2 \times 2$) in which there are two levels of each of two independent variables yielding four conditions

**Two-tailed test** test that places the rejection area at both ends of a distribution

**Type 1 error** probability that the null hypothesis is rejected when it is in fact true; equals the significance level

**Type 2 error** failure to reject the null hypothesis when it is in fact false

**Unobtrusive measures** measures taken from the results of behavior not the behavior itself (see *nonreactive*)

**Unobtrusive observations** (see *nonreactive*)

**Validity** refers to whether an observation or procedure is sound or genuine

**Variable representativeness** determination of generality of results across different manipulations of an independent variable or different dependent variables

**Variables** the things in research that are measured, manipulated, or controlled (see *independent variables* and *dependent variables*)

**Variance** measure of dispersion; the standard deviation squared

**Volunteer problem** volunteer subjects differ from those less eager to participate; may be a source of bias in research

**What–if research** research performed to see what might happen rather than to test a specific hypothesis

**Within-groups variance** a measure of the dispersion among subjects in the same group in an experiment

**Within-subjects design** an experimental design in which each subject is tested under more than one level of the independent variable

# |||| Name Index

Adams, J. A., 14
Ahbel, K., 101
Aiken, L. S., 50
Allen, K. E., 165
Alsip, J. E., 73
American Psychological Association, 77, 78, 87, 88, 89, 90, 92, 93
Anderson, N. H., 236
Anisfeld, M., 272, 273
Atkinson, R. C., 151, 234

Bachman, J. D., 221
Bacon, F., 19
Baddeley, A. D., 237
Barber, T. X., 227, 228, 240, 264
Barefoot, J. C., 262
Baumgardner, M. H., 136
Bem, D. J., 237, 281, 306
Berkowitz, L., 236
Binet, A., 14
Blaney, R. H., 78
Blecker, D. L., 259
Blondlot, M., 195
Boe, R., 166
Boice, R., 194
Boring, E. G., 45, 100, 131
Bouffard, J.-P., 35, 36
Bowd, A. D., 86, 90
Bower, G. H., 215, 234, 235
Boyer, J. L., 91
Brady, J. V., 116, 119, 121
Brazelton, T. B., 182, 207–8
Broadbent, D. E., 29, 71, 151, 152
Brooks, C. I., 112, 113
Buchanan, W., 46
Buell, J. S., 165

Cairns, R. B., 14
Campbell, D. T., 47, 49, 99, 115, 179, 182, 191–92, 200, 203, 214, 252, 253

Carre, F. A., 132
Carver, C. S., 225–26, 228
Castellan, W., 112, 113
Chapman, P. F., 78
Chezik, D. D., 73
Cicirelli, V., 252, 253
Clark, W. C., 163, 164
Cole, M., 234
Coleman, A. E., 225, 228
Comish, S. E., 283
Cone, J. D., 194
Conrad, D. G., 116
Cook, T. D., 47, 49, 99, 115, 179, 191–92, 200, 203, 214, 219, 222, 224
Cornsweet, T. N., 160
Craik, F. I. M., 189

D'Agostino, P. R., 264
Darley, J. M., 23
DeGreene, K. B., 26
Dewing, K., 142, 143, 144, 145, 146
Dipboye, R. L., 225, 236
Donnerstein, E., 236

Ebbinghaus, H., 155
Edwards, A. L., 221
Egeth, H., 259, 261
Eibl-Eibesfeldt, I., 181–83
Elkin, I., 91
Elmes, D. G., 29, 78, 112, 150, 264
Erlebacher, A., 252, 253
Eriksen, C. W., 258
Erikson, M. T., 194
Eron, L. D., 189–90, 191, 194, 204
Eskridge, V. L., 132
Etaugh, C., 73
Evans, J. W., 253
Evans, T. J., 223, 225, 226

Fechner, G. T., 155, 158
Feingold, B. F., 167

# |||| Subject Index